Jesus in Galilee

Jesus in Galilee

Risk Analysis and Recovery of Jesus' Exorcisms, Activity, and Appearances in the Context of First-Century Galilee

ROGER S. BUSSE

RESOURCE *Publications* • Eugene, Oregon

JESUS IN GALILEE
Risk Analysis and Recovery of Jesus' Exorcisms, Activity, and Appearances in the Context of First-Century Galilee

Copyright © 2021 Roger S. Busse. All rights reserved. Except for brief quotations in critical publications or reviews, no part of this book may be reproduced in any manner without prior written permission from the publisher. Write: Permissions, Wipf and Stock Publishers, 199 W. 8th Ave., Suite 3, Eugene, OR 97401.

Resource Publications
An Imprint of Wipf and Stock Publishers
199 W. 8th Ave., Suite 3
Eugene, OR 97401

www.wipfandstock.com

PAPERBACK ISBN: 978-1-6667-0961-2
HARDCOVER ISBN: 978-1-6667-0962-9
EBOOK ISBN: 978-1-6667-0963-6

10/20/21

This book is dedicated to Tami—
my love, best friend, supporter, and partner in life.

Thanks to Hunter Busse for proofing the book, to my copywriter
Griffin Edwards, and to my typesetter Savanah N. Landerholm.

Thanks to my Harvard advisor, Helmut Koester,
who encouraged my studies.

I would like to thank Stephen J. Patterson for his continued
encouragement and support, vigorous discussions, criticisms, and
suggestions over the course of the last decade.

Christos Anesti

Contents

Preface		ix
Introduction: Recovering the First-Century World of Jesus		xiii
1	Those Who Controlled Evil Forces	1
2	The Socio-Economic Risk Conditions in Galilee	14
3	Sacred and Haunted Waters: Demons, Evil Spirits, and Mitigations	23
4	Jesus in Galilee: Defeating Satan-Practices, Exorcisms, and Control	32
5	The Galilean Exorcists Trained by Jesus	64
6	How to Destroy an Exorcist: The Death, Entombment, and Curse Placed on Jesus	90
7	The Urgency to Neutralize Jesus' Exorcists Post-Crucifixion	104
8	Encountering Jesus in Galilee: The Risk and Historical Context	110
9	Mark: Recovering the Original Risk and Historical Context of Galilean Appearances	120
10	Matthew: Recovering the Original Risk and Historical Context of Galilean Appearances	150
11	Luke: Recovering the Original Risk and Historical Context of Galilean Appearances	180
12	John: Recovering the Original Risk and Historical Context of Galilean Appearances	190

13 Non-Canonical Gospels: Recovering the Original Risk and Historical Context of Galilean Appearances	195
14 Summary: Jesus in Galilee	202
Bibliography	205
Subject Index	221
Scripture Index	249

Preface

In the summer of 1974, freed from college work, I went to Israel. By August, I stood in the ruins of Capernaum, which is owned and controlled by the Franciscans. What was left were various ruins nestled along the shore of Galilee. It was a very hot, dry day, and few were there, and I don't recall any attendants initially other than at the entry area. I was not well, having contracted strep throat, which my local doctor treated by having me drink extremely hot coffee—as hot as I could stand it on those blistering days—which puzzled almost everyone at the restaurants and taverns I visited and ordered it. And it didn't help. But, I made it to Capernaum. I was a cinema student at USC then, and had a keen interest in filming archaeological sites as a project, and I had finished a course in New Testament led by a professor Bennet, who dabbled in archaeology (You could always find him in the basement with the artifacts). He suggested I visit the Middle East and Israel, and especially Capernaum. But the camera was not working well, and I felt terrible, so I decided to use my Konica 35mm still camera and take just a few shots. I began slowly wandering around.

At that time, almost nothing was blocked off and you could actually wander through some of the remains of the basalt foundations of the small houses along the walking path, as the foundations were all that were left. I was struck by what I found. They appeared to mark out small, narrow rooms. The basalt foundation stones were clearly hand-hewn, rough with course stonework, with either dirt or cobblestone floors, a single entrance, all of which surrounded a small open area like a courtyard—clearly the small, simple homes of poor working peasants. I had already been to Ephesus and saw some of the excavations of the terrace houses, which were Roman-period villas of the rich built into a sloping hill of the Bulbul mountain—stucco painted walls with elaborate frescos, tiled and stone floors, elegant brick walls with arches and columns, kitchens, interior plumbing and airflow to cool rooms, even several with an interior peristyle courtyard and fountains. Capernaum's ruins were the exact opposite of those at Ephesus—none of these luxuries were evident. These were homes of subsistence peasants.

Nearby were the stunning remains of a third- or fourth-century synagogue, just feet away from these foundations. It had some beautifully carved support columns standing. Made of white limestone blocks, what remained of the synagogue stood in sharp contrast to the rough, cramped village foundations. Whoever built this synagogue had money. It was believed to stand on top of the foundation of the original synagogue from the time of Jesus, but no excavations had been done (It has since been shown to be so). The sweltering heat and dust that day, even with being near the lake, gave me a sense of how difficult living in this village must have been in those stone homes—perhaps they had no choice, caught in poverty and under oppression.

Not far off to the east of the foundations was what looked like a larger octagonal foundation structure, which was much nearer to the lake, and only about ninety feet away from the synagogue. It was not marked distinctly or clearly identified, at least that I could see at that time, and then no modern church stood over with a glass floor to view into the structure as exists today (built in 1982). At that time, you could look into the area and get quite close, as clearly it was something different from the foundations nearby, which ran right up to it. I had no idea that these were the remains of an octagonal church foundation (typical of fourth-century Byzantine structures that covered holy sites, as eight was the symbol of the resurrection). It stood over a specific first-century home. There appeared to be a central area in the octagon that led to foundations of a room that was larger than most of the nearby houses. Curious, I finally found and asked one of the attendants walking about what this structure was, why it was so different. "Peter's house," he said, and I took a step back and just stared and studied it for what must have been an hour—Peter's house, where Jesus lived, cast out a demon from Peter's mother-in-law, and met the constant crowds pressing to be freed from demonic control until late into the evenings. It was stunning to think about all of that on this hot, dry, dusty day among the small and rough basalt foundation stones scattered around the area.

I'll never forget how I felt. Like a jolt, the real Capernaum seemed to come to life for me for the first time—and it was nothing like what I thought it would be. This was no idyllic life for the fishers living in these tiny homes only feet from where they worked. Here was the lake, but then these tiny homes made of stones that would have had had only mud and stick roofs. This was no metropolis, city, or even town—it was a village of the poor—workers who had a synagogue, but not much more. Jesus and Peter were impoverished, struggling for survival. The average life span for villagers was only twenty-four years, and almost 40 percent of children died before the age of twelve, most shortly after childbirth. The roughness of those stones spoke through the ages to me—this is what it was really like in Galilee, occupied by Rome, controlled by the rich elite and saturated with demonic forces. Somehow, I now could read Jesus' message in a new light, the risks he and the fishers that followed him took, all in a contextual setting fraught with peril as rough as those stones. My perspective was forever changed. Every picture I took and still have was about the roughness of those stones—the reality of Jesus' world.

The remains of the octagonal structure around that original home were only a stone's throw from the lake, which I could hear lapping on the shore with the slight breeze. It became clear that a central room of the original home was once revered, i.e., the focus of the entire structure. I wanted to go into it, but this time there was an attendant, and he prevented me—simply shook his head. What a journey it must have been for those early pilgrims who would come to this site from around the ancient world. What did they imagine they would see or feel when they got there? Certainly, they would have come to be near the place where Jesus slept, walked, ate, and met the possessed. But would they have felt as I did, humbled by the actual location and what it showed life was like in Jesus' time? Did the church "dress it up," making it incongruous with its actual rough and difficult surroundings, as many sites did for me during that summer? Impossible to know, but I felt changed, and perhaps they were too. For me, this all set the context for encountering Jesus as he truly was in Galilee.

Roger Busse
Eugene, Oregon
Easter Week, 2021

Introduction

Recovering the First-Century World of Jesus

To Be Near the Fire, *Jesus Resurrected*, and *The Enemies of Paul*[1] established contextual risk analysis to be highly effective in recovering the perilous risks and risk mitigations used by Jesus, Paul, and their enemies to neutralize the threat of the other in their contemporary settings. Theirs was a world believed to be inhabited by demons, curses, spells, retributive spirits of the dead, and an active conflict between the agents of Satan and the agents of God; where poor subsistence peasants struggling for daily survival under severe oppression, such as those in a dozen or so tiny villages on the shores of Galilee, were hopelessly vulnerable and powerless, often victims, caught between these vying forces.

When this contemporary context is fully recovered, important new insights have emerged. Both Jesus and his enemies employed distinctive, efficacious, but also dangerous and sometimes illicit charismatic practices to neutralize or even destroy the other—actions of another world and time. Risk analysis has shown that for Jesus, his very public and controversial control, conversations and exorcism of demons heralded the emergence of the kingdom of God and coming fall of Satan, and with it, the end of the demonic imperialism under which they suffered. His was not just a vocal

---

1. Busse, *To Be Near*, *Jesus Resurrected*, and *Enemies*. Risk analysis has its roots in human conflict and mitigations to neutralize risk, similar to scientific analysis of "affect heuristic," confirmed in the research of Slovic, et al., "Risk as Analysis," 311–22; see also Slovic and Weber, "Perception as Risk," 1–21. Also see the works of Kahneman, Slovic, and Tversky, *Judgment under Uncertainty*; Drabek, *Human Systems and Response to Disaster*; Fischoff et al., *Acceptable Risk*; Bernstein, *Against the Gods*; Burton, *Perception of Risk*; and Pidgeon et al., *The Social Application of Risk*. Risk analysis is effective when used in a consistent contextual methodology, based on a recapture of risk environment, in identifying historical conflict in its original setting, or *sitz im leben*.

threat; there was dramatic and public witness to his control over multiple demons and spirits of the dead that demonstrated he could be dangerous to the Roman sympathizers and powerful elite, including Herod Antipas and the High Priest, who feared Jesus' retributive powers, particularly necromancy, believed to have been derived from Beelzebul. For Paul, his charismatic powers came by his being possessed by the Spirit of Christ, confirming the divine authority of Jesus Christ risen from the dead, who would soon return. Paul claimed his powers, which included casting death curses and turning enemies over to Satan, legitimized his apostleship. But his claim was publicly scorned and rejected, often violently, by vicious opponents, including "apostles" from Jerusalem, whom he said were possessed by Satan. The goal of both Jesus' and some of Paul's enemies was not just to silence but annihilate them body and soul, using very specific and intentional practices of the ancient world, only recoverable through a contextual risk analysis of the first century. The evidence for the complexity and vibrancy of the risk conflicts in which each engaged is overwhelming when fully recovered.

When we enter this world using an unbiased application of contextual risk analysis, a new, broader, and much more complex and dangerous ancient setting emerges before us; whether that context is found in the New Testament, non-canonical literature, Jewish rabbinic traditions, the Dead Sea Scrolls, ancient historians, or magical papyri and pagan literature. Risk analysis provides a new portal in which to read and understand these texts in their original setting and how they inform the contemporary conflicts. The application of risk analysis always follows a distinct pattern: In-depth research into the relevant contemporary context that is recoverable; placing the core risk conflicts and practices used to neutralize threats and peril in that context; application of other disciplines and scholarship where appropriate; and the emergent findings, wherever they may land, which quite often can be discomforting and even disturbing to us today.[2] Using this

---

2. Risk analysis identifies a perception of "perilous risk," or danger of imminent serious material harm, which is thought to be a real threat to the stability or survival of an entity under analysis in the recoverable historical setting. This perilous threat is usually an assault on the entity's religious, social, economic, or political environment(s). Risk analysis assesses both the scope of those threats and the entity's vulnerability, then evaluates the effectiveness of potential measures employed to cancel them out. If they are successful, these countermeasures are usually patterned, replicated, or embellished by the entity, thereby attracting other adherents and related standard practices. However, when countermeasures fail, devastation, catastrophe, or even physical harm or death can ensue. Where there are two conflicting entities, additional criteria apply that are particularly applicable. When two entities in a common historical context perceive one another as a perilous risk, the countermeasures each employs to cancel the other out almost always isolates a verifiable historical conflict. As noted, the level of risk conflict in these instances, evidenced in the scope and scale of countermeasures to neutralize enemies,

approach, we enter a very alien and foreign world to our own—the world of the ancients—and tactilely encounter the very raw actions they intentionally employed to control, infect, disable, curse, poison, possess, or kill their opponents. These are the multiple recovered perilous conflicts that confront us vividly using risk analysis, which can give us pause, but also newly inform our view of the actual life situation of Jesus, his opponents, and the peasants and villagers of Galilee. As callous as this may be, many of these practices were commonplace in the ancient world, which alone is disturbing.

Once the original historical context is fully recovered using rigorous analysis of primary and secondary sources, the specifics of the core risk conflicts can be accurately evaluated and assessed in their contemporary life setting (i.e., the *sitz im leben*). Source, textual and ethnographic studies can then be employed, along with the tools of critical scholarship, to assist in this process.[3] Indeed, the application of risk analysis allows unparalleled and unbiased entry into that ancient world—a world filled with demons, malevolent and retributive ghosts, angels, exorcists, magicians, and sorcerers, curses and spells used to attack, disable, infect, torture, or even kill.

---

demonstrates the severity and level of the threat. In other words, the intensity of the mitigations employed to neutralize risk is equal to the scope and danger of the opponent perceived, and so can give rise to the identification of that opponent. In almost every case, the core risk issues are uncovered, and often they provide a basis for assessment of the factual nature of the escalating conflict and the countermeasures employed (e.g., actions, sayings, or events). Many times, obscure, distracting, or irrelevant issues, such as later embellishment and exaggeration of the original conflict for new purposes or situational needs, can be identified and set aside. The goal of each of the conflicting entities is victory, rarely a negotiated settlement, which usually occurs only when perilous risk assures mutual annihilation. Even if a negotiated settlement is reached, it is usually temporary, since each opponent urgently seeks and ultimately employs any advantage to eliminate or neutralize their opponent. In case of failure, the entity or its followers may shift to a different strategy, usually more clandestine, in order to survive. Most interestingly, when this method is applied, the results can provide unqualified conclusions about the materiality and likelihood that risk events will or have occurred in highly specific ways. The method is applicable to any historical conflict of crisis and peril, even those set in a different cultural context, as long as that risk context can be adequately recovered. This has important implications for the application of qualitative risk analysis to the New Testament and non-canonical sources. Consequently, risk analysis suggests conclusions as to the activities of Jesus and his contemporaries in countering perilous risk, all in a new context of historical risk and human conflict to cancel out competing perils. It can also provide clarity to the original conflict between Jesus and his opponents, as well as to the nature and intent of his activity, including the sayings that defined that activity and resulted in his capture and execution.

3. Alternative approaches first employ ethnographic and redaction-critical tools (see the recent study by Bazzana, *Having the Spirit*, 24–60) but ignore the risk conflicts so evident in the ancient sources as primary to these risk discussions of exorcism and mitigation conflicts. Both are fruitful for this critical analysis that has long been ignored by New Testament Scholars.

We take the view of these ancients and enter these conflicts from their perspective. New and ancillary discoveries about controversial events, esoteric sayings, and practices, particularly many of the traditions concerning Jesus' activities in Galilee, are revealed, giving sometimes new and startling contextual and contemporary insights. Penetrating into the world of first-century subsistent peasants (including Jesus), witnessing their oppression, poverty, and conflicts with rich and powerful elitists aligned with Rome, all come into sharp focus, including the form and function of actions they employed to control and neutralize the perilous risks they faced, human or otherwise. For the first time, the contemporary figures of Jesus and his opponents begin to emerge in startling clarity, deepening and enriching our understanding and appreciation for the perilous risk they not only faced but also took, even if it meant an agonizing death and complete annihilation of the soul. We come to understand why Jesus' opponents believed themselves of God, justifying their violent actions against one whom they believed was a dangerous, dark, satanic Galilean exorcist. We encounter the sacred and haunted environs of Galilee; its angelic and demon-possessed springs and waters; the exorcists and village heroes/villains that expelled demons and malevolent spirits; the archaic words and practices used by them to bind and disarm dark forces; and the terrifying demonic retaliation that took place against those who attacked them, which included possession, infection, and malady, or madness. For the peasants of Galilee living harsh lives of poverty and oppression, they struggled to survive in the midst of a viscious, epic conflict of forces and were too often its victims—in the conflict between the kingdom of Satan, which included demonic imperialism taking over their land, and the kingdom of God, which they hoped and prayed they would survive to see. They witnessed this conflict most often as its helpless victims—the afflicted and possessed, the poor and starving—fought on their soil in the villages, towns and on the lake.

Jesus, who publicly announced that he was compelled to enter into this deadly struggle after his ecstatic experience during John's baptism and conversations with Satan, only heightened after the capture and murder of John, confronted demonic forces by claiming the authority of the "Finger of God"—a claim of divine possession, unlike any other of his contemporaries. For Jesus, the collaboration of the Jerusalem religious elite with the Romans had fostered proliferation of a "demonic imperialism" and pollution of the land, the villages, and even the Temple—and the murder of John. The kingdom of Satan was overrunning and dominating virtually everything for Jesus. And it was this perilous risk conflict that led to his brutal death by those aligned with Rome, i.e., the pagan invader that had brought its foreign gods and demons into the land and appointed, empowered, and selected sympathizers from among the Jewish elite families in Jerusalem whom they enriched. Accompanied by a band of exorcists he selected and trained in esoteric practices we can partially recover, each adopting their own technique in exorcism,[4] Jesus assaulted the demonic forces village by village in Galilee, then in certain towns of Decapolis when accepted, as well as villages in Samaria and Judea. He encircled Jerusalem, ultimately intending to displace Satan there and reclaim the Temple.[5] If not, all was lost. The perilous risks were too high to not act.[6] Consequently, his exorcisms were more than simply protection of villagers from evil (i.e., as for other exorcists, magicians, and "healers" who were compensated, including exorcists already operating in Galilee); they were aggressive acts to free the village of demonic control, unseat Satan, and bring about the return of the kingdom and sovereignty of God.[7] Consequently, these were intense, hostile, and violent conflicts with demons intended to take back what was lost.[8]

Jesus' repeated encounters with the darkest of forces of his contemporary world (including a shocking, self-admitted encounter and conversation with Satan in the demon-possessed Judean desert where he lived for several weeks) included his authority to take control over multiple forms of possession by demons and malevolent ghosts of the dead, some of which attempted unsuccessfully to take control of Jesus using his own techniques! Unlike any of the contemporary exorcists or charismatics of his time, Jesus' authority over demonic forces raised intense fear about the danger he presented to powerful enemies (again, Antipas). Could he conjure demons and spirits to move against them—such as the dead spirit of John seeking retribution? This peril led them to mitigate and neutralize their risk by crafting a way to destroy him using special steps and techniques of the ancient world to ensure he would not return from the dead, or could be conjured by his followers.

---

4. These will be explored more fully in the next chapters.

5. Josephus also believed the Temple was destroyed because of corruption; see Josephus, *Ant.* 20:8, 4–5.

6. Robinson, *The Problem of History*, 42.

7. Evans, *Jesus and His Contemporaries*, 373–88.

8. "The hostility that Mark expresses in his descriptions of the conversations is confirmed by an examination of what was said. Bauerenfeind has shown [*Die Worte Der Demonen Markusevagelium*, 3] that the three sayings spoken by demons to Jesus (1:24; 3:11; 5:7) are all closely parallel to incantations of witchcraft in the magical papyri and elsewhere. Therefore the words could very well for Mark and his readers give the impression of a defensive magical incantation. This hostility is of course only accentuated by the reference in the demon's sayings to Jesus; destroying (1:24) or 'tormenting' (5:7) them, as well as by the opening challenge (1:24; 5:7): 'What have you to do with us?' In 5:7 the demon appeals to God against Jesus in language commonly used *against* demons; *horkizo de ton theon*." Robinson, *The Problem of History*, 37.

Consequently, Jesus' conflict with dark forces was not something ethereal—it was real, messy, violent, and deadly, pushing him and his band to starvation, and only coherent in a recovered contemporary setting established through contextual risk analysis. Only when the world of first-century Galilee is recovered can Jesus' techniques be fully understood, as well as the risks he took. Jesus was a first-century Jewish peasant exorcist that was accused of possession by his enemies for what he said his exorcisms represented—the end of their rule. He was both a frightening and welcomed figure to the Galilean villagers and peasants that he protected from demonic infection and attack—able to control the fishes, perform necromancy on the dispossessed and poor (primarily innocent children), publicly converse and expel demons, negotiate and drive them away. Virtually all of these events occurred in Galilee. He had survived past the average life expectancy of Jewish Galilean male peasants at that time, which was only twenty-four years. He spoke a distinct Galilean Aramaic dialect that was often ridiculed in Jerusalem as that of an uneducated country bumpkin.[9] But even to those who wanted him silenced, he held authority over the darkest forces of his time. In this risk-recovered contemporary setting, Jesus remained beyond what some scholars could recover or understand, handicapped by modern views and debates over contemporary theological issues, never entering that alien world and first setting context to inform their methodologies. Only contextual risk analysis can most clearly recover this original setting, its conflicts and outcomes, leaving the dust on our shoes from those times.

To his enemies, Jesus then was a dangerous, feared, and illegal dark magician, an "evildoer," and an illicit necromancer worthy of immediate death under Jewish and Roman law.[10] Only a specific ritual death was believed able to neutralize his dark powers or retributive return that he warned them about—a cursed crucifixion that annihilated a Jew, both body and soul according to Jewish law; but more, then the application of unusual extra steps. The placement in a sealed stone tomb, a special dressing for the body to ensure the retributive spirit was trapped, and a ritual guard to ensure a successful annihilation to be confirmed after three days. The combination of these neutralizing practices was highly unusual, yet they speak

---

9. The Talmud, *Mishnah Erubin* 53b: Ridiculing of a Galilean in the Jerusalem marketplace for trying to buy *amar*: "You stupid Galilean, do you want something to ride on [*chamar*: a donkey]? Or something to drink [*hamar*: wine]? Or something for clothing [*'amar*: wool]? Or something for sacrifice [*immar*: a lamb]?"

10. We will discuss Roman law and the Twelve Tables in later chapters. Judaism forbade magicians. Deuteronomy 18:10–11: "No one shall be found among you who engages in divination, or is a witch, an enchanter, or a sorcerer, or one who casts spells, or who consults spirits, one who is a wizard or a necromancer."

volumes about the risk that his opponents believed he posed even in death. Such practices were to secure their safety, that he would never return and seek retribution against them, or that his apprentice exorcists would conjure and manipulate his spirit.

Consequently, to fully understand this risk context and recover the perilous risks Jesus embraced for the sake of the kingdom of God, it is necessary, indeed essential, to enter this other world to fully appreciate the rich and complex history of the origins of Christianity in its contemporary setting; to rediscover what was distinctive about Jesus and grasp his striking demand to practice *agape* as the only efficacious mitigation to evil and demonic powers and keep them at bay. Jesus' sayings are reset in a compelling new understanding of risk and mitigation. Only *agape* completely neutralized demons and could begin to dismantle the kingdom of Satan, evidenced by what Jesus saw, Satan "falling like lightning." Indeed, no other contemporary exorcist claimed *agape* as a charismatic power of divine protection able to disable and defeat satanic power.[11]

The implications of entering this alien world and fully understanding Jesus' risk mitigations in their contemporary setting that neutralized and disbanded the kingdom of Satan have a profound impact for Christians today, whether in the faith, practice, or preaching of the church. Even Bultmann realized this over seventy years ago:

> We cannot use electric lights and radio and, in the event of illness, avail ourselves of modern medical and clinical means and at the same time believe in the spirit and wonder world of the New Testament.[12]

Only by carefully uncovering the *sitz im leben* of the first century can we translate his activity into today's context and fully understand actionable faith and *agape*, or find clarity about the perilous risks he embraced and fully grasp the deep meaning of his appearances for us today. Such are the rewards of studying the origins of Christianity through the lens of risk analysis.

---

11. The efficacious power of *agape* to mitigate evil was reaffirmed by Paul repeatedly, most notably in 1 Corinthians 13. See Busse, *Enemies of Paul*, 174–84, 200–04.

12. Bultmann, *New Testament and Mythology*, 4.

1

Those Who Controlled Evil Forces

It is immediately evident even from a cursory reading of all primary sources that the Roman world of the first century, including the provinces of Judea and Syria and the tiny villages surrounding the lake of Galilee, is completely alien to our own. In fact, it is difficult to recover its otherworldly risks and dangers given our modern biases. Phantasms, malevolent spirits, demons, gods, angels, spells, curses, and possession, along with efficacious ecstatics, *magoi*,[1] *goetes*,[2] and exorcists, were all accepted as the norm—albeit some were considered evil and dark fringe actors. For the ancients, all of these were not only thought to exist but were known to be active within their world as reflected in their recorded experiences, actions, practices, poetry, oral stories, myths and writings; in their fears, dreams, daily rituals, and responses to mitigate risk recorded in multiple traditions and by contemporary historians—regardless of whether one was a struggling subsistence peasant or a member of the wealthy elite. Entering into this life setting requires not only tenacious investigation but also openness to embracing an altered perspective of reality, one that is grossly foreign and even disturbing to us. Yet, it is into this alien world that we must enter in order to approach

1. *Magos*, or magician, including dark magicians that practices black magic, illegal in the Roman world.

2. *Goetes*, a sorcerer, which included the ancient practice of magic, alchemy, wizardry, and efficacious control of esoteric knowledge.

Jesus in his historical context and fully comprehend the original form of the oral reminisces of his activity in Galilee, as well as the deadly risk conflicts he chose to confront, both human and otherwise. Risk analysis is an effective, new entryway into this world. To begin this journey, we must first recover the risk context of life in the first century.

RECOVERING THE FIRST CENTURY SETTING

Ghosts (*phantasms*), which included malevolent spirits of the dead, also identified as "unclean spirits" and "demons," were accepted as aggressively active in the ancient world.[3] The fear of possession, evidenced by torturous illness, personal afflictions of all types, madness, and even death, was terrifying. Indeed, malevolent ghosts and demons were known to be the cause of almost every malady, deformation, bad fortune, and death in the ancient world regardless of status or wealth.[4] Multiple contemporary pagan and Jewish sources demonstrate that demons and the conjured dead were simply assumed to be active and prevalent, including in first-century Palestine and Galilee.[5] These demonic spirits were considered voracious and sought out victims, and were particularly active at night.[6] Other retributive demons wandered through villages, and on special days were expected to attack the innocent, so peasants hid in fear and special protective measures and practices were employed.[7] In the most extreme cases, demons possessed and then killed their victims by inciting suicide or committing violent acts that led to death, or else deceived or possessed others to destroy their victims by suffocation, stabbing, strangulation.[8] They often drove victims to madness, then into the desert or to graveyards.[9] As such, demons were known to roam

---

3. Josephus, *War* 7:6, 3.

4. From Peter's (in Aramaic, *Kepha*), mother-in-law's fever (Luke 4:38–40) to being mute (Matt 4:10) and even death (Mark 5:36–43).

5. Rousseau, "Exorcism," 88–93, as well as Penny, "By the Power of Beelzebul," 620–50, and Ben-Zvi, *Studies on the Texts of the Desert of Judah 10*. Generally exorcism and protection against demons is emphasized, e.g. 4Q510–11, 4Q560, and 11Q11; Evans, "Jesus and Psalm 91," 541–55.

6. Canaan, "Haunted Springs and Water Demons in Palestine," 153–70. See also Ferguson, *Baptism*, 56–93.

7. The female demon in particular, Lilith, in *Songs of the Sage* (4Q510–11).

8. Ogden, *Magic*, 158; Cicero, *On Divination* 1.57.

9. Philostratus, *Life*, 4.8; *T. Sol.* 22, for examples of demons driving people into desolate places.

near tombs,[10] which were to be avoided particularly at dark.[11] They were thought to be the cause of the very high mortality rates among innocents and infants, terrifying families.

The prevalence of demons was so pronounced in daily life that they were labeled and categorized by the ancients. Apuleius,[12] *De deo Socratis* 15 (later second century CE), provides a general "taxonomy of ghosts," some of which are termed *Di manes*, or "demons," which predate his writing by generations and reflect this world view:

> Another variety of "demons" consists of the human soul that abandons its body when it has finished with its services in life. I note that in the old Latin language these used to be termed *lemures*. Now, to some of these *lemueres* was allotted the care of their descendants. These occupy houses with a propitious and peaceful attitude, and they are called *Lares* of the family. But others, because of their misdeeds in life, are punished with a kind of exile, namely with the denial of a home and with undirected wanderings. They can only be harmless terrors to good men, but they are dangerous to bad men. People usually call these *larvae*. When it is unclear what category of ghost one is dealing with, whether it is one of the *Lares* or the *larvae*, the term one uses the term *Di manes*.[13]

These *Di manes* often left physical evidence of their presence in the form of a foul smell, smoke, vapor, or wind, a shadow or an ethereal appearance; in some cases there was a form of *soma* (body), with a material presence sufficient to touch, strike, wrestle, punch, or even rape a victim.[14] When present, they refused to leave until a *magos* or exorcist arrived and either negotiated with, threatened, or by ritual practice absorbed or drove them out, sending them to wander desolate places, which included the desert, such as the Judean desert, a place even Satan and other demons roamed,[15] or to be trapped in waters, including the lake of Galilee.[16]

10. Ogden, *Magic*, 147; Mark 5:5.

11. See Mark 5:1–20 for a demon that possessed a man near the tombs.

12. Lucius Apuleius Madaurensis (124–170 CE), a Roman from Numidia in North Africa, was a poet, writer (author of the *Metamorphses*), and Latin Rhetorician who studied Platonic philosophy in Athens, traveled widely, and joined several Greco-Roman cults, and was a priest of Asclepius. He was accused of using magic. See Ogden, *Magic*, 149.

13. Ogden, *Magic*, 149.

14. Ogden, *Magic*, 314; Xenophon of Ephesus, *Ephesiaca*, 5.9.7–9.

15. Luke 4:1–3; Matt 4:1–11; Mark 1:12–13.

16. Luke 8:26–39.

> But you don't need to take my word for it. Everyone knows the Syrian from Palestine who is such an expert at this. He takes anyone who falls down at the sign of the moon, twist their eyes and foams at the mouth and sets them on their feet again and sends them out sound in mind, delivering them from their affliction for a large fee. Whenever he stands over them as they lie afflicted and asks from whence they have come into the body, the sick man himself makes no response, but the demon answers, speaking in Greek or the language of its country of origin, and explains how and when it entered the person. The Syrian adjures it to leave, and if it does not obey he drives it out with threats. I saw one leaving; it was black and smoky in color.[17]

Malevolent demons were often termed "restless."[18] This restlessness was defined by their encounter with the living and can be categorized into groups, although these categories often overlapped.[19] They are as follows in Greek:

> *Aoroi*—those dead before their time who seek revenge in to haunt the living.
> *Bi(ai)othanatoi*—those violently killed in war, including executed criminals, with murder victims and those committing suicide the most active and angry.
> *Agamoi*—those dead before being married, which includes particularly bitter female ghosts seeking revenge.
> *Ataphoi*—those who died and were not buried or given funeral rites.

All of these were encountered, as reported in ancient literature. Many of the restless dead (i.e. the beheaded or mutilated, soldiers or criminals who had been killed or murdered) were excluded from Hades and, as noted, wandered the desolate places, including deserts and waters.[20] Because they wandered and sought retribution they would seek out innocent victims, particularly the poor (which included subsistence laborers, such as tenant farmers and fishers that populated the villages surrounding Galilee), or the frail, or those vulnerable to attack (e.g., by evil actions, greed, corruption, or hatred). Sometimes these demons appeared as deformed and decaying bodies. These were particularly feared and were known to be active daily,[21]

---

17. Lucian, *Philopseudes* 16, quoted in Ogden, *Magic*, 50.
18. Ogden, *Magic*, 146–78.
19. Ogden, *Magic*, 146.
20. Deserts, lakes, rivers and even springs.
21. Ogden, *Magic*, 148–49; Virgil, *Aeneid* 6.

and when they appeared in dreams they could do great harm because their victim was helpless.[22]

Tertullian of Carthage,[23] the "father of Latin Christianity" and polemicist against heresy writing about 190–200 CE, provides a remarkable account of various encounters with demons and the "restless dead and dead by violence." His account is clearly intended as an attack on popular magicians and sorcerers, some of whom date to the first century, and particularly those known to evoke the ghosts of the dead, which demonstrated their known prevalence in his society. Tertullian's list cites the most famous, including Simon and Elymas, the Jewish sorcerer reportedly blinded by Paul.[24] A passage from *De Anima* (56-7) contends that the appearance of these demonic phantasms evoked by these famous magicians and sorcerers were actually not the dead souls of criminals (for Tertullian all souls of the dead are transported to Hades to await judgment, which is in contrast to other ancient sources), but instead were demons that existed within the soul that became detached at death. These demons may have had a part in bringing on the untimely death of the man or woman, and could appear with a material presence, although he asserts that the manifestation was a spiritual substance, not corporeal (i.e., not flesh and blood).

Tertullian reports that dark magicians could conjure and control demons for monetary gain, satisfying a purchaser's intent to harm or destroy an enemy or targeted victim. The demons evoked by these magicians were retaliatory and used for evil purposes. It was tantamount to sending an assassin to eliminate an opponent. He states that these demons could be forced to rightly identify their true identity, i.e., as the demon of the dead. By negative affirmation, then, Tertullian fully confirms both the contemporary belief in the existence of demons as well as encounters that date from the first century to the third century.

Rabbinic tradition also confirms the pervasive activity of demons and rabbis who were exorcists.[25] These demons not only possessed and tormented their victims, but contaminated waters, preventing consumption from springs on certain days of the week, times of the month, and under unexpected circumstances that brought on illness, affliction, or even death. Water could only be drawn on certain days and times. This included the

---

22. Ogden, *Magic*, 146–47.

23. Quintus Septimius Florens Tertullianus, 160–225 CE, of the Roman province of Carthage; the Christian writer and father of Latin theology, and later a Montanist. See Ogden, *Magic*, 149–50.

24. Acts 13:6–12.

25. See Chajes, "Rabbis," 69–72, and sources cited therein.

region of Galilee and the lake, as well as the springs and rivers that fed it, which will be discussed in detail later in our study.[26]

The first century ruling elite in Palestine and Galilee, which included Herod Antipas, members of the Sanhedrin, and the High Priestly families appointed by the Romans,[27] unequivocally believed that demons and dark forces were active,[28] and that they were particularly at risk of attack or harm by local conjurers. Herod, who was ruler of Galilee and Perea,[29] was terrified that such an attack would be forthcoming as retribution for his murder of John the Baptist;[30] that John's retributive spirit would be taken and controlled by a dark magician, then used to attack him or destroy his rule.[31] Indeed, John's charismatic baptismal rites "cleansed," or, better said, drove out evil into the water and protected those heeding his call from possession and attack, returning them to the divine protection.[32] He condemned the Jerusalem elite as demonic and possessed, and that their power was a demonic imperialism. Like John, Jesus rejected demonic imperialism. He claimed that his exorcisms and authority over demons, casting them into waters or to desolate places, were evidence of successfully reclaiming the kingdom of God and driving Satan from the land.[33] The first-century Jewish historian Flavius Josephus recounts a famous tradition concerning the defeat of Herod's army by Aretas of Petra. The Jews believed that "the destruction of his army was sent as a punishment upon Herod, and a mark of God's displeasure to him."[34] In this case, it appears that God stood aside and allowed evil forces to destroy Herod's army as punishment against Antipas.

As such, dangerous malevolent spirits and demons were believed by all social strata of Palestine and Galilee to be both active and prevalent during

---

26. Bar-Ilan, *Exorcism by Rabbis*.

27. Busse, *To Be Near*, 9–11, 20–26, 29–30; Hanson and Oakman, *Palestine*, 146–54.

28. Busse, *Jesus Resurrected*, 52, and Busse, *To Be Near*, 54–59.

29. Herod Antipas (20 BCE to 39 CE) ruled as tetrarch of Galilee and Perea.

30. John's baptism was charismatic and was understood to be a rejection and rebellion against the Temple elite; see Webb, *John the Baptizer*, 203–05.

31. Busse, *To Be Near*, 16–17; Busse, *Jesus Resurrected*, 24–25; Luke 9:7–9.

32. See below on the expulsion of demons into waters to entrap or destroy them evidenced in the activity of Jesus. This was a contemporary practice, particularly in sacred waters and springs that were thought visited or protected by angels. Bar-Ilan, *Exorcism by Rabbis*: "Some springs have a complete family of spirits living in each; it is understood that hot springs, as in Tiberias (Galilee), are heated by spirits (acting on the basis of the commands of King Solomon). It can be generalized that there is hardly a source of water in the land of Israel without a spirit (one or more)." Bar-Ilan cites as additional support the *Pesachim* 112 p. 1, two *baraitot*.

33. See *T. Sol.* 5:11; Carter, *Matthew and the Margins*, 123.

34. Josephus, *Ant.* 18.109–19.

the first to third century of the Common Era. Not surprisingly, descriptions of various forms of phantasms and demons and their activity are remarkably similar to descriptions found in the New Testament Gospels, Acts, and the writings of Paul.[35]

THOSE WHO CONTROLLED EVIL FORCES

Exorcists (*exorkistes*), magicians (*magoi*), and sorcerers (*goetes*) were understood to be able to expel, conjure, consult with or even enlist malevolent demons or spirits of the dead to do their bidding. Sometimes dark magicians[36] were paid by clients to send demons to possess or torment targeted victims and bring on illness, suicide, or even commit murder.[37] When exorcised by prayer, command, use of names, ritual technique, song[38] or incantation,[39] a material substance was often encountered or seen (i.e., the sign of a departing demon), or departure was evidenced by the overturning of cups or pails of water.[40] Exorcists often went into a trance, rolled their eyes (as if in a seizure), and spoke in undecipherable languages; they sometimes used ancient incantations ascribed to other exorcists. Most forced the demon to identify itself by name[41] in order to take control over it.[42] Witnesses were plentiful and spellbound, and since most were illiterate peasants, oral traditions and lore recounted their deeds. Those who were literate recorded striking examples of their activity.

35. See Hull, *Hellenistic Magic*, 116–41; Busse, *Jesus Resurrected*, 88–89.

36. By 50 BCE the Romans had come to disapprove of magicians and sorcerers for their ability to control forces, sometimes leading to illness, death by curse, incantation or spells, and their attempts and ability to control the spirits of the dead, calling on them to obey their will. These were dark magicians. Practices by the early first century were outlawed (by the Twelve Tables), and penalties included immediate execution. See an excellent summary of the Greco-Roman period; Dickie, *Magic and Magicians*, 136–76.

37. Dickie, *Magic and Magicians*, 152, 154.

38. Of the Dead Sea Scrolls, in the *Genesis Apocryphon*, 11Q5, exorcistic songs of David are cited. See also Sorenson, *Possession and Exorcism*, 69, where the *Hymn Against Demons* (4Q560) is "an important fragment . . . which includes references to indwelling possession and its relief through exorcism." See also Morris, *Warding Off Evil*, for an excellent presentation.

39. For another excellent presentation on exorcism practices and formulae, see Leicht, "Mashbia' Ani 'Alekha," 319–43.

40. Eleazar the exorcists. Josephus, *Ant.* 8.45–48.

41. See Smith, *Jesus*, 128.

42. To know the demon's name is to take control: Judg 13:6; *T. Sol.* 2:1, 3:6, 4:3–4; *PGM* IV 1017–19.

Flavius Josephus mentions several incidents of possession and exorcism.[43] Techniques used by the exorcists included burning certain herbs and immersing the individual in water to draw out the demon. He personally witnessed a Jewish exorcist named Eleazar expel a demon while in the company of the emperor Vespasian, his generals, and his sons. According to Josephus, Eleazar employed special techniques that originated with king Solomon.[44] Solomon was known to have been a very powerful Jewish exorcist: "God also enabled him [Solomon] to learn that skill which expels demons." His words, incantations, efficacious rituals, and spells had been passed down and used by Jewish exorcists for hundreds of years and were in wide use in Palestine in the time of Jesus.[45] In Josephus's account, Eleazar drew a demon out of a victim using a special ring placed at the nose as he repeated Solomonic incantations (some of which are still found in ancient texts).

> The manner of the cure was this: He put a ring that had a Foot of one of those sorts mentioned by Solomon to the nostrils of the demoniac, after which he drew out the demon through his nostrils; and then the man fell down immediately, he adjured him to return into him no more, making still mention of Solomon, and reciting incantations which he composed. And when Eleazar would persuade and demonstrate to the spectators that he had such power, he set a little cup or basin full of water and commanded the demon, as he went out of the man, to overturn it, and thereby let the spectators know that he had left the man.[46]

Josephus continues the passage, stating that when the cup or bowl of water was overturned, "the skill and wisdom of Solomon was shown very

---

43. Josephus, *Ant.* 2, 5, 8, 45–48.

44. Ogden, *Magic*, 167–68: "So great was the intelligence and wisdom that God bestowed on Solomon that he outstripped the abilities of the ancients. The Egyptians are said to surpass all men in their understanding, but even they were outstripped by Solomon . . . God permitted him to learn the craft of demon control, since it was a helpful and healing one for men. He composed incantations to relieve diseases and left behind him methods of exorcism for the expulsion of possessing demons in such a way that they never return."

45. When Jesus says, "Someone greater than Solomon is here," he is describing his power and authority over demons as superior to the power derived by contemporary exorcists, as they draw from the techniques and incantations of most revered exorcist in ancient Judaism, Solomon. Jesus claims his authority as directly from God via his possession by the "finger of God." Jesus is making a striking claim in comparison to the authority cited by others. See Luke 11:31; also Busse, *To Be Near*, 40.

46. Josephus, *Ant.* 8:46–49; See Duling, "Solomon, Exorcism, and the Son of David," 235–52.

manifestly; for which reason it is, that all men may know the vastness of Solomon's abilities and how he was beloved by God." He notes that the Solomonic methods of cure remained of "great force unto this day." Indeed, Jewish exorcists remained plentiful, famous, and active.[47] Exorcists who mastered these techniques, including those who employed substances to the nostrils to draw out demons,[48] were considered powerful.

Qumran literature found near the Essene community at the Dead Sea similarly confirms a contemporary and prevalent belief in exorcisms and knowledge of demons, evidenced in hymns attributed to David.[49] In another fragmentary document (4Q510–511, late first century BCE), known as the Songs of the Sage (or the Songs of Maskil), an incantation of exorcism is recorded which specifically protects against demons that are listed. This suggests that there may have been exorcisms at Qumran. The magical papyri also demonstrate multiple examples of exorcism and active exorcists.[50]

Exorcists typically forced the demon to confess its name and origin to take control of it, and then either expelled it by force (by command or incantation as noted) or negotiated its departure (e.g., forcing the demon into a desolate place,[51] or agreeing to let it possess a herd of swine).[52] Other physical techniques were also employed. For example, an exorcist's spittle was thought to be imbued with authority and was sometimes applied to the affected area to draw out demonic affliction, such as the blinding of the eyes,[53] blocking the ears or preventing speech.[54] The spittle was sometimes mixed with mud or clay to create a saliva ointment[55] to expel the spirit, as well as pronounced special words. In some cases, the exorcist spit into the

47. This included to the time of Origen (285 CE), *Against Celsus*, 4.

48. Ogden, *Magic*, 171; an exorcism spell from the eighth Book of Moses: "If you say the name to a man possessed by a demon while applying sulphur and bitumen to his nose, the demon will give voice at once and depart."

49. *Qumran Hymn*, 11Q5, 11Q ps 27.9–10.

50. See Betz, *Greek Magical Papyri*.

51. Talmud, "Treatise Berachoth," fol. 3a; and Tobit 8:3; Luke 11:24; unclean spirit wanders in waterless places looking for a resting place. Q 11:24–26, Luke 11:24–26, Matt 12:43–45.

52. See Lucian's *Philopseudes* 16 as quoted by Ogden, *Magic*, 50–51.

53. Twelftree, *Jesus the Exorcist*, 83–84. Mark 8:22–26, Jesus wasn't successful at first, and he used spittle. The story was dropped in Luke and Matthew due to its embarrassing nature and possible association with magic.

54. Smith, *Jesus*, 128.

55. Saliva is mentioned by ancient authors as used in cures by exorcists, healers, and even the emperor of Rome, Vespasian. According to Tacitus, Vespasian cured a blind man by spitting on his eyes and cheek. The cure worked, but only insofar as the man could see light (Tacitus, *Histories*, 4.81).

eyes of the afflicted, or touched the tongue with the spittle. At least three of Jesus' exorcisms reflect these practices.[56]

During the first century, other charismatics were operative in northern Palestine using various techniques, including those that drove out malevolent forces. The three most prominent were Hainina ben Dosa (approximately 60–80 CE),[57] Eleazar the Exorcist (about 70 CE, discussed above),[58] and *Choni Ha-Me'aggel* (Choni the Circle Drawer, 65 BCE).[59] Hainina lived in Galilee and was popular and respected among the people for his piety and humility, despite his remarkable powers. His fame as an *anshe ma'aseh*, or wonder worker, came as a result of his efficacious prayers. One of the more famous events came at the request of Johannan ben Zakkai, Hainina's teacher, on behalf of his very ill son. Zakkai was a famous wise man, a *Tannaim*, or sage of the first century. Hainina acceded to Zakkai's request and his prayers were immediately effective, driving the illness out of the son. In a second instance, Gamaliel II (the second leader of the Sanhedrin after the destruction of the Temple in 70 CE) requested the healing of his ill son. He had sent messengers asking that Hainina pray, which he was glad to do. Despite being some distance away, Hainina's prayer was immediately effective, driving out the fever.[60] Hainina knew if his prayers had been heard and approved if they "flowed freely." Once he asked God, "master of the universe," to cease the falling rain as he travelled, which was immediately granted. When he reached his destination, he prayed again and rain returned. These traditions confirmed Hainina's favor, familiarity, and intimate relationship with God.

In the case of Choni, tradition states that God had not sent rain, even into the winter. Choni drew a circle and stood in it saying to God he would not leave the circle until he made it rain. A light rain fell, but Choni complained it was not satisfactory and he would not leave the circle. The rain then fell hard, but Choni complained it was too much. Finally, normal rain fell. For his action, Choni was threatened with excommunication by the local Jewish authorities but was saved because "Choni had a special relationship with God." Choni's grandsons, Abba Hilqiah and Hanan the Hidden, continued on Choni's charismatic practices in Galilee and were contemporaneous with Jesus. Like Choni, they too were credited with miraculous

56. Mark 8:22–26; Mark 7:31–37; John 9:6.

57. Undoubtedly, Hainina was Onias in Jospehus, *Ant.* 14.22–24.

58. Josephus, *Ant.* 8:45–48; Josephus describes the exact manner in which Eleazar performed his exorcisms and the effect on the individual.

59. See Mishnah Ta'anit 3:8. For his death see Josephus, *Ant.* 14.2.121.

60. This tradition is strikingly similar to the description of Jesus' healing of the royal official's son while at some distance while in Galilee, John 4:46–50.

deeds, but they were not alone. The Gospels record Jesus acknowledging that there were several exorcists practicing in Galilee.[61]

Ecstatic experiences of holy men and exorcists included their testing, including attempted possession by demons that wanted to destroy them. Survival of these confrontations (such as the attempts to destroy Jesus in desert wilderness of Judea by Satan[62]), meant they might obtain authority over demons, where demons would serve the exorcist as slaves, or the exorcist would negotiate with the demon to leave or permanently vacate the victim because those spirits feared torment. Others reported a vision, where voices were heard and spirits descended and possessed them, or where the spirit of that god or God was made available to act and control evil, such as Jesus' authority given by "the finger of God" after his baptism. "Finger of God" was a term used by some ecstatics and magicians to identify possession of the power and spirit of a god, or God.[63] However, as we shall see, Jesus' linkage of his charismatic authority by the "finger of God" with the arrival and authority of God's kingdom (a kingdom that displaces satanic rule, and by implication, eradicates apostasy and imperialism)[64] was completely unique in its contemporary setting.[65] Jesus is reported to have successfully exorcised all demons but one; curiously, the possession of Judas Iscariot. Satan possessed him and Jesus knew it.[66]

Consequently, the numerous reports of encounters with demons included all segments and strata in Roman and Hellenistic society. They were active in cities, rural areas, and provinces. In the canonical and non-canonical writings of ancient Judaism, Satan was known to employ demons (fallen angels and spirits of the dead), and Beelzebul, the prince of demons[67] (a fallen angel, a.k.a. the "strong man"), was active in manipulating the demons

---

61. Matt 12:27, Luke 11:19, Mark 9:38–40.

62. Luke 4:1–13, Matt 4:1–11, Mark 1:12–13.

63. Qumran's *War Scroll* includes a link between exorcism and God's hand.

64. That this was understood by Jesus as a possession by the "finger of God," see Mathew 12:28, which has softened the claim by Jesus, replacing the "finger of God" with the "Spirit of God;" see Bazanna, *Spirit of Christ*, 52.

65. Smith, *Jesus*, 130

66. John 6:7; Luke 22:3. See also John 13:27, as it is when Judas eats the bread that Satan enters his heart, i.e., a substance that had become infested with evil for him.

67. Beelzebul was the highest-ranking demon: see *T. Sol.* 3:5–6; Origen, *Against Celsus*, 8.25; Hipplytus, *Haer.* 6.34.1. Beelzebul is associated with Belial in Qumran texts, 4Q286 (4QBer a) 7.2.1–4. In both Mark and Q, the title "prince of demons" does make this equation. May be northern Galilean milieu per Humphries, *Christian Origins*, 16, 2–20. Linked with *zbl ba'al-u ars*, Jesus was linked with foreign gods, which were understood in Judaism as demons, Ps 95:5, *Jub.* 22:1–17.

he controlled in his war against God and his angels, viciously attacking, deceiving, and terrifying God's people.[68]

Of note, the demons and spirits that were controlled and expelled by Jesus and his exorcists were not necessarily portrayed as active and malevolent ghosts of the dead in the New Testament. They were sometimes considered malevolent spirits or fallen angels,[69] and yet, although the origin of demons is obscure in the Gospels,[70] Luke 11:24 and 4:33 confirm that they originally were termed "unclean spirits," which is also reflected in the earliest Gospel, Mark (perhaps the most original description reflecting a Palestinian milieu).[71] The term "demon" was more prominently used in Matthew and especially Luke, much later Gospel productions (70–85 CE), where the term "demon" fit better in a Greco-Roman setting outside of Palestine. In either case, they were the wicked dead and those employed by Satan or his minions, such as Beelzebul. Other ancient sources also confirm that demons were active spirits of the wicked dead,[72] and in most cases acted malevolently, seeking retribution by possessing and harming their victims.[73] Jesus is able to identify them by name and converse with them to take control.[74]

As we will discuss, Jesus announced that demonic forces were attempting to overtake the kingdom of God,[75] and that Satan was employing all means to succeed, whether his demons, fallen angels or the occupying pagan rulers and their sympathizers. Demonic attacks included destroying the opponents of these forces—most notably for Jesus, John the Baptizer.[76] The

---

68. Luke 11:14–28; see Josephus, *Ant.* 9:2, b1.

69. *T. Sol.* 6:1–4.

70. Meaning that they were presumed to be part of that world, infiltrating every aspect of life, with risk and dangers.

71. Unclean Spirits are demons in Mark, and this shifts to "demon" in Luke, *anthropos, en pnuemati akaharto*, a more familiar term to Hellenistic readers. Given this, the more original description, reflecting typical Jewish purity and uncleanliness associated with possession, is "unclean spirit," which has a Palestinian origin and milieu. See also Wahlen, *Jesus and the Impurity of Spirits*, 167, 174. Equated similarly in the *Testament of the Twelve Patriarchs*, for example, in *T. Sim.* 3:5; 4:9, *T. Levi* 5:6; 18:12, *T. Ash.* 1:9.

72. Josephus, *War* 6.3.

73. Again, see Philostratus, *Life*, 4.8, *T. Sol.* 22, demons driving people into desolate places.

74. Luke 8:30, i.e., "Legion," meaning multiple demons with many names.

75. Busse, *To Be Near*, 22–43; To know the demon's name is to take control of the demon, Judg. 13:6, *T. Sol.* 2:1, 3:6, 4:3–4, *PGM* IV 1017–19.

76. Jesus was devastated by the murder of John and withdrew to a secluded place. Tradition later implied that John was second cousin to Jesus. From his seclusion, Jesus emerged determined to destroy Satan's control over the land; see Matt 14:13–14; Josephus, *Ant.* 18.118. On Jesus' words about John see Luke 24–35; Matt 11:7–19.

peasant exorcists of Galilee had only their contemporary understanding of demonic world assailing the villagers. They lived and died threatened by these malevolent forces in the socio-economic status of oppression, occupation, and poverty, all of which was believed to be due to Satan's activity. Jesus stood with them, and as a Galilean exorcist and peasant, but he battled these forces to reclaim the land for God. It is this socio-economic context of Galilee that we must now recover more fully.

2

The Socio-Economic Risk Conditions in Galilee

There were primarily two fertile agrarian production regions in the Middle Eastern Roman provinces during the first century—the Nile Valley in Egypt, and the territory around the lake of Galilee in Palestine. Both were completely exploited for the benefit of the elite in power and the cities of the empire; that is, for the benefit of the wealthy aristocracy and landowners that made up less than 1 percent of the population, as well as the rulers empowered by Rome, who placed onerous production quotas on the villagers and levied and collected taxes. This included Herod Antipas, Tetrarch (governor) of Galilee and Perea (4 BCE–39 CE). Antipas not only exploited these resources and the people who supplied them, he built two new opulent cities, placing an even greater burden on the subsistence peasants already struggling to survive.[1]

Antipas began with Sepphoris, which he built as a lavish Hellenistic city populated with pagan temples. He completed its massive reconstruction in 10 CE and renamed it *Autocratoris*.[2] Archaeology of the site also

---

1. Freyne, "Herodian Economics," 23–46.

2. Autocratoris, meaning "bird" due to the view from its height on a hill, was completed between 8–10 CE. Antipas had his northern residence there until he constructed Tiberias on the Sea of Galilee. Autocratoris was only four miles north of the small village of Nazareth, where, appropriately, carpenters and other artisans would have lived

confirms a strong Jewish presence with several ritual baths, *mikva ot*, dating to the first century, as well as a Jewish synagogue.[3] Antipas's father, Herod the Great, had originally constructed Sepphoris. It became his northern stronghold until its leveling by the Romans after the rebellion of Judas, the son of bandit Eleazar.[4] When Antipas was finally granted approval by Rome to rebuild the city, he made it what Josephus called the "ornament of Galilee."[5] This description is supported by the significant archaeological finds there, which include large Roman villas, elegant and elaborate frescoes, mosaics, baths, colonnaded streets, an elaborate water and sewage system, and a theater. More important, Josephus's depiction of the city underscored the immense funding and taxation that was required to rebuild it, which placed an egregious burden on the nearby villages of Galilee not only in the form of additional taxation, paid through the confiscation of fish and agricultural production, but for the ongoing resources it demanded to feed its population. Indeed, the sustained monetary and production resources demanded were overwhelming.[6] Sepphoris became so wealthy that the Jewish elite who lived there aligned with Rome and refused to join the Jewish revolt (66–73 CE). Instead, they minted special "peace" coins, *eirenopolis*, "the city of peace," to demonstrate their allegiance to Caesar and opened their gates, thereby sparing the city.

As if resources were not already strained, Antipas then built a second city around 20 CE he named Tiberias (after the Roman emperor Tiberius)[7] on the shores of Galilee atop the older village of Rakkah, and, contrary to Jewish law, near an old necropolis (i.e., cemetery).[8] Antipas moved his northern capital here after completing his palace. The wealth and prestige of Tiberias, which was primarily pagan in the first century,[9] was so great that the lake of Galilee was renamed the Sea of Tiberias. Scholars have recently estimated the population of both cities, Tiberias and Sepphoris, at ten to

---

during its reconstruction.

3. While some reports claimed Sepphoris had up to eighteen synagogues, only one has been found, and it has been dated to the fifth century, although certainly there were synagogues dating to the first century. See Meyers, Netzer, and Meyers, *Sepphoris*, 29.

4. Josephus, *Ant.* 17:271.

5. Josephus, *Ant.* 18:27.

6. Horsley, *Archaeology, History, and Society*, 29.

7. Tiberius, and the nearby Hammat Tiberias, had several hot springs that were believed to contain powers to absorb evil and cure ailments. Josephus, as we will see, called this city Emmaus in his writings.

8. Josephus, *Ant.* 18:36–38.

9. But later becoming a center of Judaism and one of Judaism's four holy cities: Jerusalem, Hebron, Safed, and Tiberias, after the Jewish war with Rome.

fifteen thousand, and when compared to the tiny villages of Galilee where the laborers lived, ranging from a few hundred to a one or two thousand, they dominated and demanded much if not all of the resources that could be produced.[10] Consequently, life for Galilean peasants along the shore of Lake Tiberias was a struggle for survival in the first century.

As such, there was virtually no consideration given by the elite to the subsistence-based, desperately poor, indebted, and powerless Jewish peasants living in small villages on the shores of Galilee.[11] These villages had simple names like Capernaum (Nahum's village), Magdala (the tower) and Bethsaida (fish house). The plight of the villagers was no better than that of chattel slaves, surviving at the pleasure of the Romans, the elite, and their authorized agents: "Fishing was controlled by the ruling elite. The local rulers (king, tetrarch, prefect) sold fishing rights to brokers (*telonai*, commonly translated as 'tax collectors,' or 'publicans'), who in turn contracted with fishers."[12] They labored daily to meet production quotas under strenuous contracted requirements, strictly overseen by Roman-licensed masters,[13] tax collectors and landowners, leaving little if any food or money to sustain extended families in desperately poor villages where bartering dominated.[14] Starvation and destitution were only a single injury or illness away. Their survival was solely tied to their success in providing for their overseers, whether in the fields or on the dangerous waters of Galilee—harvesting and processing grains, olives, and olive oil; fishing and production or preservation of various types of pickled and salted fish, or the highly sought Galilean fish sauces (Galilee was famous for these products), which were *all for export*. All production was directed to the wealthy and cities of the Roman Empire,[15] most of them far from Galilee and its villages.[16] "The impact of the Hellenistic and Roman influence on Jerusalem's elite is evident in nearly

---

10. Horsley, *Archaeology, History, and Society*, 45.

11. Josephus reported that there were 204 villages and cities in Galilee during the first century, which scholars now agree is an exaggeration. Josephus, *Life* 235.

12. Hanson and Oakman, *Palestine*, 106.

13. No Roman garrison was stationed near Capernaum in Galilee until the second century at Legio (Safrai, "The Roman Army in Galilee," 103–14). However, Roman soldiers did patrol the area and the *Via Maris*, which ran past Capernaum.

14. Safrai, "The Roman Army in Galilee," 106; note the excellent summary of the Galilean fishing economy also on 107.

15. Hanson and Oakman, *Palestine*, 110: "Besides supplying the Palestinian population, Galilean fish were exported to other sale-points. The distributors' route would most likely take them from Bethsaida in the north, to Tarichaeae on the western shore, through Cana to Ptolemais/Akko, the port city on the Mediterranean."

16. Sawicki, *Crossing Galilee*, 27–30; and Hansen, "The Galilean Fishing Economy," 99–111.

all aspects of Jerusalem's material culture, with a wide range of imported and locally produced consumer goods."[17] All benefits were to the minority elite, including gentile culinary foods and non-kosher Italian/Roman plates, pottery, and pans. All of this only further demonstrated that the elite were Romanized:

> The heavy dose of Roman cultural influence in Jerusalem around 20–15 BCE should be understood within the context of contemporary events. It was during these years that Herod undertook the reconstruction of the Jerusalem Temple. He established a theater and an ampitheater (or hippodrome) in Jerusalem, in which athletic competitions, chariot races, and musical and dramatic contests were held (Josephus, Ant. 15.8.1).[18]

Clearly, the "style of life—and death—of Jerusalem's elite was heavily influenced by Roman culture."[19]

Consequently, Galilean peasants lived and worked in an unforgiving, uncertain, and dangerous world. They believed that their desperate condition resulted from forces outside their control, exacerbated by a demonic imperialism—an invasion of evil—brought on by the occupying forces.[20] They waited for divine rescue. In their daily struggle, aptly captured in Jesus' prayer, they relied on the combined resources of extended family, including kin. Unless infirm, everyone worked, including children when they survived birth and the first few years. This was the only means of providing any financial safety, as droughts could suddenly reduce or devastate fish populations and production or dry up the Jordan River's essential inflow to the lake; weather, overfishing, or damage to a boat or a lost net could reduce daily or seasonal catch; landowners could simply change peasant laborers based on bias, competitive production, or a whim, affecting one member or the entire family. All of these were believed to be the result of evil influence. In desperation, even children could be sold into slavery to satisfy debts, thereby avoiding the expulsion of the family and starvation.[21]

There was no escape from this poverty. Galilean peasants had nothing. They were illiterate and uneducated, other than learning the oral traditions and religious rituals taught at synagogue gatherings (if the village had a gathering place).[22] To provide mitigation to their perilous lives and bring

17. Magness, "Ossuaries and Burials," 139.
18. Magness, "Ossuaries and Burials," 139.
19. Magness, "Ossuaries and Burials, 140.
20. Busse, *Jesus Resurrected*, 33–34.
21. See Corley, *Women and the Historical Jesus*, 39.
22. Approximately fifty different synagogues have been located in Galilee, making

order and safety, they relied on customs, superstitions, and practices passed down by short-lived generations, as life expectancy was less than thirty years. The greatest perpetual fear centered on demonic activity leading to misfortune, whether injury, illness, or possession. Exorcists and ecstatics that could counter demonic forces, drive out demons and illness, bring about rain[23] or more abundant catches, were both feared and welcomed into villages, such as Capernaum, where they were fed and housed in exchange for protection, healing, and safety.[24] This was the troubled life setting for the peasants of first-century Galilee.

OPPRESSION, POVERTY, AND SUBSISTENCE EXISTENCE IN GALILEE AS THE RESULT OF DEMONIC ACTIVITY AND INFILTRATION OF FOREIGN OCCUPIERS

Galilean peasants would never rationalize and believe that their desperate condition was the result of bad economics. Their land was possessed, overseen by foreigners, and the foreign gods considered demonic. Jerusalem and the religious elite had become wicked and supporters of these invaders.[25] The land was now under demonic control. To assess this alien world, we must examine more closely the details of life in Galilee based on independent sources available to us, as well as some of the earliest sources of the Jesus tradition. We will begin with the setting and context of fishers and their families, then turn to various sources, including the most primitive Gospel that can be recovered, Q, whose origin has been convincingly established to have been in first-century Galilee.[26]

What is certain is that the typical picture painted by some scholars, theologians, and writers—those who tend to portray fishers as living almost an idyllic life with bountiful surplus, and as if market forces and capitalism were the norm—is completely errant and foreign to Jesus' world. As noted,

---

it the most concentrated site for early synagogues at that time, including Meron, Gush Halav, Navorin, Bar Am and Bet Alfa and Korazim, and Capernaum, dating from the first to the second century.

23. Choni the Circle Drawer, as noted by Josephus.

24. Jesus of Nazareth, Luke 5:4–6.

25. Evidenced by the Dead Sea Scrolls of the Essenes of Qumran, i.e., the "wicked priest," 1QpHab 12:3–5, 8–9, 1:13; 8:8–12; 9:9. Contextual analysis also shows that John the Baptist saw the Jerusalem religious elite at the progenitors of the crisis. See also Ehrman, *New Testament*, 255; and Crossan, *Historical Jesus*, 313–20.

26. See Patterson's excellent presentation in *Lost Way*, 66–109, "The Galilean Gospel," which is a compelling and thorough analysis or the origin and original setting of Q in Galilee.

it was a life of poverty, indebtedness, and struggle for even a subsistence existence in first-century Galilee. Recent archaeology and studies have demonstrated this. For example, excavations in Capernaum,[27] primarily a fishing village where Jesus resided, have revealed some first-century Roman ruins, but a much larger poor peasant area with crowded multi-room family enclaves that dominated most of the original site.[28] These crude and simple one-level structures, made with black basalt fieldstones and rubble-filled walls, dirt or cobblestone floors, topped with branch, grass, and mud roofs, provided only the barest of subsistence living conditions for extended families.[29] Where families had once owned and worked land, they now huddled in small rooms, gathering around a central cook stove and grain-milling stone in a small central courtyard. There were absolutely no luxuries. Simple clay pots, dishes, amphorae, and small lamps have been found, along with fishhooks and pieces of fishnets. There were no hygienic areas, as the homes were without drainage. Sewage was carried out and dumped. These were working homes of the poor—certainly not the houses of any middle-class folk—shelters of the impoverished, heavily taxed, struggling families. Virtually every daily action they took had to be conducted carefully and with ritual precision and patterns of behavior to avoid the risk of evil infection or demonic attack. Water had to be drawn only on certain days, never at night or on Fridays, and consumption of water and food was only conducted at certain times to prevent malevolent contamination.[30] "He who drinks water towards evening steals it from the dead, who are led to the springs at this time."[31] Wednesday nights were particularly dangerous: "According to T. Canaan, the springs are especially dangerous on Wednesday evenings and nights, because it is then that the demons go to the springs with their skin water bags."[32] Even sitting under certain trees at certain times could lead to demonic attack.[33]

27. For exorcisms in the synagogues of Galilee and archaeology including Capernaum, see Runesson, "Architecture, Conflict, and Identity Formation," 231–57.

28. Horsley, *Archaeology, History, and Society*, 115.

29. Horsley, *Archaeology, History, and Society*, 115.

30. Busse, *Jesus Resurrected*, 23n9; also Dalman, *Work and Customs in Palestine*, 19: "But demons can also have a bad influence at certain times. One did not go out on the night before Wednesday and the Sabbath, in order not to be hurt by them (*b. Pes.* 112b). The belief was so strong that rain seemed to be especially welcome during these nights since it did not harm anyone."

31. Dalman, *Work and Customs*, 20, referencing *Midr. Teh.* 11, 6.

32. Cited by Dalman, *Work and Customs*, 18, citing Canaan, *Aberglaube und Volksmedizin*, 12.

33. Dalman, *Work and Customs*, 61.

As such, the real social, political and economic situation for poor peasants and their families during the time of Jesus' activity in Galilee is captured in the daily struggle for survival under harsh tenant/landlord relationships,[34] and the constant risk of demonic influence and attack that brought on their poverty, illness, maladies, and death. They worried about their daily and seasonal production, then watched as it was delivered, counted and sorted, then sent away to the larger urban cities, "leaving nothing for the peasant producers themselves to live on."[35] It is only in this context that the prayer Jesus taught to the Galilean exorcists he trained can be fully appreciated: It was a plea for one's daily bread, the forgiveness of debts (i.e., unpaid sums owed to landlords or licensed Roman agents for food, rent and supplies when production quotas were missed or bad production seasons occurred), and safety to avoid being expelled. It was a plea for protection from evil, recognizing God as king and coming deliverer.[36] As such, the villagers of Galilee were the *ptochos*, the truly destitute.[37]

FISHING AS SUBSISTENCE SURVIVAL IN GALILEE

Galilean fishers lived and died under backbreaking catch quotas—a cycle of poverty controlled by overseers, tantamount to economic enslavement, akin to tenant sharecropping. They had absolutely no rights or voice. Antipas and Roman officials licensed these overseers, who were in turn protected by Roman soldiers, to count and collect what was due. Speculation among some scholars that these fishers (including Kepha,[38] Yohannes and Yecob),

---

34. Patterson, *Lost Way*, 69: "Ancient cities were parasitic. Each was assigned a *chora*, a large agricultural area surrounding it, upon which the city could draw for its basic food supply and income."

35. Horsley, *Arcaheology, Society, and History*, 45; Horsley references another excellent article: Reed, "The Population of Capernaum," 24.

36. Patterson, *Lost Way*, 71.

37. Patterson, *Lost Way*, 202.

38. Shimon ben Yonah was renamed "the Rock" by Jesus after being trained as his exorcist. In Greek, "the rock" is *Petros*, but in Aramaic, *Kepha* (pronounced in Kee-phah by some translators, or Kaypha by others), the "s" being added to adjust the Aramaic ending "a," implying a feminine ending in Greek, thereby making it masculine in Greek, i.e., Kephas. Consequently, Cephas, commonly used by scholars, should be Kepha, the original Aramaic. The other translation of Cephas improperly drops the hard "k" of Aramaic. The name *Kepha* is rare in the Hebrew scriptures, and is found in Jeremiah 4:29 and Job 30:6, here meaning mountain peaks or mountain crags. This creates interesting possibilities, e.g., is Jesus renaming Shimon to the exorcist-name, "the Peak," or High One, or is it a reference to his activity with Jesus in the mountains where visions were encountered? More likely, "the rock" on which Satan and his demons are broken, a foundation for the inbreaking kingdom of God.

were of "moderate means," presuming that they owned their boats and were fairly well-off is completely false.[39] Such idealized views have been shown to be absurd by K. C. Hanson.[40] There was no such thing as a "moderate" or "middle class." Their fishing cooperatives (*koinonoi*) with other family clans (the "Yonah-Zebedee" cooperative) demonstrate this—it was a matter of survival. Cooperatives were organized by necessity, certainly due to being burdened with multiple taxes—Roman, from Antipas, and the Temple tax.[41] Taxation was so heavy there was no surplus, as all production above subsistence was confiscated and sent to the urban centers and the elite for consumption and profit.[42] The cooperatives with other families were provided with refurbished and repaired boats at additional fees as part of their cooperative leases and paid for by their catch.[43] The first-century Galilee fishing boat recovered from abating waters by archaeologists in 1986 shows that it was repaired for decades[44] before sinking, as it finally failed. It sank with a cooking pot and pottery in it.

> Peasants did not voluntarily supply labor for the elite, nor did they work willingly for wages. Most traditional peasants are devoted to self-sufficient household economy as the elites are to the welfare of their estates.[45]

As such, Galilean fishers were desperately poor, indebted, and at risk on water and land. They lived day-to-day under duress and operated in what they believed were the dangerous, haunted waters of Galilee that could be deadly. They faced demonic attack from winds, waves, ghosts, and malevolent spirits that sought to draw them into the water.[46] When they returned, they even faced the scrutiny of "game wardens" that monitored catch, ensuring that no "sacred fish" were harvested, which they would confiscate. They were victims of theft, as these overseers took bribes or increased fees to line their own pockets and were hated and despised by the locals. Escaping this cycle of poverty was virtually impossible.[47]

39. Including Jeremias in *Jerusalem in the Time of Jesus*.
40. Hanson, "Galilean Fishing Economy," 99–111.
41. Matt 17:24–27.
42. Hanson, "Galilean Fishing Economy," 115.
43. The recovered Galilee boat was a refurbished boat, repaired repeatedly, using as many as 40 different woods: Shelley Wachsmann, *Sea of Galilee Boat*, cited by Hanson and Oakman, *Palestine*, 110.
44. Rabinovich, "'Jesus Boat' Causes Ripples."
45. Hanson and Oakman, *Palestine*, 119.
46. See Busse, *Jesus Resurrected*, 36. Matt 14:22–36; Mark 6:45–56; John 6:16–24.
47. Freyne, *Galilee, Jesus, and the Gospels*, 161.

In the villages, fishers often employed rituals to mitigate risks from demonic attacks by spirits and ghosts that wandered in and around Galilee. These included not only prayers but also sacrifices and sometimes divination, particularly among Hellenized Jews and gentiles who looked for protection and safety on the waters and from forces below. The sacred and haunted waters of Palestine and Galilee were an integral part of the life of Palestinian Jews. Understanding the risk context of these waters is therefore critical.

3

Sacred and Haunted Waters

Demons, Evil Spirits, and Mitigations

In the ancient world, springs, cisterns, rivers, and lakes were carefully encountered and thoughtfully consumed because they were believed inhabited.[1] Waters could be sacred gifts, providing safety and health, or contaminated with evil forces, making one susceptible to possession, illness, misfortune, or even death.[2] Those who controlled the water's inhabitants were believed to be imbued with divine authority.[3] This has important implications for how Jesus was received by the villagers and fishers of Galilee. Consequently, recovering the risk context of these waters provides important insights into the activity of Jesus and other charismatics in their contemporary setting.

---

1. For an excellent article on pre and post–modern oral traditions on water demons inhabiting Palestine, which is still cited by scholars, see Canaan, "Haunted Springs and Water Demons."

2. Even later rabbinic tradition, *Leviticus Rabbah* 24:3, reports the exorcism of a well using iron implements and oral sayings.

3. Inhabitants of the waters of Galilee were thought to include demons, phantasms, evil spirits and, of course, the fish. Those who controlled the fish were particularly esteemed by the fisher peasants, as fish could be directed into their nets.

SACRED AND HAUNTED WATERS

The identification of sacred waters in Palestine and Galilee as an event of God's intervention, often for the benefit of the afflicted, extends from the ancient traditions in Genesis to the New Testament Gospels. Many locations were named in honor of a direct encounter with God and the angels that took place there, which continued to be well known into the first century[4]:

> The pregnant Hagar who sought refuge from the Negev sun and heat while escaping danger from Abraham's wife, Sarai, was rescued by God: "And the angel of Jehovah found her by a fountain on the Way to Shur. And he said, Hagar ... return to thy mistress ... Behold thou are with child and shall bear a son, whose name shall be Ishmael (God Listens), because Jehovah has heard your affliction ... And she called the name of Jehovah that spoke to her, 'Thou art a God-That-Seeth-Of-The-Living-One-Who-Seeth' ... Wherefore the name of the well was called Be'er-la-hai-ro'i, 'The-Well-Of-The-One-Who-Seeth.'"[5]

The event of rain in the arid Palestinian climate was also understood as divine intervention for those in need:

> The wilderness and the dry land shall be glad; and the desert shall rejoice and blossom as the roses ... Then shall the lame man leap as a stag and the tongue of the mute shall sing; for in the wilderness shall waters break out and streams in the desert.[6]

Early oral traditions of premodern Palestine also recorded specific days when even approaching certain waters was dangerous and required ritual behavior.

> Bathing children Fridays is harmful. One also does not go to the water on Fridays and also at night, because of the danger of demons. According to T. Canaan, the springs are especially dangerous on Wednesday evenings and nights, because it is then that the demons go to the springs with their skin water bags ... One did not go out on the night before Wednesday and the Sabbath in order not to be hurt by them. The belief was so

---

4. For example, Genesis 33:18–20: the Patriarch Jacob's return to Shechem from Paddam Aram where a well was found and associated with him, then mentioned in John 4:5–6, where Jesus encounters the Samaritan women from Sychar at that well.

5. Gen 16:7–14.

6. Isa 35:10.

strong that rain seemed to be especially welcome during these nights since it did not harm anyone.[7]

It was around these springs, wells, rivers, and the lake of Galilee that the villages were settled, all reliant upon the waters provided by God, or to non-Jews, the gods, and were named. Josephus assumes that the powers within these waters are angels and spirits that protect them or demons that could cause harm if improperly used. For example, in Galilee, it can not escape us that he describes the efficacious powers of the warm waters.[8] Springs and waters in Galilee were considered possessed by spirits and demons, i.e., that the waters were under their control and could even be cursed.

> Some springs have a complete family of spirits living in each; it is understood that hot springs, as in Tiberias [Galilee], are heated by spirits (acting on the basis of the commands of King Solomon). It can be generalized that there is hardly a source of water in the land of Israel without a spirit (one or more) . . . The rabbis learned: "One should not drink water from rivers or lakes at night. And if he drinks, he risks his life because of the hazard. What hazard? The hazard of demons."[9]

Another warning from rabbinic literature:

> He who drinks water towards evening steals it from the dead, who are led to the springs at this time.[10]

Practices that continued to premodern periods with waters were conducted for protection:

> The *tashlikh* prayers of the Jews, which are to be recited on the afternoon of New Year's Day (1 Tishri), next to a body of water . . . this takes place at cisterns and in Safed on roofs, from which one can see the Lake of Tiberias. People throw bread into the water while praying to be purified from sin.[11]

Even certain plants that grow near waters were to be avoided:

> The carobeam (Ceratonia siliqua, Ar. *kharrub*) is also considered to be a tree inhabited by demons, and thus not suited as a resting

---

7. Dalman, *Work and Customs*, 18–19. See Dalman's comment on handwritten notes by Beshara Canaan.

8. Josephus, *War* 4.1.3.

9. Bar-Ilan, *Exorcism by Rabbis*, cites as additional support the *Pesachim* 112 p. 1, two *baraitot*: Also cited in Canaan, "Haunted Springs and Water Demons," 153–70.

10. Dalman, *Work and Customs*, 20, citing *Midr. Teh.* 11, 6.

11. Dalman, *Work and Customs*, 35, citing Luncz, *Jerusalem*, Volume 1, 37f.

place, although its dark, sparkling . . . evergreen leaves give a particularly dense shade. 'Abd el-Wali did not want to have even a stick from its wood because it would bring bad luck, and called this tree, which graces its surroundings, as well as the tamarisk of the Jordan Valley, *makruh*, "loathsome." The rustling of the latter is interpreted as a mysterious *allahallah* coming from a demon, a reason why one should not sleep under it or be under a sycamore tree.[12]

The importance and danger of waters in the ancient world can not be understated:

It is an old and widespread belief in all Semitic countries that springs, cisterns, and all running waters are inhabited. The djinn—demons—live in the first place in the interior of the earth, whence they come out. The Hebrew *ob*, the Syriac *zakkura*, and the Arabic pre-Islamic *'ahlul'art* illustrate this. They come from the lower world and therefore we meet them generally in places which have a direct connection with the lower regions: trees whose roots go down in the interior of the earth; cracks, caves, springs, and wells . . . with the above-named original abode of demons . . . springs, wells, caves, and lonely valleys . . . It is to be noted that everything mentioned in this list has a direct connection with demons, talismans, or sorcery.[13]

Of course, the rains were known to have as their origin from God, and it is to this gift many traditions, practices, and prayers were offered in every season and for virtually every festival. These waters filled the wells, river, springs, and lake of Galilee, which flowed down the Jordan to the Dead Sea. Galilee gathered these waters from the springs and rivers, and each had their own significance in the life and practices of the villagers.

Indeed, the most important waters known to be inhabited were both the hot springs and the waters that came from caves, cracks, or channels that formed the beginning of a spring.[14] While angels protected some of the springs, most were possessed by demons. The waters in Emmaus of Galilee were more than just warm springs that aided in health; they were considered transformative and powerful, able to pull out and absorb demons and spirits by the work of angels.[15] Exorcists and ecstatics such as Jesus would have frequented these sites, employing charismatic prayers, commands, and

---

12. Dalman, *Work and Customs*, 59.
13. Canaan, "Haunted Springs and Water Demons," 153–54.
14. Canaan, "Haunted Springs and Water Demons," 155.
15. A similar tradition is reflected in John 5:4.

ritual authority to call on these same angels to assist in freeing the possessed by trapping their demons in the sacred waters. Indeed, demons feared water, as it could be used to capture and hold them.[16]

> Now there is in Jerusalem near the Sheep Gate[17] a pool, which in Aramaic is called *beth hesda* [or *beth Zatha*],[18] and which is surrounded by five covered colonnades [i.e., porticoes].[19] Here a great number of disabled people used to lie—the blind, the lame, the paralyzed—and they waited for the moving of the waters. For time to time an angel of the Lord would come down and stir up the waters. The first one into the pool after each such disturbance would be cured [*hugeis egineto*, became sound, or freed] of whatever disease they had [or, *depote kateicheto*, they had been bound].[20]

By entering the pool, the demon that possesses the victim is absorbed and trapped.

Jesus was *intentionally* at that pool of *beth hesda*. This must have been a common practice, where he and his exorcists went to witness demons being drawn out with the aid of powerful angels, whose presence was made known by stirring waters.[21] In the tradition noted from John 5, Jesus acknowledges the power of the angel(s) to capture demons at these sacred pools and *mikveh*. Later he states that he was able to call on a legion of angels

---

16. That demons feared waters and being trapped in the first-century world can be demonstrated; Carter, *Matthew and the Margins*, 213. As Carter shows, water was a place to contain demons until the judgment. See also *T. Sol.* 5:11, 11:6. The practices to capture demons in water included incantation bowls. Over seventy-two in Jewish Aramaic, thirty-three in Mandaic, and twenty-one in Syriac were discovered buried under house corners. These were to not only keep evil away, but to capture these spirits and even reverse binding and attacking spells.

17. The sheep gate may have been near the Temple, where the sheep to be sacrificed were cleaned before being submitted to the priests. There the waters may have been considered sacred or part of an act of sanctification. See Rousseau, "Exorcism," 178–79.

18. A translation could be either the "house of shame" or the "house of grace," but more than likely the former.

19. In this case a five-sided pool, which has been confirmed in recent archaeology

20. John 5:1–4 (Many manuscripts do not include verse 4 in whole or part, but the inclusion of this information was problematic and omitted for that reason).

21. Our study has demonstrated that the waters of Galilee and some of the springs and waters near it were considered the home of demons. This is the place the demons requested Jesus send them as noted, in the tradition of the Gerasene demons, who possess swine and run into Galilee.

for assistance, which would include these sites if needed, to assist him in controlling and expelling demons.[22]

As demonstrated in Mark,[23] Jesus employed many techniques to expel demons, which included using his saliva to absorb demons, drawing them out of victims.[24] In other cases he combined the use of his saliva to permanently dispose of demons, sending them into sacred waters. For example, Jesus expels a blinding demon using the powerful waters of the pool of Siloam (John 9:1–10). Common to the use of multiple practices in some of his more difficult exorcisms, Jesus here employs powerful substances, some considered magical in the Greco-Roman world, and he does so in stages. First, he mixes his saliva (his spittle, the "water" that contained his authority as an exorcist),[25] with soil to make an expulsion-clay to draw out the demon (i.e., a substance that was used in many of his exorcisms).[26] Saliva, sometimes mixed with clay, was known in the ancient world,[27] and among the Essenes,[28] as an efficacious substance used to ward off or to control evil.[29] Next, Jesus then rubs the mixture into the eyelids, transferring his authority and power to the area of demonic control. He then commands the demon to "go!" (*hupage*, i.e., this is not a command to the man, but the demon to enter the special clay), followed by the command to the man to "wash!" at *Siloam*, the pool meaning "be sent." In this last stage, the demon cast into and captured by the water-mixed clay, the moist substance of the exorcist and

22. Matt 26:53.

23. Mark 7:33, 8:23.

24. Jesus takes the possessed aside in private, a common practice for him. In the example of the man blinded by a demon in Bethsaida, Jesus uses his hands and physical contact, including contact with the location of demonic possession, the eyes, to help rid the man of his demon, Mark 8:22–26. In another, Jesus places his fingers in the ears of one possessed. The contact passes the authority of Jesus to the site of demonic attack and then the expulsion by command is given, Mark 7:31–37. See Busse, *To Be Near*, 83–84.

25. Jesus' water was considered powerful, transformative, and able to commute his authority to others. For example, even at the cross, the tradition of his side flowing with water was the release of his authority and power, like that used in his saliva. John 19:34, and much later in 1 John 5:6.

26. That this tradition omits the use of spittle and mud (a magical clay) in Matthew and the tradition is missing altogether in Luke constitutes strong evidence that this controversial practice of Jesus (considered magic in the ancient world) was used frequently as one of his expulsion techniques., just as he put his fingers in the ears of the deaf man to absorb the demon into himself through his hands (Mark 7:32–35).

27. Graves-Brown, *Dancing for Hathor*, 165. Isis tricks Re by using his spittle and clay to obtain his name and gain power.

28. Frayer-Griggs, "Spittle, Clay, and Creation," 659–70.

29. For example, Pliny, *Natural History*, 28:7; Petronius, *Satyricon*, 131.

the earth, is "washed" or expelled into the waters of Siloam (John 9:1–7), a sacred *mikveh*.[30] The tradition of John has retained the translation of Siloam known to locals for its power: "[Siloam] . . . which is interpreted, Sent (*apestalmenos*)," because it was where demons and evil spirits were expelled into its waters. Recovery of this risk practice is now made remarkably clear to us.

Consequently, the "healing waters" of Emmaus that absorbed demons would certainly have been at a location where Jesus and his fellow exorcists would have been active, and a village he would have liberated from demonic control. It is likely that few if any gentiles would have visited an area where the Jewish sick, diseased, possessed, and lame waited by waters, and where many continued to be taken for years, long after Jesus and his exorcists were active. As such, Galilean Emmaus would have been a village to where his followers may have fled post-crucifixion and been in hiding, having vacated both Jerusalem and Capernaum for fear of spies and capture.[31]

JESUS AND THE WATERS OF GALILEE

The waters of Palestine and Galilee were an integral part of the daily life, practices, fears, and risk mitigations of villagers. Sacred waters also played a significant role in the activity of Jesus, including his exorcisms and teachings, which recognized and employed the sacred and profane waters of Palestine and Galilee that were inhabited. Examples are plentiful: Jesus' command to give the helpless a cup of *cold water*;[32] the waters of the Jordan, where John the Baptist immersed Jesus as part of his ritual to exorcise and capture "sin," i.e., demons that infected the victim with illness and death;[33] Jesus' command to his followers that they must be to be baptized of water and the spirit—the drawing out of evil and the reward of protection by spiritual possession;[34] the vision of Jesus stilling the storm over Galilee and rescuing Kepha from drowning;[35] his discussion about drinking living

---

30. Just as the waters of Bethesda were influenced by the angel in the Mikveh.

31. Mark 1:21–28. Jesus confronts the elite from Jerusalem in Capernaum, including their decision to try and capture and destroy him. It appears that Jesus is accused of being possessed by Satan there as well. From Capernaum he is followed and then hunted. See Iwe, *Jesus in the Synagogue of Capernaum*, 59–61.

32. Matt 10:42, Mark 9:41. A cup of cold water on the right day and time was free of demonic pollution.

33. In *Antiquities*, Josephus also cites examples of demons being drawn into the water when the exorcist immerses them (see Josephus, *Ant.* 2, 5, 45–48).

34. John 3:5.

35. Matt 14:22–23, now made abundantly clear—the terror of fishermen being

water,³⁶ i.e., his teachings that liberated adherents from demonic control if followed;³⁷ and drawn from actual life in Galilee—the parable of casting the net into the water and keeping the good fish.³⁸ Indeed, his control over the fish, directing them to nets, was such a powerful and potent authority that Jesus was fed, housed, and served by the village of Capernaum, as well as followed by some of its peasant fishers who abandoned their trade to be trained by him as exorcists. Water also played a critical role in other sayings ascribed to Jesus, such as in the *Gospel of Thomas*, where water became an efficacious metaphor for life to be found in his words; i.e., "drinking" from Jesus becomes a union with him that is immediately salvific, freeing one from evil and pollution, just to name one example.³⁹

SUMMARY

Given the dire context of life for Jewish village peasants surrounding Galilee, where they were subject to demons, illness, poverty, occupation, and an unending bond to a subsistence survival, their inability to even control the safety of the waters that gave them life is striking. Other than through ritual practices that might afford some protection, they lacked even the ability to mitigate the many risks of simply drawing water, let alone taking drink, without fear. It is abundantly clear that anyone who held authority to ensure their protection and control these forces was embraced by the villagers, and more, what they said mattered because it touched their daily lives and safety.

With the risk contexts that were operative in first-century Galilee recovered, we can now turn to Jesus' activity in this *sitz im leben*. Our contextual analysis should now provide new and critical insights into the perilous risks Jesus faced and the mitigations he employed to neutralize the proliferation of demons in Galilee and the threat of demonic imperialism that was overtaking the land and villages. Even more, we can begin to understand the perilous risk context present when Jesus linked his exorcisms

---

taken by demons that were trapped in Galilee, but overcome by the authority of Jesus over the demonic waters.

36. For rituals and purification, cistern water was not allowed according to Jewish law. In contrast to this was "living water," i.e., running water of streams and rivers that came from rains and not touched by humans. This is why *miqvaot* collected rainwater for ritual purification. Jesus is using a practice and rule familiar to the Galileans by claiming that his words and practices are pure and come from God, not from the hands of men, and so carry authority to expel evil. See Sawicki, *Crossing Galilee*, 23.

37. John 4:10, 7:37–39.

38. *Gos. Thom.* 8.

39. *Gos. Thom.* 10.8.

to the arrival of the kingdom of God, something that was unparalleled among his contemporaries,[40] and represented a dangerous threat to the elite and the forces, human and otherwise, that had elevated them to power and continued to sustain them.[41] It was their kingdom that Jesus claimed was satanic and being overthrown, evidenced by his actions.[42] He was casting out their demons, even their "legion" of demons, into the waters of Galilee to be trapped and neutralized, freeing the land and its people from peril by the "finger of God."[43]

40. Q links the kingdom of God and exorcism: Q 11:13-14, 17-20.

41. Jesus' exorcisms were a powerful countermeasure to the elite of Galilee, Judea, and the High Priestly families, which were put at great risk to their rule: see Guijarro, "The Politics of Exorcism." Jesus was considered a deceiving dark magician. Both John and his accusations of his enemies being "possessed" and a "brood of vipers" were demonic accusations and dangerous to the elite.

42. Mark 3:27, i.e. entering and overthrowing the strongman; Mark 5:1-17.

43. Mark 8:28-34.

4

Jesus in Galilee

Defeating Satan: Practices, Exorcisms, and Control

> And he went throughout all of Galilee, preaching in their synagogues and casting out demons (Mark 1:39).

Whether one was a peasant or a wealthy landowner, a member the Herodian ruling class or Roman aristocracy, the appointed high priest or the *praefectus Judaeae*,[1] Galilee was known to be inhabited by dangerous, malevolent phantasms, demons, and evil spirits—the lake, its springs and streams, the nearby caves, *necropoli*, and its villages. The evidence is overwhelming. For the village peasants, the proliferation of demonic activity in Galilee exploded with the invasion of pagan forces and their gods.[2] This "demonic imperialism" overwhelmed every aspect of life with the Roman occupationand only

---

1. *Prefect*, or governor of Judaea, such as Pontius Pilate, the fifth Roman governor from 26 CE to 36 CE; other titles applied to this appointment being *procurator* (per Tacitus) or *epitropos* (according to Josephus and Philo). The Latin inscription in the excavated theatre in Caesarea used the title *Praefectus Iuda*. See Hansen and Oakman, *Palestine*, 78.

2. Witmer, *Galilean Exorcist*, 172–73; Witmer provides a convincing argument that the occupation of the Roman army was associated by the locals with a proliferation of demonic activity. Furthermore, archaeological evidence has shown Romans present in Galilee in the first century prior to the Jewish war.

further exacerbated the already tenuous struggle for safety and subsistence survival of the villagers.[3] There was no escape from the burden of foreign occupation that brought corrupt overseers,[4] heavy taxation,[5] rampant indebtedness, the constant threat of destitution and starvation, and the intensified peril of demonic activity that could ravage them.[6] These dangerous realities affected every part of the daily life and practices for generations of Galilean Jewish peasants huddled in these poor villages: from which days and even hours that water could be safely drawn from springs and consumed to avoid infection or be poisoned by water demons,[7] to the terror of night fishing on Galilee to meet onerous fishing quotas, where dangerous phantasms floated over the waters seeking victims[8] they could drown to become demons.[9] Virtually every aspect of life had a corresponding habit or practice to mitigate peril and prevent vulnerability to evil forces.

Exorcists who could repel, control, subjugate, and expel demons that inhabited these waters or attack villagers, while feared, were cautiously

---

3. Josephus, *War* 1:128, 141, 143, 145-47, 149-51; and *Ant.* 14:61-70. For a discussion of Josephus and the intervention of Rome, see Bellemore, "Josephus, Pompey, and the Jews," 94-118. The Roman occupation began in 63 BCE when Pompey the Great conquered Jerusalem, defeating the Hasmonean kingdom under Judah Aristobulus, and was replaced by the Romans with John Hyrcanus. From that time forward, Palestine became a Roman province and was garrisoned, overseen by Roman governors. Rome appointed the kings and rule, controlled the local leadership, the High Priesthood (even the priestly vestments), and chose the priestly ruling families. In addition, Roman rule established strict taxation and law over the province, relinquishing only certain rights to local leaders. But more, the Roman occupation brought with it an embedded Roman religion in Palestine, in its buildings and public inscriptions; see Hansen and Oakman, *Palestine*, 78.

4. Hansen and Oakman, *Palestine*, 106-07, particularly with regard to the Galilean fishing economy.

5. Hansen and Oakman, *Palestine*, 114-16, on onerous Roman taxation that "flowed upward" for the benefit of the elite.

6. These were poor peasants whose worlds were inundated with otherworldly forces out of their control. In Galilee they were totally reliant on local resources, primarily a diet of bread, olives, and fish, where the whims of evil forces haunting Galilee could quickly force them into starvation.

7. Canaan, "Haunted Springs and Water Demons," 153-70.

8. Craffert, *Life*, 226.

9. For example, see a late first-century tradition in John 21:1-4, Mark 5:1-9, and Luke 8:26-39. Busse, *Jesus Resurrected*, 36.

allowed entry,[10] and sometimes housed and fed by the local peasants.[11] This was done in the villages not only to garner the protection afforded by the exorcist's presence, thereby mitigating the perilous risk of demonic attack (e.g., a family member's fever was not only expelled but the demon was prevented from return),[12] but also in the hope that the exorcist held sway over the fish so as to direct them into their nets[13] (i.e., animistic powers),[14] increasing catch and sustaining their subsistence day-to-day existence by helping to meet the harsh contracted requirements of the local Roman *publicani*.[15] And we know of one Galilean exorcist who could do all of these

---

10. Jesus was invited to remain at Cephas's house after healing his mother-in-law, Mark 1:29–31, Matt 8:14–15, Luke 4:38–41. However, Jesus was forbidden to enter not only villages that feared him but territories as well. See Busse, *Jesus Resurrected*, 25, and Matt 8:34.

11. Jesus' "home" was identified as the fishing village of Capernaum (Mark 2:1, Matt 4:13), but he left after a short time to continue his war on Satan, possibly within just a few weeks or months. By the end of the first century, rules were established to limit the amount of time an exorcist could make claim to hospitality, as these rights were abused. This indicates that wandering charismatics and exorcists of the Jesus tradition had been expecting long-term hospitality, placing too great a burden on individuals. See Jonathan Draper, "Weber, Theissen, and 'Wandering Charismatics'" and "The Jesus Tradition in the Didache."

12. Most notably, Cephas's wife, Matt 8:14–5, Mark 1:29–31, Luke 4:38–39; also indirectly, Mary and Martha, John 11:1–44.

13. Luke 5:4–6; John 21:6–8; either the trammel, drag- or cast-net that were used in Galilee; see also Hansen and Oakman, *Palestine*, 109–10.

14. For Jesus directing fish into the net, see Luke 5:1–11 and John 21:1–14. Also in Matt 17:24–27, Jesus directs Cephas to throw out a fishing line. The first fish he catches will have a four-drachma coin in its mouth, which is to be used to pay the temple tax for both Jesus and Cephas. See Hull, *Hellenistic Magic*, 104. Jesus is accused of being possessed by Beelzebul, who controlled the demons of Galilee, and is able to control the fish for the benefit of subsistence fishermen (to deceive them, according to his enemies); thus, the accusation that Jesus is empowered by Beelzebul, Luke 11:15–17.

15. *Publicani*, or Roman-appointed and -paid tax collectors, thought to be notoriously corrupt in Palestine, who monitored catch and contracted requirements, collected sums due.

things—Jesus,[16] the son of Mary,[17] the exile of the village of Nazareth,[18] who was given a room and board for having exorcised a demon of fever from the mother-in-law of Kepha, a subsistence fisherman of Capernaum.[19]

JESUS IN THE VILLAGES OF GALILEE AND THE CHARGES BROUGHT AGAINST HIM

The majority of Jesus' exorcisms were conducted in insignificant villages of only a few hundred peasants adjacent to the fresh water lake there[20] (thirteen miles long by 8.1 miles wide, with a maximum depth of 141 feet),[21] including Capernaum (the "village of Nahum,"[22] perhaps with four hundred villagers),[23] Tarichaeae ("place of processed fish," also known as Magdala, famous for its salted and pickled fish),[24] Bethsaida ("house of the fish god"),[25]

16. Busse, *Jesus Resurrected*, 160, 245; Luke 5:4 is one of several examples of Jesus' charismatic direction and ability control animals to assist his villagers, see Mark 1:16–20, Matt 4:18–22, Luke 5:2–11, John 21:6; Matt 17:27.

17. *Yeshua*, "son of Mary" (Mark 6:3) is the earliest attestation of Jesus to any familiar affiliation, even though she is mentioned only twice in Mark. It is significant that within the highly important kinship affiliation system of sustenance and support in first-century Palestine (see Freyne, "Herodian Economics," 42–43), that Jesus is thrown out of his village in Nazareth, is rejected by his brothers and sisters, and that Joseph disappears from all later narratives. Jesus is called "mad," possessed by a demon, and so is alienated. Jesus fails to provide support for his kin, rejecting them (Mark 3:35), and instead supports a band of exorcists from various fishing villages along Galilee. See also Neyrey, "The Loss of Wealth," 139–49.

18. Matt 4:12–13 says that after John was put into prison, Jesus left Nazareth for Capernaum, which omits being expelled. Likely, though, the timing of both events may have been related (i.e., the villagers of Nazareth wanted nothing to do with Jesus, who was a supporter of John).

19 After almost having been killed, Jesus was expelled from Nazareth for this claims and charismatic activities; see Luke 4:14–30.

20. For Capernaum, archaeologists now estimate the population as being between eight hundred and 1,500.

21. Josephus, *War* 3.506 slightly differs on the size of the lake.

22. The identification of Nahum is not known, as there is no association with the Hebrew prophet.

23. Horsley, *Archaeology, History, and Society*, 114. Josephus correctly identifies Capernaum as a village; see the discussion in Mason, *Flavius Josephus*, 160; on Capernaum as embellished to be a city in the Synoptics, see also Reed, *Archaeology and the Galilean Jesus*, 166–69; for Capernaum's location near a major trade route and the likelihood that it attracted less-desirables, including prostitutes, see Reed, *Galilean Jesus*, 146–48.

24. Strabo, *Geogr.* 16.2.45.

25. Hansen, "Galilean Fishing Economy," 99.

and Chorazin (perhaps "the little village" or "farm village").[26] All of these were within walking distance of each other, the furthest being ten miles away. Archaeologists have yet to locate first century Chorazin[27] (but recently perhaps some of Bethsaida), mentioned in the earliest Gospel source, Q,[28] as it was so small that no trace has been found.

> These villages are not places of mythic importance, like Jerusalem or Sodom. Neither are they well-known cities in Galilee, like Sepphoris, near Nazareth, or Scythopolis (Beth-shean), to the south of the Sea of Galilee. Q never mentions these larger places. Instead its range is focused on these tiny villages.[29]

It is from these small villages that Jesus also selected and trained a small band of subsistence fisher peasants, suffering under this cycle of poverty, foreign occupation, and demonic attack, to become apprentice exorcists, enlisting them to drive demons from the villages, thereby, according to Jesus, inaugurating the *euangelion*, the return of the kingdom and rule of God and the end Satan's occupation.[30] Unfortunately, these were the same villages on which he later placed a deadly curse for rejecting both him and his exorcists by refusing to "change their ways."[31] Poor, hungry, often homeless, sometimes gathering the raw grain from fields to eat,[32] Jesus and his exorcists continued to enter these villages when allowed[33] and drive out their demons before all was lost.

As such, the context and social setting for Jesus' confrontation with demons was set in these insignificant villages where he engaged in multiple, aggressive exorcisms of the possessed peasants (usually on the Sabbath), to free both the villagers and their synagogue assemblies of multiple demonic

---

26. Mentioned independently of the New Testament in the Talmud, *b. Menahot 85a*.

27. Excavations have yielded third- to fourth-century CE coins. The synagogue, constructed of black basalt stones (15 x 21 m.), includes a stone "seat of Moses," where an elder or "judge" of the law, recognized by the synagogue, would sit, i.e., a place of honor and authority.

28. Patterson, *Lost Way*, 66–84.

29. Patterson, *Lost Way*, 66.

30. Mark 3:15, 9:1, 38; but also included women, such as Mary renamed by Jesus, "The Tower," or the *Magdala*. See Busse, *Jesus Resurrected*, 115n46; also see Brooten, *Women Leaders*, 87–88.

31. Matt 11:20–24; Luke 10:13–15.

32. Mark 2:23, heads of corn; Matthew 12:1, heads of grain. Luke 6:1 confirms they were heads of grain, as they rubbed them in the palms of their hands to free the grain from the chaff.

33. Jesus was forbidden from entering at least two villages: Luke 9:51–56, Mark 5:17.

maladies, and so, Satan's control.³⁴ He began these village-by-village incursions immediately following his baptism by John,³⁵ and then intensified his efforts³⁶ after John's murder by Herod Antipas, *tetrarch* of Galilee,³⁷ the Roman appointee and imperialist sympathizer. With the Romans came their rulers, like Antipas, educated in Rome, and their foreign gods (i.e., new pagan demons),³⁸ which for John, Jesus, the Zealots (including the Zealot extremists, the *sikarioi*, the "knife men" or "assassins"),³⁹ and Essenes⁴⁰ resulted in such a saturation of demonic presence in Palestine that it possessed and corrupted even the religious elite controlling the Temple, including the High Priest, who was himself appointed and controlled by the Roman demonic imperialists. Indeed, for Jesus, the High Priest and Antipas represented the embodiment of demonic imperialism brought on by Rome, evidenced by John's murder. Jesus believed that this proliferation of evil must be overturned by any and all means.⁴¹

34. The reliability of the exorcism tradition as originating in the context of Jesus' historical activity is now uncontested; see the excellent analysis of Evans, *Jesus and His Contemporaries*, 214–43, as it predates any messianic claim and is controversial (Why would the church create so many controversial stories about Jesus, many of which in Mark are later dropped or softened?). Evans demonstrates their historicity and their distinctiveness from any contemporary Jewish charismatic. The tradition also can not be simply associated with Jesus as a "holy man" (Vermes, *Jesus the Jew*) or a magician (Smith, *Jesus*), but is complex and must be associated with his mission to drive Satan and demonic imperialism from the land.

35. Mark 1:9–11, Matt 3:13–17, Luke 3:21–22.

36. If, as reported in Luke 1:36, John and Jesus were second cousins, they shared ecstatic gifts, despised the Jerusalem religious elite, typified them as possessed, and both announced the coming of the kingdom of God and displacement of evil. This is an interesting set of perilous risk parallels that deserves further investigation.

37. Tetrarch, or "ruler of a quarter" of Palestine, the Roman client state, approved and selected by Rome to oversee Galilee and Perea; on his divine punishment for killing John the Baptist. See Josephus, *Ant.* 18.109–18.

38. Busse, *To Be Near*, 58; Busse, *Enemies*, 137: foreign gods were considered demons by Jewish peasants and scripturally trained Jewish pharisees. Excavations of a temple in Sepphoris demonstrate the proliferation of pagan worship in Galilee, and confirmation of a significant pagan population in that city and Tiberias in the time of Jesus.

39. See Josephus, *Ant.* 14.158–60, 20.102; *Wars* 1.204.5, 2.254–57, 2.443–48, 4.400–405.

40. See Beall, *Josephus's Description of the Essenes*, 100–114: "Evidence from the scrolls also points to the antagonism between the sectarians and the Romans. Numerous passages in the *Pesharim* and the *War Scroll* refer to the Kittim (*ktyym* or *kty'ym*) as a strong, greatly feared military power." See also Brownlee, "The Wicked Priest," 1–37.

41. See Lewis, *Ecstatic Religion*, 35, as to the circumstances that encourage ecstatic response: "Thus, as in peripheral cults, the circumstances which encourage the ecstatic response are precisely those where men feel themselves constantly threatened by

At John's death, Jesus retreated to Galilee and immediately took up John's public and vociferous condemnation of the elite, accusing Antipas and the Jerusalem religious establishment of being possessed and under satanic control.[42] But Jesus went further than John: He stated that his exorcisms were proof that their control was ending. They would ultimately be expelled like the demons he cast out, as the kingdom and rule of God were now inbreaking, displacing them and satanic forces.[43] Jesus was therefore at war with Satan and his minions, moving from village to village, and then on to Jerusalem, to evict all demonic hold on the people, land, and ultimately the Temple, reclaiming it for God.[44] Consequently, Jesus was radically different from any contemporary exorcist or ecstatic in what he said his exorcisms represented, taking an unparalleled risk of remarkable courage. But he had no choice, for to fail to pursue the expulsion of demons meant the rule of Satan would prevail and all would be lost. The multiplicity of Jesus' public exorcisms and his linking of them to the end of demonic imperialism and arrival of the kingdom of God were too widely known for him to escape notice and later the wrath of powerful enemies, which included not just the elite but Satan's demons that violently resisted and tried to possess and destroy him during several exorcisms, which we will discuss shortly.[45] This was the reality that Jesus faced daily and the world in which he lived, ate, drank, and slept as an itinerant exorcist.

While Galilean villages relied on local exorcists for protection before Jesus' arrival in Capernaum, associating with any of them carried great risk.[46] Exorcists in the ancient world were socially marginalized:[47] They were

---

exacting pressures which they do not know how to combat or control, except through those heroic flights of ecstasy by which they seek to demonstrate that they are equal with the gods. Thus if enthusiasm is a retort to oppression and repression, what it seeks to proclaim is man's triumphant master of an intolerable environment"—exactly the mission of Jesus and his small band of exorcists to overturn the rule of Satan and demonic imperialism to bring forward the kingdom of God.

42. Busse, *To Be Near*, 9–11, 20–26, 29–30; Hanson and Oakman, *Palestine*, 146–54.
43. Luke 10:18, 11:20, 17:20–21.
44. Busse, *To Be Near*, 1–39.
45. Busse, *To Be Near*, 40.
46. Luke 11:19; Matt 12:27.
47. See Lewis, *Ecstatic Religion*, 27, i.e., possession of those on the margin of society. However, these oral traditions stand out and resonate as stories against oppression of ruling classes, being freed from outside control: Freedom from spirit possession expresses this freedom, and those who could give it were revered.

reclusive,[48] wore distinctive clothing,[49] and kept odd diets,[50] but more, they were considered dangerous and sometimes unbalanced.[51] Exorcists would enter into ecstatic trances and seizures, terrifying onlookers;[52] they spoke in special and sometimes indecipherable words, used special incantations[53] or esoteric songs while conversing with and expelling demons;[54] they could cast deadly curses, including on entire villages, which caused actual harm, illness, and suffering;[55] they could not be controlled by either the peasants or the elite.[56]

Jesus exhibited many of these traits—he had been witnessed in trances,[57] groaning,[58] eyes rolled up and uttering ecstatic words and prayers,[59] and casting curses.[60] He publicly conversed with demons—the villagers of Nazareth and his own family were convinced this proved him mad, and so possessed by satanic forces.[61] The fear of Jesus and his claims to authority led to his violent expulsion from Nazareth, but only after he escaped being thrown off a cliff.[62] Even after Jesus was banished from Nazareth, his family

48. Busse, *To Be Near*, 73–74.

49. Busse, *Jesus Resurrected*, 25.

50. John the Baptist, Matt 3:4, locusts and wild honey.

51. Jesus is refused access to Decapolis, Mark 5:17.

52. Crossan, *Jesus: A Revolutionary Biography*, 92; Smith, *Jesus*, 32–2; Lewis, *Ecstatic Religion*, 37–57.

53. See specific examples, including the invocation of the name of Solomon in Kee, *Origins*, "Magical Incantations," 84–89.

54. Twelftree, *Jesus the Exorcist*, 32–34.

55. Matt 11:20–24; Luke 10:13–15; Acts 4:32–5:11, 8:4–15, 13:4–12; 1 Cor 16:22; Gal 1:8, 2:4.

56. Some would sell their services to the highest bidder.

57. "I saw Satan falling like lightning" (Luke 10:18) lends credence, via the criterion of coherence, to other traditions, i.e., that Jesus had ecstatic visions and entered into trances (as did Cephas, Acts 10:9–16).

58. John 11:33.

59. Mark 7:34: "Jesus looked up toward heaven, and with a groan he said, '*Effatha!*' which means 'open up.'" Craffert, *Galilean Shaman*, 233, quotes Marcus Borg: ". . . verbal prayer is only one form of prayer in the Jewish-Christian tradition. Indeed, it is only the first stage of prayer; beyond it are deeper levels of prayer characterized by internal silence and lengthy periods of time. In this state, one enters into deeper levels of consciousness; ordinary consciousness is stilled, and one sits quietly in the presence of God . . . One enters the realm of Spirit and experiences God."

60. Mark 11:12–25, cursing a fig tree. Matthew 11:20–25, Jesus curses Bethsaida, Korazim, and Capernaum.

61. Jesus *eksitemi* is to be understood in the most emphatic way, "lost his mind," like most ecstatics.

62. Mark 7:34; Luke 4:29.

sought to silence him, and one time attempted to seize, restrain, and gag him.[63] They did this not because of the startling number of exorcisms he performed, but they doubted the origin of his authority, their controversial nature (including necromancy), and what he said his exorcisms signified; i.e., the displacement of demonic imperialism and elite with the arrival of the kingdom of God.[64] This claim made him more dangerous than any of the other exorcists operating in Galilee,[65] placing not only his family, including his brothers and sisters, but the entire village at risk of retribution from Romans sympathizers, landlords, and overseers supporting their subsistence existence, as hungry and eager informants had infiltrated every village and town waiting to be paid Roman silver.

It is not surprising then that Jesus was quickly identified by elitist sympathizers. Spies were assigned to track him, and one paid assassin infiltrated his group. When his accusations against the elite were confirmed, representatives were sent from Jerusalem. To discredit, silence him, and crush any support, they issued the direst warning possible in the ancient world—Jesus was a deceiver empowered by Satan, specifically possessed by the demon Beelzebul, and so by dark and evil forces:[66] These were his masters,[67] and anyone seen supporting him were subject to the same penalty as Jesus—being cut off from God, banishment, starvation, and an annihilating death under a curse if they continued. The risk of supporting Jesus was too great. Consequently, Jesus was anathema, condemned and rejected as a deceptive fraud, a possessed blasphemer. Such traditions carried on in Jewish writings well into the second and third centuries.[68]

Indeed, some of Jesus' publicly-witnessed ecstatic practices represented the *darkest of magic* in the Greco-Roman world,[69] particularly his practice of necromancy, the manipulation and raising of the dead by

---

63. Attempts to restrain him *kratesai* because he was out of his mind in a trance or ecstatic state are clear. See for example Crossan, *Jesus: A Revolutionary Biography*, 92, and of course Smith, *Jesus*, 32–42. The fact is *elegon gar hoti ezeste* is a statement confirmed by bystanders that he lost his mind, i.e., that Jesus was possessed by a demon.

64. Luke 4:19, citing Isaiah 61:2, coupled with Jesus' explicit claims that his exorcisms heralded the arrival of the kingdom of God.

65. Mark 1:17; Matt 4:19.

66. Mark 11:28; Luke 11:20, Matt 12:1–21, 22–37; John 18:29–30.

67. See Busse, "The Beelzebul Controversy," *To Be Near*, 54–60.

68. *Sanh.* 43a: "On the eve of the Passover Yeshu was hanged. For forty days before the execution took place, a herald went forth and cried, 'He is going forth to be stoned because he practiced sorcery and enticed Israel to apostasy.'" *Sanh.* 107b: "The Teacher said: 'Yeshu practiced sorcery and corrupted the minds of Israel.'" *Shab.* 104b, "Did not Ben Stada bring forth sorcery from Egypt by means of scratches [tattoos?] on his flesh?"

69. Luke 11:20; see also Hull, *Hellenistic Magic*, 61–62, 68–72.

rejoining the spirits of the dead with their bodies.[70] That these "sleeping" dead could be raised at judgment was a common expectation, including by Herod Antipas and the rabbis, as this belief was prevalent in ancient Judaism, except among the Sadducees.[71] But any attempt to unite the spirit and body, or even contact the dead, was strictly forbidden. Both Roman and Jewish laws expressly prohibited any form of necromancy, threatening immediate arrest and execution if witnessed.[72] Jesus ignored this danger in three recorded instances (certainly there were more), two in Galilee (for children), and another just outside Jerusalem in Bethany (for a sympathizer).[73] It was this last event near Jerusalem that was witnessed by spies who literally ran from the site and reported it to the Jerusalem elite, specifically to the Herodian guards.[74] Shortly after this event, a plan was formed to find a safe time (i.e., when Jesus could not cast a curse or use his powers on those sent to seize him) to disable, bind, capture, and ritually "destroy" him,[75] as an illicit and dangerous dark magician, an "evildoer."[76]

70. Ogden, *Magic*, 192–205.

71. Mark 6:16; see also Daniel 12:2 and rabbinic literature, such as *Sanh*. 90b and 91b: "From the Torah: for it is written: 'And the Lord said to Moses, Behold you shall sleep with your fathers; and this people will rise up' [Deuteronomy 31:16]. From the Prophets: as it is written: 'Your dead men shall live, together with my dead bodies shall they arise. Awake and sing, you that dwell in the dust; for your dew is as the dew of herbs, and the earth shall cast out its dead' [Isaiah 26:19]; from the Writings: as it is written, 'And the roof of your mouth, like the best wine of my beloved, like the best wine, that goes down sweetly, causing the lips of those who are asleep to speak [Song of Songs 7:9].'"

72. Specific references include the Twelve Tables, Crimes, Table VII.3 and 15, also Table VIII.9 See also du Plessis, *Borkowski's Textbook on Roman Law*, 5–6, 29–30; Ogden, *Magic*, 275–99. For condemned exorcists, a ritual execution—such as a cursed death for a Jew by crucifixion, Deuteronomy 21:22–23—was employed to disarm and neutralize the spirit of the exorcist to prevent retribution or to block other magicians or ecstatics from taking that spirit for evil purposes. It is interesting to note that when Jesus raised Lazarus from the dead,(John 11:46–47, 53–54), spies witnessing Jesus' activity immediately raced to the ruling elite with evidence in hand that he must be executed. Jesus had to go into seclusion. He was now subject to a death sentence if captured.

73. In Bethany, two miles from Jerusalem.

74. Two children: Luke 7:11–17, the widow's son in Nain (a village two miles south of Mt. Tabor, during a funeral procession); and the twelve-year-old daughter of Jairus, an official in a local synagogue in Galilee, who died of a fever.

75. Some interpreters go too far in translating *pos ton apolesosin*, "destroy," as "to kill," likely a derivative of the Hebrew, *abaddon*, namely "the destroyer." The term does denote that this group of Pharisees, politically sympathetic to the Herodians, clearly understood that Jesus and his band of followers should be silenced, or scattered, or that they wanted Jesus crucified.

76. Smith, *Jesus*, 41. See for example Luke 11:20, and especially John 18:28, 30. Jesus is portrayed not just as a criminal, but instead, as an "evildoer," a term in the ancient

Clearly, all of this meant that associating with Jesus, particularly housing or calling him "master," was a perilous risk that could prove fatal—not only for the sympathizer but their entire family and even village.[77] For this reason, some villagers would not allow Jesus or his exorcists to even set foot in their village or region.[78] And yet remarkably for his most ardent followers, the perilous risk of being an exorcist for Jesus, even in the streets of Jerusalem, was fully mitigated by the remarkable control he exhibited over all satanic forces, particularly the infection of death. What could harm them, as Satan was falling "like lightning?"[79]

Understanding this danger in the context of first-century occupied Galilee is essential. Only those who fully accepted that Jesus' authority over demons as originating from God, and that this authority would neutralize the risks of demonic imperialism and bring an end to satanic rule (thereby protecting their traditions, family and livelihoods) would risk associating with him, let alone become one of his fellow exorcists. To that point, the count of his supporters, particularly those willing to follow him into Jerusalem and take such an incredible risk was small; only a handful of men and women, largely comprised of desperate and suffering peasants, mostly Galilean fishers turned exorcists that he had trained and supported. They recognized the danger and some stated they were willing to die.[80] But the villages where Jesus performed the majority of exorcisms, including Capernaum and Bethsaida (also the very home villages of his exorcists), ultimately rejected him out of fear of demonic-Roman retribution.

---

world equivalent to an illegal, dangerous dark magician. Pilate certainly knew Jesus' reputation as an exorcist and necromancer. It is he alone who ordered his crucifixion, a form of death known to neutralize retribution by the dead against their executioners (see below). Also see Smith, *Jesus*, 41, 109, 175. Smith states: "'Doer of Evil' = Magician: Codex *Theodosianus* IX.16.4; Codex *Justinianus* IX.18.7, citing Constantius; compare 1 Peter 4;15 and Tertullian, *Scorpiace* 12.3. Selwin, *1 Peter*, understood 4:15 correctly and cited Tacitus's use of *malefica*, *Annals* II.69."

77. The fate of Galilean rebels, troublemakers, or religious extremists under the Romans was deadly. For example, in 4 BCE the Roman General Varus crucified two thousand Galilean rebels along the road between Sepphoris and Galilee (Josephus, *War* 2.5.2; *Ant.* 17.10.10); a Samaritan and his followers that convinced others to follow him to Mt. Gerizin to find temple artifacts were slaughtered by the Romans (Josephus, *Ant.* 18.85–7). Jesus was similarly captured and executed when he reached Jerusalem.

78. Luke 9:51–10:15.

79. Luke 10:18–19.

80. John 11:16.

For the paid spies sympathetic to Rome and the Jerusalem elite,[81] such as those sent to track Jesus[82] (including Judas Iscariot, "the strangler," an informant and assassin of the Jerusalem elite who infiltrated his small band of exorcists), there was already ample evidence to justify his capture and execution prior to the event at Bethany.[83] First, and as noted, Jesus publicly announced that his exorcisms were proof that all pagan rulers *and their sympathizers*, which included the Herodian and Jerusalem elite, were doomed.[84] This meant the end of the elite's economic and political power, which Jesus also expected soon.[85] Such a claim could not be ignored, as Jesus pointed to his authority over the demons (which included the foreign gods of demonic imperialism) as confirmation that their rule was *now* coming to an end—a new kingdom, the *Basileia tou Theou*, was emerging, evidenced by these successful exorcisms of all types. This made Jesus' pronouncements about what his exorcisms signified also *seditious*, justifying execution.[86]

Second, Jesus was labeled an "evildoer," a *kakourgos*, which is a technical term given to those charged with evil practices and dark magic[87]—an agent of evil and Satan[88]—and therefore feared because of the threat he posed;[89] both from the growing number of peasants that supported his exorcisms in a rebellious Galilee[90] as well as the dangerous powers he both pos-

---

81. Rome had its *Frumentarii* in the second and third centuries, spies attached to Roman legions that occupied or were stationed in various portions of the empire, including Palestine, but also were a secret spy network in Rome. *Frumentarii* were preceded by the long-standing practice of recruiting paid spies from the local populace that would inform on seditious activity and instigators. Both Herod and Pilate used spies, with Pilate infiltrating a crowd with soldiers dressed as civilians (Josephus, *War* 2.175–177). The religious elite of Jerusalem also sent spies with questions to trap Jesus into making seditious claims, Luke 20:20–26. See also Jane Crawford, "Spies and Spying," 71–74, for Rome's use of spies as early as 55 BCE.

82. Luke 20:20.

83. Busse, "Judas Iscariot," *To Be Near*, 27–30.

84. Luke 11:20; Matt 12:28; Jesus' woes on the religious elite, Matt 23:14–36, i.e., that they will not enter the kingdom of God; see also Matt 17:17, 12:39, 16:4, par. Luke 11:29, and particularly Luke 20:9–19, the parable of the wicked tenants ending with the saying: "Everyone who falls on the stone will be broken to pieces; anyone on whom it falls will be crushed."

85. Hansen and Oakman, *Palestine*, 126–27.

86. Following the outbreak and Jewish revolt in 4 BCE, Varus, the Roman legate of Syria, brought legions and put down the insurrection. All those suspected of rebellion and sedition were crucified, as noted by Josephus, *Ant.* 10.

87. John 18:30.

88. Luke 11:15.

89. Luke 9:7; Mark 6:14.

90. When Herod the Great died in 4 BCE, no less than three messianic rebellions

sessed and controlled, which were more feared than any mob or rebellious crowd. It was this control over demons and dark power that could be turned on them, stronger and more dangerous than any army.[91] Herod Antipas was terrified of Jesus.[92] Indeed, Jesus was witnessed conversing with and controlling all manifestations of malevolent demons and spirits of the dead that he confronted—those that caused death, disease, disability, deafness, loss of speech, and insanity. He could even call the souls of those infected with death back to their bodies.[93] Clearly, Antipas, the Jerusalem elite, and their supporters understood Jesus to be the epitome of a Hellenistic dark magician, perhaps even an Egyptian *goetes* (and there were contemporaneous accounts of Jesus having spent time in Egypt).[94] Only an agent of evil could control such demons and the spirits of the dead—the very powers that could be directed against them. Consequently, witnesses were plentiful[95] and eager to be paid for information leading to the capture of a single Galilean peasant exorcist[96]—particularly for thirty pieces of *arguria* (i.e., Roman denarius silver coins), equivalent to over a month's wages and the price of freedom if a slave. As such, Jesus carried in word and deed the risk of unrestrained retribution that must be neutralized.

Jesus openly acknowledged his control over demons, but not by satanic magic or powers placed in his control or that possessed him.[97] On the contrary, he claimed his authority over demons was from God, his *Abbá*,[98]

---

took place, including those of Judas the son of Hezekiah, Simon of Perea, and Athronges the Shepherd; Judas rebelled in Galilee and succeeded in taking Sepphoris and looting the armory. Judas's rebellion led to the capture and crucifixion of two thousand Jews in 6 CE according to Josephus, *War* 2.433, and *Ant.* 18:1–10, 23.

91. See Bolt, "Life, Death, and Afterlife," 55–59.

92. Busse, *To Be Near*, "Herod Antipas," 16–17, and his fear of John and Jesus.

93. Smith, *Jesus*, 126–27.

94. Luke 2:14.

95. In John 11:46–47, the raising of Lazarus, an illegal act of necromancy in Judea, was witnessed by multiple informants who immediately went to the elite, leading to the intense effort to capture and kill Jesus before he left Jerusalem.

96. The informant in Jesus' case would seek a time and place where his charismatic powers were limited so that he could be taken without use of his powers to cast curses or overcome enemies. For this reason, Judas chose Gethsemane. See a discussion of Gethsemane as such a place in Busse, *Jesus Resurrected*, 44–46.

97. Luke 11:20.

98. *Abba* (in Aramaic, Ab ba`, accent on the later syllable), an intimate word (but not "daddy"; see Barr, "Abba Isn't Daddy," 28–47), was used to address one's own father, and was the unique and characteristic address of Jesus in his speech about and prayers to God, multiply-attested as having originated with Jesus. See Jeremias, *The Prayers of Jesus*, 54–55. It is attested in all strata of the tradition—Q, Mark, Matthew, and Luke, John and Paul; Paul's use the term *Abbá* in Galatians 4:6 and Romans 8:15, i.e., an

and of his being possessed by the "finger of God."[99] Yet to his opponents, Jesus' claim was an evil ruse: Satan, or his chief demon, Beelzebul, possessed him, affording him unbridled malevolent powers:[100] Jesus was a dangerous deceiver, a perilous risk that must be neutralized. Indeed, it was publicly known that Jesus by his own admission had conversed multiple times with Satan in the Judean desert—the desolate and forbidden place where demons, including the queen of demons Agrath bat Mahalath,[101] were expelled and roamed[102]—a terrifying confession.[103] This admission made Jesus a uniquely dangerous figure, only further confirmed when other exorcists successfully invoked his name to take control of demons.[104] His name was efficacious. Indeed, Jesus' own exorcists employed his name to expel demons in Galilee and beyond (Later Christian exorcists, as well as pagan and Jewish magicians and sorcerers,[105] used the invocation of his name to control and expel malevolent spirits for centuries).[106]

Consequently, what Jesus claimed as evidence of his relationship with God as *Abbá*, evidenced by the multiplicity of his exorcisms via possession by the finger of God, informants claimed to be evidence of his possession by Satan. As a hero to the village peasants he freed from demonic infections, he at first drew significant popular support in Galilee, making a public arrest and execution there problematic (particularly after the unpopular murder of John the Baptist for sedition).[107] Yet, after the public practice of necromancy

---

Aramaic word in the Greek-speaking world of his itinerant activity, is decisive proof that this was the way in which the historical Jesus' addressed God. Jesus authorized his exorcists to do the same in their ecstatic prayer, similar to the Lord's Prayer.

99. Matt 12:27, Luke 11:20: This is critically important—Jesus is stating emphatically that he needs no rituals, incantations, spells, or use of the name of Solomon, like other exorcists. His authority is of God by his "finger," the direct power that has been bestowed on Jesus and possesses him. See also Meier, *Marginal Jew, Vol. 2*, 461. For a discussion on the Beelzebul controversy and Jesus being possessed see also Bazzana, *Spirit*, 34–35, which also finds support in ethnographic studies cited.

100. This phenomenon has been confirmed in other ecstatic cultures: "We shall find that those who, as masters of spirits, diagnose and treat illness in others are in danger of being accused . . . For if their power over the spirits is such that they can heal the sick, why should they not also sometimes cause what they cure?" Lewis, *Ecstatic Religion*, 33.

101. Costa, "Exorcisms and Healings of Jesus," 133.

102. Matt 12:43.

103. Smith, *Jesus*, 104–06.

104. Mark 9:38–40.

105. There are numerous examples in the Talmud, e.g., T*osefta Hullin* 2:22f.

106. Smith, *Jesus*, 62–64, 114–15; also see *bSanh.* 43a.

107. See Lewis, *Ecstatic Religion*, 32–35, on the popularity of ecstatics by the poor and downtrodden.

at Bethany near Jerusalem, Jesus could no longer be left wandering nearby. Now, as he approached Jerusalem, the center of control of the elite, he posed too significant a threat and danger, justifying arrest and a ritual execution to annihilate him body and soul to ensure there would be no retribution—crucifixion under a curse and his body sealed in a rock tomb to prevent a retributive return as one of the untimely dead.[108]

THE METHODS AND TECHNIQUES OF JESUS' EXORCISMS IN GALILEE

Whether follower or enemy, the variety and number of Jesus' exorcisms in Galilean villages was striking;[109] from driving out demonic infection or ill-

---

108. See Busse, *Jesus Resurrected*, 47–59.

109. Cephas's mother-in-law in Capernaum, Mark 1:29-31; Throngs of the possessed by demons causing all types of maladies in Capernaum outside his village dwelling one evening, Mark 1:32-34; his control of the fish and enhancing catch, Luke 5:1-11; a leper in Capernaum, who, once freed, spread the news to several Galilean villages, Mark 1:40-45; the Roman soldier's paralyzed servant in Capernaum healed by Jesus' command alone, Luke 7:1-10; a paralyzed man let down to Jesus by tearing open the mud-and-stick roof of his village dwelling in Capernaum, exorcised by Jesus' words alone, Mark 2:1-12; man with the palsied hand, Mark 3:1-5, stretching out his hand presumably touched by Jesus (his exorcism on the Sabbath, a work that led to the religious elite claiming blasphemy and seeking his death); his control of the demons who rose the sea of Galilee against them by wind by command, Mark 4:35-41; in Gergesa on the eastern shore of Galilee, Jesus casts out the demons, who call themselves Legion, by command, out of a possessed madman, sending them into a herd of swine—they race into the waters of Galilee to drown and release the demons into the lake (here the demon again tried to take control of Jesus by calling him by name), Mark 5:1-20; a woman touches his garment and is healed near Galilee, Mark 5:25-34; Jesus crosses by boat back to the western shores of Galilee and is begged by a synagogue leader, Jairus, to heal his daughter, who dies, but Jesus casts out death using special words and touching her hand, Mark 5:21-24, 35-43; in Capernaum, Jesus casts out demons causing blindness by touching their eyes, Matthew 9:27-31, and expels a demon that caused the inability to speak, Luke 9:32-34; In Gennesaret, a village south of Capernaum, Jesus casts out demons by touch, or by the victims, laid out in the market place, touching his garment, Mark 6:53-56; Jesus expels a demon from a man in the region of Decapolis (eastern shore of Galilee), both deaf and unable to speak, by taking him apart privately, putting his fingers in his ears, spitting, and touching his tongue, then entering into an ecstatic state, sighing, and uttering special words, Mark 7:31-35; in Bethsaida, a fishing village on the northern shore of Galilee, a blind man, who he again takes by the hand apart privately out of the village, spitting in his eyes and touching him but fails to cast out the demon, and lays his hands on his eyes—Jesus warns him not to return to the village, presumably because the demon could return more forcefully, Mark 8:22-26; after his trained exorcists failed, Jesus casts out a demon in Galilee that was violently seizing a child, causing convulsions, throwing the boy into "fire and into the water to destroy him," and does so by command, Mark 9:14-29; and Jesus assisting with a catch

ness by command to the very personal and private interactions with victims by touch, using various techniques. The multiplicity of his encounters with demons was so great that it became problematic to the early church, as Matthew and Luke temper many of the exorcisms found in Mark (or omit them completely) because of their troubling nature.[110] But this demonstrates their historicity, underscored by contextual risk analysis,[111] as the scope and breadth of demonic encounters were too widely known to gloss over.[112] Certainly, the one practice that would have been omitted was the most illegal and controversial, as it clearly tied Jesus in the Greco-Roman world with the darkest of magic—necromancy. It was so controversial that the oral traditions about these encounters were ultimately associated with the Christology of resurrection, that is, as a sign that Jesus was Lord and Master over death, the one to return and inaugurate the resurrection of the dead.

Jesus usually exorcised the demonic infection of death from village children in very personal, intimate, and touching scenes.[113] Death was "sleep" in ancient Judaism that resulted from its infection; it literally drove the person's spirit, or soul, out (or led to it being "carried away," sometimes by angels), and the body became lifeless without a soul. Jesus understood this "sleep" not as final death, but a state that could be reversed by the power of God, reuniting the spirit and body.[114] Nothing one could witness was more powerful (or more fraught with risk if associated with the practice) in the ancient world. The authority over death, exorcising, and the recalling of the spirit to a lifeless body, was almost unheard of in Judaism, except by the prophets Elijah and Elisha, or reported attempts by pagans.[115] Jesus' actions would be either revered or considered evidence that he was connected to the very evil spirits he could conjure and control.

In each instance, Jesus employed personal contact and special words to expel death. In one event, he takes the child's mother and father, as well

---

of fish by directing them into nets again on Galilee, John 21:4–11. All of these can be summarized in Mark 1:39: "And he went throughout all of Galilee, preaching in their synagogues and casting out demons."

110. See, for example, Jesus' exorcism of the Syrophoenician women, Mark 7:24–31.

111. As well as critical tools of analysis employed by scholars, such as the criterion of embarrassment; see Meier, *Marginal Jew, Vol. 1*, 170.

112. Busse, *To Be Near*, 40.

113. The Synoptics primarily report young individuals; John reports the resurrection of Lazarus, an adult man, John 11.

114. 1 Cor 15:51; 1 Thess 4:13–18.

115. Elijah, 1 Kings 17:17–24; Elisha, 2 Kings 4:32–37; they each lie on the body of the dead boys repeatedly and pray to revive them.

as Kepha, Yacob and Yohannan, to the inner room where the body is laid (so this recollection must be attributed to one of them):

> And he said, "The child is not dead but sleeping." And they [those present] laughed at him. But he put them outside, and took the child's father and mother and those who were with him, and went in where the child was. Taking her by the hand he said to her, "*Talitha cum!*" which means, "Little girl, I say to you arise." And immediately the girl got up and walked, for she was twelve years old.[116]

The Gospel editor translates Jesus' words, but there are parallels to these words (in other texts) that are used by ecstatics as a command to drive out evil.[117] Their meaning is now unknown and indecipherable, but it is highly likely that these words of authority employed by Jesus were familiar to other exorcists. In fact, based on other examples that have contemporary parallels (which will be discussed), there is every reason to believe that Jesus employed common techniques that were both expected and familiar to Palestinian Jews to affect exorcism and overcome evil spirits. In the case above, the ruler of the synagogue's daughter is given freedom from death.

Aside from these few encounters, demons resisted Jesus at virtually every exorcism, and sometimes attempted retaliation. For example, when a demon called Jesus by name it was a chilling attempt to overpower and possess him; that is, it used Jesus' own technique of taking control of demon by demanding its name(s).[118] Jesus, recognizing the danger, rebuked and expelled it, which violently convulsed the victim as it left, stunning the

---

116. Mark 5:39–42.

117. See Smith, *Jesus*, 95.

118. Virtually all of these attempts took place in Galilee, and more precisely Capernaum, Jesus' village and center of activity in battling demonic forces. For example, the demon in Capernaum tries to take control of Jesus, crying out in recognition, *anakrazo*, Mark 1:21–28. This tradition must be authentic and pre-Markan. The demons in their attempt to take control of Jesus also use, "I know," i.e., who you are (see *PGM* VIII.6, for example, the "Holy One of God,"). The identification of Jesus as both the Holy One and his village, "Jesus of Nazareth," are clearly not later Christian additions—this is the demon attempting to take control of Jesus by using his name. But the demon is rebuked: Jesus commands the demon (*epetimesen*) to be silent (*phemotheti*) and come out (*phimoteti sai ekzelthe ekz autou*), be muzzled. Jesus' words reverse the attempt by taking control of the demon. The only words that are similar to language in the *PGM* relate to being muzzled, and so the demon is disabled and violently convulses his victim. The description of this event in Capernaum must be accurate, and it bears all the evidence of a terrifying demonic encounter that would have been troubling to those outside of Palestine familiar with demonic encounters. The evidence of this concern is confirmed in that Luke completely neutralizes the troubling encounter.

villagers at the synagogue assembly.[119] The intense risk of these encounters is best revealed in the pattern Jesus employed when exorcising demons.

The Pattern of Jesus' Exorcisms in the Villages, Synagogues, and Towns of Galilee

Like other exorcists, Jesus was able to converse with and expel demons, but unlike other exorcists, he did so regularly, publicly, *and intentionally* at the village's small Sabbath gatherings, where he cleansed ("expelled") the synagogue assemblies and its village of demons until sunset,[120] as the Sabbath was the holy day *when demons were vulnerable*.[121] There he followed a ritual pattern: He entered the village and synagogue assembly on the Sabbath if welcomed. He called out the demons that were present, particularly those that afflicted or harmed local victims (all ages, male and female, mostly Jews) and demanded that they identify themselves. The demons recognize Jesus (sometimes before they are called out) and either try to take control of Jesus by using his name and origin, or they insult him. Jesus compels the demon to reveal its name or origin, allowing him to take control.[122] Conversing and sometimes negotiating with the demon, he then commands silence and expels it into nearby waters (e.g., sacred pools or springs controlled by angels or into the waters of Galilee) or to the wilderness (the desert or other desolate places).[123] When expelled, the demon is violent, destructive, and "intends to cause injury or death."[124] That demons often forced their victims to kneel or fall to the ground before Jesus must not obscure the hostility of

---

119. Mark 1:21–26; Luke 4:31–36: This tradition was very troubling in that a demon attempts to take control of Jesus using the same techniques he employed, which was a terrifying tradition in the first century. This tradition would have been omitted if it had not used by Jesus' enemies to attack him, i.e., that he was known to demons, and that they attempted to take control over him, bringing into question whether they did. When the demon was expelled, the man was thrown to the ground, but according to the tradition in Luke, was not harmed.

120. Matt 8:16–17; Mark 1:32–34; Luke 4:40–41.

121. Busse, *Jesus Resurrected*, 26.

122. Busse, *To Be Near*, 31–53 ("Palestinian Judaism and Demonic Possession"), 58–60 ("the Beelzebul Controversy"), 70–88 ("Jesus' Attack on Satan and Demonic Imperialism").

123. See Jesus' description of where the expelled demons go, Luke 11:24.

124. Robinson, *Problem of History*, 39.

these confrontations[125] and the terrorizing visage witnessed by the villagers, as when the demons came out they violently convulsed their victims.[126]

There are striking similarities in Jesus' activities to other exorcists recorded in ancient literature—except Jesus does not invoke the name of Solomon, Moses, or another exorcist as do other contemporaries; he does so under his own authority on behalf of *Abbá*.[127] The Jerusalem elite assumed that Jesus employed techniques of other exorcists (particularly Jewish exorcists), such as those that invoked the Solomonic practices and teachings, reciting written incantations, all of which were widely known in all strata of society to be highly effective.[128] Jesus claimed that the authority given to him by *Abbá* and the finger of God was superior to any of Solomon's incantations and power.[129] He had no need of Solomon's authority.

The tradition in Mark accurately reflects Jesus' practice of entering the Synagogues of Galilee.

> And immediately there was in the synagogue a man with an unclean spirit; and he [the demon] cried out, "What have you to do with us, Jesus of Nazareth? Have you come to destroy us? I know that you are the *holy one*[130] of God."[131]

125. Robinson, *Problem of History*, 36: "The hostility that Mark expresses in his descriptions of the conversations is confirmed by an examination of what was said. As noted earlier, Bauerenfeind has shown [Bauerenfeind, *Die Worte*, 3] that the three sayings spoken by demons to Jesus (1:24, 3:11, 5:7) are all closely parallel to incantations of witchcraft in the magical papyri and elsewhere. Therefore the words could very well for Mark and his readers give the impression of a defensive magical incantation. This hostility is of course only accentuated by the reference in the demon's sayings to Jesus; destroying (1:24) or 'tormenting' (5:7) them, as well as by the opening challenge (1:24, 5:7): 'What have you to do with us?' In 5:7 the demon appeals to God against Jesus in language commonly used *against* demons; *horkizo de ton theon*."

126. Robinson, *Problem of History*, 37.

127. Ogden, *Magic*, 167: "The Judeo-Christian affiliation aside, exorcism sequences in ancient literature tend to conform to the following pattern: The demon is ordered out, but does not initially obey; the demon is ordered out once more again, with terrible threats, and does not obey; often the demon is adjured in the name of a particular powerful sorcerer, using the names of Solomon, Moses, or Jesus; the demon is made to confess its name and identity, and this act is often in itself tantamount to expulsion, as confirming the presence of a demon is more than half the battle; the demon gives a physical token of its departure—either it is visible as it departs, usually in the form of a dark figure, or it is made known over an external object on its outward flight."

128. Josephus, *Ant.* 8.2.5 and Eleazar before Vespasian; Jesus states, "One greater than Solomon is here," Luke 11:31.

129. Luke 11:31.

130. See below. Here, "holy one" is not a messianic term as implied by the text (later translated as "son of God").

131. Mark 1:23–25.

Verbal confrontation with demons in the synagogues of Galilee was the norm.[132] Demoniacs also attempt to intercept him before he enters significant villages and towns. As he approached the town of Gadara, six miles southeast of Galilee across the Jordan, two demoniacs living among the Jewish tombs (the "desolate places")[133] confront Jesus. Gadara was the Roman provincial capital of Decapolis. Clearly, Jesus is assaulting the Roman provincial capital, intending to expel its demons from the synagogue and announce the inbreaking kingdom of God in a stronghold of the Roman occupiers. They speak to him:

> "Have you come here to torment us before the time . . . can you cast us out into the heard of swine?"[134]

Learning of this, local authorities are terrified and come out to the edge of the town, refusing Jesus entry, perhaps threatening him with stoning, arrest, or other violence. They order him and his band of exorcists to leave at once. Jesus fails to enter Gadara or cleanse the synagogue, and so moves on to the next village. The problematic and embarrassing nature of Jesus being rejected by villagers underscores the reliability of these traditions.[135]

Confrontation with demons and evil possession typically continued into the evening following events in the synagogue. Jesus intentionally remains in the vicinity of the synagogue or in a nearby home where he stays for food and rest.[136] If the location of Jesus' temporary residence in Capernaum is accurate, he stayed in a modest peasant house only a short distance from the synagogue.[137] Jesus knows that he will be sought out, whether by

---

132. Luke 6:24–26.

133. The man with "unclean spirit" living near tombs mirrors first-century accounts, but more is reflected in madmen described in the Mishnah (ca. 200 CE—m. *Ter.* 1:1), and Tosefta (230–300 CE, *t. Ter* 1:3).

134. Matt 8:29.

135. By the *criterion of embarrassment*, as the early church would have not created such a negative tradition, where Jesus was rejected and forbidden entry following an exorcism; see Meier, *Marginal Jew, Vol. 1*, 168, 170, 174–75, 317.

136. Jesus' instruction to other exorcists is detailed in Matt 10:11–13, which include their inquiry to find "who is worthy in it," and enter their house taking hospitality, a Jewish tradition dating to the time of Abraham, who entertained angels unaware. Undoubtedly, this is what Jesus, too, did after his cleansing of the synagogue.

137. There are multiple articles that debate this location, but it is highly likely this was where Jesus resided while in Capernaum, as it certainly fits with the findings of qualitative risk analysis as to Jesus' modus operandi and intent to remain near the cleansed synagogue and continue to expel demons and exorcise evil spirits of the infirm. See Strange, "House Where Jesus Stayed."

demoniacs or by others who seek release from evil spirits that infect or possess family or loved ones.[138]

Often villagers go to extraordinary measures to reach him, as when crowds overwhelmed the entrance to the modest house in Capernaum. The details in Mark 2:4 strongly suggest a Galilean eyewitness was present. Desperate to reach the exorcist Jesus, four men carry a paralyzed male to the entrance of the house, but they are unable to push through the crowds. They tie the *teknon*, a young man or child, to a pallet and climb to the roof, pulling him up with rope about ten feet. They find the edge of the roof and begin tearing it up by hand in order to make a hole large enough for them to drop him through. They break up clay and separate the branches underneath. The description of dismantling (literally "digging") accurately portrays roofing structures found in Galilee (and Palestine) and certainly in the poor homes of workers in Capernaum.[139] This can only be one of dozens of vivid memories captured in the oral tradition that were associated with Jesus' exorcisms on these evenings and make coherent reports of his inability to eat and sleep which led him to be considered "mad."[140]

The Tactile Aspect of Jesus' Exorcisms

The tactile aspect of Jesus' exorcism of evil is reinforced repeatedly in the texts. Jesus is most commonly surrounded by the infirm, particularly after his synagogue cleansings, when he retires to a local village home he has chosen (they must offer hospitality), sometimes the home of a "ruler" of the local synagogue.[141] Touching Jesus' garments or cloak, including the "fringe of his garment," would drive out evil spirits or Satan's torment.[142] When this happens, Jesus reports that he feels "power had gone forth from me."[143] To touch Jesus was to gain protection from malicious spirits and demons. It is for this reason that young women bring their children and infants to Jesus

---

138. Mark 1:32–34; Matt 8:16–17.

139. Atop the basalt stone support walls, un-hewn crossbeams were laid. Across these beams were branches and saplings as cross support. Specially-prepared clay was packed on top of the branches to make a water-resistant surface. Typically a roller remained in the roof to spread out the clay in the winter months to seal cracks and prevent leaking. Examples of first-century rollers have been found.

140. Mark 3:20–25.

141. Jesus was likely heading to the home of Jairus, head of the synagogue. Jairus knows of Jesus' common practice of entering the synagogue to exorcise and teach and meets him on his way there, Mark 5:21–43.

142. Luke 4:19, 6:17–19, 53–56, 8:25–33; Mark 3:10, 6:56; Matt 14:36.

143. Luke 8:46.

to touch him, that is, to protect them from evil and illness, particularly given the high mortality rate among children in ancient Palestine.[144] This is a moving scene, consistent with the risk context of peasant life and given Jesus' reputation. Other exorcists attempt to hold them back, but Jesus does not refuse. The resulting saying is completely coherent with the risk context of Jesus' countermeasure to free Palestine and Galilee from evil; i.e., those who embrace his exorcisms as evidence of the inbreaking kingdom and practice forgiveness and mercy are the children of God, while those that reject him and harm the children of God are doomed:

> Let the children come to me, do not hinder them; for to such belongs the kingdom of God.[145]
> Whoever causes one of these little ones who believe in me to stumble [or sin], it would be better for him if a great millstone were hung round his neck and he were thrown into the sea.[146]

They, possessed by a demon, will be trapped in the sea and annihilated. This saying captures the essence of Jesus' actions and how he characterized them for the peasants of Galilee.

Aside from verbal commands to "go," Jesus sometimes employed special techniques in his encounters to expel demons, some of which have parallels with other ancient exorcists. For example, he created an efficacious substance with his spittle, which was mixed with dirt to make a dressing to absorb and draw the demon out. On rare occasions, Jesus was forced to use multiple techniques to successfully exorcise demons, such as in Bethsaida.[147] Mark reports that he spit into the eyes of a blind man, but then also had to manipulate the eyes with his hands.[148] The use of spittle, combined with other techniques of manipulation to draw out the demon, was then effective. Regardless of his techniques, Jesus aggressively cast demons out of their victims, sending them to wander desolate deserts so they would not return,[149] or drove them into the waters of Galilee, where demons dwelt and

---

144. Mark 10:13–16.

145. Mark 10:14b; Luke 18:15–17.

146. Mark 9:42.

147. That Jesus was not immediately successful must be considered historically accurate, as the early church would have certainly suppressed this information.

148. Twelftree, *Jesus the Exorcist*, 83–4. Mark 8:22–26: Jesus wasn't successful at first, and he used spittle. This tradition was dropped in Luke and Matthew due to its embarrassing nature—Jesus was unsuccessful, a common experience of some exorcists on the first attempt—and possible association with magical practices.

149. Mark 3:21. The return of demons back to those exorcised or on the exorcist himself is acknowledged by Jesus, Matt 12:45; the "strongman" is not bound, so he would "plunder" the house, meaning that the demon will turn on the exorcist, Luke

were trapped, such as the demons that possessed the Gerasene demoniac.[150] The demons often spoke through their victims, admitting their fear of his power. Consequently, these were not calm encounters, but violent confrontations, where demons shouted back at Jesus in front of terrified villagers.[151] "Jesus is not conversing with demons; he is disposing of them."[152]

When Jesus' trained exorcists are successful in cleansing a village or synagogue, he acknowledges that the exorcist has attained special standing with God, one that ensures that they will be welcomed into the kingdom when it fully arrives: "rejoice that your names are written in heaven."[153] In a clear Semitism, Jesus equates their successful expelling of demons and spirits with their treading on "serpents and scorpions, and over all the power of the enemy . . . and nothing shall hurt you."[154]

The Garments of Jesus and His Exorcists

Jesus' appearance as an exorcist when entering a town or village must be considered unique as well, drawn from sayings attributed to him.[155] He describes what his own itinerant exorcists should take and wear, both men and women, when sent out, likely in teams of two.[156] First, the pattern of entry is familiar: "Whenever you enter a town or village and they receive you . . . heal the sick [those possessed by evil spirits] in it and say to them 'The kingdom of God has come near to you,' . . . and eat what is put before

---

11:14-22. See Smith, *Jesus*, 32-33.

150. Mark 5:1-17; Luke 8:26-37.

151. Robinson, *Problem of History*, 36: "We do not find calm conversations, but shouts and orders. The demons 'shout' at Jesus: 1.23; 3.11; 5.7; 9.26. In 5.7 the demon 'adjures' Jesus. Jesus 'orders' the demons (1.27; 9.25), or 'reproaches' them with an order (1.25; 3.12; 9.25). The only passage approaching normal conversation is 5.9-13, after the struggle is over and the authoritative word of exorcism has been uttered (v.8). This conversation does not serve to place Jesus or the demons in 'normal' relations, but rather to accentuate the completeness of Jesus' victory, a trait which recurs normally in the Markan narrative."

152. Robinson, *Problem of History*, 36.

153. Luke 10:20b.

154. Luke 10:19.

155. See Matt 10:7-9, 10a, 11-13; Luke 10:1-16.

156. Jesus sent followers as exorcists, Mark 6:7-13 Matt 10:5-15, Luke 9:1-6, Q 10:4-9; *Gos. Thom.* 14.2, as the tradition is multiply attested, and so authentic. Crossan, *The Historical Jesus*, 334-5; Crossan argues for a male/female team, those who had been healed, and Pauline text 1 Corinthians 9:5 being accompanied by a "sister-wife." All evidence related to the proclamation of repentance of the kingdom of God is early, therefore supporting its authenticity.

you."[157] Next he describes the distinctive physical appearance of the exorcist. When entering, there is to be no money carried, or belt (a leather belt) worn, only a single tunic, the base garment that covered the loincloth; no bag to carry supplies or extra sandals (bare feet if sandals fail), and no walking staff (used for protection as well as balance, the sign of a traveler). There are to be no traditional greetings on the road, only silence, an obvious suspension of Jewish Palestinian custom of greeting, kissing, and blessing. This marks the entrant as a religious ascetic, exorcist or prophet, separated from the local folk, clearly a striking and noticeable entry. While Jesus goes to the synagogue, he instructs his exorcists to find "who is worthy" in the village or town first, likely a leader of the local synagogue, or one of position.[158] They are to take advantage of the tradition of Jewish hospitality, i.e., of welcoming and feeding travelers, a Semitic practice that dates to the time of Abraham, who unknowingly entertained angels. It is known that Jesus wore a tunic, a *chiton*,[159] but also a mantle with tassels or a fringe, as those who touched it were freed from evil spirits, illnesses, or possession.[160] The entrance of the exorcists then was clearly identifiable, austere and intended to be striking, underscoring the serious risk present and the authority of the one approaching the village.

What Distinguished Jesus From Other Exorcists: Eleos and Agape

Yet, what also separated Jesus from other contemporary ecstatics, exorcists, and charismatics (such as Choni or Hainina ben Dosa)[161] was his insistence on the practice of readmitting those he freed from possession back into the village and synagogue fellowship,[162] ending their destitution and social marginalization, and to provide for them as if family—as protected children of the kingdom of God[163]—through the practice of mercy, *eleos*, and active and efficacious love, *agape*.[164] For the leaders of the synagogue who

---

157. Luke 10:8–10,.

158. Jesus was known to head to religious leaders' homes in each village and seek traditional hospitality. Jairus, the "ruler of the synagogue," understood this and met Jesus on the way to the synagogue, or to his home, Mark 5:35–43.

159. John 19:23–24.

160. Luke 6:19, 4:19; Mark 3:10, Matt 14:36.

161. As discussed in our earlier chapters.

162. For example, Mark 5:19, Luke 8:39.

163. Mark 10:13–16.

164. Matt 5:44, Luke 6:27–36; Matt 22:37–39, Luke 10:27.

witnessed his exorcisms, he demanded a change in the view of sin and judgment; that demonic illness, poverty, possession, suffering, and lowly status had nothing to do with wrongs committed by those afflicted.[165] These must not be the cause of continued separation and condemnation.[166] It was the work of demonic oppression, augmented by the apostasy of the elite and religious hypocrites—they were casualties of Satanic aggression permeating the land.[167] Because his demands to readmit the marginalized and dispossessed were punctuated with multiple exorcisms, confirming the emergent kingdom of God and end of satanic rule, he spoke as "one having authority, not like the Scribes (of Jerusalem)."[168] Mercy and forgiveness must predominate in preparation for the kingdom's arrival, evidenced by the mercy had been shown to the possessed:[169] "So the last will be first and the first last."[170] The eschatological reversal had begun, and those that were in power must become the servants of the ones who are oppressed by Satan and his dominion. The reversal evidenced in Jesus' actions then also becomes a dire warning to the elite—they will be dispossessed unless they turn to the same mercy and love and become children of God, not of Satan.[171] Of course, Jesus was directing his comments at the village leaders and peasants. Nonetheless, the message was clear—Jesus was plainly stating that the practice of love, mercy, and forgiveness now displace the corrupted Temple and its sacrifices. Indeed, for Jesus the entire Torah was summed up in the command to love overcoming the need for them.[172] This was a saying fraught with risk for Jesus, but one that captures the dramatic conflicts at play that all began in the obscure villages of Galilee.[173]

For Jesus, *agape* was more than an attitude—it was a charismatic practice, a power that warded off demons and spirits of the dead, preventing not only their return to the victim, but expelling them from the village, thereby

---

165. On giving to the poor and good treatment, Mark 9:41, on freeing the possessed from bondage, Luke 13:15; there are multiple examples.

166. Luke 17:1-2: "Things that make people sin are sure to come . . . but how terrible it will be for anyone who causes these things to come!"

167. Matt 23:1-36, ending with "I tell you solemnly, this judgment will fall on this very generation." Jesus is exposing himself to retribution and death by his charges of hypocrisy and warning that the religious elite are doomed to judgment now upon them.

168. Mark 1:22.

169. In Jesus parables: The lost sheep, Luke 15:1-7; the prodigal son, Luke 15:11-32; the good Samaritan, Luke 10:25-37.

170. Matthew 20:16.

171. Matthew 18:1-5.

172. Mark 12:31, just as it was for Paul, 1 Corinthians 13.

173. Matt 9:13.

facilitating that the inbreaking of the kingdom of God[174] and ending the rule of Satan.[175] Once the village is cleansed, Jesus demands that the synagogue leaders and elders, indeed the village assembly itself, reject Jerusalem and its elitism, the sign of Satan, and accept the "lost."[176] The authority for this demand is Jesus' claim that he is "master" of the Sabbath; more clearly, he is the master over all demons.[177] Like *agape*, mercy afforded protection from demonic return.[178] Therefore, Jesus' command of *eleos* and *agape* ensured freedom from re-possession, which could be seven-fold worse.[179]

Jesus and *agape* are irrevocably intertwined in this battle with Satan, as *agape's* power was immune from demonic control, as its presence was evidence of divine protection. God, the true King, their *Abbá*, was soon to arrive and bring the kingdom and with it the general resurrection of the dead and the vindication of the just.

Jesus' Troubling Admissions in Galilee

To provide context to the villagers as to these demands and the source of authority that empowered his exorcisms—that his authority was of God—Jesus openly admitted to a frightening origin: That of an ecstatic vision during a ritual immersion into the demon-absorbing waters of the Jordan at the hands of another ecstatic, exorcist, and preacher, John the Baptist, near Galilee. John was a voracious critic of the Jerusalem and Temple elite, whom he dangerously labeled demonic and possessed (i.e., "vipers").[180] As Jesus emerged from the demon-neutralizing "living waters" (which flowed from Galilee), he went into a trance, heard the voice of God.[181] Immediately, Jesus said that he was possessed by what he later identified as "the finger of God"[182] and was driven into demon-controlled lands in the desert wilder-

---

174. Luke 10:18, 17:20–21.

175. Luke 11:20.

176. Luke 14 presents in full Jesus' demand on acceptance, particularly Luke 14:1–14.

177. Matt 12:8.

178. The outcome of the exorcisms is a return to normal life and acceptance, Robinson, *Problem of History*, 41.

179. Matt 12:45.

180. Matt 3:7, i.e., demons: see Busse, *To Be Near*, 4.

181. As our study will show, the waters of Galilee were entrapped demons, as the waters were considered a desolate place holding demons and unclean spirits, just as deserts did.

182. Luke 11:20.

ness of Judea,[183] where both villagers and the religious elite knew the most feared malevolent spirits and demons roamed, seeking victims.[184]

There, like other ecstatics, Jesus resisted demonic attack[185] and had survived numerous possession attempts, as well as a satanic invitation to kill himself.[186] But unlike other exorcists and ecstatics, Jesus confessed to having had multiple conversations with Satan—a terrifying admission unparalleled in contemporary Jewish literature or Hebrew scripture.[187] With this public admission, Jesus made himself vulnerable to accusations of being under satanic control, which continued to haunt his reputation in Galilee among the villagers,[188] and was repeated by his enemies long after his death.[189] Herod Antipas sought to annihilate him for this reason.[190] As noted, Herod believed Jesus was using John's powers by taking control of his spirit.[191] This confirms both John and Jesus were believed to be dangerous ecstatics and exorcists by Herod *and the elite*. But for Jesus, his encounter with and possession by the "finger of God" coupled with his successful resistance to demonic control that proved favor by God, not Beelzebul or Satan. Jesus' confession about these events and his prevailing against Satan were intended to be proof that the source of his authority to exorcise demons, and his demand for the practice of *agape*, were of God. Jesus was at war with

---

183. Parallels with Moses' forty days and confrontation with Satan, in the form of the demon Azazel, appearing in the form of an unclean bird. Azazel tests Abraham to leave his angel Joael for food. Apocalypse of Abraham in a midrash on Genesis 15 is similar to the Markan report: Kelly, "The Devil in the Desert," 190–220. *The Apocalypse of Abraham* 14:1–14; *Jub.* 10:8–11, here Abraham is tempted by Mastema. Jesus' encounter to overcome evil in the form of demons and wild beasts in the wilderness, similar to Testament of Naphthali 8:4–6, Kee, "Testament of the 12 Patriarchs," 775–81.

184. Luke 11:24, Busse, *To Be Near*, 65.

185. Cross-cultural parallels include ceremonial initiations, such as in desert places, which is common for healers; see Winkelman, "Shaman and Other 'Magico-Religious' Healers," 334. Also the role selection of mediums and shamans begins with spontaneous spirit possession (334), where they learn directly from the spirits (335).

186. Busse, *To Be Near*, 60–69.

187. Busse, *To Be Near*, 65–69.

188. Busse, *To Be Near*, "The Beelzebul Controversy," 54–59.

189. See for example *BT Sanh*.43a.

190. Josephus, *Ant.* 18.5–2; Busse, *To Be Near*, 16–17.

191. Mark 6:4; Matt 14:2.

Satan; he was binding Satan[192] and his demons,[193] and reported his ecstatic vision of such.[194]

Other accusations were also troubling. Jesus did not behave like other contemporary Jewish sons. He did not support his family or kin, who, like other peasants, were struggling in Galilee. This was not just customary but essential for survival of the family unit. The Galilean villagers knew of his troubled background. It can not pass notice that Jesus had left his kin and family behind in Nazareth[195] after having been almost killed by the villagers.[196] He was accused by village leaders, the *rosh ha-knesset* or *archisynagogos*, at the Sabbath assembly of being of Satan—in essence, he was a dangerous, delusional villager possessed by demons,[197] and a blasphemer, claiming that he had the authority to communicate with and control demons through his being possessed by the "finger of God."[198] His family did not try and protect him, nor would they, given the risks they faced from their village and losing subsistence support—and he would not help them.[199] Leaving or abandoning family or being expelled by them on accusations of being mad and possessed, unless true, was one of the most serious risks to survival of subsistence-based central family units, as well as their social standing in the ancient world. And so, Jesus' trances, his ecstatic prayers, admission of conversing with Satan, that his exorcisms signaled the end of elitist rule, all led those who he grew up with to abandon him and want him silenced.

We know this because of this irrefutable, truly embarrassing tradition, one that the early church would like to have extinguished if possible, but it was already well-known and repeated by its enemies—that Jesus broke with

---

192. Jewish writings speak of binding and evil spirits: *Tob.* 8:3; *Jub.* 10:3–8; 1 En 10:4. *PGM*, second century BCE to third century CE, also describe the binding of demons, *PGM* IV.1244–5.

193. Jesus successfully bound Satan. So now he is the thief plundering his house, the kingdom of the royal house of the prince of demons is being destroyed; see Meier, *Marginal Jew, Vol. 2,* 417.

194. Luke 10:18.

195. Horsley, *Archaeology, History, and Society,* 109.

196. Luke 4:29.

197. Mark 6:3–5. In Luke 4:14–30, the original conflict of rejection and attempt to kill Jesus as a charlatan and dark magician has been expanded into the rejection of the Jews for the gentiles. Salvation is now for the gentiles, i.e., the thrust of the Lukan theological program.

198. Luke 4:20–30 and 11:20; for Jesus emphatic use of "I" in his description of this authority by the finger of God, see Twelftree, *In the Name of Jesus,* 93. See also "finger of God," in Q 11:19–20: Luke 11:19–20; Matt 12:27–28.

199. Luke 4:24–28.

kin and family on the worst of terms in the ancient world. The criterion of embarrassment absolutely confirms this tradition to be reliable.[200] This rejection of Jesus by his own family was shocking in the ancient world and to the villagers of Galilee and continued to be orally circulated for generations. Indeed, it eventually became embedded in the written gospel tradition to explain and neutralize opponents' claim that Jesus' own family agreed that he was mad and possessed, and why they would not stop his illicit and radical behavior. Clearly then, the conflict between Jesus and his family was one of certainty; it was vehement and public on both sides, as each tried to mitigate the risk of the other's rejections.[201]

Jesus survived his banishment. He was provided subsistence support (a meal, a roof, and clothing) in Capernaum and later other villages of Galilee, ironically only a few miles from Nazareth.[202] Undoubtedly, he was also compensated with whatever subsistence peasants could provide for his exorcisms, however meager. If the location of Jesus' temporary residence in Capernaum is accurate, he stayed in a desperately poor village area. Less than ninety feet away was the synagogue. This is where Jesus met the victims of demonic possession and illness and performed his exorcisms on the Sabbath; often unable to even leave the shelter he shared with his host family. It was those he freed from demonic possession and those who risked all in giving him shelter and joining with him to defeat Satan that he now called his brothers, sisters, and mother.[203]

PEASANT EXORCISTS

As such, Jesus was operating among the heavily oppressed Jewish populace of first-century Galilee. After exorcising demons, he disappeared for days into the hills of Galilee, where he is said to have "prayed," only to be sought out by those in desperate need. While Jesus was not the only exorcist operating in Galilee, his control and authority over virtually all demons was so well-known and sought out that when he chose peasants to join with him and assist, they immediately agreed.[204] Those who became his followers and

---

200. See Meier, *Marginal Jew, Vol. 1*, 168.

201. Jesus' public rejection of his kin: Mark 3:35; Matt 12:46–50; Luke 8:21. His family's rejection of Jesus, Mark 3:21 and John 7:1–9 (certainly authentic given the negative implications of Jesus and his kin who rejected him).

202. See also Mark 2:1 and Luke 4:38. Jesus being a guest in Kepha's home after exorcising a demon causing the illness of Kepha's mother-in-law, Luke 4:39.

203. Mark 3:31–35.

204. Mark 1:16–20.

were trained to use his techniques to expel the demonic proliferation by invoking his name risked not just Roman punishment and crucifixion, but also the agonizing possibility of failure, and so possession, illness, madness, and death.

> And he went up into the hills and called to him those he desired . . . And he appointed twelve to be with him and to be sent out to preach and have the authority to cast out demons.[205]

This small band of exorcists, mostly fishers and some women ecstatics, were his new family, bound together in a desperate and dangerous war on Satan. They were to expel demons, announce the inbreaking kingdom of God, and demand the practice of *agape* and mercy as the efficacious power that kept demons at bay, preventing return.

SUMMARY ON THE VILLAGE SETTING, JESUS IN GALILEE, AND PERILOUS RISK MITIGATION

Because Jesus and the exorcists he trained came from a subsistence setting,[206] we have labored to understand the social and religious context of first-century Galilean villages using multiple primary and secondary sources. In this setting, we have assessed and recovered the countermeasures Jesus employed to mitigate the perilous risk of demonic possession of the villages of Galilee and the invasion of their homeland after the murder of John the Baptist. Moreover, we have established that to follow Jesus was to embrace perilous risks of demonic possession or ritual execution by Roman authority, i.e., to be "near the fire."[207] Indeed, for this conflict that these young, desperately poor men and women joined,[208] each accepted the risk of starvation,[209] demonic possession, loss of family and kin support, and the likelihood of arrest, followed by a brutal execution. Yet, they joined. For them it was a worthy risk, as following Jesus was the one countermeasure to demonic rule and freedom from their plight—the promise of the displacement of satanic rule and demonic imperialism by the kingdom of

---

205. Mark 3:13–19, 31–35.

206. Luke 9:60.

207. *Gos. Thom.* 82.

208. Jesus' statement, "I come to bring the sword," is a contemporary reference to a special brass sword that was imbued with "powers" to drive demons and phantasms away. More will be discussed on this below.

209. Once starving, they picked the remaining heads of grain in a harvested field on the Sabbath, Matt 12:1.

God. Accused of being possessed by Beelzebul, abandoned by family and called mad,[210] (*exeste*), tracked by spies of the Jerusalem elite who waited to seize and silence him, Jesus accepted these risks for his *Abbá*, demanding *agape* until Satan was defeated. In sum, our successful recovery of the risk setting of Galilee in its social, religious, and political setting[211] has revealed a unique risk-based dimensional view of Jesus of Nazareth in his contemporary setting. It is now clear that his exorcisms and ecstatic activities and practices, particularly those that were most troubling, along with his condemnation of the elite and announcing their displacement by the kingdom of God, were remarkably perilous in their historical setting, and so bold and courageous.[212] Facing Roman wrath was perilous enough, but Jesus also faced off against countless demons and evil forces that not only confronted but tried to take control of him, terrifying onlookers.[213] Jesus successfully resisted, possessed by the "finger of God," expelling and forcing these demons into the most desolate places, which included the waters of Galilee,[214]

---

210. Matt 12:22–25, 46–47 (the rejection of his family standing nearby), and Mark 3:21; Jesus' use of your "sons," Mark 9:38–39, and "by whom do your sons cast them out," 9:19, support that other were exorcising that were accepted by the Pharisees or some other religious Jewish group in Galilee authorized.

211. Hanson provides an excellent critical bibliography as follows: Corcoran, "Roman Fishing Industry"; Freyne, "Urban-Rural Relations," 75–91; Freyne, "Geography, Politics, and Economics," 75–121; Freyne, "Herodian Economics" 23–46; Hanson and Oakman, *Palestine;* Nun, "Cast Your Net," 46–56, 70; Nun, "Ports of Galilee"; Parásso, "Lease of Fishing Rights." 89–93; Oakman, "The Archaeology of First-Century Galilee," 220–51; Raban, "The Boat from Migdal Nunia," 311–29, and *Marine Archaeology*, 957–965.

212. Matt 12:27.

213. Virtually all of these attempts took place in Galilee, and, more precisely, Capernaum, Jesus' village and center of activity in battling demonic forces. For example, the demon in Capernaum tries to take control of Jesus, crying out in recognition, *anakrazo*, Mark 1:21–28. This is likely authentic and pre-Markan. The demons in their attempt use, "I know," i.e., who you are (see *PGM* VIII.6 for example: The "Holy One of God"). The identification of Jesus as the Holy One, and his village, "Jesus of Nazareth," are clearly not later Christian additions—this is the demon attempting to take control of Jesus by using his name. But the demon is rebuked: Jesus commands the demon (*epetimesen*) to be silent (*phemotheti*) and come out (*phimoteti sai ekzelthe ekz autou*), be muzzled. Jesus' words reverse the attempt by taking control of the demon. The only words that are similar to language in the *PGM* relate to being muzzled, and so the demon is disabled, and violently convulses his victim. The description of this event in Capernaum must be accurate, and its bears all the evidence of a terrifying demonic encounter that would have been troubling to those outside of Palestine familiar with demonic encounters. The evidence of this concern is confirmed in that Luke completely neutralizes the troubling encounter.

214. See Bar-Ilan, *Exorcism by Rabbis*. Also cited by Canaan, "Haunted Springs and Water Demons," 153–70. The waters of Galilee were considered to be filled with

a practice the earliest Jesus tradition supports.[215] Now Satan was "falling like lightning." The very waters that demons once controlled at night now contained the demons and ghosts of the dead Jesus exorcised.[216] Indeed, Jesus now held mastery over the waters of Galilee, whether through silencing or muzzling the wind and waves, or sending fish into nets, an authority known to only a few charismatics, ecstatics, and some rabbis[217]—and to illegal magicians of the Roman world.[218] The demons of the springs and rivers no longer held control over the lives of the villagers struggling for survival. As such, Jesus, the thirty-year-old Jewish Galilean peasant-exorcist was embraced by some of the village peasants, but was a grave danger to the religious elite he condemned, and so to Rome. His intentional engagement and violent confrontation with the demons of Satan was a high-risk battle to establish the kingdom of God before it was too late, and before he was silenced.

> And when Jesus had called the people to him with his disciples also, he said to them, "Whosoever will come after me, let him deny himself, and take up his cross, and follow me. For whosoever will save his life shall lose it; but whosoever shall lose his life for my sake and the gospel's, the same shall save it."[219]

---

demons and spirits, as were all the springs around Galilee.

215. Mark 6:45-56. A deadly encounter with a malevolent ghost was feared. Also, the tradition concerning the demon, Legion, that Jesus exorcised is additional testament to the demonic infection of Galilean waters. Legion requested to be cast into swine, then driven by their request to be thrown into Galilee, that is, into a place of refuge for demons; from Q, Luke 8:26-39.

216. Jesus walking on water can also be seen as his mastery over the demons of the waters. Other Hellenistic traditions also exist, see Ogden, *Magic*, 175.

217. Evans, *Jesus and His Contemporaries*, 241-42 and the chapter "Jesus and Jewish Miracle Stories" as a whole.

218. Ogden, *Magic*, 125 (Tibullus's, the story of changing the course of rivers, 27 BCE), 25 (the Telchines, able to induce clouds and rain, hailstones and snow, first century BCE), and 269 (a magic amulet provided to divert hailstones, second century CE).

219. Mark 8:34-35.

5

The Galilean Exorcists Trained by Jesus

In the first-century Mediterranean world, the average life expectancy was less than forty years.[1] Infant mortality for Roman children was almost thirty percent.[2] Life expectancy for Jewish peasants during the Roman periods was estimated at twenty-four years at birth, and twenty-six years by the age of ten.[3] For children of Galilean peasants, infant mortality was certainly higher, some estimations being 40 percent by the age of ten, and this heartbreaking loss was attributed to evil forces and demons occupying the land that brought hardship and poverty, elitist control and debt, drought and death. The peasant villages along the shores of Galilee were made up of the surviving kin and extended family, the most important affiliation for every villager struggling to stay alive, and it is where their children and ancestors were buried. Consequently, they did not move to find better farming or fishing, as the village was their world, and there was no such freedom to do so. All this means that Jesus' followers were likely desperately poor, generational peasants and subsistence workers in their late teens or early twenties.

1. Hanson and Oakman, *Palestine*, 14.
2. For Romans, it was 28 percent up to the age of one, and up to 40 percent by puberty. In first-century Palestine, the rate was like much higher among the peasants; see Bar-Ilan, "Infant Mortality."
3. Naggar, "Human Osteological Database."

Male Jewish peasants had virtually no rights in the Roman world and were kept in debt.[4] They were not citizens and could be compelled into labor at any time by the occupying Roman soldiers.[5] They did not own land and had few possessions. They received no education other than the family trade and religious instruction at the synagogue.[6] Virtually all were illiterate,[7] although some by necessity were bilingual.[8] They were rugged, most, like Jesus, no taller than five feet five inches,[9] with dark complexions, and were descendants of northern Israelites, distinct from Judeans, who looked down on them.[10] There are multiple traditions in the Talmud that show Galileans were considered ignorant, rubes, and silly country folk by the elite in Judea.[11] But they were also dangerous, having raised violent rebellions against onerous taxation and foreign rule.[12] Jewish women had virtually no rights, other than inheritance in the event of a husband's death. According to the Mishnah,[13] in Jerusalem and Galilee widows had the right to remain in the home and live off the husband's property, but not in Judea. Heirs could sell the husband's property and dispose of the widow by giving her the amount of her original dowry, the *kethubah*.[14] This also created a number of wealthy widows, who became patrons.[15] They made their own clothes, pottery, flaxen line, and nets from skills taught by father to son and mother to daughter. They strictly served the production needs of the estates and elite, who controlled the army, lending, and taxation, making the peasants powerless. Families specialized in certain skills, whether making simple leather sandals or harvesting fish, and bartered for necessities, as there was little if any coin in their hands. This was no idyllic life, but a harsh and dangerous existence.

4. Hanson and Oakman, *Palestine*, 117–18.
5. Matt 5:41, referring to the Roman impressment law.
6. For a very early recreation of first-century synagogue practice and order of worship, see Burton, "Ancient Synagoge Service," 143–8. According to the Talmud, there were 394 synagogues in Palestine up to 70 CE (Talmud, *Ket*. 105a.).
7. Luke reports that Jesus could read Hebrew, Luke 4:16–20.
8. Aramaic and Koine Greek, see Horsley, *Archaeology, History, and Society*, 248.
9. Based on archaeological surveys of ancient Palestinian Jews, likely dark brown hair, brown eyes, olive brown skin, darkened further by work in the Mediterranean sun.
10. Josephus, *War* 2.510.
11. Collins, *Jesus, the Sabbath, and the Jewish Debate*, 210–14. They may have spoken with accents, but this has been recently challenged; see Mitchell, "Matthew 26:73."
12. See Loftus, "The Anti-Roman Revolts."
13. Mishnah, M. Ket. 4.12a.
14. Hanson, *Palestine*, 48.
15. See Busse, *Enemies*, 30, 124–25, 215.

The elite controlled fishing via Roman-licensed brokers, who in turn contracted with local fishers they selected and enforced heavy fishing quotas. The brokers controlled everything, leasing boats and essential equipment at onerous rates. Their intent was to keep the fishers enslaved to debt, thereby increasing their dependency. Uncertainty and the ever-present risk of displacement and starvation left them no choice but to take significant risks on the waters. These included fishing in dangerous weather and at night, which were both under the control of demons.[16]

The boats were primarily made of cedar and oak (26.5 feet long and 7.5 feet wide) and had a mast and sail.[17] They were heavy, frequently repaired, and required a crew of five—four staggered oarsmen and a man on the tiller—just to manage them. Fishing cooperatives that used these boats were formed by necessity; not because some fishers were middle class and "well off"—there was no middle class, only poverty and dependence—but to meet contracted catch requirements.[18] To leave kin and the village, abandon their contracts and boats, meant risking everything for themselves and their families, who could be attacked, tortured, abused, and imprisoned.[19]

Why then did those Jesus trained to be exorcists leave their villages and fishing? Why did they risk losing their critically important kin relationships, face starvation and social rejection, vacate normative responsibilities of Jewish sons and daughters for their peasant families, abandon subsistence survival,[20] and accept the threat of imminent arrest and death, all to be trained by an exorcist many thought was possessed by Beelzebul? A man thrown out of his village, called "mad" by his own family and the powerful religious leaders for what they charged were the dark and demon-possessed practices of an evildoer; a former recluse who now claimed to be possessed by the finger of God, and most dangerous for them, whose exorcisms he claimed heralded the end of the Jerusalem elite and demonic imperialism with the inbreaking of the kingdom of God? Why take such onerous risk?

16. Busse, *Jesus Resurrected*, 39–40.

17. Rabinovich, "'Jesus Boat' Causes Ripples."

18. An example is mentioned in the New Testament: The Jonah-Zebedee cooperative, whose peasant sons were Kepha, Andrew, Jacob, and Yohannes, all in their teens or early twenties when they encountered Jesus.

19. Philo, *Special Laws* 3.159, as cited by Hanson and Oakman, *Palestine*, 129: "Recently (early first century) a certain collector of taxes was appointed in our area [Alexandria, Egypt]. When some of the men who apparently were arrears because of poverty fled in fear of unbearable punishment, he laid violent hands on their wives, children, parents, and other relatives, beating and trampling and visiting every outrage upon them to get them either to betray their fugitive or pay up on his behalf."

20. See Hanson and Oakman, *Palestine*, 106–09, and further discussed below.

Was it to escape unforgiving debt and the burden of ever-increasing taxation and fishing quotas by their overseers, leaving family behind to suffer a worse fate? Or was it to join forces with Jesus and drive demons from the land, thereby protecting family and becoming an exorcist of God, a "fisher of men," to draw villagers from demonic control? Analysis of such questions is of paramount importance in developing our understanding of the risk and the countermeasures embraced by Jesus' tiny band of uneducated and desperately poor peasants he collected from the shores of Galilee who became exorcists to this master.

Scholarship unanimously accepts that all of Jesus' closest followers became exorcists,[21] but most important, at least six came from subsistence life as village fishers under oppressive production quotas, or from related practices: Brothers Shimon (Kepha, the new "exorcist" name given to him by Jesus,[22] translated from Aramaic,[23] the "rock," on which demons are broken) and Andreas (the "warrior"); brothers Yecob and Yohannes (renamed by Jesus,

---

21. Luke 9:1, Matt 10:1, Mark 6:7–13. A mountain in Galilee (likely Mt. Tabor) was sacred to Jesus; it is where he escaped, had ecstatic encounters and prayed (Mark 6:46), sometimes for days, and where he selected and trained his exorcists (Mark 3:13–19; Busse, *To Be Near*, 76).

22. The tradition of Jesus awarding trained exorcists a new "exorcist" name, either to protect them from demonic attack or to use in attacking demons and to signify their power and authority, is founded upon multiple attestations in the synoptic, Johannine, and Pauline writings: Shimon Kepha (the rock, i.e., leader of the exorcists and the rock on which Satan is broken); Mary the Magdalene (the fortress, overcoming and taking control of multiple demons—seven in all [Luke 8:2], indicating a multitude of demons that she overcame); Yecob (and Yohannes) *bane-reghesh* (in Greek, Boanerges, the thunderers, or the ones who drive out demons); Levi to *Mattay* (*Sanh.* 43a, Mattai, or Mittithyahu, "God's gift"); Toma *Didymus* (twin, i.e., equal to Jesus in authority); Simon *Kanna' im* (the Zealous, i.e., zealous to overtake satanic control; not a designation of a "Zealot," one of the "Fourth Philosophy" that led armed resistance against Rome during the Jewish rebellion, 60–70 CE; see Eisenman, *James the Brother of Jesus*, 132–35, and Morrison, *The Turning Point*, 2014); Yacob, *Mikros* (the child, i.e., of *Abbá*); Judas Iscariot (according to Joan Taylor, "the choker"; see Taylor, "The Name Iskarioth," 129, 210, 369–85. The "choker" would be one that expelled demons into the waters to trap or destroy them, or one who may have burned certain herbs that choked the demon out of the victim when inhaled, forcing it to flee. See also Cohen, *Primitive Mind*, 147, as well as a choking possession referenced by Josephus as understood by Avioz, *Josephus's Interpretation*, 63); Saul to Paulus *Apostole*. This practice of renaming adherents likely originated with the charismatic baptizer, John, i.e., *Yoannes ho Baptizon* (who immersed in water to capture evil spirits and demons). This practice was continued by Jesus and then his followers. Paul identifies Jesus as Iesus *Christos*, Jesus Christ; in the Synoptics and Q, Jesus is renamed *Iesus bar enos* (Greek, *uios tou anthropou*), the Son of Man.

23. See page 20n38.

Boanerges, "sons of power/the thunderers");[24] Toma ("my twin," from Bethsaida); and Mattaym (likely one of the Galilean-licensed assessors of catch, i.e., a tax collector licensed under Antipas to collect production quotas for the elite). Their reliance on the lake of Galilee and fishing, and their radical decision to risk all and leave this trade, must be carefully explored.

To begin, these tenant fishers and their kin knew that demons and evil inhabited the land, and that the refuge of demons was under the waters of Galilee, a fact even the earliest Jesus tradition supports.[25] Malevolent phantasms roamed over the lake, particularly at night, and for this reason, fishers would have only continued to fish after darkness if they were desperate, or willing to risk all for their catch.[26] During the day, immediate changes in the weather and wind were thought to be brought about by evil forces that were real and dangerous, seeking to capture the souls of those drowned if possible.[27] As such, the waters were known to be the haunt of demons[28] and ghosts by the Jews of Palestine.[29] Mastery of the waters, whether through silencing or muzzling the wind and waves, was regarded with awe; it was considered an authority known to only a few charismatics and ecstatics (and some rabbis)[30]—including Jesus[31]—and to magicians in the Roman world. When Jesus did muzzle the wind and waves, the words employed are the same as when he cast out demons.[32] Consequently, the first century recount of Jesus walking over these waters among the fishers, certainly from oral tradition originating in Galilee, was *the* demonstration of this authority to trample over demonic powers of the lake, so feared by these fishers and villagers. This

24. Mark 3:17.

25. Mark 6:45–56. A deadly encounter with a malevolent ghost was feared. Also, the tradition concerning the demon, Legion, who Jesus exorcised, is additional testament to the demonic infection of Galilean waters. Legion requested to be cast into swine, then driven by their request to be drown into Galilee, that is, into a place of refuge for demons; from Q, Luke 8:26–39.

26. Mark 6:49–50; see Combs, "A Ghost on the Water," 345–58 for an excellent analysis of the tradition, the appearance of the apparition, the terror of the disciples during the fourth watch while on the lake of Galilee.

27. Craffert, *Life*, 226.

28. See the tradition of Pausanias on the defeat of a ghost, a demon, that sank into the water, 2.65–11.

29. See page 63n216.

30. Evans, *Jesus and His Contemporaries*, 242, and the chapter "Jesus and Jewish Miracle Stories" as a whole.

31. We must reject our scientific assumptions or understanding of sudden waves or wind as detached from their world of demons, spirits, or even God. This would be alien to Galileans.

32. Craffert, *Life*, 301.

event or vision is one of the reasons it was remembered and recounted by these fishers in oral lore, later to be crystallized in the written Gospels, i.e., Jesus had control over the haunted and dangerous waters of Galilee.

As such, Jesus' charismatic authority, particularly in his repeated village confrontations with satanic demons, the retributive dead, and spirits of the lake,[33] was markedly different from those ascribed to other contemporary charismatics, including Hainina be Dosa.[34] This context is critical in understanding the decision of the fishers to embrace perilous risk—adopting a subsistence existence as an itinerant exorcist over the daily struggle to meet ever-increasing quota contracts so as to avoid starvation and the homelessness of one's family. A single drought or seasonal climate change could devastate catch and production, and likely did during Jesus' time.[35] That Jesus is at least twice reported to have assisted with catch, and they were forced into high-risk night fishing, underscores that these may have been extraordinarily difficult years for Galilean fishers and their families.[36] Indeed, poverty was rampant in first-century Galilee, particularly among peasants.[37] Most likely, they were starving, indebted, facing eviction, infected with illness associated with demons, and were penniless. These would be attributed to evil, demonic forces occupying the lake and villages of Galilee, brought on by demonic imperialism, all of which Jesus was successfully mitigating and driving from the villages. Years of suffering and struggle, prayers for daily bread and forgiveness, unrelenting demonic attacks on family and children, ever-increasing debt burdens, the Romanization of Galilee via the building of Tiberias and Sepphoris, and a sense of hopelessness, were daily realities for them.[38] *Indeed, one would only immediately respond to Jesus' invitation to become an exorcist if convinced that his authority over all these dark forces would prevail and provide safety and mitigation, ending these perilous risks, and that they too could offer this safety to their families and others. Then the risk of being trained as an exorcist and publicly naming Jesus as kyrios, "master," would not only be justified, but essential to survival and an act of piety to God.* This also allowed them to provide for kin via donations and payments

---

33. Which included the demons he drove into the lake of Galilee, Mark 5:1–20.

34. Freyne, *Galilee, Jesus, and the Gospels*, 234–35.

35. Jensen, "Climate, Droughts, Wars, and Famines in Galilee."

36. Luke 5:4–6; John 21:6–8.

37. Häkkinen, "Poverty in First-Century Galilee." This is an excellent article and summary study of poverty in first century Galilee that draws on all major research conducted by foremost scholars of Galilee, such as Freyne, Fresen, Hansen, Horsley, Oakman, Crossan, and Reed, with multiple citations of Josephus, including *Ant.* 17.6.7, 18.2.2, 18.60–62, *War* 2.4.2.3, 2.5.2, 2.175–77, and recent archaeology.

38. Mark 11:25; Matt 6:5; Luke 11:2–4.

received.[39] Indeed, we are told that all the fishers he invited to join him responded without hesitation,[40] and based on these facts, there is every reason to believe this accurately reflects historical events based on a risk analysis of peril and mitigation. To be blunt, that these fishers were willing to embrace this deadly risk only underscores just how intolerable and desperate life had become and how clear was the mitigating risk option to join Jesus in his battle with Satan. Villages all over Galilee, including Bethsaida, held fishers eager to embrace his authority and his control over the demonic waters.

Bethsaida, home to two of Jesus' exorcists, Yecob and Yohannes, was a small village on the northeastern shore of Galilee, only 2.5 miles from the village of Capernaum. Its name is most often translated "the fishing village," but is more accurately translated as the "place of the fish god's temple (or house)."[41] This ancient village name is important, as it underscores the common view of the lake as spirited, controlled by gods and demons—dangerous, requiring homage and sacrifice. Fish were one of the most important foods of subsistence existence, and so were used in magical practices and incantations, and were associated with control over others. Uses of certain sacred fish were employed in rites to silence enemies or even harm others and were feared in ancient times.[42] Practices to appease malevolent spirits and ensure the benefits of a safe catch were undoubtedly used, including in Bethsaida. It is of interest that Jesus places a curse on Bethsaida, along with the other villages of Chorazin and Capernaum, for their rejection of him and their "unbelief," suggesting that the local villages were unwilling to abandon their practices to mitigate risks from the lake for the protection of Jesus and his exorcists. But for Jesus, rejection brought doom and the risk of satanic control that required they "kick the dust" off their feet,[43] a Palestinian practice, not only to signal condemnation, but also to cast off any demonic pollution and leaving it there.

Yohannes and Yecob, given the exorcist names "the thunderers" by Jesus, asked that he allow them to place a curse on their village by calling down fire from heaven to destroy it, likely by invoking his name.[44] This pericope, certainly drawn from Galilean oral lore, is immensely important,

---

39. Luke 22:35; John 12:6.

40. Mark 1:18; Matt 4:20; Luke 5:11.

41. Hanson, "Galilean Fishing Economy."

42. Ogden, *Magic*, 129 (i.e., the "Drunken bawd-witches: Old women pass on her skills to girls," where the witch uses magical ingredients, sewing them into a fish head, to "silence" enemies; written about 8 CE), also 287 (relating to charges in court against Apuleius for using fish in incantations and magic, second century CE).

43. Mark 6:11.

44. Luke 9:54.

as it confirms why these fishers risked all and joined Jesus in his war on Satan—that joining with Jesus as an apprentice exorcist could mitigate the evil that had infiltrated and dominated their world as peasant fishers, exchanging powerlessness for a visible demonstrated authority that was efficacious and protective, and one that was made accessible even to them. Even they, simple peasant exorcists, could request the annihilation of God's enemies under Satan's control in the name of Jesus. Consequently, everything had changed, overturning their once hopeless and dangerous world, as now the kingdom of God was emerging in their daily defeat of Satan, and by their own hands.

THE EXORCISTS OF JESUS AND THEIR CONFRONTATION WITH DEMONS

Within a few months of their selection and training, Jesus sent his exorcists into the villages of Galilee to expel demons and proclaim the kingdom of God (Mark 6:7–13, Matt 10:5–15, Luke 9:1–6, Q 10:4–9; *Gos. Thom.* 14.2). This tradition is multiply attested, and so authentic and uncontested. Just as certain is that these young, desperately poor apprentice exorcists were not always successful in expelling demons, even when employing his name—an embarrassing tradition to the early church, and so certainly historical.[45] To this point, Mark 9:14–29 provides the most detailed and graphic description of a violent possession in the New Testament (and perhaps in the ancient world) and, just as stark, the inability of his exorcists to take control and expel the demon from a boy, making them dangerously vulnerable to retributive attack and deadly possession.[46] Only Jesus could drive it out, and did. Nonetheless, Jesus continued to send these exorcists into the villages facing this perilous risk, which provides the critical context for the instructions he gave and their importance, which survive in Mark, Q, Matthew, and Luke, and indirectly in the *Gospel of Thomas*.[47] From a risk perspective, such instructions must be considered to have been the mitigation to the perilous risk of demonic attack, or else why give them? Consequently, they provide a remarkable description of the actual practices Jesus required of his peasant

45. Mark 9:14–29; Matt 17:14–21: This tradition is also certainly authentic because it is embarrassing to the early church, i.e., that Jesus' exorcists were not always successful in expelling demons, by the criterion of embarrassment. Also see Sterling, "Jesus as Exorcist," 467–93.

46. As we noted, an exorcist that could not take control of the demon was vulnerable to being possessed if the demon calls them by name.

47. *Gos. Thom.* 35, which is strikingly similar to Mark 3:27, and so may be a direct reference to the exorcism of demons in Galilee.

exorcists to protect them, which were passed on to later generations of itinerant exorcists[48] and embellished to fit their life setting.[49] How did each of these mitigate risk of possession?

With the danger of demonic possession and injury to the exorcists high and potentially deadly, Jesus was not only explicit in his instructions, but he also commanded (*pareggelien*) that they follow them. The exorcists (both men *and women*)[50] must enter a village *in pairs*, never alone,[51] wear only specific clothing,[52] never carry certain objects, and avoid customary behaviors and greetings.[53] There was a specific pattern of entry required:[54] "Whenever you enter a town or village and they receive you . . . heal the sick in it [i.e., exorcise the evil spirits from those possessed by demons] and say to them 'The kingdom of God has come near to you' . . . and eat what is put before you,"[55] or in Mark, "Stay there until you leave the place [village]," usually the next day, presuming a meal would be provided and shared.[56] Jesus directly links the exorcists' expulsion of demons with the proclamation of the "nearness," or immanent inbreaking and even presence of the

---

48. Here Koester's "criterion" applies, i.e., that practices retained are the most direct reflection of the authority that established them, which in this case was Jesus of Nazareth. Koester, *From Jesus to the Gospels*, 231.

49. Compare Matt 10:9 and Mark 6:8 on the type of money that should not be carried. In Mark, bronze coins are forbidden, signifying an early tradition when the exorcists were poor, while in Matthew, gold, silver, and bronze coins are forbidden, a much later tradition from a later generation operating in the Hellenistic cities. See additional footnoted comments below referencing the tradition in Mark 6:6b–13.

50. While the gospel tradition lists twelve men, as we shall see this tradition has intentionally omitted one of Jesus' leading exorcists and leaders, Mary the Magdalene, the "Tower."

51. Crossan, *Historical Jesus*, 334–35; see also page 54n156 in this text.

52. Mark 6:9; Luke 9:3; Matt 10:9. These same traditions are repeated in the traditions in the sending of the seventy in Luke 10:1–16, obviously a parallel tradition underscoring the number of itinerant exorcists still active two generations later.

53. See Matt 10:7–9, 10a, 11–13; Luke 10:1–16.

54. The history of this tradition is complex, as Mark represents the earliest form, Mark 6:6b–13 (also Luke 9:1–6), evidenced by Jesus' command to carry no "bronze" coins, reflecting the low status of the exorcists, versus Matthew's gold, silver, and bronze coins (see Hanson and Oakman, *Palestine*, 122–23). Matthew and Luke share a similar tradition in Q (Matt 9:35, 10:1, 9–11, 14; Luke10:1–16) of the sending of the "seventy" exorcists, certainly a later tradition than Mark's and perhaps a conflation of traditions that were originally prescribed only to Jesus' exorcists before the composition of twelve was well defined. While some of the practices may apply to itinerant exorcists in the post-apostolic period, these traditions were certainly retained as originating with Jesus and the apostles. See Koester, *From Jesus to the Gospels*, 231.

55. Luke 10:8–10.

56. Mark 6:10.

kingdom of God, which signals the *inauguration of the messianic age*.⁵⁷ This connection is confirmed by Jesus' insistence that they must also stay and share table fellowship with the villagers,⁵⁸ whether kosher or not, as the meal is a celebration, long expected in Judaism,⁵⁹ which anticipates the "messianic banquet" to be held in the emerging kingdom of God.⁶⁰ Jesus had already established this celebration meal with his exorcists⁶¹—Satan was being defeated and a new age was dawning, evidenced by their success.⁶² Just as they must celebrate with Jesus, his exorcists must celebrate with the villagers who have been freed of satanic control. It was, therefore, an ecstatic practice of protection, acknowledging the reality that the kingdom was already emerging in "their midst,"⁶³ and in which they participate as a new community of *Abbás* own family, i.e., mother, brothers, and sisters.⁶⁴ When placed in the context of Jesus' war on Satan, where Jesus' exorcisms and daily ecstatic activity were overcoming Satan village by village as he approached Jerusalem to reclaim the Temple,⁶⁵ the communal meal, whether Jesus with his exorcists or they with the villagers, was an ecstatic and powerful countermeasure to evil in the context of perilous risk and the

---

57. Pitre, "Jesus, the Messianic Banquet, and the Kingdom of God," 155–61: For the most comprehensive and excellent analysis of the kingdom of God in the literature of ancient Israel, apocalyptic and Qumran literature to the time of Jesus, see Perrin, *Jesus and the Language of the Kingdom*, 20–69.

58. Which Jesus celebrates with his exorcists; see Vassiliadis, "The Eucharist in the New Testament Ecclesiology," 121–46.

59. Celebrating the kingdom's near arrival as a banquet and its historicity, see Sanders, *Jesus and Judaism*, 307; Dunn, *Jesus Remembered*, 425–27; Theissen and Merz, *The Historical Jesus*, 254; and on the kingdom of God in the preaching of Jesus, Jeremias, *New Testament Theology*, 96; Perrin, *Rediscovering the Teachings of Jesus*, 54.

60. Koester, "The Memory of Jesus' Death," 335–50.

61. Koester, "Story and Ritual in Greece, Rome, and Early Christianity": "Now, is it possible to infer that the Christian community meal has indeed its origin in meals that Jesus celebrated with his disciples? And my answer to this question is yes. There is indeed good evidence that Jesus celebrated common meals with his disciples and friends. What is told in the reports about Jesus' last meal, as well as in other information, indicates that these common meals must have been understood as *anticipation* [my italics] of the banquet of God, the banquet in the kingdom of God."

62. Luke 10:17–20.

63. Luke 17:21; *Gos. Thom.* 113, it is "spread out over the earth and men do not see it."

64. Mark 3:31–35. The history of this saying is complex, particularly how it is modified and also appears in Q (e.g., Luke 11:27–28). The debate about what is pre-Markan, or the result of Markan editorial work, only underscores its very early ascription to the ministry of Jesus.

65. Luke 11:20.

daily threat of demonic counter-attack.⁶⁶ Jesus certainly instituted it for this reason. Moreover, consuming food, such as the traditional herbs, bread, and wine, combined with apotropaic prayers taught to them by Jesus and rhythmic songs, all provided protection from demonic attack, not dissimilar to multiple examples found in the Dead Sea Scrolls and its community (which also included incantations).⁶⁷ *Abbá* had provided *to daktulo tou theou* to possess and protect Jesus from satanic attack and to control demons,⁶⁸ and now Jesus protected his exorcists with these specific practices, and, more, allowed them to address God as *Abbá*. Consequently, the meal and a special prayer preserves the exorcists and villagers, protecting from "falling into the hands" of Satan, i.e., from being possessed and tormented, just as those that they had rescued.⁶⁹ Jesus warned that they could be overwhelmed by the demons that returned seeking retribution.⁷⁰ Satan could still attempt to possess them, even that evening, like a thief at night when demons roamed⁷¹ seeking victims, if they did not strictly adhere to his instructions and practices.⁷² Consequently, the practice of entry, exorcism, and ecstatic meal provided protection from perilous risk of possession, particularly the demonic dangers present at night, while also celebrating the day's victories and union with those who were rescued, the new children of the kingdom of God. Satan and his kingdom were collapsing, "falling as lightning."⁷³

The apotropaic prayer said at the outset of the meal must have been similar to the Lord's Prayer. It followed a solemn, liturgical pattern,⁷⁴ similar to contemporary Jewish prayers, but was more urgent.⁷⁵ Indeed, the reason the exorcists had requested the prayer *was because it afforded protection*, just as it had for John the Baptists' followers.⁷⁶ The prayer cries out from the

---

66. Matt 12:45.
67. See Lichtenberger, "Demonology in the Dead Sea Scrolls."
68. Luke 3:21–22.
69. Jeremias, *The Prayers of Jesus*, 104–06.
70. Similar to Matt 12:45.
71. Similar to 1 Peter 5:8, but found in the Dead Sea Scrolls, 1QH 5:9, 13–14; 4QpNah 1:5–7; 4QpHos 1. While alluding to individuals, the image still stands as how Satan seeks his victims, even through human manipulation.
72. Luke 12:39; Matt 13:19, or when Satan possesses, Luke 22:3.
73. Luke 10:18.
74. Jeremias, *Lord's Prayer*, 15.
75. Such as the *Qaddish* and *Shema*; Jeremias, *Prayers*, 77–78; but transformed into a charismatic, urgent plea and invocation for protection and power in the face of perilous risk and danger.
76. Luke 11:1.

context of perilous risk.[77] Paul confirms that Jesus spoke it at the evening meal and that he continued to practice it.[78] It was uttered, perhaps even sung, while holding bread and breaking it, so as to imbue it with protective power.[79] When it was ingested, the bread and food acted as the communal and numinous nourishment against Satan's forces. But if the exorcists are refused entry into a village, there can be no exorcisms, announcement, and meal. They are vulnerable and the village is dangerously possessed. They are to immediately leave, publicly kick the dust of the village off their feet, as the village is polluted, under the control of Satan, and so is cursed.[80]

Jesus also prescribed the distinctive clothing and physical appearance of his exorcists (described on pages 55 and 56). These practices identified them as followers of Jesus.[81] When entering, there is to be no gold, silver, or copper money carried in a belt, or belt worn (i.e., a leather belt), only a single tunic,[82] the thinner base garment that covered the loincloth; no bag to carry supplies or extra sandals,[83] or a walking staff (the sign of an itinerant traveler).[84] There are to be no traditional greetings on the road, only silence, an obvious suspension of Jewish Palestinian custom of greeting, kissing, and blessing. This marks the entrant as a religious ascetic, exorcist, or prophet, separate from the local peasants—clearly a noticeable entry. In Matthew, Jesus instructs his exorcists to find "who is worthy" in the town first, such as a leader of the local synagogue (an actual practice of Jesus), but this may be a later addition.[85] Mark again reflects the more original instructions for peas-

---

77. Jeremias, *Lord's Prayer*, 22.

78. 1 Cor 11.

79. See also Chase, "The Lord's Prayer," 147–51, in the section, "Deliver us from the Evil One," on "Note on the 'Songs' in St. Luke's Gospel in Relation to Ancient Jewish Prayers."

80. Mark 6:11.

81. Matt 12:27.

82. Jesus is said to have worn a single tunic (John 19:23–24), as it is noteworthy that John the Baptist asked that his followers give away their second tunic (Luke 3:11), indicating Jesus would have done so.

83. The tradition is unclear here if Jesus is prohibiting a second pair of sandals or sandals at all. On the rough roads in Palestine, it seems that sandals would be a necessity. Nonetheless, given the context here, it appears that Jesus is prohibiting sandals.

84. Mark 6:8–9 permits a staff, while Matt 10:10 and Luke 9:3 prohibit it. Why the contradiction? Here, Mark has priority, as the staff was a common feature in Palestine for travelers. Both Matthew and Luke are likely referring to a cudgel or baton used for protection in the Hellenstic-Roman world familiar to travelers. Since the Greek word could mean either, Matthew and Luke are reflecting a next generation practice used by itinerant exorcists.

85. Matt 10:11.

ant exorcists; i.e., "where you enter a house,"[86] meaning that it is not certain they will be welcomed. Moving into villages in the morning or after dark, they were easy to spot, and were likely taken into small homes where they were urgently needed. They lived an itinerant life and survived from the often paltry donations given for their exorcisms, carrying a single communal purse—but were often still starving, evidenced by their picking grain left after harvesting from the barren fields.[87] They are allowed to employ Jesus' name to take control over demons and to use the techniques taught them to exorcise and free the victim, as noted, sometimes with limited success.[88]

These practices also identified them as followers of Jesus. The poor and disenfranchised that accepted them also protected them from retribution of the urban pagan rulers.[89] They were welcomed by the dispossessed and outcasts, but particularly by the subsistence laborers, i.e., the impoverished strata. No one else stood up for the desperate poor, the subsistence peasants,[90] nor offered protection against demonic illness, injury, starvation, death, unending poverty, and social persecution.

If betrayed to satanic rulers, they could be quickly captured and executed as "evildoers";[91] and Jesus warned them about this.[92] For Jesus, Roman legal prohibitions (e.g., *Lex Cornelia de sicariis et veneficit*),[93] which included the penalty of death and by crucifixion under a Jewish curse, were ever-present—but this outcome was unthinkable to Jesus' exorcists, and only would confirm that evil had prevailed.[94] This perilous risk was being mitigated; that is, to warn that following him could lead to crucifixion was

86. Mark 6:10.

87. Mark 2:23.

88. Mark 9:18–20. Certainly, this is not the only time they could not exorcise, otherwise the record would not have been remembered by later Christians who also failed to do so, but called on the spirit of the risen Lord Jesus for assistance and success.

89. See Lewis, *Ecstatic Religion*, 32–33.

90. Patterson, *Lost Way*, 75.

91. John 18:30 may be the most historically reliable tradition confirming Jesus' identification as a dark magician, "an evildoer." Pilate's wife fears contact with Jesus due to an ecstatic dream. Dreams were considered wholly reliable as forewarnings of evil and danger, and so, this tradition fits the contemporary setting. Pilate thereafter interrogated Jesus as a dark magician and attempted to turn him over to his accusers as such. Pilate acceded to their demands that he be crucified, so as to kill both body and soul and, as noted, prevent retaliation. Considered a dark magician and dangerous even after death, Jesus must be annihilated and his power vacated by executing him under a divine curse, i.e., crucifixion (Deut 21:22–23).

92. Mark 8:34.

93. Ogden, *Magic*, 288. This law was introduced by Sulla in 81 BCE.

94. Smith, *Jesus*, 75–76.

also an expression of confidence that the exorcisms assured the kingdom was not only in their midst, but fully coming, and that they would feast in the kingdom soon.[95] This same confidence filled both the men and women trained by Jesus who were sent to drive demons from the land, and who exclaimed, "Master, even the demons submit to us in your name."[96]

THE WOMEN IN JESUS' BAND—MARYAM

In Luke she is called *the Magdalene* (*Maria he kaloumene Magdalene*, or in Hebrew, *Maryam*), which is commonly associated by many scholars with her having resided in the village of Magdala on the western shore of Galilee. The village's name, Magdala,[97] derives from a tower that stood there and the fish brought for market, i.e., "fish tower." This is where the various fish caught on Galilee were taken and processed,[98] whether salted or pickled. This is also where fish oil was extracted to create very popular and sought after sauces, all for export throughout the Roman Empire, generating important revenue for the Romans and Herodians. Magdala, also known as Taricheae (the contemporary Greek name of the village, meaning "fishville"),[99] may have been the largest settlement along the lake (perhaps 1200–1500 people, mostly peasants) prior to Herod Antipas's construction of Tiberius about 20 CE, three miles south. The location of the village and its first-century synagogue[100] containing a carved stone block (the "Magdala Stone") with the oldest Menorah found to date in Israel (it also includes a remarkable "three-dimensional" view of the second Temple),[101] have been

---

95. The parables of Jesus underscored that they would share in the messianic feast of the kingdom now inbreaking: Luke 14: 7–14; 15–24; and see Jeremias, *The Parables of Jesus*, 176.

96. Luke 10:17.

97. Josephus, *War* 1:8, 9; in Aramaic, the native language of Galilee, it was *Magdala Nunayya*, "tower of fishes."

98. From Bethsaida and other villages to Magdala, then on to the coast for export from Caesarea or Akko.

99. Hanson and Oakman, *Palestine*, 110.

100. Dating was determined by pottery and coins during the excavation, including some that dated to 29 CE, the time of Jesus' activity in Galilee.

101. The block is twenty-four inches long, twenty inches wide, and eighteen inches high, showing the seven-branched Menorah (on the side that faces Jerusalem), and was carved by someone who must have seen the second Temple, as it appears to be a three-dimensional view of the Herod's temple by someone who had seen it. The stone is the correct size to hold a Torah scroll. The carved images include the sacrificial altar, a large oil lamp, and water containers on each side, engraved steps, some of the utensils used, and perhaps even the veil that divided the Temple from the Holy of Holies. The stone

excavated, along with ritual Jewish baths (*miqva' ot*, still fed by springs) and other buildings, including a marketplace adjacent to a harbor where fish were sold and processed and portions of the main road built with basalt and limestone.[102] The synagogue was finished with stucco walls (red, yellow, blue, black, and white) and beautiful mosaic floors with stone benches surrounding the central structure, as well as two courtyards. The synagogue had wealthy patrons. Certainly, Jesus visited this village and its synagogue.[103] It was on the main road from Nazareth to Capernaum and Bethsaida.

In the traditional view, she is identified as Mary *of* Magdala, suggesting that Mary came from this village, although this is never mentioned in the New Testament. Mary is said to have "ministered (*diekonoun*)" to Jesus and his exorcists, implying to some scholars that she provided monetary and subsistence support, which has been shown to be wholly probable as other first-century Jewish women held monetary power and even religious authority.[104] Mary may have very well been a "patron to Judaism," supporting the synagogue as a benefactor, receiving an active and important title of leadership. That such roles and titles for Palestinian Jewish women were prevalent has been demonstrated based on archaeology and inscriptions.[105] Consequently, a wealthy Mary of Magdala is possible, as one of the women mentioned in Mary's company was Joanna, the wife of Chuza, Herod Antipas's householder (the head of financial and business affairs of the emperor or his designee), an *epitropos*, who would have had the means to provide support to Jesus.[106] Joanna was one of the women from whom Jesus is reported to have expelled demons. Certainly, she could have become an acquaintance of a wealthy Mary.[107] However, this is problematic. If Joanna were to have been a supporter of Jesus, this would mean that Herod's fear of

---

was excavated in the center of the synagogue indicating it created a sacred space, which is contrary to what many scholars have held, i.e., that the synagogues were assembly and meeting locations for reading the Torah. This stone directly relates the synagogue with the sacred space of the Temple. Consequently, Jesus was entering sacred space and exorcising demons that had invaded and polluted it; just what he intended to do when he reached the Jerusalem Temple itself.

102. Avshalom-Govi and Najar, "Migdal," 121–25.

103. Jesus visited multiple synagogues in Galilee and beyond: Matt 9:35, Luke 9:2.

104. Kraemer, *Her Share*, 174.

105. Brooten, *Women Leaders*, 15–64, 141–44; see also Kraemer, *Maenads, Martyrs, Matrons*, 27–32, 90–99.

106. *Epitropos* was an important position, evidenced by Josephus's use of the term to describe the role of the procurators (Josephus, *Ant.* 14.143). The name Chuza has been found in Nabataean inscriptions, and so would be someone from the area from which Herod came, i.e., he was trusted and a countryman of Antipas.

107. Josephus, *Ant.* 18:3.2.

infiltration into his inner circle by an enemy was not a paranoid delusion but a reality, making Jesus all the more dangerous a threat.[108] Consequently, it is more likely that the tradition of Mary "ministering" to Jesus is just another of several examples in the Synoptic and Johannine Gospels of intentionally diminishing her role, which we will explore in detail later in our study.

The more accurate translation is Luke's, Mary, *the Magdalene*,[109] which in Hebrew and Aramaic is translated as a proper name, the "the tower," "fortress," or the "high one."[110] In fact, none of Jesus' other exorcists or followers had their village linked with their name, only, as we have shown, the exorcist name given to them by Jesus. Consequently, it is this identification and description given to her by Jesus that renders the proper understanding of Mary's position within the original band of Jesus' exorcists in the perilous risk context of Jesus' activity of exorcising demons and proclaiming the kingdom of God; that is, it was Mary's new name, "the fortress," "high one," the "tower," awarded by Jesus, designating her authority and position among his band of exorcists in their village-by-village war to expel Satan's demons.[111] Indeed, this is the very tradition retained in early Christian literature,[112] repeated by Jerome in 412 CE in his letter to Principia, recounting the life of Marcella: "And how specially Mary Magdalene—called *the tower* for the earnestness and *glow* of her faith, [glow here can also infer ecstatic and healing activities]—was privileged to see the risen Christ first before the very [male] apostles."[113] She was a charismatic among Jesus' exorcists, "*the* tower," and was undisputedly the first to witness and speak with the risen Lord (multiply attested), the first *apostolos*. But even Jerome could not bring himself identify her as such. Why is this?

If Jesus renamed her "the tower" it was to designate her authority and place among his small band of followers, confirmed by the fact that she was the first to encounter the risen Jesus. Then why are the traditions about Mary so remarkably sparse in the Synoptic and Johannine Gospels? For example, Mary is mentioned only briefly at the end of Mark 15: In 15:40, watching the crucifixion from "afar"; in 15:47, witnessing where the body was laid in a rock-hewn tomb from a distance; in16:1, finding the empty

---

108. Busse, *To Be Near*, 16–17, and his fear, even terror, of John's retributive spirit being resurrected by Jesus to bring harm on him for John's murder.

109. Luke 8:2.

110. Kraemer, *Maenads, Martyrs, Matrons*, 181.

111. Luke 8:1–3.

112. Koester, *Ancient Christian Gospels*, 79–128; note particularly the discussion of Mary, 128, where females must become like the perfect ascetic male to be admitted to the group.

113. Kraemer, *Maenads, Martyrs, Matrons*, 181.

tomb and then encountering a young man dressed in a white robe (but running away, "trembling" and "telling no one"); and finally in 16:9 (the appendix to Mark), witnessing a nondescript appearance of the resurrected Jesus. Mark seems to intentionally limit her role only to these final events, albeit they are significant; as if to minimize her role she had with Jesus and his band in their war on Satan, saying the most innocuous thing possible, that she "ministered" to him.[114] There is further evidence. The editors of Matthew and Luke (who used Mark as a source) continue to diminish her role. Luke omits Mary's encounter with Jesus, while Matthew describes her as frightened, running away.[115] Moreover, John (writing 95–110 CE) portrays Mary as silly, confused, frightened, ignorant, and subservient to the men, *particularly Kepha*.[116] But if this was so, then why is Mary at the cross (the others fled and abandoned him), the tomb, and granted the first appearance that clearly circulated in the earliest oral traditions, while Kepha's encounter, the supposed leader of Jesus' exorcists, is never described in the Gospels? Where was Mary before this? It is clear that she travelled with Jesus and the other male exorcists for some time, which is problematic in ancient Judaism—that is, *unless she was some form of an ecstatic and exorcist*.

Indeed, Mary must have held an important role in Jesus' band to have received such a distinctive and impressive name from him and be allowed to travel with the band while engaged in high-risk warfare against Satan, demons, and demonic imperialism. Clearly there is a significant incongruity evident. What risk did she pose to early Christian communities to have been diminished? It is apparent that the Synoptics and Gospel of John would have left Mary out if possible—*except*, she was universally recognized as the first witness to the resurrected Jesus, which linked her to a specific "orthodox" trajectory that was critical to certain communities reliant on Jesus' resurrection as the salvific event in history and in apocalyptic revelatory theology. Mark had no choice but to include Mary, as the Synoptic and Johannine Gospels center around the resurrection and empty tomb as the salvific event, and Mary the Magdalene was inextricably linked to it and their apocalyptic worldview.[117]

---

114. Mark 15:41.

115. Luke 24 omits Mary's having an encounter with the risen Jesus (!) and, further, Matthew describes her has being frightened and running to the males to report events, diminishing her role significantly and making her subordinate to the males. See Schaberg, *Resurrection of Mary Magdalene*, 264–66.

116. Mary is not only named last now in the group of women, but she does also not believe the empty tomb indicates Jesus is risen, even after seeing two angels (John 20:11). Jesus forbids her to touch him, as if she is unworthy.

117. See Koester, "One Jesus and Four Primitive Gospels"; Patterson, *Lost Way*, 134–39.

Employing risk analysis as a tool to analyze these stark contradictions is revealing. It is evident that the multiple, intentional attempts to suppress and limit Mary's role only confirm that they represent an effort to mitigate a perilous risk so significant that one is left with a striking conclusion: Mary must have once held a prominent role in Jesus' band, but this role became so dangerous to certain Christian communities that it was not just diminished but virtually eradicated, elevating Kepha to the leading role. This conclusion is confirmed when examining other early Christian literature.

In contrast to traditions that suppressed Mary, she is presented in a significant and separate trajectory of non-canonical literature that predates the Gospel of Mark by perhaps two decades and honors her prominent role during Jesus' activity in Galilee.[118] In this trajectory, Mary is presented as Jesus' preeminent disciple, having personal conversations with him concerning esoteric wisdom contained in his words alone that when grasped is salvific.[119] This she does repeatedly, and so is portrayed as more favored than Kepha, Matthew, or the other male exorcists—all of whom complain and try to silence her! The *Gospel of Thomas* emphasizes this leading role and close relationship with Jesus. Saying 114 specifically demonstrates Mary's priority. Here she converses with Jesus as if an equal- something that made the male exorcists angry and jealous. Saying 114 records their response:

> Simon Peter said to them, "Let Mary leave us, for women are not worthy of life."

Clearly, Thomas represented a trajectory that was in conflict with those communities claiming Kepha as the sole source of their legitimacy. The communities embracing Mark's Gospel, asserting the authority of Kepha, were later followed by those tied to Matthew, Luke, and then later John. So, how significant was the perilous risk that Mary and the competing trajectory presented to these communities?

Exploring further, the *Gospel of Philip* (150 CE) also portrays Mary as a close companion of Jesus, above that of the male disciples (59:6–11), receiving a kiss (a blessing and conveyance of authority and power), making the other disciples jealous (63:30–64:9). Clearly, Mary stands above all of the male disciples and has the closest relationship with Jesus. The *Gospel of Mary* is the most striking of all the non-canonical Gospels with regard to Mary's preeminence. Karen King argues for composition between 30–130

---

118. *Gos. Thom.* (dating as early as 50 CE, earlier than Mark), particularly sayings 21, 114 (see Robinson, *Nag Hammadi Library*, 126–38; also Patterson, *The Fifth Gospel*). *Pistis Sophia* similarly is a Gnostic text dating to the late fourth century. Jesus instructs his disciples, including Mary, in salvation by divine wisdom that he brings.

119. *Gos. Thom.* 21.

CE.[120] For example, in Mary 5, it is she who takes control of the panicked male disciples, fearing for their lives after the crucifixion and is *asked by Kepha* to share with them the teachings of Jesus she has received from the risen Lord, i.e., secret knowledge only she knows, received from him. It is she who becomes the leader of the disciples, not Kepha. In fact, Levi criticizes Kepha for being cruel, and Mary's leadership is reconfirmed.

Mary also has a prominent role in the *Dialogue of the Savior*, joining with Didymus Judas Thomas and Matthew in discussions with the risen Lord. This is an esoteric wisdom text (150 CE), but it continues the tradition of Mary's prominence in the early church within this wisdom salvation trajectory, where Jesus, particularly the risen Jesus, offers salvation to those who heed his words:

> If you become my disciples and hear my sayings, then these stones will minister to you . . . Whoever knows them will not taste death.

What then can we make of this trajectory and the perilous risk she presented, and what does this tell us about Mary's actual role as part of Jesus' band?

When reviewing the evidence, the conclusion is clear—canonical sources intentionally obscure the history of Mary's role among Jesus' band because of the controversy it would cause among Jewish and Hellenistic males in certain communities, particularly followers of Kepha, but more, because the trajectory that is said to have originated with Jesus and Mary did not require a physically resurrected Jesus to achieve salvation.[121] Mary having a dominant role, combined with this trajectory, was intolerable and even heretical for these communities;[122] but the primitive movement could not obscure the widely-known oral traditions that it was *only* Mary who had first witnessed three critical events: the crucifixion, the place of burial, and had a vision of the risen Lord,[123] while all the other exorcists (other than the "disciple that Jesus loved"[124]) had fled, abandoning him—even Kepha.

---

120. King, *Gospel of Mary*, 148.

121. For an excellent article summarizing the intentional diminished role of Mary see Miller, "Subordinate Women."

122. Confirmed by the *Gospel of Mary* and the debate is intense between Kepha and Levi noted above.

123. See Brock, *Mary Magdalene*, 70; Haskins, *Mary Magdalene: Myth and Metaphor*, 126–38.

124. The tradition in the Gospel of John (19:25–27) that the "disciple whom Jesus loved" (said by later tradition to be John, although this is disputed because of Mark 10:38, which may indicate James and John were martyred) was with Mary near the cross. It is this disciple that stands behind the traditions in the Gospel of John according to the community. Having him with Mary at the cross certainly enhances the reliability

Consequently, the traditions of Mary were a perilous risk. Given this risk context, we must explore whether there are grounds for broadening the role of Mary and her time with Jesus, pre-crucifixion.

In the context of Jesus' war on Satan, Mary's exorcist name, "the fortress," is significant and must be considered to have been equal or greater in importance to those Jesus awarded his male exorcists. Like Kepha, "the rock," who was given the "keys" (that is, the techniques and methods to access the authority of the "finger of God" to "bind and loose" victims from demonic possession in Jesus' name),[125] Mary is similarly given a title that designates her authority over demons. Is there evidence then that Mary was an exorcist or healer?

Luke 8:2–3 states that seven demons had "come out of her." This tradition led to erroneous, even outrageous accusations that she was a possessed prostitute.[126] Luke places her in a group of women who had "been cured of evil spirits and diseases"; i.e., a familiar theme of Luke's effort to diminish Mary's role by making her and all the other women who followed Jesus possessed, thereby implying they were less than reputable.[127] None of the male exorcists were ever accused of being possessed or had demonic challenges. What was the original context of this saying?

It is more likely that Mary had taken control of at least seven demons,[128] a common trait of ecstatics and exorcists, i.e., to take on and absorb exorcised spirits.[129] Consequently, the tradition that Mary simply had been possessed by seven demons because she was evil is erroneous.[130] As I. M. Lewis had demonstrated, exorcists and shamans, i.e., "masters of the spirits," exorcise or control demons by taking them in from victims and absorbing them.[131] Mary must have been a "healer," that is, an exorcist who had

---

of the traditions and practices they follow, which differ substantially from those represented in the Synoptic tradition.

125. Matt 16:19.

126. Solidified by Pope Gregory I (591 CE), who blended the tradition in Luke 8:2–3 with Luke 10:29, the woman of Bethany, and Luke 7:36–50, the sinful woman who anoints Jesus' feet. This remained doctrine until 1969, when it was changed by Pope Paul VI.

127. Schaberg, *The Resurrection of Mary Magdalene*, 264–66.

128. In Jewish traditions, seven represented a multiplicity, many, and so the tradition could mean seven, or many more.

129. A common trait, i.e., to take on and absorb exorcised spirits. See Lewis, *Ecstatic Religion*, 51.

130. See King, *Gospel of Mary*, 3.

131. As Lewis has demonstrated, the exorcist would absorb demons and keep them. For a completed discussion of practices, see Lewis, *Ecstatic Religion*, 37–57. While the tradition in Mark 16:9 was late and recasts Mary as the possessed (a devaluation of her

done just this "seven times," as "seven" in ancient Judaism was the perfect number, implying a multiplicity of times successfully. It is this risk perspective that underscores her importance to Jesus and his war on Satan, as well as her acceptance into his band and her acceptability as a travel companion. Jesus likely freed her from the demons, either by his absorbing or loosing and then sending them into the waters of Galilee or to the desert wilderness. Only her role as a powerful exorcist can adequately explain her title, and more, why she alone accepted the perilous risk of going to a tomb before dawn, i.e., at the time voracious demons roamed seeking victims; or why it is she who has the first ecstatic post-crucifixion experience with Jesus and can then order the other exorcists off to Galilee in Jesus' name;[132] or have private conversations with Jesus post-crucifixion, indeed salvific wisdom and esoteric dialogues with Jesus, that Kepha asks she reveal.[133] Based on this risk perspective, the name "the tower" or "the fortress" fits the role.

Now it is clear that the reality behind the tradition in Luke 8:1–3 is that Mary was not a wealthy patroness, but an itinerant exorcist and healer who traveled with Jesus from village to village in his war on Satan.[134] The living conditions of an itinerant ecstatic were subsistence level, and for women even more difficult. In the Greco-Roman world such women were considered wandering magicians and sorceresses who were to be avoided and were considered dangerous, or were religious ascetics.[135] Furthermore, by joining with Jesus, she was counted with him and therefore considered possessed by Satan and an evildoer by the religious elite. Like Jesus, she was considered a demonic servant of Beelzebul, a deceiver and blasphemer. This conclusion allows for a contextual reconstruction of *the Magdalene*, the "fortress," a leader of Jesus' exorcists.

Mary must have embraced the perilous risk of joining with Jesus, an "evildoer." Like Jesus, she was watched, if not hunted, by spies because she

---

role as noted), it still may reflect an authentic tradition where Jesus would have taken these demons within himself from Mary or set her free from them without any intent to devalue her role—it was an act that Jesus, as possessed by the Spirit, would have been able to execute for other exorcists.

132. Matt 28:1–10; in the expanded ending of Mark 16:1–8; Luke 23:1–11; also see *Gospel of Peter* 12:50–13:57.

133. *Gos. Mary* 1–6.

134. It is possible to see the tradition of her support as the example of what women patrons were expected to provide "out of their means." However, Mary, as an exorcist, would have received donations, which would have contributed to the common purse. Klutz, *The Exorcism Stories in Luke-Acts*, 119–21.

135. See for example some traditional analyses by Gager, "The Social Practice of Magic"; See also Dickie, *Magic and Magicians in the Greco-Roman World*, especially chapter 8; in addition, we will discuss healing ascetics in detail below.

too was considered possessed and an illegal dark magician. Jesus had made powerful enemies—Herod Antipas[136] and the Jerusalem elite[137]—and now she was associated with him. Herod himself considered Jesus a conjurer of the dead and dangerous threat—that Jesus had both raised and invoked the spirit of the beheaded John the Baptist in order to seek revenge.[138] Consequently, Mary's deliberate association with Jesus was fraught with perilous risk, which included capture and execution. For Mary to travel with men who were considered possessed was to embrace scandal and certain controversy, including charges of being a prostitute. If Mary had property, it would have been confiscated and sold.[139] What was Mary's possible contextual setting and social background? Would it fit into this perilous risk perspective?

While she may have been a dispossessed subsistence worker who knew the other exorcists and embraced the opportunity to abandon that life under the harsh conditions in Galilee, Mary was more likely a well-known charismatic, a female Jewish healer and ascetic, who joined with Jesus. Contemporary examples confirm there were charismatic women,[140] and several who traveled or lived among male ascetics and charismatics, not only as equals but also as more powerful healers and leaders than the males.[141] Most interesting, examples point to communities of ascetics who lived along lakes that were famous healers, both men and women.[142] The Therapeutae (20

136. Luke 13:32, Herod as "the fox," and Jesus, being hunted, has nowhere to lay his head, Luke 9:58.

137. Mark 3:6, 12:13.

138. Mark 6:14.

139. See Cicero, *De legibus*, III.3.6; Schiller, *Roman Law*, 178–80.

140. See Lesses,"Exe(o)rcising Power," 343–75.

141. The authentic letters of Paul (42–57 CE) unanimously confirm the active and charismatic role of first-century women ("there is neither male nor female," Galatians 3:28), including those who traveled as itinerant missionaries and exorcists, and women who were leaders, both deaconesses (Phoebe) and apostles = "co-workers" (e.g., Junia, who according to early oral tradition recorded in Mark included, if they were legitimate apostles, the authority to exorcise demons, 6:17). As discussed, such practices of accepting women with male exorcists must have originated with Jesus (Koester, *From Jesus to the Gospels*, 231). Paul greets Junia and identifies her as a renowned apostle who preceded him in the Jesus movement, "outstanding among the apostles" (Romans 16:7), indicating more than simple missionary work or the role of a patroness. This designation meant that not only was she a witness to the risen Jesus and had encountered him receiving a commission, but that she was imbued with charismatic authority like that of Paul's, including exorcism and healing (see Hammer, "Wealthy Widows and Female Apostles"; and King, "Women in Ancient Christianity." Women identified by Paul in just these letters include Priscilla (Romans 16:3), Mary (a Jewish woman, 16:6), Persis (16:12), Julia (16:15), Nereus's sister (16:15), Tryphena and Tryphosa (16:12), and Chloe (1 Cor 1:10, 11).

142. The Therapeutrides, 20 BCE–40 CE; see also Brooten, *Women Leaders*, 87–88.

BCE to 40 CE) were adherents of a Jewish ascetic community contemporary with the Essenes and active in the first century.[143]

Unlike the Essenes, this sect included Jewish women as equals, called the Therapeutrides. They were not only educated in Hebrew scripture but were also healers and teachers. They cut their hair, wore men's clothes (including special robes), and lived throughout the Greco-Roman world. The name derives from the Greek word *therapeuo*, "to heal, cure, and restore," indicating that these women cured maladies which in the ancient world suggested that they were able to control spirits, exorcise demons, and did so near lake waters. Galilee was the most prominent lake in Palestine. Philo (*Da Vita Contemplativa*) confirms that the Therapeutae were living in many locations throughout the world.[144] In Alexandria, they lived along lake Mareotis in caves or small cells or structures. Villages along the lake of Galilee were known for spirits inhabiting waters. Mary being a Therapeutae would explain why she would be living among non-kin Jewish males, and cohabiting in a socially acceptable practice, particularly having become like a male. This attribute of Mary becoming like a male is striking, as this transformation to what was considered the complete human being (i.e., a male in the ancient world) is found repeatedly. Paul utilizes a pre-Pauline formula, likely repeated in rituals during early Christian baptisms, that there are neither "male nor female" adherents.[145] The *Gospel of Thomas* confirms Jesus helping adherents (saying 22), and particularly Mary (saying 114), to become unified, a solitary one, like a male;[146] and early baptismal rites report rituals where gender was shed at baptism. With regard to ecstatic powers, Philo states that the Therapeutides were "physicians [healers] of souls as servants of God," or the gods (e.g., in pagan religion, as in association with the Therapeutae of the god of healing, Asclepius). In addition, Philo states that the Therapeutides were literate:

---

143. For the differences between the two (most notably, women active only in the Therapeutae), see Shurer, *The History of the Jewish People*, 591–97; Taylor and Davies, "The So-called Therapeutae."

144. Taylor and Davies, "So-Called Therapeutae," 21–22.

145. Patterson, *Lost Way*, 227–28, on the pre-Pauline formula and its use in early Christian baptism, which Paul includes in Galatians 3:27–28. Patterson also discusses the Gospel of the Egyptians, recorded in Clement of Alexandria's *Stomateis*: "When you have trampled on the garment of shame, and when the two become one, and the male together with the female are neither male nor female [*Stromateis* 3.13.93]." The *Gospel of Philip* also confirms, "Christ came to correct the separation that existed from the beginning and to unite the two, to give life to those who died because of the separation and unite them," Gos. Phil. 70.13–17.

146. See Koester, "One Jesus and Four Primitive Gospels," 174–75.

"The entire interval from dawn to evening is given up by them to spiritual exercises. For they read the holy scriptures and *draw out in thought and allegory* their ancestral philosophy, since they regard the literal meanings as symbols of an inner and hidden nature revealing itself in covert ideas."[147]

They thought and taught in *parables and allegories*, which as a major and unique feature of Jesus' teachings,[148] particularly in the *Gospel of Thomas*, where Mary is prominent.[149] Mary and Jesus may have shared much in common, particularly in the development of the parables, allegories, and esoteric wisdom teachings that we know today in the Synoptic Gospels and *Thomas*. Indeed, Mary may have had a significant impact on Jesus' teachings, making her a leader and influencer as well as a healer and ascetic. Perhaps this is why the disciples questioned Jesus on teaching in parables and repeatedly asked about their meaning, while Mary never questions his use of allegories and parables and is included in non-canonical literature as a major participant in this trajectory. Did Mary indeed have "secret knowledge" and spiritual understanding that "healed the soul," i.e., that was salvific, unlike that of the other male apostles? Most likely, yes, which later caused a major rift between male-dominated communities linked to Kepha and those that embraced Mary. This conflict between salvific wisdom found in the words of Jesus (linked with Mary) that healed the soul and the demand for faith in the resurrection alone as the salvific event (associated with Kepha) certainly engendered risk mitigations between these communities, ultimately leading to Mary being suppressed and relegated to Gnostic wisdom literature labelled heretical.

In the new association of men and women in Jesus' war on Satan, Jesus proclaimed those with him as his kin and under his protection, i.e., his true mother and brothers and sisters,[150] and more, the women who joined his band had become like men. Saying 114 in the *Gospel of Thomas* has Jesus defending Mary and addressing this very concept. Jesus says to Kepha: "See, I myself will lead her so as to make her male so that she also may become a living spirit like you males. For every woman who will make herself male will enter the kingdom of heaven."[151] This is exactly what Mary would have

---

147. Taylor and Davies, "So-Called Therapeutae," 21–22. Emphasis added.

148. The current definitive works on the parables being Jeremias, *The Parables of Jesus*; and Crossan, *In Parables*.

149. Koester, "One Jesus and Four Primitive Gospels," 175–83.

150. Mark 3:35, Matt 12:50.

151. For a discussion that assumes this saying is part of a Gnostic tradition, see Buckley, "An Interpretation of Logion 114."

done as a Therapeutides. As such, this saying accurately reflects why Mary, a healer and exorcist, was accepted and lived with the other males, and was on equal footing with them; and why there was no controversy about her traveling and living with males from village to village. Consequently, it is evident that Mary the Magdalene was a member of Jesus' band of exorcists, undoubtedly further trained and empowered by Jesus, but who came with prior esoteric practices and powers to control demons and spirits, and allegories and parables that may have significantly influenced the teachings of Jesus. Moreover, she was the first to have post-crucifixion encounters and ecstatic experiences near the tomb. Clearly, this evidence demonstrates that *the Magdalene* was a significant member of Jesus' exorcists, forming the foundation of a trajectory of allegories and wisdom teachings that set her apart from the other disciples.

In sum, the leading role of *the Magdalene* is multiply attested in all layers of tradition, i.e., in the four canonical Gospels,[152] non-canonical Gospels,[153] esoteric writings and in *Thomas*.[154] She is reported as having had multiple direct conversations with Jesus, both pre- and post-crucifixion. She was said to be in conflict with Kepha, and yet considered an equal, and Jesus demands her acceptance and authority. The trajectory of salvific wisdom found in the words of Jesus that "healed the soul," complimentary to Mary's historical context as a likely Therapeutae, was suppressed post-crucifixion by those communities that found salvation through faith in the resurrection alone. Consequently, even Mary's conversations with Jesus post-crucifixion were severely diminished in trajectories associated with Kepha, further demeaning her role and portraying her as a confused, frightened, and ignorant messenger of the resurrection event, running to Kepha and the other male exorcists to announce the news and nothing more.

We must conclude that Mary the Magdalene was not just considered a powerful exorcist but was as well-respected as Kepha in certain primitive communities for her salvific wisdom teachings that originated with Jesus, and for her courage, her authority, and close relationship with Jesus. The Magdalene had not abandoned Jesus like the male exorcists (led by Kepha, who announced he was returning to fishing and fleeing to Galilee). Indeed, she went to the tomb and successfully encountered Jesus. Consequently, gospel traditions of her being possessed are evidence of collusion in devaluing the role of Mary by a male-dominated hierarchical church in the late first century, which continued into the second century and beyond; just as it

---

152. Mark 16:9–10; Matt 28:1–8; Luke 8:2, 24:10; John 20:18.
153. *Gos. Mary, Codex Berolinensis* 8502; *Gos. Phil.*; *Pistis Sophia*.
154. *Gos. Thom.* 114.

was for Junia, as later scribes changed her name to *Junias*, i.e., a male name. As Helmut Koester notes about Paul's list of women:

> Most of the persons named in this list are not simply personal friends of Paul in the church of Ephesus, but associates and co-workers. This is shown by the repeated references to their functions. The fact that such a large number of women appear in this list is clear and undeniable evidence for the unrestricted participation of women in the offices of the church in the Pauline congregations.[155]

In 1 Corinthians 14:34, Paul is said to require that women remain silent, but this passage has convincingly been shown to be a later emendation and not Pauline.[156] In 1 Corinthians 11:5, Paul states that women prophesied (including speaking words inspired by the risen Lord) as well as participated in ecstatic prayer, and so had an indispensable role in the primitive community, which must have originated in Galilee and Palestine. Women leaders, such as Magdalene, Junia, and Phoebe (a full letter of recommendation was written by Paul for her and her authority) held preeminent roles among the exorcists and apostles in the early Jesus movement, and one is indisputably named an apostle equal with Paul.

Here we must count the Magdalene as one of the Galilean exorcists who shared in the perilous risk of associating with Jesus. While there is no confirmation that she continued exorcisms, non-canonical traditions confirm that Magdalene was an active and influential member among the remaining exorcists in Galilee and provided instruction to them about her vision of Jesus and her continuing relationship with him. This communication is remarkably portrayed as prior to their reengagement in their itinerant activity—indeed that she was a catalyst for doing so.

---

155. Koester, *Introduction*, 139.
156. Koester, *Introduction*, 215.

6

How to Destroy an Exorcist

The Death, Entombment, and Curse Placed on Jesus

History has shown that most Palestinian Jews who were an annoyance or danger to Rome or its sympathizers[1] were quickly captured and dispatched, whether by soldiers, mobs, or assassins,[2] and then thrown in the city dump or quickly buried in trench or cist graves.[3] A few were publicly executed, but not usually—take John the Baptizer for example, a popular ecstatic and preacher, considered a prophet by many Jews, including Josephus.[4] He was beheaded[5] during a drunken party at Antipas's fortress at Machaerus where he was held prisoner.[6] Most were simply thrown off a high wall, stoned, or

---

1. Such as Herod Antipas, the high priestly families, wealthy landowners, and local overseers.

2. Horsley, "The Sicarii"; Josephus also describes brutal attacks by Pilate, Josephus, *Ant.* 8.60–62.

3. In Palestine, in the second Temple period, peasants were buried in simple trench or cist graves. See Magness, "Ossuaries and Burials," 123–24.

4. Mark 6:14–29.

5. And perhaps arm-pitted, the gruesome ritual mutilation of the body to prevent retribution and escape of the consequences of the crime; see Ogden, *Magic*, 162.

6 Josephus adds more color as to the basis of Antipas's fear of John: "Herod, who feared the great influence John had over the people to put them into his power and raise a rebellion, for they seemed ready to do anything he advised, thought it best to put him

stabbed.⁷ But not Jesus. He was considered too dangerous—as much a threat in death as in life, having warned that he would rise and return if murdered in three days, even if by crucifixion⁸—a danger to his enemies, including Antipas who, like most in the ancient world, clearly did fear retribution of the dead,⁹ particularly from Jesus, or those who would conjure him.¹⁰ And this was no empty threat—paid spies and informants had witnessed multiple demonic exorcisms in Galilee, all performed through what they believed to be the power and agency of evil, specifically possession by Beelzebul. Jesus had been witnessed taking control of demons, commanding obedience, and by his own admission had conversed multiple times with Satan in the demon-possessed desert of Judea where he lived for a period of time after having been "driven" there. He openly performed necromancy, clear evidence that he was a nefarious and outlaw dark magician, raising the dead with impunity and was seen doing so right outside of Jerusalem in *Bet Hananya* (Bethany)—the back door to the elite's stronghold.¹¹ And Antipas and the religious elite believed he had conjured, i.e., "raised," John the Baptist's spirit for retributive, deadly purposes. Jesus had cursed entire villages in Galilee with tangible effect. Moreover, he dramatically expanded the perilous risks he presented to his enemies by training and empowering a band of exorcists to perform these same acts *in his name*, crisscrossing the peasant villages of Galilee, while gaining popular support; all while denouncing the Jerusalem elite and Antipas as demonic, proclaiming their end was imminent. Jesus and the threat he would pose in death meant that he could not just be killed, he had to be annihilated.

---

to death." Josephus, *Ant.* 18:5.2.

7. Josephus, *Ant.* 20.9. James was stoned on false accusations formed by Ananus, the High Priest, during the interim time between the death of Festus, Roman governor, and the arrival of Albinus. The later Christian writer Hegesippus reported that James was thrown off the Introple and then stoned to death. There are traditions of his murder recounted also by Clement of Alexandria and Eusebius.

8. Jesus was claiming that he would return after three days, exceeding the time allotted in the ancient world to ensure there had been no pseudo-death (*Sem.* 8.1), i.e., that the individuals was certainly dead.

9. Ogden, *Magic*, 160–82; a fear common in the ancient world.

10. Luke 9:7–9; Matthew 14:1–12; Mark 6:14–29.

11. Less than two miles.

THE CURSE OF CRUCIFIXION

The Romans, specifically Quirinus,[12] crucified, i.e., "killed by violence," hundreds, if not thousands, of Jews in Galilee after the tax revolt of Judas of Gamala in 6 CE.[13] The bodies of crucified Jewish rebels (and anyone associated with them) lined the road not far from Nazareth leading into Galilee.[14] Multiple crucifixion techniques were employed given the number of those killed, but all were agonizing, slow, and brutal deaths.[15] It is possible that even women and children were killed, their throats slashed while the crucified watched, which had been done before (by a Jewish ruler!).[16] This horrifying visage may have been seen by the young Jesus and some of the fishers later turned exorcists who traveled the road as children. Joseph, Jesus' own father in Nazareth, may have been taken by the Romans, as men were gathered up and crucified after the revolt. He disappears from the narrative about this time.

Those who violently murdered or killed others believed their victims could return as one of the "untimely dead," a *biaeothanati*, and curse, punish, and harm them.[17] But not Quirinus and the Romans occupying Palestine; they had no fear of encountering any malevolent phantasms of these Jews seeking retribution[18]—because of *how* they died. For Jews, crucifixion was to die under an annihilating curse according to the Torah, destroying both body and soul.[19] It was a vicious and intentional form of death for Jews. Evidence in the Dead Sea Scrolls, 4Q 169 3–4 II (*Pesher Nahum*) and 11QT LXIV, 7–13 (*Temple Scroll*), confirms that the eight hundred Jews crucified by Alexander Jannaeus prior to the Roman occupation were also believed subject to this curse.[20] Shimon b. Shetah had seventy "sorceresses" crucified in Askelon according to the Mishnah for this reason.[21] Consequently, there was no expectation by Jannaeus or later Roman occupiers that any

---

12. Appointed governor of Syria from 6 BCE until 12 CE.

13. Josephus, *Ant.*, 17:10, 18:26–8.

14. Two thousand of them; see Josephus, *Ant.* 18:1.1–10, 23.

15. Josephus, *Life* 76; During the Jewish rebellion, Josephus came across three of his acquaintances crucified and asked Titus to take them down, which he agreed to do. Titus's physicians could save only two of the three.

16. Josephus, *Ant.* 13:14.

17. Ogden, *Magic*, 152–53, 158; and as disputed by Tertullian in 200 CE, reflected in Ogden, *Magic*, 149–50.

18. Craffert, *Life*, 131, 176–77.

19. Deuteronomy 20:23, also referenced by Paul in Galatians 3:13.

20. See also Thatcher, "I Have Conquered the World," 147–48.

21. Hengel, *Crucifixion*, 84.

phantasms could seek retribution. Crucifixion was the ritual annihilation of Jews—the Hasmoneans, Herodians, and Romans knew this.

With the Roman occupation, Antipas (like all of their appointees) had no authority to crucify, unless he colluded with the Romans.[22] He used other techniques to prevent retribution from those he killed, but feared he was still at risk. For example, the mutilation of John the Baptist's body was Antipas's attempt to not only silence him but also hobble his phantasm after beheading to prevent return and attack.[23] Antipas, a Hellenized Roman sympathizer,[24] believed that phantasms of the dead did return, particularly those of the untimely dead killed by *his* violence because he could not crucify them: "[Antipas] heard of him [Jesus' control over demons] . . . and he said, John the Baptist was risen from the dead."[25] Antipas's fear that John was "risen from the dead" was not a form of corporeal resurrection, but the haunting belief (shared by all, whether a first-century peasant or a king) that a malevolent ghost or spirit, particularly one that could be manipulated by another charismatic *magos* or *goetes*, could be conjured, i.e., "raised," and brought against him. In this case, Antipas believed that John's phantasm could literally be pulled from the dead pool of wandering souls for retribution by the "evildoer" Jesus. As a result, Herod's stated "fear" of the rabble is now understood in a much more dynamic, perilous risk context; that Jesus could use the spirit of John (seeking retribution) to deceive Antipas's subjects, even his own family, and incite rebellion or attempts to kill him.[26] In fact, this is what he thought he was witnessing. When we think of "deception" today, we think of lies or rumors; but for Antipas and those of his time, deception was an evil force in the grasp of conjurers like Jesus,[27] whom

22. Hengel, *Crucifixion*, 34–35. Crucifixion was a Roman punishment for desertion, betraying of secrets, incitement to rebellion, murder, prophecy about welfare of rulers, nocturnal impiety, magic, falsification of wills, and others; Paulus, *Sententiae* 5.19.2; 21.4; 23.2, 16; 25:1, 30b.1. Crucifixion was almost always "inflicted" on the lower classes, not on the upper classes or elite. After the tumultuous events of Jannaeus actions, Herod the Great abandoned crucifixion, leaving it to the Romans, as did his family (see Hengel, *Crucifixion*, 85).

23. Ogden, *Magic*, 162.

24. Herod Antipas was a Hellenized Jew and patron of Rome. As is evidenced in the tradition of Herod's fear of John's return, that is, his fear of Jesus' claiming John's spirit and power (see Busse, *To Be Near*, 16–17), Herod would have been fully aware of the risks associated with retaliation from Jesus' ghost, particularly given the plentiful reports in the Greek and Roman world of malevolent ghosts of the untimely dead who were brought under control of sorcerers and magicians to attack their enemies.

25. Mark 6:14, 15.

26. This tradition makes doubtful that Herod was "glad to see Jesus," i.e., hoping to see him perform some miracle, as Herod was terrified of Jesus of Nazareth; see Luke 23:8.

27. Smith, *Jesus*, 97.

they feared could influence and control the populist mob, turning them into deadly enemies. Facing perilous risk and danger of illness, possession and death, Antipas thought himself in grave danger.

Consequently, it is no surprise that Antipas fully supported Jesus' crucifixion, uniting with Pontius Pilate and the religious elite.[28] If Jesus was destroyed, so too would be the threat from John. Consequently, Jesus' crucifixion was an essential step in neutralizing his retributive return by first placing the divine curse on him.[29] However, as noted, Jesus had also warned that if he was crucified, or if others of his band were similarly killed, they would not be subject to the curse, nor would they be destroyed—a shocking claim in the ancient world.[30] Unremarkably, none of his exorcists understood this warning—all fully believed crucifixion was annihilation, as did most Jewish peasants.[31] Indeed, Jesus had publicly extolled his followers to "take up the cross" (i.e., do not fear the curse, the kingdom of God was imminent), but all, except the women exorcists, fled to Galilee when he was captured and crucified fearing a similar cursed fate and annihilation—even Kepha publicly denied even knowing him repeatedly and then abandoned him.[32] As such, Jesus' warning that he would return in "three days"[33] was understood as a clear threat of retributive return *to his enemies* who were Romanized, Hellenized Jewish elite like Antipas, but was thought impossible by those who followed him.

Did Jesus actually warn that he would return in three days? Critical scholars have long rejected the historicity of any such predictions as having come from the historical Jesus, assuming the early church, looking back on Jesus' itinerant activity, inserted them.[34] However, risk analysis and the context of first-century Palestine allow that such predictions were made,

---

28. Luke 23:11–12.

29. Smith, *Jesus*, 75–76.

30. Mark 8:34—9:1; Matt 16:24–28; Luke 9:23–27. Certainly this is the meaning of this saying set in the original risk context, i.e., that you will not die, but "find life" and "see the Son of Man coming in his kingdom."

31. For the lack of comprehension which meet the criterion of embarrassment, see Mark 8:31, 9:31, 10:32–34; see also Mark 4:40, 6:51–52, 8:4, 14–21, 8:33, 9:2–10, 14:68–72; despite what Wrede stated relative to the "messianic secret" (and what many scholars have accepted), these were not fabrications of the early church, but accurate reflections of the contextual risk situation. Jesus did not "predict" his crucifixion, he warned his opponents that he would not be annihilated under that curse, i.e., placing the sayings in the original risk context.

32. Luke 22:54–62, another tradition that meets the criterion of embarrassment.

33. Mark 8:31, 9:31; also see Matt 12:38–42; Luke 11:29–32; Mark 8:11–12, the sign of Jonah.

34. See, for example, Bultmann, *Theology*, 29.

particularly since Jesus did so not as a Christological prediction but as a warning; that is, a warning and countermeasure to his capture and murder by opponents, *particularly by crucifixion*. In this context, having witnessed the arrest and execution of his mentor, John the Baptist,[35] Jesus' "prediction" was actually a stunning threat to his opponents—a countermeasure they would clearly understand. He publicly cautioned them that if murdered he would return (as one like of the untimely dead) after a period of time, three days, which was known in the ancient world as the period of time when death was unquestionably confirmed.[36] "In three days I will rise again"[37] would be perceived as a promise of return and retaliation, which they believed came by the authority of Beelzebul. Consequently, to his enemies, *Jesus was more dangerous in death than in life if not dispatched correctly*.

Based on the foregoing analysis, it is evident that the enemies of Jesus were still concerned he might return as one of the "untimely dead," those violently murdered or killed, even though crucified; a *biaeothanati*, able to curse, punish, and harm, even kill his murderers, under the authority that empowered him.[38] They had accused Jesus of being possessed by Beelzebul, prince of Satan's demons—a charge they leveled against him repeatedly and publicly. Might this possession and control of Jesus by Beelzebul make impotent the divine curse, which Jesus also claimed he would overcome?[39] Recognizing even the possibility of this perilous risk, Jesus' executioners took several additional steps that are now fully coherent in this risk context.

THE SPECIAL TREATMENT OF JESUS' BODY

Jesus wasn't the first "evildoer" (or even feared individual) whose body was sealed in a container or tomb using special practices to prevent retributive attack. There are multiple examples where those who feared retribution took a body (or remains of an enemy), placed it in a sealed container and then set it among magical amulets, spells, and tablets to trap it.[40] And there are

35. Patterson, *Lost Way*, 38.
36. Ogden, *Magic*, 152–53, 158.
37. Luke 18:33.
38. Ogden, *Magic*, 152–53; 158; and as disputed by Tertullian in 200 CE, reflected in Ogden, *Magic*, 149–50.
39. Busse, *To Be Near*, 54–58.
40. For example, the laying of a ghost into a tomb or cenotaph with controlling spells, see Ogden, *Magic*, 29–30, 164–65. The use of spells, amulets, and other means to seal the ghost into a tomb or grave are also mentioned and described below. As Ogden states: "The means by which the ghost is bound into its grave is not entirely clear: there is one reference to the use of stones, another to the use of bars, numerous ones referred

examples, including the tomb of Joseph Caiaphas, where items were placed in a tomb to protect from evil attack, notably two crucifixion nails.[41] Jesus' rock-hewn tomb was intended to be just this—a trap. The tomb could not be used again, as neither the "righteous or sinners" (i.e., Jesus) nor two enemies were to be buried side by side.[42] Consequently, the placement of a peasant's body into an expensive elitist's tomb and then the sealing it up can only be explained as an intentional act to mitigate a perilous risk. They were sealing it in stone, whatever the cost, to neutralize the risk of his return.

Moreover, according to John 19:38–42, the body had been covered with unusually large amounts of burial "spices" (over one hundred pounds of myrrh and aloes! Only forty pounds were used for the highly respected and revered Rabbi Gamaliel).[43] This is likely not an exaggeration. That Jesus' body had been dressed is certainly correct. However, based on the risk and contextual setting, Jesus' body, like that of other evildoers, was more likely covered with a concoction of special herbs, amulets, and written spells[44] to further ensure he could not escape *or be conjured by his followers*.[45] Protective amulets, as well as binding amulets, were common and widely used in the ancient world, as were spell scrolls. Consequently, the tomb was chosen by the elite, likely by Joseph of Arimathea, a member of the Sanhedrin (who likely was not "a secret disciple of Jesus," i.e., his membership was approved by the Romans), for this very purpose. Jesus' body and spirit were ritually entrapped, or better, harnessed by binding magic, common in the ancient world.

GUARDING THE CORPSE OF JESUS AND THE TOMB

They then took additional steps. Given the recovered risk context, the elite also placed a guard at the tomb,[46] making the gospel tradition reliable. They did so to ensure that the body of Jesus remained trapped for at least three days, confirming he had been annihilated. As with Jesus' death, burial was to be immediate (*Sanh.* 6:6), particularly before the Sabbath; both Jairus's

---

to with the use of iron bands or chains, apparently knotted, and one reference apparently to swords being driven down into the grave, no doubt to pin the ghost down."

41. Evans, *Jesus and the Remains of His Day*, 142–43.

42. Magness, *Burials*, 129.

43. Josephus, *Ant.*, 17:8.3.

44. Small scrolls with written text, rolled up and place on the corpse, or curse tablets written in wax, lead, or stone, even textual amulets.

45. For the use of amulets by Jewish rabbis and others, see chapter 1.

46. Only reported in Matt 27:62—28:15.

daughter (Mark 5:38) and Lazarus (John 11) were buried immediately. Often the dead were buried with personal items (archaeologists have found combs, ink wells, sandals, and sometimes jewelry), but not Jesus; apparently even remainders of his clothes were divided among his executioners.[47] Josephus states that "all who pass by when a corpse is buried must accompany the funeral and join in the lamentations" (*Apion*, 2:205), the minimum duty being to rise as the funeral procession passed (*Bik.* 3:3, 65c; *Sh. Ar., YD* 361:4); but Jesus was afforded no such rights. The body of a crucified peasant criminal would normally have been dumped, or at best buried in a trench. Criminals who died by violence did not have their body cleaned and rewrapped, they remained in the garments worn, however brutalized. This is what is remarkable about a peasant criminal from Galilee being placed in the tomb of a member of the Sanhedrin and carefully wrapped by an enormous amount of material, then sealed up. This was done intentionally to prevent escape, further mitigating perilous risk.

When placed in a tomb, bodies were laid on a stone bier to allow for decomposition. A reinternment was made after one year into an ossuary[48] (Miam. Yad., Evel, 12:8), "which first began to appear in the middle of Herod's reign (as a result of Roman influence, 20–15 BCE)," then disappeared after 70 CE with the destruction of Jerusalem.[49] A tomb, carved out of bedrock (which only the upper class and upper-middle class could afford in the Herodian period)[50] with a single entrance was selected. Late second-temple-period tombs (usually family tombs with multiple niches or chambers to place ossuaries when the bones were collected) lay outside of the walls of Jerusalem. Hundreds have been excavated by archaeologists. Most were sealed with either a heavy block stone or by a round stone that could be rolled along a trench to cover the entrance (which was low, requiring one to stoop down to enter into the main chamber). A block stone was permanent, as was a rolling stone when the trench allowed the stone to drop into a fixed grove. More commonly, a small stone was used to keep the round stone in place once positioned, called a *dofek*, allowing for reentry. In this case, the *dofek* could be removed and the stone rolled back with a lever, sometimes requiring great strength. This was commonly done to check the tomb after three days to ensure the individual was in fact dead,[51] and later to collect the bones and place them in an ossuary.

47. Magness, *Burials*, 129–30; Matthew 27:35.
48. Ossuaries were twenty to thirty-two inches by twelve to twenty inches by ten to sixteen inches.
49. Magness, *Burials*, 129.
50. Magness, *Burials*, 123.
51. See Ogden, *Magic*, 179, 181; Busse, *Jesus Resurrected*, 109–10.

Depending on its size, rolling back the stone could require two or more men on the lever. In the case of Jesus' tomb, the size described indicated that a few men would be required to move the stone. So, who were these men sent to watch the tomb and check it after three days?

It is unlikely that Pilate placed a Roman guard at the tomb. There are multiple problems with this tradition:[52] The awkward explanation as to why the soldiers were not executed for falling asleep while on duty (the required penalty) or that they were bribed by the religious elite to explain their failure (i.e., still grounds for execution); Pilate turning the guards over to the chief priests, "Go, make the tomb as secured as you know how," was certainly not a Roman practice. Most telling, when they discover the empty tomb they report directly to the chief priests, not to Pilate, and are bribed and protected by the same.[53] These were not Roman soldiers.

Given the risk that Jesus posed to the elite, the guards were likely Jewish ritual priests, *kohen*, who wore *white linen robes*.[54] They would be armed with this protective garb, powerful amulets, and iron or brass swords, as these swords provided protection from evil spirits and malevolent ghosts. In fact, there were reports of swords present when Jesus was taken, after Judas "kissed" Jesus (which was an ancient curse used to infect and disable an opponent).[55] When held up, the phantasm departed.[56] Given that Jesus' return was feared, it was this kind of ritual guard, one that could both protect

---

52. Only the *Gospel of Peter* (early second century; see Wright, *Jesus and the Victory of God*, 44–62; Crossan (*Cross that Spoke*, 16–30) argues that the Gospel predated Mark, and Koester argues that passion traditions in Peter predate the Synoptics: Koester, *Introduction*, 163), refers to the guards being Roman soldiers,(31–2); Matthew is silent.

53. Matt 28:12–14.

54. White robes were protective garb used to prevent attack from evil and Satan. For example, the Talmud states that the High Priest was to wear a white robe to appear like an angel. Lauterbach states: "The white garments were to deceive Satan, who, when seeing the high priest dressed in white, would mistake him for and angel and not seek to harm him," *Rabbinic Essays*, 63. The special ritual power of white linen robes has been confirmed both in archaeology and in literature. Over two hundred linens, many from bleached white robes, have been uncovered in caves near Qumran, are all linked to the Essenes and their ritual power as purists, standing against evil and their war against darkness. Jesus wore the mantle of an exorcist, as did those he sent into the villages. The power of ritual clothing was prevalent in early Christian literature, including Revelation, which was heavily influenced by Jewish apocalyptic and tradition. For example, in Revelation 7:9–17, the gentile righteous dead are given white robes indicating they are both angelic and priests, i.e., they are protected. White worn by the High Priest, the priests, and Essenes confirm that purity and protection were linked in the wearing of white linen robes.

55. John 18:2–3.

56. See Ogden, *Magic*, 179, 181. Pre-Talmudic literature speaks of Solomon's sword, transformed into the magic sword of Moses (Pesik 140a, Pesik R15, T. Sol.), where the sword is able to ward off evil at night, certainly including ghosts and spirits.

itself and ward off the evil spirit, that was charged with "watching" the tomb for activity. Their duties included removing the *dofek* and rolling back the stone at dawn to verify if the body was still present. Dawn marked the time when evil spirits and demons no longer roamed, seeking victims. If Jesus' body was found to have vacated the tomb, or there was a sign of activity, those involved in the execution could be warned (exactly what happened) and protection by wearing amulets could be sought, which was common in the Herodian period.[57]

This brings us to Joseph of Arimathea, donor of the tomb.[58] Despite the Gospel's portrayal of a unexpected and remarkable good deed ascribed to Joseph, it is also known that he was a member of the Roman-approved assembly of the seventy, the elite Sanhedrin,[59] which included those who had been threatened by Jesus and participated in the plan to take, secure, crucify, trap, and then guard the body to ensure his demise.[60] Jesus was betrayed by an assassin that had been funded and paid by these same men to infiltrate his band of exorcists and inform on him with the intent of killing him.[61] There are other problems as well. The gospel tradition states that Joseph cautiously approached Pilate for the body of Jesus because he was a "secret disciple"[62]—yet it is clear that such a request would be an obvious admission of support for a condemned and crucified seditious "evildoer," an enemy of Rome and dangerous necromancer *from rebellious Galilee*. Why would a member of the Sanhedrin seek out the body of Jesus and risk all—unless it were part of risk mitigation actions? To approach Pilate would not only be extremely dangerous (if not deadly) but unimaginable in the recovered risk context.[63] Consequently, Joseph, or whoever the owner of the elite tomb

---

57. Bohak, "Jewish Amulets," 328. In the second Temple period, the use of amulets was widespread, both textual and non-textual amulets. These were used to protect from disease, evil, demons, or the dead and their spirits. "There are numerous *mishnaic* references to the use of knots, coins, and such rarer items as the egg of a locust, the tooth of a fox, or a nail from a crucifixion (m. Sabb. 6:6, 9–10)" (Bohak, "Jewish Amulets," 328). It is very interesting that archaeologists discovered crucifixion nails in the family tomb of Joseph Caiaphas. Certainly these were used as protective amulets, perhaps as ongoing protection from a crucified enemy, considered an "evildoer," such as Jesus of Nazareth.

58. Crossan believes Joseph is a completely fictitious character. Crossan, *Who Killed Jesus?*, 172–73, 176.

59. One of the council of the seventy, who, like the High Priest, was approved by the Romans.

60. Mark 15:43–46.

61. Busse, *Jesus Resurrected*, 132–33; Busse, *To Be Near*, 27–30; and Busse, *Enemies*, 8–9.

62. John 19:38.

63. To mitigate the historical risk associated with such a request, the Gospel and

might have been, was clearly a member of the elite that sought to seize the body of Jesus and seal it in a tomb, entrapping it to prevent retribution, and then guard it to ensure he had been destroyed.[64] Indeed, even the gospel tradition confirms that Joseph was a not just a member of the Sanhedrin, he was a "prominent" counselor (*euschemen bouleutes*). The Sanhedrin was the elite association whose membership included the ruling Jerusalem families, including the High Priest, Caiaphas, among others approved and appointed by Roman authority—in this case by Pilate or his predecessor, Valerius Gratus (15–26 CE). What is certain is that Joseph, representative of the Jerusalem elite, is given the body of Jesus, places it in his tomb, seals it up, and tells Pilate where Jesus is buried—he is complicit.[65] All of these are risk mitigations—steps used against Jesus, the Galilean exorcist—and, remarkably, have no contemporary parallels.

EXAMPLES OF THE DEAD VACATING TOMBS

The ability to rise and vacate a tomb is believed to have occurred in the ancient world,[66] and certainly was feared by Jesus' murderers. Yet, some of the most striking accounts of vacating tombs had nothing to do with retribution, but instead, with love, or more precisely, to be with those loved after death and provide comfort and guidance. While rare, such events were recounted by credible sources (i.e., ascribed to well-known individuals) that circulated before and after Jesus' activity in Galilee.

For example, Phlegon, a Hellenistic writer and freedman of Hadrian (early second century) provides an account of a deceased girl, Philinnion, doing just this—leaving her tomb (after six months!) and physically interacting with a loved one, Machetes. In this account, Philinnion is able to vacate her tomb (still apparently sealed), appear at a location of choice, physically manifest in corporeal form, and even leave clothes and jewelry at sites visited. Her ability to do so, according to Phlegon, was allowed by "the gods." When her parents, Charito and Demostratus, alerted by a servant

---

early church make Pilate sympathetic to Jesus, and that Pilate tried to release Jesus as innocent. As Busse, *To Be Near*, 20–26 demonstrates, Pilate was brutal, cruel, and only used the ruse of releasing Jesus so that at a public hearing his spies and assassins could identify, capture, and kill any of Jesus' followers who spoke for him. This was a standard practice used by Pilate according to reports.

64. Tombs were not provided to peasants or the poor to lay the body until the bones were collected for burial. See Magness, *Burials*, 125–39.

65. Mark 15:43.

66. Even in the sense of physically touching, eating, sleeping, or harming living victims.

(a nurse) about her presence in the house, find her in a room sitting with Machetes, they grasp her in joy. But when touched, she laments and says she is unable to remain any longer, all to their despair, and disappears. When the family tomb is checked, only an iron ring is present on the bier, one that belonged to her lover. Her body is later recovered (outside the tomb) and due to the terror in the city arising from these events, she is burned by the order of a local sorcerer.

There are similarities in Phlegon's account that mirror aspects of the traditions associated with Jesus' empty tomb, such as his sudden appearances in locked rooms,[67] physical interaction with loved ones,[68] and his warning not to touch him,[69] all allowed by the power of God. It must be remembered that while Jesus' tomb was ultimately unsealed and his body found gone, this did not mean he walked out as is sometimes presumed, that is, as if he needed to be freed. Removing the *dofek* and rolling back the stone on the third day was to ensure Jesus' body was present but instead *confirmed* that it was gone, sending his opponents into panic. Like the iron ring found on Philinnion's bier, the neatly folded cloth that had covered Jesus' face and the linens lay on the spot where his body had been left.[70] Such an account is reliable confirmation in its contextual setting that entrapment in a tomb was intentional but could not contain the victim if divinely empowered to rise. Phlegon's remarkable tradition, dating from about 140 CE,[71] recounts an event ascribed to the city of Amphipolis, Greece, during the reign of Philip II, 359–336 BCE. The tradition, however, was recalled because this type of event was experienced in the Greco-Roman world contemporaneous with the activity of Jesus and his exorcists.

The Gospels reflect this characterization of Jesus' resurrection, i.e., rising by the power of God, not to seek retribution, but to comfort those he loved and promise them that he would continue to be with them until the kingdom of God arrived. In fact, not a single act of retribution is ascribed to Jesus' exorcists post-resurrection, only a call to *agape* and command to continue ecstatic practices to overcome satanic forces until the *Parousia*. Moreover, non-canonical Gospels and writings never emphasize retribution, only salvific wisdom in Jesus' words. That Jesus' Galilean exorcists did not threaten the elite is remarkable in the historical context of the first century—unless the encounters with Jesus were of *agape*, *elpis*, the promise of

---

67. John 20:19; Luke 24:36–49.
68. Matt 28:9.
69. John 20:17.
70. John 20:7.
71. Phlegon of Tralles, *Mirabilia I*, in Ogden, *Magic*, 159–60.

the kingdom to soon come and continued empowerment to drive demons out of the land in the name of Jesus, risen from the dead, who was available to and active with his exorcists.

In this risk context, Jesus' warning satisfactorily meets the criterion of dissimilarity, as it is distinct from the traditions of contemporary Judaism[72] and alien to the teachings of the early church,[73] as well as the criterion of embarrassment, as Jesus' followers (both men and women) are portrayed as oblivious to his resurrection predictions, and thus the warning to his opponents. Given this context, it is highly probable that the historical Jesus did describe the very brutal death that he might suffer, and by whom and how he would be killed; and that he gave the strongest warning possible that if he were to be murdered, he would return, but contrary to their fear, not for revenge (that would be left to God when the kingdom arrived), but to continue the war on Satan and demonic imperialism until their end and the kingdom's inbreaking.[74] He would return and be powerfully available for his exorcists. However, his opponents understood that Jesus' threat was a real, tangible perilous risk to them, and feared the worst.[75]

---

72. As established, it was the Galileans, Jesus' fellow exorcists, who rejected any such concept or expectation.

73. Jesus' predictions in the Synoptics are never expressed as a warning, but as a promise, yet still one that his disciples never understood. This portrayal of misunderstanding by Jesus' disciples employed by the early church is used to obscure the historical context of Jesus' true message to his opponents, i.e., it is a warning that if they kill him, even crucified, he will rise and retaliate against them. Peasant Galilean Jews understood the concept of malevolent and retributive ghosts, but Jesus' exorcists were unfamiliar with any such concept of a post-crucifixion return due to the curse placed on Jews executed by being "hung on a tree." Mark 8:28–30 confirms the markedly different perspectives about Jesus held by the elite and the peasant Galileans. When asked by Jesus, they report that some say he is Elijah or John the Baptist raised from the dead (clearly understood as being for retributive judgment on the enemies of God). His opponents claim he can conjure the spirits of the dead for malevolent purposes (conjured through dark magic). But their understanding is that he is not demonic. Jesus is the liberator from Satan, destined to free them from demonic imperialism. This is exactly what Busse *To Be Near,* demonstrates. Jesus' fellow exorcists presume his control of demons and Satan heralds the inbreaking of the kingdom of God. Jesus, by the "finger of God," leads the expulsion of demons and the elimination of pagan pollution and Satanic control of the land. Consequently, Jesus' original warning to his enemies is completely foreign to the portrayal found in the Synoptics and early church.

74. Mark 8:31, 10:34.

75. Matt 27:63: While this is a unique tradition to Matthew and is later (perhaps 80 CE), this tradition explains the historical context of tomb resurrection well, and the context of sealing the tomb and hiding his body from his disciples so that it can be watched, verifying it had not left to do harm to the opponents. Even though killed under a curse, Jesus' opponents were also Hellenized Jews, and feared retribution.

THE GALILEAN EXORCISTS' EXPECTATIONS

All of the Galilean exorcists but Magdalene fled after Jesus' capture. None of them expected a post-crucifixion encounter with Jesus. The testimony of the Synoptic and Johannine traditions is unanimous on this point.[76] This is a reliable tradition, as the criterion of embarrassment confirms its historicity. In fact, the male exorcists even refused to accept that Magdalene's report of the empty tomb and encounter.[77] Within the context of first-century Palestine, Jesus' capture, his beating, and bodily mutilation from being viciously and professionally scourged (*verberatio*) by the Roman *flagrum*,[78] followed by his cursed crucifixion, left little doubt that Jesus was dead in every sense to them. None of the exorcists even dared remain or carry Jesus' body to burial for fear of being contaminated by the curse placed on him at death and fear of capture, scourging and a similarly cursed death on a cross. Only Magdalene knew where his body had been taken having followed. Kepha and the others likely assumed it had simply been thrown into the city dump, which was a common practice. The stark human fear portrayed in these traditions, indeed, the perilous risks associated with any overt action or affiliation with Jesus after his betrayal, are all certainly reliable from a risk analysis perspective.

And they now faced new perilous risks, human and otherwise. They were recognizable *because they were Galileans*. They spoke "Galilean"; that is, Aramaic with a distinct accent that was ridiculed by Judeans who considered them country rubes.[79] They wore special clothing (as had been required by Jesus).[80] They were poor, uneducated, and with little means of bribing or paying their way to an escape. Contrary to some of the Gospel accounts, particularly in Luke, the Galileans immediately fled Jerusalem and went into hiding with village kin to avoid capture. Fearing the elite was one thing, but now there was the risk of demonic retaliation. There were no countermeasures available—their master had been destroyed by the forces of Satan. All was lost. Moreover, they were sought out by that the elite who still feared they would conjure Jesus. It is to this perilous risk, the threat of the remaining exorcists to the elite, that we now turn.

---

76. Matt 9:18, 19, 23–25; par. Mark 5:22–24; Luke 7:11–15; John 11:1–44.

77. Luke 24:11, the disciples at the report of the women.

78. A "cat of nine tails," or whip with multiple leather strips whose ends held metal strips or balls designed to lacerate the flesh, so that the victim was near death from pain and loss of blood; limited to slaves, non-Romans, and criminals.

79. Matt 26:73.

80. Mark 6:9.

7

The Urgency to Neutralize Jesus' Exorcists Post-Crucifixion

JESUS' GALILEAN EXORCISTS AS A PERILOUS RISK TO THE ELITE

Upon discovery of the empty tomb, the Jerusalem religious elite immediately charged Jesus' Galilean exorcists with a capital crime punishable by death—grave robbing. In the first century, grave robbing meant the body had been taken for evil purposes—necromancy and dark magic (i.e., to summon the soul of the dead back into its body and take control of it for evil purposes).[1] In other words, it was not simply a charge that Jesus' followers had stolen his body to fake his resurrection—it meant much more in the ancient world. We must first take the view of the elite in order to understand the charge as a countermeasure to perilous risk. It is this context that will establish the risk conflict for the elite, which is not necessarily the same for the Galilean exorcists. In fact, the risk perception of the elite, who were Hellenized Roman sympathizers, and thus the countermeasures employed, may not even have been comprehensible to the Galilean peasant exorcists who fled Jerusalem.

---

1. Ogden, *Magic*, in his section on necromancy, 179–209; Smith, *Jesus*, 118.

THE ELITE AND RISK: JESUS' FOLLOWERS WERE MORE DANGEROUS THAN OTHER GALILEAN REBELS

For the elite, Jesus was a not just a dangerous illegal magician and exorcist,[2] he was an agent of Satan,[3] and therefore feared because of the threat he posed to them,[4] both from the rabble that supported him in rebellious Galilee and from the dark powers he possessed that could be brought against them.[5] As noted, paid spies of elite had witnessed Jesus controlling all classes of malevolent demons and spirits—those that caused death, disease, disability, deafness, loss of speech, and insanity—and announcing that the expulsion of demons signified the end of the current rule, which was demonic. Moreover, he called the souls of those infected with death back to their bodies.[6] For the peasants, Jesus was a protector, a charismatic empowered by God, the return of John the Baptist. To the elite, Jesus was the epitome of a Hellenistic magician, perhaps even an Egyptian *goetes* (a sorcerer, as there were contemporaneous accounts of him spending time in Egypt).[7] Only an agent of evil, indeed of Satan, could control such demons and spirits of the dead. Indeed, Jesus had admitted to having conversed with Satan in the Judean desert just outside of Jerusalem; the desolate and forbidden place where demons, including the queen of demons, Agrath bat Mahalath, were expelled and roamed[8] (except Wednesday and Sabbath nights)[9]—a terrifying and threatening admission.[10] While Jesus made claim to this power by the "finger of God," for his opponents this was a ruse—it was Satan's chief demon that possessed and gave him unbridled malevolent control over demons to deceive and come against them. The elite did not see themselves as evil or possessed, but the blessed that were given position and power by God. Jesus and his name were feared[11]—even

2. John 18:30.
3. Luke 11:15.
4. Luke 9:7; Mark 6:14.
5. See Bolt, "Life, Death and Afterlife," 55–59.
6. Smith, *Jesus*, 126–27.
7. Luke 2:14.
8. Matt 12:43.

9. Costa, "Exorcisms and Healings," 133; Jewish Virtual Library, "Demons & Demonology."

10. Smith, *Jesus*, 104–06.

11. Even after his death, later Christians, as well as pagan and Jewish magicians and sorcerers used the invocation of his name to control and expel malevolent spirits for centuries. There are numerous examples in the Talmud, e.g., *Tosefta Hullin 2:22f*; 62–64, 114–115; also see *bSanh.* 43a. See Origen, *Against Celsus*, 6:40.

the mob that came to take him in Gethsemane fell over each other backing up to get away as he approached them.[12] Jesus' authority over demons, his claims against the elite that they were corrupt, possessed servants of the kingdom of Satan and demonic imperialism and whose rule would soon end, meant that Jesus was a perilous risk. And so, each were set on a collision course to neutralize the other.

To the elite's horror, Jesus' tomb was found empty three days after he was crucified, just as he had warned. The fear that he might escape the tomb and be active or be available to his exorcists for retaliation was now realized. Ironically, the most dangerous threat to the elite now *became the empty tomb*, as Jesus had overcome even a cursed death and entrapment in stone. He was active, available and dangerous—and so, just as Paul later states, Jesus' "name" was "above" (greater than) all spirits;[13] he was "raised," with the undisputed "empty tomb" as proof—a fact accepted even by his most ardent enemies.[14] Faced with this perilous risk, the elite immediately responded to extinguish the new threat of an active Jesus, whom they believed was now available to Galilean exorcists (i.e., just as they had believed the spirit of John was available to Jesus). It is this risk response that informs the magnitude of the contextual response of the elite to the empty tomb, evidenced by the deadly charges brought against the Galilean exorcists.

THE GALILEANS AND RISK: ESCAPE CAPTURE, JESUS HAD BEEN DESTROYED

Grave robbing and necromancy were clearly the furthest thing from the minds of the Galileans. They were desperately trying to hide and then escape Jerusalem after the capture and execution of Jesus. The infiltrator, informant, and assassin, Judas, had compromised their secret nighttime retreat, a large cave with an olive press in the grove of Gethsemane that offered protection from evil that roamed at night—until Judas showed up with a debilitating curse and kissed Jesus, disarming him.[15] Ultimately, they were forced to hide in an "upper room," where they had only hours before shared their last communal meal with Jesus. They had entered into a

---

12. John 18:4–6.

13. Ephesians 1:21. While not Pauline, this passage reflects the continuation of earlier practices where Jesus' name could take command of any evil spirit or demon, as more powerful that all others available. Koester dates Ephesians to the end of the first century: Koester, *Introduction*, 273.

14. Koester, *Introduction*, 67.

15. Busse, *Jesus Resurrected*, 44–46.

protective union with their master's spirit by mystically participating in a ritual where they ingested bread and wine, his body and blood—a practice similar to magical rites of the Greco-Roman world also used for union and protection.[16] But the mystical security afforded them was made impotent, dissolved, by Jesus' capture and then death under a divine curse by men they perceived as possessed and under the control of satanic forces. The Galileans were uneducated peasants having witnessed their master taken by the very demonic forces he had said were "falling like Satan," knowing that he would be destroyed by crucifixion. They were terrified of being captured and killed, even annihilated like Jesus, no longer protected by Jesus and "the finger of God."[17] At least three of his band abandoned or betrayed Jesus— Kepha (one of Jesus' leading exorcists),[18] Thomas,[19] and of course Judas (the elite's embedded assassin, infiltrator, and informant).[20] It is clear that after Jesus' death the male exorcists did not completely trust each other.[21] Indeed, everyone in Jesus' band fled when he was taken by his opponents in Gethsemane—no one stayed with him;[22] and despite the tradition that a young disciple was present with Jesus' mother Mary near the cross,[23] it is uncertain if this was even one of his exorcists. In the context of dire risks facing Jesus' band, it seems quite improbable that it was. Even Magdalene hid, only going to the tomb before dawn on the third day.

The risk response of the Galileans in the context of their dire situation *absolutely confirms that grave robbing and necromancy was not a possible or even conceivable countermeasure.* Everything they believed about Jesus, his mission and authority, as well as the powers he had given them to control demons in his name, had been made moot. Perilous risks now surrounded them, and they were want for any countermeasure but to escape, get to kin, and hide. Indeed, their escape is an embarrassing tradition that only confirms its historicity.

---

16. Smith, *Clement of Alexandria*, 217–19.
17. John 20:19.
18. Mark 14:66–72.
19. John 20:25–27.
20. Busse, *To Be Near*, 27–30.
21. Some apparently decided independently to escape to Galilee.
22. Mark 14:50.
23. John 19:26–27.

THE CHARGE OF GRAVE ROBBING—
NEUTRALIZING GALILEAN RETRIBUTION

Consequently, from the perspective of the elite, Jesus' threat to return after three days was understood as a threat to make himself available to his followers after death, i.e., that his spirit could be conjured by them for malevolent purposes. As such, the Galilean exorcists would be perceived as capable of bringing the retribution of the murdered Jesus against them—physically, politically, and spiritually.[24] To neutralize this threat, the elite would use any and all countermeasures to destroy the remaining exorcists before this could occur. The most effective risk mitigant would be to make them *targets meriting immediate capture and execution*. Matthew provides the most accurate representation of the elite's actual countermeasures to accomplish just this.

Matthew 28:11-20 reports that the elite charged Jesus' exorcists with stealing his body from the sealed tomb. Recovering the original risk setting, it is clear that the elite charged the Galileans with the most heinous and repugnant of all crimes immediately punishable by death, namely, taking the body of Jesus *for dark magical purposes—necromancy*.[25] If they were to conjure their master and use his name to take control of demons and retaliate, their lives and souls were in danger. Thus, this accusation against the Galileans of stealing Jesus' body is a weighty countermeasure to the perilous risk they faced, and therefore certainly historical in its contemporary setting. It represented to the elite the most potent response to perilous risk that they believed the exorcists could employ against them once back in Galilee.[26] The charge empowered anyone to immediately inform (for money), or even attack, stone, and kill a follower of Jesus if discovered—exactly what happened later to one of Jesus' band,[27] and exactly the commission of the paid informant and assassin, Saul of Tarsus. Interestingly, this is the earliest charge brought against Jesus' followers, that is, that they practiced necromancy and dark magic, and so were to be associated with Satan—a charge that followed them and the early church.[28]

---

24. Ogden, *Magic*, 152-53, 158; and as disputed by Tertullian.

25. Burton and Grandy, *Magic, Mystery, and Science*, 150-51.

26. Remarkably, however, this possibility is completely absent from all traditions, including antagonistic writings against Christians, other than general comments such as a "disgusting" or "evil superstition"; see Tacitus, *Annals*, 15:44. Consequently, something else was ascribed to the empty tomb, completely absent any tradition of this sort, and the least concern for such a body theft.

27. Acts 7:54-60.

28. Roman historians such as Suetonius (69-122 CE) and Celsus (second century CE).

In the context of the first-century Greco-Roman world, multiple traditions report that the stealing and manipulation of dead bodies for magical practices, reanimating them to affect some spell or action, or even to learn the secret of life, were prevalent.[29] The rites surrounding this dark magic were strictly forbidden under Roman law under penalty of death.[30] The body was stolen and manipulated, ultimately set up standing, filled with magical ingredients and potions and commanded to speak to reveal secrets or perform acts to the benefit of the magician or sorcerer. Examples included consultation and oracles, understanding dark secrets and mysteries, correcting drought, visiting one's dead relative and speaking again with them, or harming others in the most vicious of ways.[31] Jesus used none of these techniques, but was known for reanimating the dead, as noted, usually children to grieving parents. Consequently, his followers were believed to have learned these techniques. The charge, therefore, led them to flee Jerusalem for Galilee, and why, when they returned to Jerusalem, they were arrested and sentenced to death. Galilee, hiding among peasant kin in villages, was the safest escape, exactly as reported in the Synoptic and Johannine Gospels.

SUMMARY

The charge of grave robbing and necromancy, arising from the fear of the evocation of Jesus' spirit and power by the disciples, was thus perceived by the elite as a countermeasure to the empty tomb and way to quickly find and capture the remaining Galilean exorcists. The intent of the charge was to find and kill them before they could harm those who executed Jesus and evoke his powerful and retributive spirit. They failed because they all escaped to Galilee. There, kin protected them. Yet, they became active again as exorcists after a series of remarkable, perilous risk events in Galilee.

---

29. Ogden, *Magic*, 179–209.
30. Smith, *Jesus*, 75–76.
31. Smith, *Jesus*, 152–53, 184, 199–201.

8

Encountering Jesus in Galilee

The Risk and Historical Context[1]

TRAUMATIZING POST-CRUCIFIXION ENCOUNTERS AS EVIDENCE OF A RISK EVENT

Tradition is consistent in portraying the exorcists' response to the first post crucifixion encounters with Jesus as one of shock and surprise, discomfort and denial—even fear, as most fled to Galilee, abandoning him to satanic enemies. Some of them even ridiculed those who claimed to have had any form of encounter, particularly Magdalene,[2] while others continued to doubt, or struggle (*distazo*), altogether.[3] At first, only his enemies are said to have remembered that Jesus warned of a three-day return.[4] These and similar traditions were inescapable for the early church, and so all meet the criterion of embarrassment, making them early and reliable.[5] The church would never have invented these troubling events, nor would it have admitted that the exorcists hid behind locked doors if there were any expectation

---

1. See also Busse, *Jesus Resurrected*, 66–74.
2. John 20:19; Luke 24:37.
3. Matt 28:17.
4. Matt 28:63.
5. Luke 24:44.

of post-crucifixion encounters. Consequently, it is certain that there was no expectation of encountering Jesus post-crucifixion, *particularly* by the Galileans.

There are at least thirteen post-crucifixion encounters embedded in the four canonical Gospels. Some of these have been recast as events occurring during the life of Jesus. These will be described in more detail below. At the outset, it must be stated that any attempt to harmonize these encounters is simply impossible, confirmed by critical analysis.[6] Moreover, it is apparent that these traditions were quite varied and circulated independently even after they were gathered into what is known as the "passion narrative." The editors/evangelists themselves make no attempt to bring coherence to the tradition, even though Matthew and Luke, and certainly John, may have known the narrative framework and events about the passion recorded in other Gospels. As Willi Marxsen correctly states: ". . .there was no longer a unified view in the primitive church about the mode of the Easter happening."[7]

Part of the reason for the varied accounts is that encounters with the dead could take a multiplicity of forms in the ancient world, and this is exactly what is found in the various gospel accounts. Yet, evidence will show that the majority of the encounters were taken from their original contextual setting and adapted for theological purposes, and so, were disassociated from their original perilous risk context. Consequently, the resurrection appearances should be understood as a reflection of the editors/evangelists' theological intent in serving the communities to whom their Gospels were directed.[8] Each evangelists had one objective—to confirm that their community is an extension of the activity of Jesus, who is still active and alive, the Lord and Son of God, and whose encounters with disciples engendered the legitimacy and on-going activity of his *ekklesiae*.[9] While the dates of

---

6. Marxsen, *Resurrection*, 72–74.

7. Marxsen, *Resurrection*, 76.

8. Marxsen, *Resurrection*, 77: "It can be shown, for example, that Luke works out his conception with the help of geographical information, among other things. The Church starts from Jerusalem. Galilee's greatness is a thing of the past. Hence Luke, in contrast to his Markan source (16:7) leaves out the sending of the disciples to Galilee. Instead, he reminds his readers of what Jesus *had earlier programmed* in Galilee (24:16). Consequently, the Easter events are localized in and around Jerusalem."

9. Koester, *Introduction*, 83–86; "The resurrection and the appearances of Jesus are best explained as a catalyst which prompted reactions that resulted in the missionary activity and founding of the churches, but also in the crystallization of the tradition about Jesus and his ministry," 84. This is echoed in Paul's statement: "And if Christ be not risen, then is our preaching vain, and your faith is also vain" (1 Cor 15:14).

final composition of these traditions are suggested below, it is recognized that they circulated orally for decades.

The post-crucifixion encounters embedded within the four canonical Gospels are as follows:

MARK (65–72 CE)

- The original ending of Mark, Mark 16:1–8, records no post-crucifixion encounters with Jesus, only discovery of an empty tomb. However, the appendix, Mark 16:9–20, does include the report of several encounters. Some scholars claim that this section is a conflation of later gospel narratives of events, and so a later addition (105–125 CE).[10] The ending is not included in most key manuscripts. When it is included, there are varying iterations. Most significant, at the conclusion of this section is an interesting "signs" statement attributed to the risen Jesus and addressed to his exorcists; i.e., that they will be able "*in my name to cast out demons, they will speak in new tongues, they will pick up serpents, and if they drink any deadly thing, it will not harm them; they will lay their hands on the sick and they will recover.*" This appearance and list of "signs" is unique to Mark, as it does not appear in any other New Testament document. Therefore it must be considered a separate encounter with Jesus that circulated independently only to be absorbed into the Markan appendix. These charismatic activities are coherent with the activities of Jesus during his ministry. As such, this encounter should be evaluated on its own merits and tested.

- Mark 9:2–8: The ecstatic experience of three exorcists, Simon (i.e., Kepha), James, and John, known as *the transfiguration*, was most likely a post-crucifixion encounter with Jesus re-inserted into his itinerant activity. The literary unit begins, "After six days . . ." (an appropriate timeframe after the crucifixion to escape), and is set in Galilee, which is consistent with the aforementioned risk context with the exorcists fleeing Jerusalem and encountering Jesus there (a command given to the Galileans in Mark).[11] The nature of this ecstatic experience is markedly different than the other post-crucifixion encounters. As it is an ecstatic vision, its placement as a resurrection encounter would certainly be problematic to those communities that proclaimed a corporeal resurrection only, such as the community of Mark.

---

10. Funk and the Jesus Seminar, *Acts of Jesus*, 449–95.
11. Mark 16:7.

MATTHEW (75-85 CE)

- Matt 28:1-10: Mary Magdalene goes to the tomb, then later with "the other Mary" meets the risen Jesus on the way back to Jerusalem (who hold onto Jesus' feet). He tells them to instruct his fellow exorcists (including Magdalene), to "go to Galilee where they will see me."
- Matt 28:16-20: Jesus meets the exorcists (or a larger crowd) on a Galilean mountain. Some doubt even after seeing the Jesus (indicating a larger circle perhaps than the reported twelve exorcists). He gives them a commission to go out into the world and "make disciples of all nations, baptizing them . . ." He promises to return at the end of the age (as messiah).

LUKE (80-85 CE)

- Luke 24:13-35: Two followers of Jesus, one named Cleopas, walking to a village Emmaus (in Galilee), meet a stranger who they ultimately recognize as Jesus, but he vanishes out of their sight at supper when he breaks bread. They return to Jerusalem to let others know they had "seen Jesus."
- Luke 24:34: Then the two Emmaus travelers return to Jerusalem, they are told that the "Lord has risen indeed, and has appeared to Simon [presumably Kepha]." There is no expansion of this provided in the canonical Gospels; however, Paul later confirms the primacy of the encounter in his listing, 1 Corinthians 15:1-5.[12]
- Luke 24:36-39: Hiding in Jerusalem, Jesus suddenly appears in a locked room. Those present think they see a *phantasm*, but Jesus shows his wounds and invites them to handle him to see he has flesh and bones. There is no indication they do. They disbelieve "for joy." Jesus eats in front of them. The disciples are instructed to remain in Jerusalem until they receive power "from on high."

---

12. Conzelmann, *1 Corinthians*, 248-57. Conzelmann agrees that the primacy of Kepha's encounter with the risen Jesus as recorded in Paul's listing (taken itself from a very early formulae) is a variant tradition of a primitive event recognized by the earliest church as primary to the confirmation of Jesus' resurrection and therefore is not reliant on Luke 24:34.

- Luke 24:50–53: Jesus takes the followers to Bethany, blessed them, and then "parted [*dieste ap auton*, withdrew] from them." The implication is that he dematerialized or ascended to heaven.

JOHN (50, 95–110 CE)

- John 6:16–24 (also Mark 6:45–56 and Matt 14:22–36): Jesus is seen walking on the Sea of Galilee at night. The exorcists leave shore without Jesus, for "he had not yet joined them." They row against heavy winds toward Capernaum, about three or four miles out. Jesus later approaches the boat, walking on water. The exorcists are terrified when they see him, but when he is helped into the boat they suddenly appear at the shore of Capernaum.[13] This tradition has led to debate as to its original setting. Recent analysis has shown that this event was most likely a resurrection account, later transposed into Jesus' Galilean ministry.[14] The tradition was problematic as a resurrection event, as Jesus was identified as a *phantasm*, a ghost, reducing the experience as ethereal, subjective—a common ghost story. By placing the tradition back into the ministry of Jesus, concern that the resurrected Jesus was nothing more than a ghostly experience is eliminated.[15]

- John 20:11–18: Jesus appears to Magdalene outside the empty tomb, she assuming he is the gardener, until she hears his voice calling her name. She attempts to hold him, but he stops her, saying he has not yet "ascended."

---

13. This event is also found in Mark 6:45–56 and Matt 14:22–36. In Mark, Jesus is trying to pass by the disciples without notice about 3–6 AM as they fight the strong winds, but the exorcists see Jesus and think he is a *phantasm*. He joins them in the boat and the wind ceases. In Matthew, Jesus sees them in trouble and comes directly to assist. Again, they believe they see a ghost. Kepha tries to join Jesus on the water but begins to sink, only to be taken by Jesus' hand and rescued. The winds cease.

14. Patterson, *Beyond the Passion*, 113–4; Madden, "Jesus Walking, on the Sea."

15. The development of the tradition is also apparent. While Mark and Matthew use the word *phantasm*, Matthew expands the tradition with the inclusion of Kepha, showing that Jesus was more than ghostly; he was material and extraordinarily powerful. John eliminates *phantasm* altogether and has the boat arrive at its destination when Jesus boards. Mark's version is the earliest form. The event happens in Galilee, where the exorcists are to meet Jesus after the crucifixion. They row onto the sea, where ghosts roam at night, and they encounter Jesus. Jesus has no plan to assist them but tries to pass by. The risen Jesus, as a *phantasm*, is encountered. This is a resurrection account.

- John 20:19–23: Jesus appears to the exorcists despite the doors being locked (for fear of the "Jews"). He shows his hands and side and is recognized and gladly received. While the appearance feigns materiality, there is no indication it is material. Jesus breathes the Holy Spirit, authorizing them to forgive sins or "retain" them, and they are sent out to do so. Not all the exorcists are present.

- John 20:26–29: Eight days after the foregoing appearance, Thomas, who has reluctantly returned and found refuge from the elite with some of the other exorcists, refuses to accept that Jesus is active and risen. He takes their experience as ghostly. Jesus materializes behind closed doors and asks Thomas to feel his wounds, although it is unclear if he does. Thomas falls to his knees and believes. Jesus blesses those who believe without seeing him.

- John 21:1–23: The longest of the resurrection encounters of the four Gospels, Jesus appears at dawn on the shores of Galilee, cooks breakfast and eats with Kepha, Thomas, Nathanael, James, and John, and two others—seven exorcists. Kepha is fishing with these men off the shore at night, and they catch nothing. At dawn, Kepha sees a figure standing on the shore, who calls out and asks about their catch. They answer that they have caught nothing. Jesus, famous for controlling the fish of Galilee, orders them to cast their net to another spot. The quantity of the catch is overwhelming. "The disciple whom Jesus loved" identifies the figure as Jesus. Kepha dives into the water. They meet the figure. Curiously, Jesus is not necessarily recognized, just the actions that have taken place identify the man, but "they dare not ask him, 'who are you.'" Interestingly, the section ends with this event being the "third" time Jesus was revealed. Obviously, the appearance to Magdalene was not counted (consistent with the devaluation of Magdalene discussed earlier).[16] Rather, there was only a single witness, which was unacceptable as "proof."[17]

---

16. For example see Josephus, *Ant.* 4:219.

17. The discussion between Jesus and Kepha, commanding him to feed his sheep (John 21:15–24), is clearly a later Christian tradition. Its purpose is to explain the reinstatement of Kepha as the primary leader of the church (apparently James, Jesus' brother and leader of the Jerusalem *ekklesia*, was forgotten) and provide the prediction of his death, and the tale of "the disciple whom Jesus loved," the source of many of the accounts in the Gospel, who lived to an old age, but who did not live to see the return of Jesus as expected (creating dissonance in his community).

SELECTED NON-CANONICAL GOSPEL ACCOUNTS

- *Gospel of Peter* 37–41 (150–90 CE): The "elders," a centurion Petronius, and soldiers guarding the tomb witness two figures from heaven enter and walk out of tomb with a third figure, a cross following behind. There is no speaking or identification of the figure, but it is presumed to be Jesus. There are three witnesses, despite a combination of groups and individuals, which was required for confirmation of an event. It is also important that all of the witnesses are independent of the disciples of Jesus.

- *Gospel of Mary* is a fragmented document of the second century,[18] but may have traditions that predate the canonical Gospels, which reports Magdalene's discussion with Kepha and other exorcists as to her interaction with Jesus post-crucifixion, and Jesus' defense of Magdalene as an equal to the male exorcists, i.e., her becoming male.[19] Her presence with them would indicate that Magdalene continued to be considered an exorcist post-crucifixion. Consequently, contextual evidence suggests that Magdalene was considered an exorcist. She likely never abandoned her role as such.

Pagan sources are void of post-crucifixion encounters with Jesus. They are primarily polemics against Christianity as a "vile superstition." These include Roman writings of Tacitus[20] and Pliny.[21] Flavius Josephus, a Romanized Jew, in the infamous *Testimonium Flavianum* (likely a "Christianized" passage that has corrupted Josephus's original report[22]), alludes to Jesus being seen alive again, but nothing more.[23] References in the Talmud refer to Jesus as a magician, sorcerer, and deceiver, that he was punished in hell, thereby denying the resurrection (for him or his followers), and so provide no additional information.[24]

---

18. King argues for composition between 30–130 CE; King, *Gospel of Mary*, 148.

19. If she becomes like a "male," i.e., what was perceived in the ancient world as the complete human being reflected in male form. See Meyer, "Making Mary Male," 554–70. For this she would have cut her hair and wore male clothing. See below on the discussion of the *Gospel of Mary* and analysis by Karen King.

20. Tacitus, *Annals*, 15:44.

21. Pliny, *Epistles*, 10:96.

22. Busse, *To Be Near*, 18–19.

23. Josephus, *Ant.* 18:63–64.

24. The references to Jesus in the Talmud may not predate the fourth century, and they presume a comprehensive knowledge of the canonical Gospels, but they also likely capture earlier traditions ascribed to sages who lived in or around the time of the early

RISK ANALYSIS OF THE POST-CRUCIFIXION ENCOUNTERS IN THEIR CONTEMPORARY SETTING

It is possible to analyze the various traditions that relate these encounters using risk analysis, seeking those that are contextually coherent with risk and criteria employed in this study. The results of this analysis should isolate the most reliable encounters and forms within the original setting, rendering conclusions as to the "contextual historicity" of the resurrection encounter. Risk analysis can thus suggest which encounters in their original form are coherent with that setting.

Based on our foregoing analysis, the risk criteria to be employed are as follows:

1. Qualitative risk analysis: The encounter can not be a countermeasure to the elite (this is a later development of the church), but must heighten the perilous risk of the Galileans.

2. The criterion of dissimilarity: Encounters must differ from the needs of the early church on the one hand and the context of first-century Judaism in Palestine on the other.

3. The criterion of embarrassment: Encounters should create embarrassment for the early church or create additional perilous risk.

Once these risk criteria are employed, the remaining encounters must pass contextual coherence tests using the contemporary setting recovered in this study, with emphasis on Galilee, including Jesus' activity there among his exorcists—a world controlled by Satan, whose demonic influence had previously motivated the Galilean exorcists to risk everything, abandon subsistence existence, and follow Jesus into perilous danger. The encounter must therefore be coherent with the sociological risk setting, including the subsistence struggle of the Galileans, the background from which they came to join Jesus' band of exorcists.

The contextual risk tests are as follows:

4. Encounters with original members of Jesus' band of Galilean exorcists, those who faced capture, death, and social isolation and starvation, are given priority.[25]

Christian movement. By assigning Jesus to punishment in hell, these traditions deny the resurrection for Jesus, or for his followers.

25. However, because of their problematic nature (see the criterion of embarrassment), encounters with the Galilean women (also original members of Jesus' band) should take preference over those reported with men.

5. Encounters should be consistent with the ecstatic practices of Jesus that engendered the original perilous risk with his opponents.[26] Specifically, encounters that encouraged the remaining exorcists to continue the ecstatic activity of Jesus and his war on Satan are preferred.[27]

6. Encounters near or on the lake of Galilee, particularly related to subsistence fishing, and similar to the animistic control exhibited by Jesus, are preferential (i.e., the remaining exorcists escaped there).[28]

7. Finally, encounters that may have led the Galileans to again risk all and abandon subsistence existence (i.e., to which they returned for survival post-crucifixion[29]) are also preferred.[30]

---

26. Koester, *From Jesus to the Gospels*, 231: "Historians are on very thin ice if they try to recover the historical person of Jesus through a critical analysis of the sayings tradition. A person of past history can only be understood if the extant sources reveal the traditions to which such a person belongs as well as the subsequent structures, practices, and institutions of a community in which the memory of this person is preserved." This risk test does not violate the criterion of dissimilarity in that we are not finding coherence with the early church, but what may have existed that was continued, not being a help to the church, but remained problematic to it, but originated with Jesus. This is a further confirmation that the criterion of dissimilarity has been met.

27. Koester, *Introduction*, 84: "There is at least no doubt that whatever was experienced was not without relationship to a previous direct or indirect knowledge of or about Jesus."

28. Because of the nature of Jesus' activity there, combined with tradition that the men returned to Galilee to take up their subsistence existence, any activity on or around Galilee relative to how they became followers of Jesus, i.e., as exorcists having witnessed Jesus' ability to employ animistic control (see the previous discussion on how Jesus' charismatic activity assisted with survival in a subsistence existence), such activities should be given preference.

29. There is ample evidence that the exorcists returned to subsistence fishing after the crucifixion of Jesus and their having fled to Galilee. Both John and the *Gospel of Peter* reference Kepha's decision to return to Galilee and fishing. As Brown notes: "The verb 'to fish' has the form of an infinitive of purpose which is rare in John (iv. 7, xiv 2) and more frequent in Matthew and Luke; MTGS, 134–35, reports that this construction was becoming increasingly popular in Greek from ca. 150 BCE on. McDowell, 430, argues that the present tend of the verb 'to go' expresses more than momentary intention: Peter is going back to his earlier way of life and will stay with it. The point of the story, then, is that Jesus caused Peter to change his mind, especially in v. 15: 'Do you love me more than these (nets, boats, etc.)?'" Brown believes that this may be dubious, but it is compelling in a perilous risk context, so we must accept the premise; Brown, *Gospel of John*, 1068–69.

30. Slovic and Weber, "Perception of Risk," 473, a recast of Slovic's classic article in *Science*, "Trust, Emotion, Sex, Politics, and Science," 280–85. A discussion with Professor Slovic confirms that the human response to perilous risk has not changed in millennia, only the context of that risk. For the Galileans to perceive risk and perilous, but accept it as necessary, is a clear test of historicity, when the historical context can be adequately recovered.

The original form of these post-crucifixion encounters can then be recovered. These traditions circulated orally for decades and were retained for the benefit of the early church, but the use of these criteria will enable us to render the most original form of the tradition within its original context.[31] From this effort, conclusions as to contextual historicity of the encounter can be suggested, and perhaps affirmed, using these criteria of risk analysis. This methodology will now be applied to those encounters only in Galilee.

---

31. An empty tomb is discovered by the guards placed by the elite to at ensure the body and spirit of Jesus is still, that is, dead. The elite's worst fear is realized: the spirit of Jesus, whom they believed had been annihilated, is roaming, likely seeking revenge. In fear of the exorcists of Jesus who may conjure Jesus' spirit for malevolent purposes and retaliation the elite charge them with necromancy. The Galilean exorcists are baffled by the empty tomb, quickly deny it, and go into hiding. Some flee Jerusalem for Galilee, while others stay in hiding. Those who go to Galilee return to subsistence fishing.

9

Mark

Recovering the Original Risk and Historical Context of Galilean Appearances

The evaluative risk criteria will be applied to two traditions in Mark associated with resurrection encounters in Galilee. Mark is the earliest of the four canonical Gospels,[1] and was used as a source for Matthew and Luke. When applied, the criteria will attempt to recover the original risk and historical context of the encounter and reveal the instructions of the risen Jesus to his exorcists and followers. Some of the results will forever change the understanding and risks associated with these encounters and the dangerous context in which the earliest followers of Jesus brought forward their ecstatic activity into a hostile, demon-filled world, to continue Jesus' war on Satan.

MARK 16:1-8: JESUS' INSTRUCTIONS TO HIS EXORCISTS

Several key Markan manuscripts end only with the discovery of an empty tomb (16:1-8),[2] no resurrection appearances or encounters reported. Other manuscripts provide a list of encounters as well as the criteria to be used

---

1. Between 67-70 CE.
2. Manuscripts S, B, and in sy Clement and Origen; also Koester, *Ancient Christian Gospels*, 12.

in identifying legitimate exorcists, almost as if as an afterthought.³ This list may have been added as an appendix much later, or it could have been original. If original, it is a very puzzling aggregation of events, but more important, it incorporates a very primitive exorcist tradition that is rather startling in its placement, as the risen Jesus defines his legitimate apostles *only as charismatics and exorcists*. In addition, the editor of Mark appears to have inserted resurrection encounters back into the ministry of Jesus. Why? Each of these issues will be discussed in turn.

MARK 16:9–20—JESUS DEFINES THE PRACTICES OF HIS LEGITIMATE EXORCISTS

Because Mark 16:9–20 is missing in a number of ancient manuscripts,⁴ some scholars hold this section to be an "appendix" that conflates all post-crucifixion encounters from the other canonical Gospels, and so is non-Markan and a later addition (105–125 CE).⁵ The different vocabulary and style of the unit is cited, and the text includes a classical Greek term that is unique to the New Testament. This has led to debate as to its date and origin.⁶ More recently, scholars, such as Koester, have defended the section as Markan.⁷ Embedded in this unit is a striking post-crucifixion "signs" saying of Jesus that is addressed to his exorcists and charismatics. It is a separate encounter from those recorded in Mark or the other canonical Gospels, and so stands alone. This raises important qualitative risk issues, as the saying not only echoes but demands the continuation of the same charismatic activities that brought Jesus into deadly confrontation with his opponents, thereby creating continued perilous risk for Jesus' exorcists in Galilee. According to Mark 16:17–18, Jesus commands the following:

> . . . *in my name* to cast out demons, they will speak in new tongues [or in heavenly language, *glossais*, in ecstasy], they will pick up serpents [*opheis*], and if they drink any deadly thing, it will not harm them; they will lay their hands on the sick and they will recover.⁸

---

3. For example, A, C, D, W and others; see Throckmorton, *Gospel Parallels*, 191.

4. Other examples include ℵ, B, 304, syr, and several others noted.

5. Funk and the Jesus Seminar, *Acts of Jesus*, 449–95.

6. Snapp, *Authenticity of Mark*, one of the most exhaustive analyses by a textual scholar.

7. Koester states that the language is compatible with the Gospel of Mark; see Koester, *Ancient Christian Gospels*, 295.

8. Mark 16:17–18.

Bultmann claims that this saying is a conflation of events found in the Synoptic Gospels and Acts of the Apostles,[9] and is a reflection of the "signs" source of charismatic events that were embedded into the Gospel of John by its editor.[10] But, if so, questions immediately arise that challenge this view. Why would charismatic acts, indeed those of Jesus and the men he trained to be exorcists, need to be legitimized by Jesus *after* the crucifixion by repeating all the events found in the Synoptic Gospels and John? Mark is filled with these events, and Jesus chose his band because they could be trained to be exorcists and drive demons from the land.[11] Indeed, charismatic practices and authority are clearly and authoritatively placed throughout the context of Jesus' activity in Mark—no more need be said.[12] The very formation of Mark recognizes the empty tomb, Jesus as risen Lord, and, as such, sayings of Jesus in the context of his ministry carry the same weight for the community, i.e., there is no need to have these practices reauthorized by Jesus.[13] Indeed, this is why the community retained such sayings; i.e., to legitimize their charismatic practices and activities post-crucifixion. Consequently, this saying concerning "signs" in a post-crucifixion encounter in Mark is puzzling, even question-begging, and deserves special attention, particularly as to its risk function in the context of first-century Galilee and among Jesus' exorcists immediately after the crucifixion. Consequently, this saying will be evaluated as a separate post-crucifixion encounter with Jesus that has been absorbed into the Markan appendix, not as a conflation of events.

We begin with an application of qualitative risk analysis. Jesus appears (Mark 6:14, *ephanerothe*, i.e., "he was manifested") during a communal meal of the eleven remaining exorcists, chastising them for their stubborn unbelief (*skaerokardian*, i.e., "hardness of heart").[14] The location of the encounter is not specified, but it is likely Galilee. Jesus commands the exorcists to go into the world to proclaim the *euangelion* (the end of satanic rule and the kingdom of God) and baptize those who will believe. Those that refuse the charismatic message to be baptized are immediately *cursed* (they are of Satan), meaning separated from God and condemned, i.e., they are damned (*katakrithesetai*). A similar commission is found in Matthew. The location is on a mountain in Galilee, but there is no mention of a curse, and the

---

9. Acts 2:4, 5:15, 28:3.

10. First proposed by Bultmann in his commentary on John (Bultmann, *Gospel of John*). See Brown, *Community of the Beloved Disciple*, 31.

11. Mark 3:14; Busse, *To Be Near*, 66–69.

12. Matt 17:19; Mark 9:38; Luke 9:1–6, and so on.

13. Mark 3:14, 6:7–13, 9:28.

14. Mark 6:14.

command to baptize is linked with liturgical rites of the early church, i.e., baptizing in the names of the Father, Jesus, and the Holy Spirit.[15] Mark's version is clearly earlier; it is a charismatic act (i.e., the curse for refusal) and shows no reliance on Matthew. The commission is therefore linked with *continuation of charismatic activity* of Jesus' exorcists and, therefore, heightened risk when compared to the tradition in Matthew. Luke has no such commission. John has a commission, but it is tied solely to Kepha who is warned that he will be captured and murdered.[16]

Mark 16:17–18 then radicalizes the post-resurrection community by narrowing the legitimate followers of Jesus to those who successfully continue dangerous, and illegal, public charismatic practices. They must evoke "signs" (*semeia*); the very charismatic activities that created the perilous risk and conflict between Jesus and his opponents are to be continued. In Mark, the risen Jesus demands that his exorcists battle against the demonic pollution of the land just as he did. When true followers invoke his name, demons will flee—a reflection of the very experience of Jesus' exorcists in Galilee.[17] Consequently, to continue exorcism and release of demons is to continue Jesus' war on the satanic pollution of the land, and, by implication, demonic imperialism.[18] This is a Galilean setting. Indeed, for the community to embrace these practices is to dramatically heighten the perilous risk of the post-crucifixion followers.

To employ Jesus' name in public exorcisms, particularly in Galilee, was to employ the name of an executed magician, condemned by the elite under Roman law;[19] an "evildoer" and "deceiver" who accused the elite of being under satanic control; a possessed agent of Beelzebul, who not just labeled the Temple polluted, but warned that it should be destroyed if not redeemed from satanic influence.[20] Here the perilous risks for these exorcists are just as extraordinary as they were for Jesus when he was in conflict with demonic forces and his opponents.[21] But this is the first sign expected of legitimate followers of the risen Lord.

---

15. Matt 28:16–20.

16. John 21:18.

17. Luke 10:17, Mark 9:38–39.

18. Busse, *To Be Near*, 70–88.

19. Roman Law, *The Twelve Tables, Crimes*, Table VII.3 and 15, also Table VIII.9. See du Plessis, *Borkowski's Textbook on Roman Law*, 5–6, 29–30.

20. Mark 14:58.

21. Lewis, *Ecstatic Religion*, 88–89, for the discussion on the battle between the oppression of the elite and possession, as well as the reliance of lower castes on exorcists (as "masters of the spirit"), both as a cultural phenomenon that crosses all cultural barriers.

The expectation of "speaking in new tongues (*glossais*)" is listed as the next sign of legitimacy. Some scholars have cited this sign as principal evidence that this section is a conflation of later practices in the early church.[22] But it was this very charismatic practice that became problematic in Corinth, claimed by itinerant "apostles" as the sole true test of legitimacy well before the composition of the Gospels. These "super apostles" from Palestine arrived in Corinth[23] (CE 52–54) and made claim to this charisma as proof of their apostolic authority.[24] 1 and 2 Corinthians confirm the importance of this sign and that it must have originated with the risen Lord, just as reported in Mark. Indeed, Paul has to devalue it as the principal "charisma" of legitimacy, as his opponents pointed to it alone as proof their apostleship, and Paul's as illegitimate since he did not practice or teach its practice in Corinth.[25] The Corinthian confrontation points to a time when the early tradition in Mark had developed into specific practices. Paul's devaluation of *glossolalia* as just one of the charisma is an affirmation that Markan tradition is early and not a conflation.

The term "new tongues" has been interpreted as foreign languages, reminiscent of the events at Pentecost reported in Luke-Acts.[26] However, here in Mark the linkage is with demonic expulsion, indicating that these tongues were those that controlled demons and drove them out. Paul admits that he is able to speak in tongues more than any of the other itinerant apostles in Corinth, but finds it unnecessary to do so, implying it was a practice associated with the early exorcists, including the Galileans with whom Paul counts himself.[27] Interestingly, Paul speaks of *glossolalia* in terms of the language of angels (which he can understand and speak), which implies there is also a language of demons.[28] Jesus is never explicitly tied to speaking in tongues in the synoptic or Johannine traditions; however, the multiple interactions with demons, identifying and silencing them, his groaning in spirit and prayer,[29] must be assumed to have included understanding and speaking in angelic and demonic language.[30] Indeed, when Jesus' exorcists

22. Mann, *Mark*, 673–76.
23. 2 Cor 11:5–6.
24. Busse, *Enemies*, 259–62.
25. 1 Cor 13:8.
26. Acts 2:1–13.
27. 1 Cor 14:8; 1 Cor 15:1–9.
28. 1 Cor 13:1.
29. John 11:33, or Mark 7:34, and the use of specific words that are interpreted by the Gospel editors, but whose original use may have parallels with unintelligible words, such as his words in Mark 5:41, "talitha, koum." Smith, *Jesus the Magician*, 95.
30. For further discussion on the use of special language in Jesus' exorcisms see Smith,

fail to expel the demon of young boy, they ask why, to which Jesus replies that only prayer (implying a special type of prayer) and fasting could succeed.[31] That this expectation immediately follows the sign of exorcism is evidence that this charismatic power is associated with communication with demons, spirits, and the reception of heavenly instruction, as well as commands to exorcise demons. Curses and the ability to mute opponents were often written in secret language, or on hidden tablets.[32] Jesus and his exorcists were able to release victims from such demonic curses,[33] understanding and affecting exorcisms that neutralized them. Consequently, this practice is contextually coherent with the others in Mark 16:17–18 and is to be associated with the continued itinerant activity of the exorcists as they encounter and communicate with demons and neutralize curses and evil spirits that they must control and expel.

Jesus also commands the charismatics/exorcists to raise-up (*arousan*) serpents (*opheis*). The significance of this charismatic power is lost on many commentators, as if this were simply snake-handlers, or a recast of the events in Acts 28:3 where Paul, while picking up brushwood for a fire, is accidentally bitten by a poisonous serpent, remains unharmed. Indeed, such stories did exist and were known, as Pythagoras is said to have handled a snake without harm, as did Hanina ben Dosa.[34] But Jesus is not talking about accidental events. Jesus is saying, if not commanding, that his exorcists are to raise up, or perhaps better, "take away" poisonous serpents.[35] In the ancient world, particularly in Judaism, snakes were often the personification of Satan, evil, and capable of possession or engendering dangerous and sometimes fatal deception.[36] Consequently, this is a

---

Jesus, 95. "Talitha, koum," was also circulated without translation as a magical formula.

31. Smith believes this was "secret" prayer, but the implication is for prayers that may be said ecstatically and under the influence of the Spirit, and so in heavenly language. That fasting is associated with this prayer implies that a special state of ecstatic experience and language is possible. Smith, *Jesus the Magician*, 95.

32. Ogden, *Magic*, "A legal, tongue-binding, lead curse tablet from Selinus," 211; also see page 215.

33. See discussion above on the deaf and mute man of Bethsaida, whom Jesus commands not to reenter his village, as he likely had been cursed by someone there, i.e., a person who would repeat the process.

34. See Vermes, *Jesus the Jew*, 74; see also Vermes, *Jesus the Jew*, 178–214; Freyne, "The Charismatic," 223–58; Boxer, "Wonder-Working," 42–92. See also Kee, *Origins of Christianity*, 225–28.

35. For the various translations, see for example John 11:48, i.e., "take away."

36. See Revelation 12:9 and Genesis 3:14; also see Paul, 2 Cor 11:3, for a comparison of Eve and the serpent and the deception of the Corinthian believers. Jesus equates the Jerusalem religious elite with vipers and serpents in Matthew 23:33, again because these

charismatic directive of Jesus and appears to imply that the exorcists held animistic powers over snakes as creatures of Satan, i.e., they could take control, just as they controlled demons and rendered them harmless, or even destroy them.[37] If to destroy them, this raises interesting and contemporary parallels where serpents are killed by "blasting." Blasting was a well-recognized charismatic power, albeit considered sometimes a dark power (conducted by incantation, or often by those who practiced manipulation of the dead, i.e., necromancy). In the Greco-Roman world, this authority was associated with powerful sorcerers or magicians, often foreigners, such as Chaldeans, Babylonians, Assyrians, or Egyptians.[38] The charismatic person, using animistic powers, would communicate with the snake(s), collect or call them together by command, then destroy them, in many cases by breathing on them with fire—i.e., blasting,[39] or would trap them in tombs. Jesus gave his charismatics a similar authority to destroy creatures that were thought to be controlled by Satan, or by his demons, *particularly snakes and scorpions* in Luke 10:19: "I have given you authority to *trample* [*pantein*] on snakes and scorpions and to overcome all the power of the enemy; nothing will harm you." This power is the equivalent of crushing serpents and scorpions, and so the original intent of this saying was to "take away" or blast the serpent, and hold it up showing it destroyed, exorcised.[40] Satan would then be shown powerless, as even the creatures of evil that attacked could be annihilated when encountered by Jesus' command and authority. Ultimately, the use of Jesus' name alone was able to neutralize serpents, including their venom, among Jews.[41] Consequently, this reference is clearly not a conflation of gospel texts, nor is it a reflection of Paul's experience in Acts. Instead, the risk setting is in the itinerant charismatic activity of Jesus and his fellow exorcists, including a post-resurrection setting and encounter in Galilee. It is unique and original. Jesus commands a continuation of the perilous conflict with Satan and his demons in the

---

creatures were controlled and possessed by Satan and demons and used to hamper or kill enemies.

37. Jesus was known to have animistic powers; the directives on draft of fishes, the coin in the fish's mouth, and others previously described, see Mark 1:16–20; Mat. 4:18–22; Luke 5:2–11; John 21:6; Matt 17:27.

38. Ogden, *Magic*, 49–50.

39. Ogden, *Magic*, 50.

40. Ogden, *Magic*, 49–50, 121–124, 238, referencing Lucian in *Pharsalia* (6.413–587), *Philopseudes* (11–13), and Ovid, *Amores* (2.1.23–28).

41. This was said by Jews about 120 CE; see Hull, *Hellenistic Magic and the Synoptic Tradition*, 71.

context of first-century Palestine, and the ability to control all of his forces that could be used against followers of Jesus.

The next command, drinking poison unharmed, is without parallel in the New Testament, with only a single reference found in Eusebius.[42] Barsabas Justus, the exorcist not selected to replace Judas, is said to have survived drinking poison. The reference to "poisons" again should not be thought of as toxic chemicals that immediately kill, but instead, are the result of witchcraft and evil potions and concoctions intended to harm the recipient in multiple ways, even driving one insane.[43] Poisons were slipped into water, wine, or other drinks, or added to foods, and depending on their intent, could be deadly to soul or body, or were sometimes even intended to engender love or eroticism.[44] Such poisons were also combined with spells and curse tablets often hidden in the walls or floors of homes by enemies, which caused illness to accelerate, or bring on death. One famous case is of this type was told about Germanicus, a powerful general and leader, rival of Piso, who died by magical assassination in Antioch in 19 CE.[45] Poisons had wide application and were placed in contact with the victim for malevolent intent, many times secretly. For the Galilean charismatics, opponents would seize every opportunity, including the use of magic and witchcraft (even hiring famous witches if needed) to kill them, a common practice in the Roman world.[46] Consequently, this charismatic expectation comes with reassurance and protection from magic, curses, and dark spells, and so Jesus' exorcists are to not fear any poison, as they will remain unharmed if ingested. This risk context of this saying is clearly to be set in the post-crucifixion itinerant ministry of the exorcists and the mission to drive Satan from the land.

In this final expectation, Jesus commits his exorcists to the *laying on of hands* (*keiris epithesousin*), as required to drive out demons of illness,[47]

42. Eusebius, *Ecclesiastical History*, 3:39.9.

43. Ogden, *Magic*, 115: "Canidia and Sagana perform necromancy and erotic magic," as reported about 30 BCE, Horace, *Satirea* 1.8: ". . . so much as the women who try to twist about human minds with spells and poisons [*venena*]."

44. Ogden, *Magic*, 117–18; a love potion considered a type of "poison."

45. Ogden, *Magic*, 217; Germanicus was the nephew of Tiberius, so the account was widely known. Piso filled Germanicus's residence with poisons, spells, and binding curses.

46. So with Germanicus. To counter the poisons and spells, Germanicus's wife hired a woman, "renowned for poisoning/witchcraft [*veneficia*] in that province [Syria]" to counter the poisons, curses, and spells found.

47. Mark 6:5, 7:32; Luke 4:40; It is important to note that Jesus' charismatic activity in Nazareth, the Galilean town where he was raised, was limited to laying on of hands to drive out illness, i.e., direct contact to convey power to drive out demons. As such,

i.e., another very specific form of exorcism, since illness was associated with demonic possession or evil, whether undeserved or, more commonly, resulting from a curse or contamination arising from evil actions or wrongs against a deity (e.g., the presumption of "sins," willful acts of defiance, committed by the victim or members of the victim's family).[48] Jesus used this practice of exorcism only after all other methods had failed in Nazareth.[49] Touching with hands was not just a soothing element, but a powerful charismatic act to drive off evil that required special technique and knowledge.[50] There are multiple examples to be found in ancient sources, both Hellenistic and Jewish.[51] Jesus affected several cures with the use of his hands, either in terms of touching the affected victim or in creating substances for application to the areas infected with evil. For example, in Mark 7:32–35, Jesus is asked to lay on his hands to a man possessed with a demon causing deafness and confused language. Jesus takes the man aside, privately, because the exorcism may not succeed. We are then provided one of the most thorough descriptions of a charismatic exorcism in ancient literature. Jesus first places his fingers in the man's ears. He then uses spittle, a substance previously described as a powerful healing substance of magicians and charismatics. Jesus spits on his fingers and touches the man's tongue. Then he goes into a trance, blows out his mouth in a "deep sigh," likely to release power and blast the demon, followed by pronouncement of a command, "*ephphatha*," or "be opened." The man is freed.

This remarkable account of "laying on of hands" provides descriptive evidence that specific practices taught by Jesus to the exorcists stood behind this command, most of which are now lost. There must have been multiple techniques employed by Jesus, evidenced by Luke 4:40. John 9:6 mentions Jesus making an application of mud and saliva. Another example is Mark 8:22–26. Here Jesus is specifically asked to lay his hands on a blind man who appears to have been cursed and attacked by a demon. Taking him out of the village of Bethsaida, perhaps to avoid those affecting the curse on the

---

Jesus' practice, the use of touch, or the laying on of hands, to drive out demons of illness was passed to his exorcists, and so references to this practice have the highest claim to authenticity.

48. See John 9:3.

49. Mark 6:5, dealing with only a few and likely in private.

50. Also to pass along charismatic power and authority: See Acts 9:17, and Acts 8:17–18, the baptized received the gift of the Holy Spirit, the dominant of all Spirits and so the most powerful available to charismatics and others who take on the risk of following the crucified man, the accused "evildoer" of Galilee. Other references include Hebrews 6:2.

51. For example, Apollonius who is said to have learned this from the priests of Asclepius in Aegae; see Eshel, "Jesus the Exorcist in Light of Epigraphic Sources," 183–85.

man, Jesus spits on his eyes. The cure is incomplete. Jesus then rubs his eyes with his hands and the man is able to see. He then orders the man to go to his home and avoid the village, indicating that Jesus was concerned that the exorcism would either be temporary, or that there was a risk of return of the demon if the man was cursed again by his attacker in the village, i.e., the attack would be repeated. Jesus would have trained his exorcists with these methods.[52]

Thus, the "laying on of hands" was common to Jesus' practice of exorcism—healings, driving out demons, and releasing the afflicted from curse or possession. As such, this final command to the exorcists, i.e., the expectation of laying on of hands and the special techniques employed, is coherent with the forgoing list of charismatic practices to be embraced by Jesus' exorcists. It is clear that this activity was also fraught with risk and danger. In Luke 10:14, Jesus was undoubtedly using a similar technique as recorded in Mark 7:32–35 when he was accused of being possessed by Beelzebul, the lightning-rod accusation that brought Jesus into deadly and perilous conflict with his opponents. Jesus, like the exorcists, would be accused of being "evildoers," dark magicians; they were possessed. Deceiving the people, announcing the end of demonic rule, and by implication the end of elitist rule that supported demonic imperialism, they would be sought out and destroyed like Jesus. Consequently, with this segment properly assessed in its contemporary setting, and perilous risk found to be inherent in its practice, we can now summarize our analysis of the qualitative risks present in Mark 16:17–18.

Recalling Helmut Koester's criterion,[53] where one can only discover the historical practices of a leader (a leader like Jesus, whose teachings and practices have become obscured by layers of theological interpretation) by looking to the practices of those who followed him or her, we find Mark 16:17–18 to be an accurate reflection of Jesus' actual activity. It was reiterated in an ecstatic experience with the risen Lord. Moreover, these charismatic activities clearly continued the most dangerous and perilous practices of Jesus' war on satanic pollution of the land, including his war on demonic

---

52. As implied by Luke 10:9, i.e., Jesus' sending of the exorcists into the towns and villages to drive Satan and demonic pollution out. They are to "heal" the sick or employ the laying on of hands and the techniques taught by Jesus to drive demons out and away. They also were effective by employing Jesus' name in exorcising demons.

53. Koester, *From Jesus to the Gospels*, 231: "Historians are therefore treading on very thin ice if they try to recover the historical person of Jesus through a critical analysis of the sayings tradition. A person of past history can only be understood if the extant sources reveal the traditions to which a person belongs as well as the subsequent structures, practices, and institutions of a community in which the memory of this person is preserved."

imperialism, which ultimately led to deadly conflict with his opponents and his execution. Clearly these sayings, embedded within the Markan appendix, are very early, and must come from a period in time when those who were Jesus' most intimate followers—the exorcists of Galilee—decided to continue the perilous mission of Jesus. From the standpoint of qualitative risk analysis, the only event that would have engendered such a radical decision would have been a post-crucifixion encounter with Jesus.

The exorcists would only have perceived more perilous risk by not engaging in dangerous behavior, i.e., continuing the very activity that led to Jesus' brutal death and execution, if they had not had an encounter with Jesus post-crucifixion. They were at greater risk by remaining silent or in hiding in Galilee as subsistence fishermen (which they attempted), doomed to demonic control and possession. Paul's own expression of dread and fear if he did not do the same is evidence that the post-crucifixion encounter was decisive.[54] Consequently, it is this encounter and the subsequent return to perilous risk behavior that authenticates the Markan tradition. We now move to our next risk tests, employing the criteria of dissimilarity and embarrassment in our assessment of Mark 16:17–18.

Applying the Criteria of Dissimilarity and Embarrassment to Mark 16:17–18

We begin with the *criterion of dissimilarity*. What is distinctive and different from both the needs of the early church and first-century Palestinian Judaism with regard to Jesus' charismatic demands placed on his exorcists in Mark 16:17–18? This is a challenging question in that if the appendix was a conflation of Gospel and Johannine materials, it would by definition serve the needs of the early church and fail the test. However, our analysis, using both contextual and qualitative risk analysis, has convincingly demonstrated that these specific sayings were not a conflation, but likely authentic sayings of Jesus that fit the context of the post-crucifixion period and reflected an ecstatic encounter. They contain rigorous and dangerous demands (one of which is found nowhere else in the New Testament), all of which created unparalleled perilous risk for Jesus' followers. As such, none met the needs of the early church. They were instead high-risk practices that were dropped in the other Gospels.

These sayings could only have been directed at Jesus' own Galilean exorcists, and in particular those who had been trained to use the techniques employed by Jesus; most specifically, the laying on of hands in conjunction

---

54. 1 Cor 9:16.

with demonic exorcism. Unfortunately, aside from a few examples noted in Mark and John, the specific practices and techniques Jesus employed have been lost to history. Nonetheless, it is clear that Jesus explained these techniques to the Galilean exorcists, as they were the source for the oral traditions as to what happened at these private exorcisms, if not the direct witnesses; whether using spittle, blasting, or breathing, special words of authority, or fingers in the ears, these were Jesus' techniques when exorcising demons. Consequently, Mark 16:17–18 stands apart from the needs of the early church, and as such represents perhaps the earliest list of post-crucifixion signs demanded of the risen Lord, and perhaps one of the earliest encounters with Jesus with his original band. What that encounter may have been will be more fully assessed below.

As to the Jewish context of these sayings, we can evaluate the contemporaneous charismatics of Jesus' time, including Choni, Hanina ben Dosa, Eleazar, and various rabbis noted earlier in this study.[55] Even though there is evidence that some of the traditions associated with these charismatics may have been altered to remove controversial and troubling activity, there still is no comparison to the radical charismatic activity of Jesus in his battle with demonic imperialism and Satan, and so he is distinct from his contemporaries. Indeed, Choni and Hanina are hailed not only as Jewish sages, but for having an intimate relationship with God. They have these powers as a gift, and as such there is little if any risk to them of physical harm or attack. Their position within the community is one of respect, coherent with charismatics who are favored by God and benefit the community. The activities demanded of Jesus' exorcists are not only controversial and divisive; they are fraught with physical peril and risk. As such, the practices demanded by the risen Lord are distinct from their Jewish context. Consequently, Mark 16:17–18 passes the test of the criterion.

The *criterion of embarrassment* identifies those sayings or events in the New Testament that created difficulties for the early church, implying that they were undeniable or else these traditions would never have been included, let alone created. To be clear, they are problematic to the early church. The betrayal by Judas (one of Jesus' chosen exorcists), Jesus' baptism by John (Why would Jesus need baptism?), and the crucifixion (Jesus was brutalized on a cross like a common criminal) are all examples of troubling events that would never have been created or included by the gospel editors were they not well known, and so undeniable. They were potentially embarrassing.

---

55. See Busse, "Palestinian Judaism and Ecstatic Activity," in *To Be Near*, 31–53; for examples, Vermes, *Jesus the Jew*, and also Kee, *Origin of Christianity*, 226–28.

When we turn to Mark 16:17–18, the test is whether the practices, in whole or part, were problematic, and therefore, could not have been a creation of the early church. That Matthew and Luke omit Jesus' commands to raise-up (or blast) snakes, as well as drink cursed or poisoned potions, stands as compelling evidence that these practices were very problematic to early communities.[56] If Mark 16:9–20 is part of the original Markan composition, then omission of the sayings provides conclusive evidence of this, as both Matthew and Luke use Mark as a source.[57] Regardless, since very specific radical, charismatic practices were abandoned or were obscured by these communities, there is sufficient evidence. For example, the charismatic techniques employed by Jesus in the laying on of hands (some of which were very similar to contemporaneous magical practices noted) are omitted or radically emended in other later Gospels. Also, the practices used in the exorcism of the blind man of Bethsaida (Mark 8:22–26) led to the entire tradition being dropped by the author/editors Matthew and Luke. Furthermore, Matthew omits reference to Jesus' common practice of the laying on of hands found in Mark 6:5, while Luke drops the section entirely. In Mark 1:29–31, Jesus is said to have to have laid his hands on Kepha's mother-in-law when driving out a demonic fever;[58] but in Luke, Jesus stands over her and commands the fever depart. In this case, Matthew omits the tradition entirely. Indeed, Matthew goes to great lengths to remove any traditions that might imply Jesus was a magician.[59]

Even the saying on exorcism, Mark 16:17, became problematic to the early church. For example, while it is clear that Jesus' sayings related to

---

56. The fact that these charismatic sayings and practices, i.e., on raising up snakes and particularly laying on of hands, are omitted in Luke and Matthew provides strong evidence that the entire section, Mark 16:19–20, was very early, and was likely the original ending to Mark. The practices are problematic to the later church communities, and so were very early, then later recast or dropped. This would explain the ending's omission in some ancient manuscripts of Mark. The development of these practices, such as the laying on of hands, dramatically changes in these later Gospels and Acts. For example, the laying on of hands for Luke becomes the ordination of apostles or leaders, e.g., Acts 18:17–18. The raising up of snakes becomes the tradition that Paul was bitten by a viper while collecting wood but remained unharmed.

57. As noted, Mark was used as a primary source by the author/editors of Matthew and Luke.

58. That fevers were demonic possession, see Smith, *Jesus the Magician*, 107.

59. Hull, *Hellenistic Magic*, 116–41. Hull makes a broad comparison, for example, with regard to the "signs," where Mark and Luke identify signs as exorcisms and the call to return to God as king, where Matthew only emphasizes one sign, the resurrection (118). "Unlike Luke, he [Matthew] refrains from drawing attention to the sign aspect of exorcism; he does not attach the demand for a sign to the actual Beelzebul controversy itself, but instead defers it" (119).

exorcism have the highest claim to authenticity,[60] exorcism was considered illegal in the Roman world, and continuation of the very practices that led Jesus into deadly conflict with the elite and Roman authorities was *most problematic*—particularly in Paul's itinerant activity in metropolitan communities of the Greco-Roman world. Certainly Paul knew of Jesus' exorcisms, and Paul's own itinerant activity continued from approximately 34 CE in Palestine to 63 or 64 CE in Rome. Yet, in his undisputed letters, where any reference to exorcisms might be detected, Paul is very careful to describe them as "working powers" (Gal 3:1–4) and "miraculous powers" (1 Cor 12:10), avoiding reference to exorcisms or to Jesus' exorcisms, particularly the laying on of hands.[61] This is true even in 2 Corinthians, where Paul links his charismatic activity to those of the apostles, but avoids the laying on of hands and exorcism.[62] Interestingly, Paul's healing "miracles" in Acts were associated with the passing on of handkerchiefs, work aprons, or cloths that came into contact with him.[63] It is the handkerchiefs and cloths that touched and healed others of illness, not Paul's hands.[64] Other charismatic events that avoided the laying on of hands included Paul's resuscitation of a young man who had apparently died (i.e., the young man, Eutychus, who fell from a third-floor loft[65] and seemed as dead);[66] the blinding of Bar-Jesus, a Cyprian sorcerer, for trying to convert Sergius Paulus;[67] the various miracles

60. Koester, *Introduction*, 78–79.

61. See also 2 Cor 12:12.

62. 2 Corinthians 12:12 includes Paul's description of his being a true apostle, which is linked to his ability to perform signs, wonders, and miracles much like Jesus' exorcists (including the "super apostles," 2 Cor 12:11–12). In fact, this section is Paul's defense of his apostleship, and by his referencing these specific activities as defining a true apostle Paul confirms that they were linked to the very activity of Jesus' exorcists. This confirms that this passage of Mark is an authentic reflection of the earliest activity of Jesus' exorcists post-crucifixion, and that Paul uses it to assert he was a legitimate apostle like they.

63. For additional reference on the use of handkerchiefs in the ancient world and magic, see Eshel, "Jesus the Exorcist," 184. The handkerchiefs mentioned in the *Greek Magical Papyri* (7:826) had incantations written on them.

64. Acts 19:12.

65. This was in Alexandrian Troas, a very large Greco-Roman seaport on the Adriatic. The site covered almost a thousand acres, including the typical public buildings, only a handful of which remain. Like other Roman cities, there were certainly three-story buildings, likely apartments like those near the forum in Rome.

66. Due to Paul's long sermon, still referenced today in many sermons as an anecdote for a preacher's long and laborious sermon; Acts 20:9.

67. Acts 13:6–11.

at Iconium;[68] and his surviving a stoning.[69] The "laying on of hands," or any other of the charismatic practices similar to those in Mark, are avoided or are intentionally diminished. Consequently, any expectation that the charismatic practices of Mark 16:17–18 were to continue post-crucifixion became problematic.

In sum, as a whole, Mark 16:17–18 reflects the most controversial activities of Jesus. The author/editor of Mark, including the Markan appendix, would never have created these expectations were they not understood to be unconditional post-crucifixion demands of Jesus. Moreover, the author would never have invented a tradition that implied that the failure to perform these practices would imply condemnation of the exorcist, or that these practices must be continued in their most radical form. Consequently, Mark 16:17–18 passes the test of the criterion of embarrassment. These were the practices of Jesus' surviving Galilean exorcists after the crucifixion and may contain the earliest instructions from the risen Lord to the Galileans.

Mark 16:17–18 and the Contextual Tests

We now turn to contextual analysis. If an encounter has successfully passed the foregoing risks tests, it must also pass four contextual coherency tests. The event must be coherent with the sociological risk setting, including the subsistence struggle of the Galileans, i.e., the background from which they came to join Jesus' band of exorcists. The contextual risk tests can be found on pages 118 and 119.

We can now turn to assess these sayings in Mark employing the contextual tests, each in turn.

Mark 16:17–18 passes the first contextual test based on our foregoing analysis. The charismatic expectations delineated in this section could only have been directed at Jesus' Galilean exorcists, i.e., those that witnessed for example the specific techniques and practices associated with the laying on of hands. Since laying on of hands as practiced by Jesus passed into obscurity very early, evidenced by its omission in other Gospels and in the authentic letters of Paul, only the Galilean men and women/exorcists, or those trained by them, could have been addressed. These were Jesus' most controversial and problematic practices and were familiar only to them. When combined with raising up snakes, or blasting, and harmlessly drinking cursed potions and other concocted poisons, there is little doubt that these practices were directed at this intimate band of followers. The risk of continuing these

---

68. Acts 14:3.
69. Acts 14:9–20.

practices was indeed perilous. Furthermore, it is unlikely that any of them, having escaped to Galilee and resumed subsistence fishing,[70] would have embraced these perilous risks if it were not for a post-resurrection encounter with Jesus that demanded their continuation.

This is also true for the second test, as the continuation of these radical charismatic practices by the Galileans is not simply encouraged but is expected and becomes the true and only valid test of charismatic legitimacy, which in turn is what defines Jesus' true and only followers. Consequently, there is little doubt that what is required is the continuation of Jesus' ecstatic practices that engendered the original perilous risk with his opponents.[71] These extend the ecstatic activity of Jesus and his war on Satan and ensured that demonic possession and pollution of the land continued to be attacked and destroyed. Satan would continue to fall from power through these exorcisms.[72]

With regard to the third test, we are unable to confirm if the encounter was near the lake of Galilee. However, some of the events listed in Mark 16:9–20 have Galilean connections. Indeed, Jesus' final encounter with his eleven was on a Galilean mountain.[73] It is clear that Luke's theological agenda was to recast the final encounter with Jesus in Jerusalem to demonstrate the spread of the gospel from Jerusalem to Rome, i.e., the focus of the Luke-Acts composition.[74] As noted, there is ample evidence that Jesus' exorcists fled to Galilee after the crucifixion and the report of the empty tomb. Consequently, the shift in location in Luke for theological purposes to Jerusalem would suggest that the original encounters with Jesus were near Galilee—indeed, the majority were. Further, with regard to the charismatic expectations, they do include animistic control, which is a power exhibited by Jesus in Galilee. Indeed, the animistic control over scorpions and snakes represents a more radical charisma than that reported about Jesus, e.g., in the repeated draft of fishes for the subsistence of Galilean fishermen. Jesus' exorcists are given unparalleled animistic authority, as they will be able to control the very creatures of Satan and render them impotent to possess,

---

70. John 21:3.

71. An interesting correlation with our tests of historicity related to risk is found in Smith, *Jesus the Magician*, 95: "Details can never be guaranteed, but those general characteristics of a tradition that accord with and explain both the opinions of a man's adherents, and those of his opponents, have a claim to authenticity far stronger than that which can be advanced for supposedly idiosyncratic sayings."

72. Luke 10:18.

73. Matt 28:16–20.

74. Koester, *Introduction*, 51.

deceive, or harm others. Consequently, while there is strong evidence to support satisfying the third test, it is not conclusive.

The final test evaluates whether the encounter led the Galilean exorcists to again abandon subsistence existence as fishers of Galilee (i.e., to which they returned for survival post-crucifixion). Risk evidence would strongly support their flight to Galilee and a return to subsistence fishing, hidden by their extended family[75] and sent out at night[76] (a great risk they were willing to take given the danger, as the lake was haunted by demons).[77] Conservative scholars cite the command of Jesus to stay in Jerusalem until they receive "power from on high," i.e., the Spirit.[78] However, this has been shown to be part of the Luke-Acts theological agenda as noted. Moreover, the supposed command of Jesus to the women to tell his disciples to meet him in Galilee is clearly an attempt to explain an embarrassing situation; all of the exorcists, including Kepha, fled Jerusalem to the safety of Galilee to hide. John 21:1–3 places at least five of the exorcists back in Galilee struggling to make their catch as nighttime subsistence fishermen. Of course, this passage contradicts all passages concerning encounters with Jesus in Jerusalem. In fact, none of the events in the Markan appendix 16:9–20, other than an appearance to Mary Magdalene, are necessarily in Jerusalem, and she tells them to flee where they will meet Jesus. As a result of this encounter in Mark 16:17–18, the Galilean exorcists once again embraced the war on Satan. Consequently, based on the foregoing analysis, the last test is satisfactorily met.

Conclusions on the Veracity of Mark 16:17–18 and Jesus' Appearance in Galilee

Based on both the risk and the analytical criteria employed, combined with contextual analysis, Mark 16:17–18 should be considered a contextually reliable post-crucifixion set of demands that relate to an encounter with the risen Jesus in Galilee. In the context of human risk experience, this encounter is reliable in its original context and setting. Such an encounter was likely

---

75. See Freyne, "Herodian Economics" 43–44, on *homophylia* and subsistence activity in Galilee.

76. As reported in John 21:1–3.

77. Keeping also in mind the events they had witnessed in Jerusalem, where the very evil forces they had attempted to cast out had overwhelmed Jesus, beginning in the olive grove of Gethsemane where they believed protection from demonic forces was certain.

78. Luke 24:49.

a group ecstatic experience where one of the exorcists was possessed by the spirit of Jesus and spoke for him, similar to Paul's own ecstatic experiences of possession, "Christ in me,"[79] words of the Lord given by dream or ecstatic experience,[80] or like the ecstatic trance conveying him to the third heaven,[81] or the encounter on the mountain of Galilee where Jesus was transformed.[82] All of these encounters in the ancient world were considered real, physical, and life changing, particularly since none of the exorcists ever expected to encounter Jesus again after the cursed death of the crucifixion. Was this the appearance to Kepha? While possible, and the encounter must be ascribed to one of the earliest encounters with the exorcists, it remains uncertain.

Corollary Observations, Mark 16:15–16

There is a demonstrable link between the perilous risks of extending these charismatic practices in Mark 16:17–18 (i.e., those that Jesus' expects his itinerant exorcists' take) with instructions that precede them. The command to baptize in Mark 16:16 includes a startling condemnation on those that refuse, as *katakrino* implies both immediate judgment and punishment, i.e., a divine curse. This is similar to Jesus' own condemnation of villages that refuse to accept and institute the changes he demands,[83] including democratized *agape*, the inclusion and acceptance of all outcasts and the former men and women possessed as a response to his exorcisms by the "finger of God." They thereby reject his and his exorcists' authority as from God and remain subject to Satan and demonic imperialism. God alone as king—a king who is coming with judgment.[84] Jesus suspended baptism due the risk of capture after the execution of John. To reconvene baptism was fraught with danger, but as such is coherent with the risk practices expected of the exorcists in verses 17–18. But why baptize? Baptism was linked with the demand to continue itinerancy and expand the "gospel," the *euangelion*. While the command to "go into the world" (*kosmos*, Mark 16:15) is later seen in terms of Luke's theological program (Christianity's expansion from Jerusalem to

79. Gal 2:20.
80. 1 Cor 7:12, 11:23, 14:32.
81. 2 Cor 12:1–4.
82. Mark 9:2–8; Matt 17:1–8; Luke 9:28–36.
83. These include the principal villages he had visited and also failed in this attempt to cleanse them and win over the village: Chorazin, Bethsaida (the village of at least two of Jesus' exorcists), and Capernaum (the village of several other followers, and where Jesus lived with Kepha, Kepha's wife, mother, and his brother's family—the typical extended family in first-century Palestine)
84. Luke 10:13; Matt 11:20.

Rome in Luke-Acts), in Mark, there was uncertainty and unlimited danger in carrying out such a demand. *Gospel* should be thought of as a verb; it was a charismatic power, imbued with authority for immediate transformation, and baptism, post-crucifixion, was the charismatic response to unite one with the Spirit of God, i.e., what Jesus had termed the "finger of God"; active in protection from the terror of Satan and demonic possession and doom at judgment, which was so near. Indeed, the exorcists could proclaim that it was this Spirit that had denied the annihilation of Jesus, the man "approved by God" by miracles, signs, and wonders (i.e., like the exorcists of Mark 16:17–18), who they had encountered to their shock post-crucifixion.[85]

These practices demonstrated the continued expulsion of demonic pollution of the land, where Satan would continue to "fall like lightning" from power, ensuring that God's rule was inbreaking. In this context, commands to continue these itinerant and dangerous practices, which by public admission given by a condemned and crucified "evildoer," an accused dark magician, is to risk everything and embrace perilous risk. Consequently, the command for itinerancy and baptism are coherent with the risk practices of Jesus and his exorcists at war with Satan. The *criterion of coherence* can be appropriately applied to support these conclusions since the criterion of dissimilarity has been employed. As Norman Perrin states: "Material from the earliest strata of the tradition may be accepted as authentic if it can be shown to cohere with material established as authentic by means of the criterion of dissimilarity."[86]

Given these findings, the most original and primitive stratum of tradition supports the authenticity of this encounter with Jesus, where these instructions were communicated to Jesus' original exorcists in Galilee. It is likely that this was the first encounter with Jesus due to the intensity of perilous risks created and contextual tests met in association with exorcism and was the encounter with Jesus' chief exorcist, Kepha, that is acknowledged in all strata of tradition,[87] the contents of which are now lost, but the event was known to the original community. It is likely that this encounter was thus to Kepha and that these instructions were given to him and then passed on to the other exorcists who had fled to Galilee.

---

85. Acts 2:22, "a man approved by God by miracles, signs and wonders," the same words used by Paul to describe the authority of authentic apostles, 2 Cor 12:12.

86. Perrin, *Rediscovering*, 20–22, and 43; also Jeremias, *Parables*, 11.

87. Paul, 1 Cor 15:5; Luke 24:34.

MARK 9:2–8: THE METAMORPHOSIS OF JESUS AS A POST-CRUCIFIXION ENCOUNTER

Mark 9:2–8 recounts the ecstatic experience of three of Jesus' exorcists, Simon (i.e., Kepha), Yecob, and Yohannes. They are separated from the other exorcists by Jesus and taken up to a high mountain (*oros hupselon*). There they witness his metamorphosis *(metemorphothe)*, also known as *the transfiguration*. The common translation of *anapherei* implies that Jesus physically leads these men up the mountain, but this word can also be translated as "carries up," as in a spiritual journey. As such, we must be cautious not to assume this event is a physical hike guided by Jesus any more than it is a spiritual journey, séance or vision, where Jesus reveals his true self—his glory.[88] There is evidence this is a shared séance or spiritual journey among Jesus' exorcists, guided by an encounter with Jesus, interrupted by Kepha's question, leading to the end of the vision.[89] Shamans are able to produce group visions, but usually through rhythmic music and dancing; however, there is no evidence this is a shamanic experience—this is something much different and impactful.[90] To recover the original form and setting of this event, the tradition should be tested using comprehensive risk analysis and rigorous contextual evaluation. This may reveal the most likely setting and use of the tradition, and more, if this event was a post-crucifixion encounter.

The unit begins, "After six days . . ." and is set on a mountain in Galilee. The count of days stands out,[91] as "six days" is the most specific description of passing time found in the Gospel of Mark aside from the predictions of the passion, a perilous risk event. As such, this unit must also have been originally tied to a similar perilous risk event, one absent from the current context. This indicates that the unit has been awkwardly placed in a new setting. Thus, in its current setting, the original risk context has been neutralized.

Form critical analysis long ago identified the event as resurrection appearance,[92] while others argue it as an epiphany or representation of

---

88. See Smith, *Jesus*, 120–22.

89. Smith, *Jesus*, 122.

90. Lewis, *Ecstatic Religion*, 53.

91. Mann, *Mark*, 359; Mann also mentions the six days that Moses was on the mountain before the voice of God called him from the cloud. While this may be an important parallel, the location and temporal reference when combined are more significant. Six days would allow the exorcists to return to Galilee after the crucifixion and be hidden by kin among night fishermen.

92. Bultmann, *History*, 259–60. Bultmann is followed by Robinson, "On the Gattung of Mark (and John)," 116–18. Robinson finds support for his conclusions based on a review of Gnostic writings, including *Pistis Sophia* 2–3 and the *Apocryphon of James*

Mark's redactional program to reveal Jesus as the glorified Son of Man at the *Parousia*.[93] However, from a risk analysis perspective, the designation of days demands a relationship with a perilous risk event, namely the crucifixion, consistent with the Markan editor's use of days elsewhere, which reference that event.[94] Consequently, Mark 9:2–8 is a post-crucifixion encounter with Jesus that has been reset back into the days of Jesus' itinerant mission.[95]

The location in Galilee is consistent with the aforementioned risk context of the exorcists fleeing Jerusalem for the safety of Galilee. According to Matthew and Mark,[96] the women share the command of Jesus to meet him in Galilee.[97] While this tradition may have been used to explain why the exorcists were in Galilee, there is little doubt that within a week they were there because they fled Jerusalem.[98] The mountain in Galilee was familiar to the exorcists[99] and to Jesus,[100] and so must have been a specific location where he sought ecstatic prayer,[101] solitude, and encounters with the divine, and likely where he trained his exorcists. Jesus' history with ecstatic mountain experiences began with his confrontation with Satan (Matt 4:8). It ends with his metamorphosis in Galilee at the "appointed" mountain.

The nature of this ecstatic experience in Galilee is markedly different than other post-crucifixion encounters reported in any of the canonical Gospels. As this event clearly could be construed as an *ecstatic vision or trance*, its placement as a resurrection event could was likely considered problematic.[102] Indeed, the three exorcists suddenly awake and find they

---

14:25–26. Contrasting this view very early was G. H. Boobyer, *St. Mark*. For a current analysis of the debate, see Litwa, *Iesus Deus*, 114n4.

93. For example, Perrin, *Christology and a Modern Pilgimage*, 8–9, 27–28; also on the Transfiguration as a proleptic of the Parousia, see Kee, "Transfiguration in Mark," 137–52.

94. Not a reference back to a theological point! Perrin, *Christology and a Modern Pilgrimage*, 8–9, 27–28.

95. Stein, "Is the Transfiguration (Mark 9:2–8) a Misplaced Resurrection Account?" 79–96; also for a thorough analysis of the account from a Christological perspective and brief review of scholarly view of the original form of the unit, see Rothschild, *Baptist Traditions and Q*, 134–40.

96. Matt 28:7, Mark 16:7.

97. Mark 16:7.

98. As we have already confirmed, Luke's theological agenda is to have the gospel preached from Jerusalem to Rome, but Mark, followed by Matthew, confirm that Jesus' followers met with him in Galilee.

99. Mark 3:13–19.

100. Matt 8:1, 14:23; Luke 5:16, 6:12; also see Mark 1:35.

101. Mark 6:46.

102. The disappearance of Apollonius of Tyana from a temple led to presumptions

are alone with Jesus, i.e., they "looked around" and saw no one else (Mark 9:8).¹⁰³ There the trance or revelatory experience abruptly ends.

Relative to this experience, we find a similar event reported by an undisputed historical figure, Paul of Tarsus, sometime between 35–42 CE. We learn of this experience from Paul's own hand as recorded in two of his undisputed letters, principally to the Corinthians (52–54 CE), and Galatians (49–56 CE).¹⁰⁴ Paul in 2 Corinthians 12:2–4 reports an ecstatic experience where he is transformed and taken to *tritou ouranou*, "the third heaven," by God ("*theos oiden*" is repeated, which implies that God was fully involved in this transportation and experience). This transport is to the highest heaven, paradise, the place where God and the angels reside, a description common in Judaism before the second century and in rabbinic literature.¹⁰⁵ It is where God takes the heroes of the Hebrews, such as Moses and Elijah. Paul is insistent that God was involved not only in this ecstatic experience, but that it was God who chose him from mother's womb,¹⁰⁶ and who "revealed [*apocalupsai*] his son to me."¹⁰⁷

The risk context of this event is defined by Paul as *optasias* and *apokalypseis*, "visions" and "revelations," that is, one of *multiple ecstatic experiences where he is taken in or out of body to be with the divine, which includes the post-crucifixion Jesus*. For Paul, these experiences redefine his perilous risk (one was now subject to attack by *messengers* of Satan),¹⁰⁸ and to disavow these encounters as anything but real was to bring on a divine curse.¹⁰⁹ Paul reports that he heard *arreta remata*, "unutterable words" that are forbidden to repeat by humans, a term used in mystery religions and rites, where the secret of the cult or divine revelations are to be kept to the initiate.¹¹⁰ Paul's

---

he was taken to paradise. The subsequent appearance of Apollonius in a dream to a follower, attempting to convince him of eternal life, is a good example of the contemporary appearance of the dead in a dream. See Philostratus, *Life of Apollonius*, 3i.

103. The experience is characterized as puzzling and ethereal, and so is less tangible than seeing Jesus with the marks of crucifixion evident on his body.

104. Koester holds that Galatians was written after the council of Jerusalem, about 56 CE. See Koester, *Introduction*, 114. The other theory is of course that Paul's discussion should be thought of a pre-council, or about 47 CE. Since Paul cites multiple revelations and visions in 2 Corinthians 12, the dating of these events is irrelevant for our purposes.

105. Schweitzer, *Mysticism of Paul*, 153–54.

106. Gal 1:15.

107. Gal 1:16.

108. 2 Cor 12:7; *aggelos*, used as angels, messengers, which in this case can also infer the demons of Satan.

109. Gal 1:8.

110. Furnish, *2 Corinthians*, 527.

transportation was immediate, and he is uncertain if he was transformed from his body or not, which is evidence a metamorphosis occurred that was beyond his comprehension to discern.

Paul's metamorphosis and charismatic experiences do not at first appear to have a direct correlation to Mark 9:2–8; however, they confirm that Jesus' exorcists and chosen charismatics (and note that in 2 Corinthians 12, Paul considers himself one of them; that he is equal to Kepha because of his charismatic powers of *signs, wonders, and miracles*) received divine visions (in dreams or by trance) and revelations (transportation with or to divine beings to receive mysteries, wisdom, or special insight) by God, where they heard divine voices directed to them. Consequently, Paul confirms that this type of ecstatic experience was *common* and *expected* among Jesus' Galilean exorcists, post-crucifixion, just as Mark 16:17–18 implies. Moreover, it was a sign of those who claimed to be true and authoritative representatives of Jesus, before and after the crucifixion, whether "fourteen years ago," or "after six days." From a risk context, it also meant that these men and women were at great risk, and if they refused to embrace these experiences as itinerant messengers (whose lives were no longer their own)[111] and the concomitant dangers,[112] their fate was set.[113] Their perilous risk rested in a refusal to accept the encounter as divine and act (i.e., to thumb one's nose at God), not in the deadly danger from enemies. They would be doomed and subject to Satan's rule.[114] This is the message Paul understood from his encounter with Jesus: To prevent Paul's believing himself superior to all men due to his multiple visions and revelations, messengers, the demons of Satan, were allowed to attack him.[115] This was a deliberate, perilous risk warning: If Paul turned his back on his commission as an itinerant *apostolos* of the "gospel," he would be turned over to Satan for destruction, something akin to Paul's curse on an adulterer in 1 Corinthians 5:5, *olethron tes sarkos*, the destruction of the flesh.[116] This is an echo of Jesus' dire warning to his exorcists in Luke 9:62, "No one who puts his hand to the plow and looks back is fit for the kingdom of God." This reflects the tenor the danger of refusal to embrace the risks of being an *apostolos,* a charismatic messenger, selected, trained, and commissioned by Jesus. Consequently, the exorcists, like Paul, had an ecstatic

---

111. Gal 2:20; and the tradition as to Kepha's fate remembered, John 21:18.
112. 2 Cor 11:24–26; Gal 1:13, 23; Acts 8:3; Acts 7:54–60.
113. 1 Cor 9:16.
114. Such as the tradition represented in Matt 12:45.
115. 2 Cor 12:7.
116. Smith, *Hand This Man Over*, 7–37.

post-crucifixion encounter that was transformative, shattering, and fraught with perilous risk if it were to be denied.

Mark 9:2–8 and Qualitative Risk Analysis

With this context set, we can begin our risk analysis of the unit, employing, first, qualitative risk. In this analysis, the encounter can not be a countermeasure to the elite, but must heighten the perilous risk of the Galilean exorcists and the conflict with opponents.

To begin, unless we hold the unit to be a post-crucifixion event[117] (near the lake to which some of the exorcists fled in terror after the crucifixion), the metamorphosis of Jesus becomes a neutral risk event slipped into his itinerant mission and war on Satan—an awkward and unlikely setting for such an event—and one whose intent must be thought to be theological, to the extent that it is the theological motif of a Markan redactor.[118] Scholars have suggested that if this were the purpose of the unit, the redactor sought to confirm Jesus' Christological standing as *bar nasha*, the Son of Man, and Son of God, i.e., the transfiguration confirmed his glorified state to be realized at the *Parousia*.[119] Or, the event becomes the pivotal moment in Mark when the benefits of being a disciple are made apparent, i.e., despite the disciples' struggles, the reward is to be with Jesus at the *Parousia*, which is near.[120]

Perhaps this was the need of the Markan community at the time of the Gospel's assimilation in late 60s CE, facing the crisis of the destruction of Jerusalem (a sign of the *Parousia*), albeit any reconstruction around such events is completely theoretical.[121] Unfortunately, when theories ignore the

---

117. This mountain was the location of several ecstatic experiences during Jesus' lifetime; see references later in this section.

118. This argument dates back to Perrin, "The Composition of Mark IX, 1," 67–70, and has continued.

119. Perrin, *Christology and a Modern Pilgrimage*, 93.

120. Morrison, *Turning Point*, 140–43.

121. We must recall the early traditions related to the composition of Mark written by Eusebius, church historian, citing Papias, bishop of Hierapolis, 60–130 CE: "This also what the presbyter said: 'Mark, having become the interpreter of Peter, wrote down accurately, though not indeed in order, whatsoever he remembered of the things done or said by Christ. For he neither heard the Lord nor followed him, but afterward, as I said, he followed Peter, who adapted his teaching to the needs of his hearers, but with no intention of giving a connected account of the Lord's discourses, so that Mark committed no error while he thus wrote some things as he remembered them. For he was careful of one thing, not to omit any of the things which he had heard, and not to state any of them falsely." Eusebius, *Ecclesiastical History*, 3.39:14–17. Mark's composition

original risk context of the post-crucifixion period in which the oral tradition was formed, such as this unit, they forgo a prudent effort to recover its more original form and function. This study has shown that the unit in some form has a well-defined risk context, and that it was originally linked with a perilous risk event that preceded it by "six days," and that the unit has been dislodged from its risk setting. The specific passing of time (the most specific in Mark) was a special designation employed by the Markan editor when speaking about the crucifixion, supporting its original setting as an oral post-crucifixion event.[122] Since the unit was displaced, we must ask what editorial work (theological redaction) was done to reset it within Jesus' itinerant mission, so as to recover its original form as a post-crucifixion experience, as the unit as it stands was likely not a unified tradition. Once recovered, perilous risk analysis can more accurately commence.

Scholars have identified the remnants of a core tradition within Mark 9:2–8 that has been expanded. As it stands today, the unit is the result of editorial work of a redactor, one whose theological intent can be recovered by examining Mark 8:27–10:52.[123] In these studies, the metamorphosis of Jesus is linked to Mark 8:38, Jesus' prediction of the coming Son of Man, which for Mark meant the all-powerful divine messianic eschatological figure, a combination of the divine attributes in *1 Enoch* and *IV Ezra*,[124] who would subdue Satan and all God's enemies in the last days. The metamorphosis confirmed for a *community* in crisis that Jesus was this figure and that their protection and hope for justification was assured.

The presence of Moses and Elijah appear to be later additions to the unit, as they serve as confirmation of Jesus' authority as the divine Son, i.e., the Son of God who now stands ready to fulfill and expound the Law and prophets. Bultmann argues that the presence of Moses and Elijah were not original to the unit, but instead were angelic figures present, similar

---

was not in chronological order, was related to the needs of Mark's community, and adapted (redacted) the traditions, and second hand. Since Matthew and Luke retain Mark almost completely and in the same sequence, it is arguable as to the apostolic composition of any of the Synoptic Gospels.

122. Mark 8:31–32, 9:30–32, 10:32–34.

123. Perrin, *Christology and a Modern Pilgrimage*, 100–101; Todt, *Son of Man*, 145–47.

124. These eschatological and apocalyptic tests provide different portrayals of the Son of Man as a messianic, redemptive, or judgmental and retributive figure. See Todt, *Son of Man*, 145–47; also Cullmann, *Christology of the New Testament*, 137–88; Bultmann, *Theology*, 30–31; Bornkamm, *Jesus of Nazareth*, 228. For a thorough discussion of sources and the Son of Man in eschatology and apocalyptic tradition see Reynolds, *Apocalyptic Son of Man*.

to those who appeared at the tomb.[125] Other scholars omit the verses altogether as part of the earliest version. However, there is general agreement that the original unit included the following: A miraculous transportation to a mountain (possibly to a sacred mountain) or to paradise (like Paul's transportation in 2 Corinthians 12); the metamorphosis of Jesus (including the change in appearance, dazzling, which likely included his face shining in glory); the appearance of an angelic figure (to confirm presence in the third heaven); Kepha's question and breaking the trance; the covering of a cloud (the sign of divine presence); a divine pronouncement; and an awakening alone with Jesus. It was an ecstatic trance or vision. It is this form of the unit that represents the original in a post-crucifixion unit.

While the vision is reported to the three of Jesus' followers, Kepha's presence is significant as leader of the male exorcists. All traditions ascribe his encounter as pivotal in confirming the others as valid.[126] Paul describes Kepha and Yohannes as "the pillars," an indication surely associated with their priority among the other male exorcists resulting from their revelations and visions of Jesus and being the principal witnesses to the event.[127] While this may have been a shared vision, there was likely one present originally, Kepha, who reported to the others his experience.

As a post-resurrection encounter of Kepha, perilous risk would have been significantly heightened. Kepha was the acknowledged leader of Jesus' male exorcists in all strata of tradition, and, as noted, the Synoptic Gospels acknowledge that Kepha's encounter was a lightning rod event for other exorcists and, ultimately, the nascent community.[128] From a risk standpoint, this event, along with Mark 16:17–18, clearly acted as the catalyst for his abandoning a kinship-assisted escape into hiding as a night subsistence fisher on Galilee. He was thrust back into the perilous risk of serving his master. This event therefore passes the test of qualitative risk analysis.

Mark 9:2–8 and the Criteria of Dissimilarity and Embarrassment

In this test, encounters must differ from the needs of the early church on the one hand and the context of first-century Judaism in Palestine on the other. To accurately test the tradition, the most original form of the unit should

---

125. Bultmann, *History*, 259–61, 309, 432–33.

126. Luke 24:34: "It is true, the Lord is risen and has appeared to Simon" (NIV); also translated, "The Lord has risen indeed and has appeared to Simon" (ESV).

127. Paul's description, Gal 2:9.

128. Luke 24:34.

be employed, as best as can be recovered. Analysis has confirmed that the unit differed significantly from the current structure, and occurs only a few days after a perilous risk event, almost certainly the crucifixion. The core tradition recovered is as follows:

> Late at night, or in heavy sleep,[129] there is ecstatic transportation by a trance or vision to a sacred mountain in Galilee, a place familiar to the exorcists,[130] or to paradise itself (e.g., 2 Corinthians 12); the metamorphosis of a risen Jesus occurs revealing his glorified state (the change in appearance, dazzling clothing, and shining face[131]); angelic figures, or Elijah and Moses, appear (to confirm presence in paradise); Kepha, in a trance[132] and likely the only one present, is terrified (*ekphoboi*), and inappropriately speaks, bringing the vision to a close; there is covering by a sacred cloud (the sign of divine presence); Jesus now resides in the third heaven with God and the angels; there is a pronouncement as God speaks and identifies Jesus as "my son"; Kepha awakes alone on the mountaintop; there may have been one or two other exorcists with him; he goes down the mountain to tell others Jesus is risen.

There are no other contemporary Jewish traditions that report an encounter between a deceased crucified criminal and exorcist, one considered a dark magician by enemies who attempted to destroy him. There is no question that the unit differs from the context of first-century Judaism in Palestine. The unit also differs from the needs of the early church. By recasting the unit as an event occurring during the itinerant activity of Jesus in Galilee, it confirms that the tradition was problematic to the early church as a post-crucifixion encounter. Indeed, 2 Peter 1:15–18 reports an independent tradition concerning a post-crucifixion encounter between Jesus and Kepha.[133] The sacred mountain is mentioned, the heavenly voice, and the "majestic glory" to which the author was a witness. This tradition confirms

---

129. Luke 9:32.

130. Shillington, *Jesus and Paul Before Christianity*, 42. As noted, the mountain in Galilee (likely modern day Mt. Tabor), was sacred to Jesus; it is where he escaped to have ecstatic encounters and pray (Mark 6:46), sometimes for days; where he selected and trained his exorcists (Mark 3:13–19; Busse, *To Be Near*, 76), and contested with Satan (not necessarily a mountain in the Judean desert).

131. Luke 9:29; While praying, Jesus' face begins to change. This tradition portrays the metamorphosis more accurately.

132. Just as he did in Acts 10:10 while praying, i.e., deep spiritual breathing and meditation.

133. For example, see Wells, *Historical Evidence*, 113n3, for a detailed and exhaustive analysis of the sources and scholars debating the original use and for of the tradition.

that Mark 9:1–8 was most likely a post-crucifixion encounter with Jesus by Kepha. Consequently, with the vision-trance content of the encounter emphasized in Mark, it became difficult to sustain confidence that the resurrection of Jesus was more than a dream of a poor, displaced Galilean fisherman turned exorcist—one who had abandoned Jesus and fled. Such an encounter was insufficient to inspire new followers to embrace perilous risk, indeed the risk of arrest, death, and annihilation under a divine curse. This is why the resurrection encounter with Kepha has been lost—it is recast in Mark. In sum, this unit differs from the needs of the early church on the one hand and the context of first-century Judaism in Palestine on the other, and as such passes the test of the criterion of dissimilarity.

The *criterion of embarrassment*[134] identifies those sayings or events that created difficulties for the early church, implying that they were undeniable or else these traditions would never have been included, let alone created. In evaluating the unit in its original form, Mark 9:1–8 meets the criteria. It was problematic to the early church as a post-crucifixion encounter, evidenced once again by its displacement and recasting as an event that occurred during Jesus' itinerant war on Satan. More, placed in its new context, the metamorphosis now served the needs of the early church, as the redactor of Mark linked the event to Jesus' prediction of the coming Son of Man, the messianic apocalyptic figure that would render justice to the righteous of God and crush all enemies. Set in the context of Mark 8:24–10:47, the metamorphosis of Jesus confirms he is both the Son of Man *and* the Son of God, revealing to his disciples his glorified self as he will appear at the *Parousia*, the judgment. Therefore, a community in crisis, one that was facing the catastrophic destruction of Jerusalem, becomes comforted by the assurance that Jesus will act as the divine Son of Man on their behalf, mitigating all perilous risk and rescuing them from destruction. As such, the unit's placement in the activity of Jesus in Galilee eliminates its problematic nature and so passes the criterion of embarrassment.

In sum, an analysis of Mark 9:2–8 has isolated the original form of the unit by employing the criteria of risk analysis. Based on this analysis, the event may be considered reliable, subject to passing the remaining contextual tests.

Mark 9:2–8 and the Contextual Tests

We now turn to contextual analyses. Here an event must be coherent with the sociological risk setting, including the subsistence struggle of the Galileans,

---

134. Meier, *Marginal Jew, Vol. 1*, 170.

the background from which they came to join Jesus' band of exorcists. Once again, the contextual risk tests previously established are as follows:

1. Encounters with original members of Jesus' band of Galilean exorcists, those who faced capture, death, and social isolation and starvation, are given priority.
2. Encounters should be consistent with the ecstatic practices of Jesus that engendered the original perilous risk with his opponents. Specifically, encounters that encouraged the remaining exorcists to continue the ecstatic activity of Jesus and his war on Satan are preferred.
3. Encounters near or on the lake of Galilee, particularly related to subsistence fishing, and similar to the animistic control exhibited by Jesus, are preferential (i.e., the remaining exorcists escaped there).
4. Finally, encounters that may have led the Galileans to again abandon subsistence existence (i.e., to which they returned for survival post-crucifixion) are also preferred.

In each of the foregoing tests, the original form of the unit recovered through risk analysis is evaluated.

To begin, it is readily apparent that the unit passes the first, third, and fourth contextual tests, as Kepha was not only one of Jesus' trained male exorcists, but he was also considered their leader even two decades later[135] and continued to practice as an exorcist.[136] Moreover, risk analysis has suggested that Kepha fled to Galilee immediately after the crucifixion, returning to agrarian subsistence existence in desperation to hide and to support his family (e.g., his wife and mother-in-law). Hiding under the protection of kin (and other fishers), they arranged night work for him, where trammel-net fishing would allow him to avoid detection and capture by spies or informants.[137] Kepha's subsequent trance and vision either on or near the sacred mountain in Galilee of the glorified Jesus (a secret or special place familiar to Jesus[138] and his exorcists; indeed the place where they were selected and trained[139]), was certainly the pivotal ecstatic experience that drove him to abandon that life and, once again, embrace perilous risk; it

---

135. Gal 2:9, written between 48–52 CE; Koester, *Introduction*, 104.

136. Acts 5:12–16, 8:14–17, 9:33, 34, 36–41.

137. For the design of the net and the methods employed by Galilean fishermen, see archaeologist Nun, "Let Down Your Nets," 11–13.

138. Luke 5:16 and 6:12.

139. Mark 3:13–19.

led him to gather up Jesus' remaining (and willing) exorcists[140]—thereby passing the second test—and report that Jesus was not only active, but in paradise and able to support them by using his name to control demons and guide them in visions and dreams, or in personal and group encounters. Kepha's trance was also consistent with the ecstatic activity of the exorcists trained by Jesus. Jesus himself experienced trances and visions, as did his exorcists, particularly Kepha, as confirmed in Acts 10:10. Later, Paul verifies that ecstatic visionary and trance experiences were confirmation of one's authenticity as an *apostolos*, such as Kepha and the other "super apostles." Given this, the unit passes all contextual tests.

Conclusions on the Veracity of Mark 9:2–8

Based on the risk and analytical criteria employed, combined with contextual analysis, Mark 9:2–8 should be considered an authentic post-crucifixion encounter with Jesus. In the context of human risk experience, this encounter is authentic in its recovered historical context and setting. Jesus is now seen as enthroned with God in the third heaven.[141] It is this event in Galilee that transformed Kepha and the male exorcists' activity from one of fear to returning to the war on Satan with Jesus as Lord.

---

140. The "twelve" were eventually gathered and selected by Kepha and included perhaps all of those chosen by Jesus on the mountain, assuming they returned to Galilee and remained, as some still were not convinced (Matt 28:17). The variation in the names of the Twelve in Gospel lists, as well as the question of who followed Kepha to Galilee, suggests that there may have been changes over time. Clearly, an early tradition confirmed that vacancy among the Twelve was filled by casting lots, a practice used by even the High Priest to decide religious issues.

141. Analysis will show below that this encounter then extends Mary's, where Jesus was clearly active and available but "not yet ascended," to his acceptance to the place with God. This difference set Kepha's encounter as significant and different from Mary's, and ultimately took precedence over Mary's in the primitive Christian tradition, and as reflected by Paul in 1 Corinthians 15:1–5.

10

Matthew

Recovering the Original Risk and Historical Context of Galilean Appearances

In this section, the evaluative criteria will be applied to two traditions in Matthew associated with resurrection encounters in Galilee. As with the previous section, when applied, the criteria will attempt to recover the original risk and historical context of the encounter and reveal the instructions of the risen Jesus to his exorcists and followers. Like the traditions in Mark, the results will forever change the understanding and risks associated with these encounters and the dangerous context in which the earliest followers of Jesus brought forward their ecstatic activity into a hostile, demon-filled world to continue Jesus' war on Satan.

MATTHEW 28:1–10: MAGDALENE AND THE DIRECTIVE TO GO TO GALILEE

In Matthew 28:1–10, Mary *the Magdalene* and "the other Mary" have the first ecstatic encounter with Jesus post-crucifixion.[1] According to the Matthean report, Magdalene had gone to see the tomb the evening after the Sabbath

---

1. The problematic nature of a report coming from the witness of Jewish women in first-century Palestine will be addressed below when applying the various risk criteria, including the criterion of dissimilarity.

"toward the dawn," which, from a risk perspective, makes her effort striking—not because it was dark, but it was exactly when malevolent ghosts, evil spirits, and demons were believed to roam, seeking victims, particularly near tombs and graveyards![2] Mary was completely vulnerable. Why would she, and perhaps other women exorcists, have taken such a perilous risk, particularly when these very demonic forces[3] had just succeeded in overwhelming and killing Jesus, once thought to be able to control all demonic forces; the man she held to be a powerful exorcist possessed by the "finger of God?" If it were only to be near the tomb, then her courage should be considered remarkable, but also quite puzzling and even incoherent. She is literally heading to the very spot demonic forces would attack and attempt to possess her. As such, qualitative risk and contextual analyses would suggest her visit to the tomb had a specific risk motivation and one that can be recovered.

To begin, both Marys, particularly the Magdalene, were most certainly itinerant ecstatics and exorcists,[4] just as were the men who followed Jesus—as has been established, a tradition that was undoubtedly later suppressed.[5] The Matthean tradition confirms that, unlike the male exorcists who fled, they made a conscious, perilous risk decision—they *chose* to

---

2. Ogden, *Magic*; see previous citations in chapter 1.

3. The satanic forces included Satan's control over the Jerusalem elite and Roman imperialism under Pontius Pilate; see Busse, *To Be Near*, 23–34.

4. Janowitz, *Magic in the Roman World*; see chapter 6 and also footnote on page 100. While not explicitly tied to women "exorcists," women were directly linked to healings (i.e., driving out demons) with more than fifty-one of those associated with women married to or associated with rabbinic families. Paul does make this association; for Junia in Romans 16:7, whom he names as an apostle (and as defined by Paul in 2 Corinthians 12:2 as one who could exorcise demons and heal and would be itinerant; one who was so named before Paul's post-resurrection encounter with Jesus and held by all the apostles to be superior). Consequently, Paul clearly supports that women were exorcists in the Jesus movement from its inception. Why then in Paul's list of appearances in 1 Corinthians 15 does he not cite Mary the Magdalene? This question has puzzled scholars for decades without definitive resolution. The most compelling argument thus far is that Paul does include women in this his lists of apostles, including a Mary he lists with other prominent apostles (Romans 16:6). Further, as his argument with the Corinthians demands unquestioned witnesses (and a woman's testimony did not carry the weight of men in the Greco-Roman and Jewish worlds of the first century), he particularly emphasized the report of Kepha, who likely visited Corinth in 54–55 CE (1 Cor 9:5; Acts 9:32).

5. See the discussion below on the suppression of women in subsequent gospel traditions, particularly Kraemer, *Her Share of the Blessings*, 130–31; We know that Junia and Phoebe were likely itinerant ecstatics, as Junia is identified by Paul as an apostle of note among the others and was known to be one long before he had his own encounter with Jesus, Romans 16:7. Paul is very clear about the qualities of true apostles like himself in 2 Corinthians 12.

remain and risk being captured, *secretly* following (at a distance)[6] to see not only who took the brutalized body of Jesus,[7] but more important, to see *where* it was taken.[8] For these two exorcists, the perilous risk of doing so is outweighed by the even greater risk of abandoning him. They watched as it was sealed in a rock tomb, the entrance blocked by a heavy rolling stone. Finally, when alone and before the guards arrived, they faced or sat and leaned against the tomb. The tomb was then guarded (as noted, by special priests).[9]

Why these women would take such a risk is critical to ascertain. Indeed, to assert there was no risk because, as women, they would be immune from attack is completely inaccurate and neutralizes perilous, dangerous actions. There are numerous contemporary accounts of brutal attacks on men and women, even innocent bystanders, by Pilate, the elite, and their spies, recorded by Josephus and others.[10] Saul, an agent and spy of the Jerusalem elite, brutalized both men and women of the early followers of Jesus' movement. Indeed, as will be seen, the actions to secure the body by Jesus' enemies is coherent with the risk context of the danger he presented to them even in death (and so are most assuredly reliable), but underscore the risk of being seen or even thought to be his supporter.[11] These exorcists must have had a different risk motivation.[12]

After the Sabbath ended, and at the most dangerous time of night, the two Marys return. Mark and Luke include that it was to "anoint the body" (Mark 16:1-2 or Luke 24:1), adding also the names of other women present

---

6. Matt 27:55.

7. Bultmann, *History*, 274, accepts the burial narrative as a recount and reliable, including the tradition about Joseph; however, this view has been challenged because of the problematic nature of Joseph's membership in the Sanhedrin, with carefully selected membership sympathetic to the Romans; see Crossan, *Who Killed Jesus?* 772-77, and Ehrman, *How Jesus Became God*, 142, 165. Bultmann is correct that the narrative is likely authentic but misses the very problematic issue that can be recovered through risk analysis, i.e., that Joseph was taking the body of Jesus to put it in stone, as he and other members of the elite feared retribution and wanted to ensure Jesus had been annihilated.

8. If these men were sympathizers of Jesus, the women would not have had to follow at a distance, or wait until their departure, and only then approach the tomb.

9. Matt 27:61; Guarding the tomb was indicative of fear of retribution, i.e., to monitor it to ensure it remains still and inactive.

10. See Horsley and Hanson, *Bandits, Prophets, and Messiahs*, 29-32, 41-42; Josephus, *Ant.* 8:60-62, 18:3.3, 18:85-89; Philo, *Embassy*, 302. See also Busse, *To Be Near*, 20-27.

11. Mark 14:70; Luke 22:58; Matt 26:73; John 18:17.

12. For a comprehensive analysis of the burial of Jesus see Costa, "Ossuaries and Burials," 1-20.

with them.[13] However, the editor/redactor of Matthew knew Palestine and that anointing a decaying body would have been inconceivable and repugnant after three days; and, with the brutalized condition of Jesus' body, simply too horrible.[14] For the editor/redactor of Matthew, such a tradition was an embarrassment, and so it was dropped. Further, carrying heavy spices at night (let alone purchasing them while in hiding) would have been difficult, if not impossible, and since the tomb was guarded and ritually sealed,[15] any approach would have led to their being attacked (i.e., the guards not knowing if they were spirits, ghosts, or exorcists of Jesus). Those monitoring and guarding the sealed tomb would have used special protective weapons, including bronze swords, magical amulets, or special tokens for driving away evil or casting (throwing) deadly protective curses.[16] Furthermore, and as noted, no anointing was needed, as according to John 19:38-42, the body already had been anointed, covered with unusually large amounts of burial spices (over one hundred pounds of myrrh and aloes, while only forty pounds for the highly respected and revered Rabbi Gamaliel).[17] That Jesus' body had been dressed is certainly correct. However, based on the risk and contextual setting previously analyzed, Jesus' body was more likely covered with a concoction of magical herbs, amulets, and written spells.[18] Large quantities of this mixture were placed on the body by enemies to ensure the dark magician's spirit, if not annihilated by crucifixion, was trapped. His enemies feared that, as a minion of Satan's demonic prince, Beelzebul, he could be "raised" or "conjured" and would seek deadly retribution against them or be used for malevolent purposes.[19]

Consequently, going to the tomb had nothing to do with anointing a decaying and mutilated body. Employing a contextual risk perspective

13. Other women are mentioned in Mark 16:1-2: Mary Magdalene, Mary the Mother of James and Salome; other Gospels have different groups and interactions, but are unanimous that women found the empty tomb and tried to report it to Kepha, only be told it was an "idle tale."

14. The very point of John 11:39 within the canonical Gospel tradition.

15. To keep the body of Jesus and his spirit trapped, preventing retributive attack on enemies as was expected by the "untimely dead."

16. Jesus' body was taken by his enemies to ensure he had been annihilated both body (they brutalized and mutilated it as a first precaution) and spirit (killing him under a divine curse, being "hung on a tree"). It was then sealed in the tomb and guarded by special priests ordered to monitor the body, rolling back the stone at dawn each day to verify it remained still, i.e., to ensure his spirit was not "restless" to seek retribution as one of the untimely dead. See Ogden, *Magic*, 179, 181.

17. Josephus, *Ant.* 17:8.3.

18. For the use of amulets by Jewish rabbis and others, see chapter 1.

19. See Busse, *To Be Near*, 55-56.

within the contemporary setting, we must postulate that, as ecstatics and exorcists who had been abandoned by the rest of the band (the male exorcists had fled) and who were desperate for escape (fearing discovery and attack), these exorcists went to seek if he had been destroyed; that is, if they could communicate with Jesus' spirit, intending to seek him and his protection, or that of the "finger of God," the spirit that possessed him. It is more likely that they brought special herbs and spices used by contemporary exorcists[20] to carry out ecstatic prayer near the tomb with the intent of having a vision, that is, to determine if Jesus' spirit had been annihilated. To accomplish this, ancient ecstatics, exorcists, and *goetes* went to the tomb of the victim, particularly during pre-dawn hours. Spices and herbs could be burned and inhaled or ingested to activate ecstatic experiences. This presents the possibility that these exorcists were responsible for the first critical encounters with Jesus post-crucifixion; all accepted and believed to be completely reliable and unexpected, and so validating, within their risk setting—the very origin of the Jesus movement post-crucifixion and primitive Christianity. Only these circumstances adequately address the contemporary risk context of the two Marys visitation to the tomb.[21]

Accordingly, the women have an ecstatic experience, whether in a trance or vision, but an encounter where they are present and Jesus is experienced (not unlike that of Kepha's at the mountain),[22] near the site of the tomb. They see the descent of an angel, felt a tremendous earthquake, and then the rolling back (*kulio*) of the large stone that sealed the tomb. Notably, the guards are nowhere to be found, indicating this is a vision. An angel of God instructs the women to tell the remaining exorcists that the tomb had been vacated. Jesus' body did not appear; the tomb was already empty, just as in the tradition of Phlegon previously noted in the account of a deceased girl, Philinnion.[23] The vision may end at this point, but the exorcists have confirmed Jesus has not been annihilated but is available and active and

---

20. A tradition of Rabbi Johanan ben Zakkai refers to the use of herbs and roots, instructing that they be burned under a possessed individual, then surrounding the victim with water, which causes the demon to flee (Kohler, "Exorcism"); a root was used by the exorcist Eleazar according to Josephus (*Ant.* 8.2.5). While the practice has been lost, the women coming to the tomb during the peak hours of demonic activity, using similar herbs and roots to drive demons away, could have augmented a state of prayerful trance free from attack while hoping for contact with Jesus.

21. See examples in Ogden, *Magic*, 64–65, 146–47, 149–52, 161–62, 164–65, on tombs and encounters with ghosts and spirits there.

22. As determined in our previous analysis of the metamorphosis of Jesus, or as in Act 10:10.

23. Phlegon of Tralles, *Mirabilia I*, in Ogden, *Magic*, 159–60.

will be in Galilee—"risen" in the risk context of the ancient world. This is a shocking, unexpected outcome.

The extant tradition then has the women rush to the male exorcists, who were either in hiding or already in the process of fleeing to Galilee. But before they reach them, they encounter Jesus on the road.[24] Jesus appears suddenly and is in a visible and substantive form. They fall, wrap their arms around his feet, and worship him. Jesus commands the women to tell the male exorcists, "Go to Galilee where they will see me." These instructions are contrary to those reported in Luke (i.e., they are to remain in Jerusalem, Luke 24:49), and so certainly reflect an earlier tradition of Jesus' first encounters, i.e., since it retains the more controversial tradition of the exorcists "fleeing to Galilee," versus remaining in Jerusalem.

The tradition of women first conversing with the risen Jesus, as well as Magdalene having equal standing with Kepha, is deeply rooted in early Christian literature. Furthermore, these traditions are multiply attested.[25] Consequently, the tradition that "the Lord is risen indeed and has appeared to Peter [Kepha]"[26] should not be understood as proof the women exorcists were ignored perhaps for days or weeks by the original group of exorcists. Any report of a post-crucifixion encounter by a male or female (e.g., Thomas, John 20:25, who rejected the report made by males), was *leros*, i.e., nonsense. When the encounter with Kepha occurred in Galilee, there was confirmation, but more, that the male exorcists had been readmitted by Jesus into his fellowship, despite having abandoned him in Jerusalem when captured. Jesus sought no retribution. Paul, like the other male charismatics listed in 1 Corinthians 15:1–8, traced their charismatic and divine authority to Kepha's encounter as confirmation of inclusiveness as male *apostoloi*, not that the report of the women was invalid. Indeed, 1 Corinthians is Paul's response to male "super apostles" that had infiltrated his *ecclesia* sent from James in Jerusalem (i.e., so Paul uses the tradition of the male encounters, listing himself among those who had encountered the risen Lord) to demonstrate his equality with Kepha, and included James![27] Consequently, until

---

24. If on a road, the tradition may have been created as an echo to Paul's Damascus experience. Were this the case, the encounter was during the trance.

25. See the excellent analysis of sources and the *Gospel of Mary* by King, *Gospel of Mary*, 175–76; Mary is known as an apostle in various early Christian writings, from the *Dialogue of the Savior*, *Apocalypse of James*; the confrontation with Kepha is recorded also in the *Gos. Thom.* 114. The multiple attestation of Mary's role as an apostle and women as apostles is indisputable.

26. Luke 24:34.

27. As confirmed in Busse, *Enemies*, 112–17, Paul must defend the legitimacy of his apostleship from the counter claims of "super apostles," all male, who demeaned women. They were sent from James to disrupt Paul's *ecclesia*, because he held firm to the

the encounter with Kepha, primitive belief in a risen Jesus was strictly associated with female *apostoloi*, thus explaining the continuing primacy of the women in the earliest tradition, and why Phoebe's and Junia's supremacy is noted in Paul's greetings and ascription to them as an *apostolos* and deacons in Romans 16 are made clear.

Matthew 28:1–10 and Qualitative Risk Analysis

With this context set, we can begin our risks analysis of the unit, employing, first, qualitative risk. In this analysis, the encounter can not be a countermeasure to the elite, but must heighten the perilous risk of the Galilean exorcists and the conflict with opponents.

Magdalene's post-crucifixion actions and the subsequent ecstatic encounter with Jesus heighten perilous risk on several levels. Risking discovery, capture, or attack, Magdalene goes to the sealed and guarded tomb that holds the brutalized body of Jesus. She does so at the hour that spirits, demons, and ghosts roam, looking for victims and souls to seize. She knows and understands this danger; that being near tombs brings contact, particularly with the untimely dead or the dead by violence seeking revenge while they wander at night. Magdalene is in perilous danger. But as an exorcist trained by Jesus, she comes to the tomb accepting the deadly risk of either conjuring or communicating with him to discover if he had been annihilated. She receives more than expected. The practices she employs were related to contact with the dead, and if discovered would have resulted in her immediate execution.[28]

For her to remain in Jerusalem was also to risk all. There was perilous danger from enemies, whether demons or the enemies that had killed Jesus, all of whom were under satanic control. Magdalene could not hide easily. She was identifiable—a Galilean with that telltale accent, wearing clothing that Jesus prescribed of his exorcists (another reason for nighttime travel and moving from place to place). She had been seen with Jesus and the

---

resurrection event being pivotal to salvation, versus their insistence on ecstatic experiences and special salvific words of Jesus as immediately transformative. Consequently, Paul must appeal to Kepha as witness to the resurrection of Jesus, and all the other witnesses who were male to defend the legitimacy of his apostleship and "gospel" of salvation by faith alone in that event prior to the *Parousia*.

28. Jesus' "laying on of hands," described in detail above, included using mixtures of spittle and mud to exorcise demons, Mark 7:33, 8:23; John 9:6. Luke 8:55, this food was likely herbs or roots to sustain her spirit's return after Jesus cast out the demon of death, i.e., the translation can be that "he prescribed she be given something to eat."

exorcists.[29] Magdalene's incursion and perilous practices near the guarded tomb can not be understood as benign.

Magdalene's ecstatic experience also heightened her perilous risk. In Matthew, the event follows a vision or more likely a "possession trance."[30] The angelic appearance signifies that the tomb has been vacated, and she immediately becomes the first witness, bearing the risk of the message and recommitment to the war on Satan—but she stands alone at this point and is completely vulnerable. The Matthean redactor attempts to neutralize her perilous risk and standing. Her role is simply to be a messenger, traveling a short distance to the male exorcists in Jerusalem, which significantly devalues both Magdalene's importance and significance of her encounter, which, as this study has demonstrated, is completely errant.[31]

Magdalene encounters Jesus and reports the experience first to the other women. Now her perilous risk is dramatically heightened. She becomes a witness that the "evildoer" Jesus is active despite the efforts of the religious elite and Roman sympathizers to annihilate him. She thus becomes complicit as a participant in the return of Jesus, the dark magician and one of the untimely dead; the servant of Beelzebul who was most certainly going to seek revenge against his enemies. Mary's action therefore meets the test of qualitative risk analysis.

Matthew 28:1–10 and the Criteria of Dissimilarity and Embarrassment

With regard to the criterion of dissimilarity, encounters must differ from the needs of the early church, on the one hand, and the context of first-century Judaism in Palestine on the other. To accurately test the tradition, the most original form of the unit should be employed. Analysis has confirmed that

29. Luke 9:3, Matt 10:10.

30. For characteristic of a possession trance, which includes introducing artificial means to produce the trance (such as spices, roots, or herbs), see Aune, *Prophecy in Ancient Christianity*, 20–22. These are typically associated with prophetic experiences, but in this case, Mary become prophetic by spreading the news of her vision and the vision's meaning, then relating the encounter. Christian prophets, described by Paul in 1 Corinthians, also may have had similar experiences (like that of Paul himself) in visions and revelations, which were then adopted as sayings of the risen Lord, paranesis and instruction, or clarification for the benefit of the community. Aune confirms that these traits were prevalent in the Greco-Roman and Jewish worlds.

31. The same fate is found in the tradition of Jesus and the Samaritan woman, John 4:1–42. According to my discussion with Stephen Patterson in 2013, Jesus' discussion with her, based on the Greek used, is harsh, but the tenor of the tradition is that she is like an *apostolos*.

the unit in Matthew 28:1–10 differed significantly from the recovered structure. The core tradition recovered by risk analysis (i.e., that Mary was herself an exorcist, not that she had demons exorcised as held by most scholars[32]) is therefore markedly different from the needs of the early church. Her role as an exorcist (and that tradition as a whole) was devalued and made subservient to the traditions of the male exorcists. But can we say that the recovered tradition differs from the context of first-century Palestinian Judaism?

Based on contextual and risk analysis in this study, Mary was a trained exorcist of Jesus, likely with origins as a *therapeutides*. Like Kepha, she was given a new exorcist's name, *the Magdalene*, the "high one" or "fortress," having overcome and taken control of multiple (i.e., seven) demons. Magdalene becomes an itinerant exorcist and charismatic with Jesus' band, taking the deadly risk of participating in his war on Satan and demonic imperialism, traveling from village to village, driving out demonic possession, and announcing the displacement of the elite and inbreaking kingdom of God—she was a threat and perilous risk. Other women were also added as exorcists or assistants to Mary (at least four) and to Jesus' band. They contributed to the common purse by sharing their donations for cures and exorcisms.

Magdalene was not wealthy, not a harlot, nor a Jewish patron. She lived a subsistence existence among the fishing villages of Galilee as a charismatic and esoteric wisdom teacher (with healing power) until she encountered Jesus and joined with him in his war on Satan. Unfortunately, her fate has been lost to history,[33] but traditions as to her importance in the early risk encounters with demons and demonic imperialism, as well as crucifixion and her incursion at the tomb, are found in all layers of the early Christian tradition, both canonical and non-canonical. This multiple attestation confirms that Magdalene held a prominent place in the early Christian movement and that traditions were recited and orally circulated for generations. Clearly, they were instrumental in the formation of the early movement based on her first encounter and subsequent interactions with Jesus post-crucifixion.

---

32. See Adna, "Encounter of Jesus," 299–300. Adna cites the tradition of exorcism of demons from Mary, and that scholars, such as John Meier, *Marginal Jew*, find that it has a reasonable claim as historical, following a detailed inquiry. However, risk analysis has recovered the original context and tradition, which has been subjugated by a male-dominated church hierarchy that owes its authority to traditions of Kepha's encounter with Jesus.

33. With the possible section of Romans 16:6, "Give my greetings to Mary, who has worked so hard for you." Although this is a Mary in Rome and this Mary in not called Magdalene by Paul, or more thoroughly acknowledged. Mary was a common Semitic name, but it is interesting that such a name was mentioned about a leader in Rome who was a Jew.

As such, Magdalene's role is unlike any known in contemporary Judaism. While there are some similarities with Greco-Roman women, particularly sorceresses and charismatics in ancient literature,[34] the closest similarity within Judaism is with women of rabbinic families who are said to have had charismatic authority.[35] However, there is no contemporary correlation. The conclusion must be that the tradition of Magdalene, "the fortress" and exorcist, is dissimilar to Palestinian Judaism. Consequently, this tradition passes the test of the criterion of dissimilarity.

With regard to the criterion of embarrassment, it is clear that the traditions of Magdalene became problematic, as they are devalued and made subservient to the traditions associated with the male exorcists, both in the canonical and extra-biblical literature. Later traditions include esoteric sayings and confrontations with Kepha.[36] While the revised tradition in Matthew and the other canonical Gospels make Magdalene the catalyst of communication with the male exorcists, this trend only confirms that these traditions were problematic, and her role was diminished. As such, the traditions relate to Magdalene's encounter meet the criterion of embarrassment.

Summary of Risk Analysis

An analysis of Matthew 28:1–10 has isolated the original form of the unit by employing the criteria of risk analysis. Based on this analysis, the event may be considered reliable in this revised form, subject to passing the remaining contextual tests.

Matthew 28:1–10 and the Contextual Tests

We now turn to contextual analyses. Here an event must be coherent with the sociological risk setting, including the subsistence struggle of the Galileans,

---

34. See the discussion earlier in this study on Magdalene; also see Dickie, *Magic and Magicians*, 93–184, on sorceresses in the ancient world to the late republic.

35. Janowitz, *Magic in the Roman World*, see chapter 6 and also footnote on page 100. While not explicitly tied to women "exorcists," women were directly linked to healings (i.e., driving out demons) with more than fifty-one of those associated with women married to or associated with rabbinic families.

36. *Gos. Thom.* 114; See Patterson, *Gospel of Thomas*, 249–51. In a discussion with Steve Patterson, August 19, 2015, we discussed the charismatic nature of Thomas, and the ecstatic nature that stood behind sayings tradition, i.e., in visions and revelations, that must have accompanied them. These sayings were likely part of visionary experiences, and so an ecstatic background to Thomas and its sapiential material must be considered.

the background from which they came to join Jesus' band of exorcists. The contextual risk tests can be found on pages 118 and 119.

Applying these contextual tests to the original tradition recovered from Matthew 28:1–10, given the risk analysis of Magdalene as an exorcist of Jesus (Luke 8:1–3) and employing the criteria of dissimilarity and embarrassment, the tradition clearly passes the first two tests.

With regard to the third, there is no evidence in the canonical Gospels that Magdalene returned to subsistence existence as an exorcist, or to activity related to subsistence fishing in Galilee.[37] However, the report of Magdalene's encounter with Jesus must have been impactful to the original band of exorcists, as the tradition is multiply attested (the Synoptics and John), and is also found in non-canonical sources. Magdalene must have contacted the male exorcists in Galilee, certainly their leader, Kepha, for this is remembered in all traditions. The risk criteria employed also confirm its impact. Both the *Gospel of Thomas* and the *Gospel of Mary* report Magdalene's discussion with Kepha and other exorcists as to her interaction with Jesus post-crucifixion, and Jesus' defense of Magdalene as an equal to the male exorcists, i.e., her becoming male.[38] Her presence with them would indicate that Magdalene continued to be considered an exorcist post-crucifixion. Consequently, contextual evidence suggests that Magdalene was considered an exorcist who would continue not only practicing but also receiving revelations and guidance from the risen Lord. She likely never abandoned her role as such. Elements of the tradition, based on risk analysis, would indicate that she reported that Jesus was active; that she had a vision at the tomb and then encountered Jesus, not as a ghost, but in a substantive form, whether in a vision or trance.[39] This tradition therefore passes the third test.

The last test evaluates whether encounters with Jesus, post-crucifixion, led the Galileans to again abandon subsistence existence and return to their war on Satan. Here we must count Magdalene fully as one of the Galilean exorcists whose perilous risk was heightened following her encounter with Jesus. While there is no confirmation that Magdalene continued exorcism in the synoptic tradition or in John, extracanonical traditions confirm that

---

37. That the tradition has Jesus ordering Mary to tell the exorcists to go to Galilee (not to a hiding place in Jerusalem, a later addition and Lukan creation that conflicts with Mark, Matthew, and John *20:17*) confirms it is original, as this is where the exorcists fled.

38. If she becomes like a "male," i.e., what was perceived in the ancient world as the complete human being reflected in male form. See Meyer, "Making Mary Male," 554–70. For this she would have cut her hair and worn male clothing. See below on the discussion of the *Gospel of Mary* and the analysis by Karen King.

39. As noted, encounters with the active spirits of the dead included material activity and contact.

Magdalene was an active and influential member among the remaining exorcists in Galilee and provided instruction to them about her vision of Jesus and her continuing relationship with him. The communication is portrayed as prior to their reengagement in their itinerant activity—indeed that she was the catalyst for doing so. The tradition of this influence is best captured in the *Gospel of Mary*, which is a fragmented document of the second century,[40] but may have traditions that predate the canonical Gospels.

> *Gospel of Mary*, Chapter 5:
> 1. But they were grieved. They wept greatly, saying: How shall we go to the gentiles and preach the gospel of the Kingdom of the Son of Man? If they did not spare him, how will they spare us?
> 2. Then Mary stood up, greeted them all, and said to her brethren, Do not weep and do not grieve nor be irresolute, for his grace will be entirely with you and will protect you.
> 3. But rather, let us praise his greatness, for he has prepared us and made us into Men.
> 4. When Mary said this, she turned their hearts to the Good, and they began to discuss the words of the Savior.
> 5. Peter said to Mary, Sister, we know that the Savior loved you more than the rest of women.
> 6. Tell us the words of the Savior, which you remember which you know, but we do not, nor have we heard them.
> 7. Mary answered and said: What is hidden from you I will proclaim to you.
> 8. And she began to speak to them these words: I, she said, I saw the Lord in a vision and I said to him, Lord, I saw you today in a vision. He answered and said to me,
> 9. Blessed are you that you did not waver at the sight of me. For where the mind is there is the treasure.
> 10. I said to him, Lord, how does he who sees the vision see it, through the soul or through the spirit?
> 11. The Savior answered and said, He does not see through the soul nor through the spirit, but the mind that is between the two that is what sees the vision and it is [. . .]
>
> Chapter 9:

---

40. King argues for composition between 30–130 CE; King, *Gospel of Mary*, 148.

1. When Mary had said this, she fell silent, since it was to this point that the Savior had spoken with her.
2. But Andrew answered and said to the brethren, Say what you wish to say about what she has said. I at least do not believe that the Savior said this. For certainly these teachings are strange ideas.
3. Peter answered and spoke concerning these same things.
4. He questioned them about the Savior: Did he really speak privately with a woman and not openly to us? Are we to turn about and all listen to her? Did he prefer her to us?
5. Then Mary wept and said to Peter, My brother Peter, what do you think? Do you think that I have thought this up myself in my heart, or that I am lying about the Savior?
6. Levi answered and said to Peter, Peter, you have always been hot tempered.
7. Now I see you contending against the woman like the adversaries.
8. But if the Savior made her worthy, who are you indeed to reject her? Surely the Savior knows her very well.
9. That is why he loved her more than us. Rather let us be ashamed and put on the perfect Man, and separate as he commanded us and preach the gospel, not laying down any other rule or other law beyond what the Savior said.
10. And when they heard this they began to go forth to proclaim and to preach.

A review of this tradition alone confirms that Magdalene was believed to have influenced the return to subsistence existence as exorcists and *apostoloi* of Jesus post-crucifixion. As such, the last contextual test is also passed.

Conclusions on the Veracity of Matthew 28:1–10

Based on the risk and analytical criteria employed, combined with contextual analysis, the tradition that stands behind Matthew 28:1–10 should be considered an authentic post-crucifixion encounter with Jesus. In the context of human risk experience, this encounter with Magdalene is reliable in its recovered contemporary context and setting. The order of appearances then is emerging as follows:

Magdalene, "the fortress," a powerful Galilean female exorcist of Jesus that had taken control of multiple demons, has been abandoned in Jerusalem post-crucifixion. All of the male exorcists fled to Galilee and are in hiding. Magdalene, desperate to determine the fate of her master, goes to the tomb, facing deadly perilous risks. She intentionally arrives at the very time spirits, demons, and evil are active and seek victims. This is also the time to engage in special rites to discover if the spirit and soul of Jesus have been annihilated. She brings special herbs and roots of the exorcist and then enters into a trance. An angel confirms Jesus' spirit has vacated the tomb and that he is free and active—he has not been annihilated under a curse. Magdalene's rites and activity at the tomb facilitate the return of Jesus by the power of the spirit that possesses him, the *daktuo theou*. Magdalene encounters Jesus. While the tradition is that she is to immediately contact the male exorcists, this tradition is clearly a subjugation of the Magdalene's encounter. Magdalene's perilous risk is significantly heightened. She has contacted a condemned dark magician executed by the powerful elite and now publicly admits she has been in contact with him. Her life is in danger, and if captured, she would be immediately killed. She escapes to Galilee and locates the male exorcists, still in hiding, protected by kin, working as fishermen through the night to avoid discovery. Magdalene communicates her encounter. There is no doubt at her report, and she begins to encourage a return to Jesus' war on Satan and demonic imperialism. Magdalene confirms that Jesus would contact them in Galilee.

Kepha, the leader of the male exorcists, has returned to subsistence life on Galilee, hiding and working through the night to help feed himself and his kin. His perilous risk is significantly heightened by his escape, and his abandonment of Jesus to his enemies. Kepha is now subject to capture and death, or attack by demons that he expelled since he is no longer under the protection of Jesus and the "finger of God." He had also abandoned Jesus to demonic enemies and to satanic forces. Kepha faces retribution. While in Galilee, Kepha encounters the spirit of Jesus who approaches and communicates with Kepha. Soon afterwards, Kepha goes to the sacred mountain where he and other exorcists had been selected and then trained by Jesus to be ecstatics and exorcists. He may have brought others with him and enters into a trance where he encounters Jesus. Kepha and the remaining male exorcists decide to abandon subsistence existence on Galilee and reenter the war on Satan. The list of practices to be embraced by the exorcists is then delineated through an encounter with Jesus, evidenced in the appendix to Mark, defining the authentic witnesses to Jesus post-crucifixion, i.e., they must demonstrate these charismatic practices to be counted among the valid *apostoloi*. This includes Magdalene.

These traditions represent the nascent post-crucifixion events that led to encounters with Jesus.

MATTHEW 28:16–20: MASS VISIONS AND TRANCES IN THE ANCIENT WORLD

Jesus is "seen," or is "perceived" (*idontes*) by the "eleven" (i.e., purportedly, the remaining male Galilean exorcists that fled Jerusalem *sans* Judas) on a mountain in Galilee. Who led them there or why they went to that particular mountain location is not fully explained, only that Jesus had "told them." Although not named, some of the eleven "doubt" (*de edistasan*), meaning they do not believe they encountered Jesus, or the same Jesus, whether materially, in a vision or trance—*a shocking admission*.[41] This implies that there were those of repute (i.e., of the original exorcists of Jesus—not necessarily those in the final lists of apostles named in Mark 3:13–19, Matthew 10:2, Luke 6:12–19)[42] who doubt that they encountered Jesus post-crucifixion, and so refused to embrace the same mitigating practices of perilous risk, i.e., returning to the war on Satan, as the other exorcists. From the tradition of Jesus' metamorphosis (Mark 9:2–8, as noted, a post-crucifixion encounter)[43] we do know the names of three who are said to have encountered Jesus on

---

41. Explanations that this "doubt" is a personal response to Jesus' command to continue proclaiming the *euangelion* do not fit this context. Personal doubt has nothing to do with the risk context of this passage, and there is no paranesis on such behavior, as there is in John 20:24–29. Here the community of John is explicit that Thomas was at one time a doubter, but when he actually is invited to feel the wounds of Jesus, i.e., a material resurrection that portends a future *Parousia*, does he then believe in the passion and resurrection of Jesus. While the Matthean passage may be a critique on a community associated with Thomas, it is not yet named. However, John was composed two decades after the composition of Matthew and likely knew of communities that held to salvific sayings associated with the *Gospel of Thomas*, so he is named. Consequently, the Matthean community may have been facing disruption from another community that held to salvific wisdom sayings versus a resurrection of Jesus and future *Parousia*, but the community here is not yet named. In John (90–110 CE), that community is known and does ascribe to salvific sayings of the Thomas tradition. The community of John combats this threat by appealing to an eyewitness, the "disciple whom Jesus loved," who attests that Thomas was a doubter, but then became the most ardent believer in the resurrection and future *Parousia*, thereby making that competing community heretics.

42. See the discussion of the identity of the "twelve" being the same as Jesus' exorcists or others that became known as "the Twelve" in Koester, *Introduction*, 8. In fact, the Twelve mentioned by Paul in 1 Corinthians 15:5 can not be exactly identical as the eleven who went to the mountain here in Matthew. Paul recounts that the Twelve were with Kepha, and all were witnesses to the resurrection, active in defending this witness (i.e., many still available to confirm their experience). Matthew allows that some of the original exorcists did not believe they had encountered Jesus, and so those listed in Mathew 10:2 likely reflect the list of those who witnessed and did not doubt, drawn from the "disciples" who followed Jesus and named by Kepha as the Twelve. See Jenott, *Gospel of Judas*, 40–44.

43. See discussion above on Mark 9:2–8 recovered by risk and contextual analysis.

a mountain in Galilee—Kepha and *Boanerges*, i.e., Yohannes or Yecob, the "sons of thunder."[44] These three clearly were never considered as "doubters" in early Christianity. So, then, why was such a troubling oral tradition of doubt retained in Mathew some fifty-five years after the crucifixion (80 to 85 CE, when Matthew was compiled by its editor/redactor)? What risks existed for the Matthean communities that necessitated recounting this tradition of doubt (it could have easily been omitted). It is an embarrassing tradition—doubt among some of Jesus' eleven original exorcists! Matthew crystallized this embarrassment in a widely-circulated community document that was read to its members and to proselytes in charismatic gatherings for decades.[45] While the scope of this study can not reconstruct the Matthean community or its practices,[46] it can examine specific risks. To mention "doubters" is a mitigation to an existing perilous risk, i.e., that some of Jesus' Galilean exorcists could no longer be considered reliable, implying they represent heretical competitive beliefs to the community. Consequently, this tradition served a risk-mitigating function for some time. What was this risk? To evaluate how it functioned as a countermeasure, the tradition must be analyzed contextually.

The most obvious explanation for its retention is rather stunning; namely, that some of Jesus' chosen exorcists (i.e., the original Galilean's trained by Jesus) did not have, or did not accept, a post-crucifixion encounter where a manifestation of the risen Jesus was present or essential. Rather, these men or women, who still claimed authority and had followings (and so were in competition with the Matthean community, or else they would be identified as "doubters"), had what they claimed were alternate ecstatic, transformational encounters that were considered dangerous or threatening to the Matthean community, and that clearly denied the need to adhere to a manifestation of Jesus and a future *Parousia*. For the Matthean community, they were not to be counted among the legitimate *apostoloi*. Is there early evidence for such communities in conflict by the time Matthew was composed in 80–85 CE?

Paul's letters, particularly in 1 and 2 Corinthians (54–57 CE), confirm a tension between claims of authority linked to various post-resurrection encounters and the practices they engendered. For example, in his chronological list of encounters in 1 Corinthians 15:1–9 Paul attempts to mute his opponents' claims to legitimacy by linking a material encounter with

---

44. Two of these are confirmed by Paul in Galatians 2:9.

45. Hengel, *Four Gospels*, 19–20.

46. See Koester, *Introduction*, 44–49, 109, and Koester, *Ancient Christian Gospels*, 317; the community likely was located in Roman-occupied Syria after the destruction of Jerusalem (70 CE).

Jesus and future *Parousia* to the legitimacy of a salvific "gospel." Paul's own post-crucifixion encounters with Jesus were different from those reported in Luke, Matthew, and Mark, as well as in John. Paul's multiple encounters appear to have been *both* visionary (trance-like experiences and spirit transportation, still considered in the ancient world as a material encounter[47]) as well as substantive (*opthe*, that is, Paul clearly states he saw Jesus *with his own eyes*).[48] They also include revelations, including spiritual insight, paranesis, wisdom, and understanding of mysteries and hidden secrets given to him by Jesus.[49] But none of this matters to Paul's opponents who have arrived in Corinth from Jerusalem. They deny a future *Parousia*, or the need to assign apostleship to a resurrection encounter. Indeed, because Paul does not adhere to their understanding of salvation, he is a liar and charlatan—a profiteer.[50] For them, salvific knowledge and transformation come through *gnosis* of Jesus' wisdom sayings and immediate unison with the divine achieved through them, which is freeing and makes them "kings," able to act as they wish in this ethereal world without harm. Death has no meaning any longer, so why would there ever need to be a physical resurrection of Jesus? He is divine and his sayings provide access to salvation now. If this view goes back to the Galilean setting, such as with Mary or another of Jesus' exorcist's authority, we are witness to a remarkable conflict over orthodoxy that emerged at the very origin of primitive Christianity, leading to multiple trajectories that claimed authoritative interpretation of the Jesus event.

Does such a community and document exist? Indeed, the *Gospel of Thomas* would suggest that there were other ecstatic experiences considered just as legitimate to some communities; ones that were not reliant on an empty tomb, apocalyptic *Parousia* and future judgment, or reliance on an encounter with the risen Jesus. Jesus was the living Lord when present and after his departure. A union with the divine was realized immediately through mystical encounter with Jesus' words as the "living" one, where charismatic sayings awakened one's spirit and were salvific—a mysterious awakening and reuniting of the true self with the divine—a transformation

---

47. Even Acts continues this tradition five decades later, Acts 9:1–19.

48. Gal 1:15–16; 1 Cor 9:1, 15:1–9, 50–54 (not a body of flesh and blood, but a spiritual body); 1 Cor 12:2 (the visit to the third heaven).

49. 1 Cor 13:2, 14:2, 15:5; 2 Cor 12:1–7; also, 1 Thess 4:17; Rom 16:25; also in the sense of *gnosis*, special knowledge, 1 Cor 12:8, but given by the Spirit. Paul's receiving instructions from Jesus, 1 Cor 7:1–12, 11:23.

50. Busse, *Enemies*, 82–147.

by encountering heavenly wisdom in salvific esoteric sayings of the divine one, reuniting one's soul with God immediately.[51]

One of Jesus' exorcists, *Toma* (the "twin," a name given by Jesus,[52] in Greek, *didymas*), is said to have been the source and authority for such esoteric wisdom sayings and practices passed to him by Jesus. Salvific esoteric wisdom trajectories, such as that in the *Gospel of Thomas*, are found in the earliest strata of tradition, originating perhaps during Jesus' charismatic activity in Galilee.[53] As noted, in 51 to 54 CE, Paul encountered well-established and popular "super apostles" (*huper apostolon*), carrying persuasive letters of recommendation on their behalf (2 Cor 3:1), most likely from James, brother of Jesus, who may have espoused the salvific *logoi* tradition ultimately captured in the *Gospel of Thomas*.[54] Paul's vigorous confrontation with these *huper apostolon* in 1 and 2 Corinthians includes his mimicking of esoteric sayings of Jesus similar to those in Thomas, or in a primitive version of Q, that stood behind the final version of Q and Thomas.[55] As Koester notes, "The basis of the *Gospel of Thomas* is a sayings collection which is more primitive than the canonical Gospels, even though its basic principal is not related to the creed of the passion and resurrection."[56] Thomas has no expectation of a general resurrection to come; access to the divine is already present in the charismatic *logoi* of Jesus. The Matthean community is one that rejected the legitimacy of any *apostoloi* who did not experience a substantive if not physical resurrection encounter with Jesus, as well as initiate new followers with baptism, a mystery rite of unification with the divine in preparation for the *Parousia*. Only these *apostoloi* had been given

---

51. See the discussion below on the *Gospel of Thomas* and Stephen Patterson's research and conclusions.

52. This may have also been an exorcist name awarded by Jesus, i.e., the "twin" being Jesus' twin, an exorcist who shares the same authority and power.

53. An example is in Davies, *Gospel of Thomas and Christian Wisdom*, XXXIV and XXXV, sayings 14 and 53. Also see Kloppenborg and Meyer, *Q-Thomas Reader*, 102, Saying 65, the parable of the wicked tenants, a familiar situation in Galilee. Both Q and Thomas may have originated from a common salvific wisdom tradition of Jesus sayings.

54. By implication, persuasive letters, like those of the super apostles, must have come from those of substantive reputation, i.e., from Jesus' brother, James, or others of belonging to Jesus' original exorcists, including Kepha or even Mary.

55. Patterson, *Gospel of Thomas and Christian Origins*, 245–46, 257, and Patterson, "Paul and the Jesus Tradition," 23–41. Koester believes that 1 Corinthians 2:9 was from an early version of Q; see Koester, "One Jesus," 158–204, and Koester, *Ancient Christian Gospels*, 58–59. The saying of Jesus would indicate that competing views of its meaning are in play very early.

56. Koester, "One Jesus," 186.

the right, through these certain rituals and practices, to affect escape from perilous risk of death and annihilation of the soul.

Consequently, Matthew 28:17 confirms there were competing risk traditions about Jesus post-crucifixion among those who followed him— some of the Galilean exorcists he trained. These risk traditions created conflict among vying communities and their ecstatic rites—rites that afforded safety and protection from evil, demonic pollution, and death. The countermeasure was to reject what were considered errant communities and deny the legitimacy of their leaders—something Paul directly experienced from powerful opponents linked with Jerusalem.[57] He was tersely rejected by the "super apostles," and earlier by men (false brothers, *psuedadelphous*) sent by James,[58] both of whom (just like the Matthean community) practiced charismatic baptism. Consequently, it is important to further explore the command of Jesus on the mountain to baptize embedded in the Matthean encounter.

For those exorcists on the mountain, Jesus approaches (*proselthon*) and makes a demand: "Having gone [Go!], instruct and make adherents [*mathetuesate*][59] of all people, *baptizing* them . . ." This encounter and the accompanying demand are similar to contemporary examples in the Greco-Roman world with the untimely dead or the dead by violence. Here the restless spirit of the deceased makes demands on living relatives, or others, in order to find rest or to seek retribution on enemies, particularly the murderers.[60] Jesus makes a similar demand on his exorcists, one that fits its contemporary risk setting and expectations of the first-century world. *However,* in this case they are commanded to remain itinerant exorcists. Instead of revenge, the exorcists' primary role is now to perform an ecstatic, mystical rite that is founded on something contrary to these other contemporary encounters with the dead; namely, a charismatic act of love, not revenge, that is salvific and a rescue[61] for those who are possessed and afflicted; liberation for the demon-possessed and Satan. Even those who killed him, if they will listen and act, can receive this rite. Consequently, instead of retribution, this post-crucifixion encounter with Jesus remarkably demands *agape*, salvific love, which can only reflect a core teaching that echoes the message and

---

57. Thus the accusations against Paul in Galatians, 1 and 2 Corinthians.

58. Gal 2:4, 11–13.

59. Greek, imperative form—teach, inform, in this case give them understanding that, when accompanied by powerful rites, is transformative.

60. Ogden, *Magic*, 146–48, 158, 322–23, and there are several other examples provided by Ogden.

61. And thus mitigate perilous risk.

practices of the historical Jesus.⁶² It is this unique response of love that differentiated the itinerancy of Jesus' exorcists from other magicians, exorcists, ecstatics, and sorcerers who interacted with or were controlled by the spirits of the dead.⁶³ There are no other contemporaneous examples of instructions like these given to the living by those killed by violence. This command and its link to baptism must be considered reliable and a legitimate extension of Jesus' war on Satan by the itinerant exorcists who continued his conflict after this encounter. This became the bridge between the Jesus of history and the post-crucifixion experiences of Jesus by certain exorcists who practiced *agape*, love, based on this encounter.

In Matthew, the risen Jesus orders a mystical baptism of unification with powerful, divine names—a command to his believing exorcists. Baptism, undoubtedly similar to the baptism of John,⁶⁴ was a substantive transformational rite, and may also have been accompanied by recitation of other sacred words. As such, baptism unites the disciple/learner with divine protection from perilous risks and death. They are to be immersed in water by legitimate *apostoloi*, those who are charismatics having had encounters with Jesus. For Matthew, legitimate charismatics and teachers of Jesus' words and wisdom, post-crucifixion, must baptize concurrent with these names being pronounced to enact a powerful union, a new being, joined with and under the protection of the Father (the *Abba* of Jesus), *Abbás* spirit, the Holy Spirit, that empowered the exorcist Jesus (i.e., by the "finger of God," who gives Jesus *pasa exousia*, unlimited authority, Matthew 28:18) and the risen "Son" who is active and maintains this authority to abolish demons and cast out the curse that brings death and who is coming with the *Parousia*. Such ritual acts "in the name of" were intentional,⁶⁵ that is, they extended the power of that entity to the individual receiving rites, thereby becoming united in the sense of imbuing or saturating the initiate with divine protection, including the *immediate* award of authority that will be (or in some cases *is*) a countermeasure to death.⁶⁶ This form of baptism was a fully charismatic

---

62. Koester, *From Jesus to the Gospels*, 231.

63. Herod assumed the spirit of murdered John the Baptist had been taken by Jesus for retribution against him, Mark 6:16.

64. The baptism of John led Jesus to have an ecstatic experience and hear the voice of God, and then be driven to confront Satan in the demon-controlled hills of Judea, Mark 1:9–11.

65. See Paul in 1 Corinthians 1:13 as an example.

66. These rites could also bring punishment and a curse of destruction, such as Paul's spirit transport to Corinth and condemnation in the name of Jesus in 1 Corinthians 5:4. There is no doubt that Paul practiced the use of Jesus' name in rites. This is exactly what is occurring mystically in this example.

and ecstatic countermeasure, i.e., an act of unison with the divine and protection from evil and satanic forces, including, as noted, possession or the disease of death that led to the capture or annihilation of the spirit. Those delivering this baptism allow the adherent to achieve protection now, and if they die, to "sleep," only to be awakened when the general resurrection comes, which was imminent—an expectation held by Paul and Jesus.[67] This is the understanding of baptism, based on the resurrection of Jesus, in Matthew. But, like the conflict between salvation through baptism by those who adhere to a resurrected Jesus from the dead, there is evidence that there was a perilous risk conflict that held baptism to be a rite of accepting the salvific wisdom sayings of Jesus and uniting immediately with the divine if conducted by *apostoloi* that insisted on this view.

Indeed, the post-crucifixion encounter and command of Jesus in Matthew 28:16-20 to baptize points to the confrontation between various groups and trajectories that associated their safety with itinerant "apostles" or "fathers" (*pateras*)[68] who baptized them in primitive Christian *ecclesiae*; a confrontation that is again evident in conflict between Paul and his opponents in 1 and 2 Corinthians. Paul is accused of being a false apostle, a charlatan, also because he does not require baptism and does not regularly baptize.[69] Paul's saving "gospel" is in the mercy of the cross and its power—the death, burial, and resurrection of Jesus (1 Cor 15:1-3)—and the *Parousia* to come for those who suffer, hold fast to faith in the risen Son, and evidence the transformation to salvation by practicing love. The sacrifice of Jesus breaks the curse of death, brought on by sin that kills.[70] His sacrifice[71] holds out a promise of justification at judgment for those who wait in faith for the return of Jesus as messiah, i.e., Jesus the *Christos*. When the *Parousia* occurs, a transformation into a spiritual body (*soma pneumatikon*), presumably like that of Jesus (seen by Paul), occurs for the faithful (1 Cor 15:44). Consequently, safety is in justification by faith (like the faith of Jesus), the countermeasure to death, not only in rites of baptism.

For Paul's opponents in Corinth, the "super apostles" (2 Cor 11:5) and their followers who are already "kings" (i.e., in a state of union with the divine and free from the fear of death, 1 Cor 4:8), baptism is the essential, transformational, mystical rite acknowledging wisdom salvation via Jesus'

---

67. 1 Thess 4:16; 1 Thessalonians was the earliest writing now found in the New Testament, written by Paul between 42-49 CE. A saying of Jesus: "Some of you standing here will not taste death until they see the kingdom of God coming with power," Mark 9:1.

68. 1 Cor 4:15.

69. 1 Cor 1:14, 17.

70. For Paul, the curse is revealed and made active by the Law evoking death.

71. 1 Cor 5:17.

efficacious sayings. Baptism must be conducted by only their special *apostoloi*; i.e., those who are the conduits of passage from death to life (where baptism is central in an initiation to safety). Baptism in these apostles' names unites the initiate with the divine immediately. Perilous risks, including death of the soul, are neutralized—one is no longer bonded to death.[72] Initiates find awakening in the *logoi* of Jesus. Shedding this body means unison with the Lord.

> I shall give you what no eye has seen and what no ear has heard and what no hand has touched and what has never occurred to the human mind (*Gos. Thom.* 17).

The saying is about the awakening, revealing one's true state as united with the divine, the child, an androgynous being. For Paul, this saying is comprehensible only if understood in the context of his "gospel" of the death, burial, and resurrection of Jesus, and thus, the future *Parousia*.[73]

> None of the rulers of this age understood it, for if they had, they would not have crucified the Lord of glory (1 Cor 2:8).

He executes a curse on anyone teaching otherwise![74] For Paul, baptism, if employed, is burial in the death and resurrection of Jesus. But this is not necessarily what the saying of Jesus in Matthew 28 implies. There can be multiple trajectories in the application and interpretation of these sayings. In fact, interestingly, Paul's opponents seem to share a similar trajectory to that reflected in Matthew 28, as Jesus further instructs, "teach[ing] [those baptized] to keep [or to act on] whatever I direct you and be perceiving." This saying of Jesus can be interpreted as a directive to the apostles to act as conduits of wisdom of the living Lord, i.e., to continue passing on divine salvific wisdom, and with them, the protection they provide (e.g., like the "living one" in Thomas) until "the end of the age." Consequently, the event on the Galilean mountain in Matthew 28 demonstrates how sayings of Jesus became the catalyst for different trajectories of their application and interpretation (i.e., to meet the needs of vying communities). Indeed, clearly, this led to the ongoing confrontation between the Pauline *ecclesiae*[75] (baptism was optional) and communities associated with the salvific sayings, such as the *Gospel of Thomas*. Moreover, they were linked to a sayings tradition whose authority rested with Thomas, who was later known in ancient

---

72. Patterson, *Gospel of Thomas*, 28, 31, 121, 137–38, 249–51.

73. Patterson, *Gospel of Thomas*, 251–58.

74. Gal 1:8. It is for this reason that Betz calls Galatians a "magical" book; Betz, "Letter to the Galatians," 352–53.

75. And so, the legitimacy of Paul's "gospel" and apostleship.

Christianity as "the doubter." As a result, while Paul is battling the super apostles' salvific wisdom and esoteric baptism, the Matthean community appears to be battling on at least two fronts—both the Pauline community (i.e., that devalued baptism for faith alone in the risen Lord) and the community of the sayings-wisdom salvation tradition and its esoteric baptism as "doubters." What is evident is the primitive battle for orthodoxy in early Christianity originated from the event on the mountain in Galilee and Jesus' sayings that were remembered by those present. What mountain was this?

The location of the Matthean encounter is most likely the sacred mountain in Galilee, the modern *Har Tavor*,[76] which, based on the number of events on this mountain,[77] must have been well known to the exorcists and the primitive community who later visited in the hopes of having a similar ecstatic experience.[78] The well-developed oral tradition repeated by Paul in 1 Corinthians 15:1–5 states that Kepha and then the "twelve" saw Jesus. In Matthew we have eleven. So who then are these twelve?

The paid informant and assassin, Judas, had been killed, and we know of one to three who did ultimately see Jesus based on traditional reminiscences of the metamorphosis (as noted, likely only Kepha has this vision). The names of the Twelve vary in the canonical lists. Acts 1:12–26 confirms that others were added to complete the Twelve, using divination by lots,[79] a practice also used by the High Priest to settle questions, as the lots were influenced by God. The redactor/editor of Matthew brings consistency to the events following the crucifixion by eliminating Judas, implying that eleven

---

76. Likely, Mt. Tabor (*Har Tavor*), held to be sacred by Jews (Ps 89:12) and Pagans (Baal Tabor, Hos 5:1), like Mt. Hermon. See Freyne, *Jesus*, 57. Not as in Luke the Mount of Olives (as has been demonstrated, the editor/redactor of Luke wishes to show the Jesus movement having successfully spread from Jerusalem to Rome). Galilee is where the earliest tradition states the exorcists encountered Jesus. Risk analysis has demonstrated that this tradition coincides with the escape of the exorcists from Jerusalem, abandoning Mary and perhaps other women exorcists behind. The Lukan theology attempts to smooth over the embarrassment of their abandonment of Jesus and flight to Galilee by having them remain in Jerusalem.

77. The selection and training of the exorcists; the location of Jesus' ecstatic prayer and retreats to solitude for days; the metamorphosis of Jesus and trance of Kepha; the teaching to the exorcists and others to name the most prominent events on the mountain.

78. The location was attested in the early second century, as 2 Peter 1:17–18 includes this tradition, which predates the letter likely by decades. In addition, pilgrims to Mt. Tabor, for example, may have been visiting sites on this mountain as early as the second century, but is well attested by the fourth century, including visits by Melito Bishop of Sardis, Origen, and Alexander from Cappadocia. See Charlesworth, *James, Jesus, and Archaeology*, 167–68.

79. Luijendijk, *Forbidden Oracles?*, 2–3. This is a fascinating analysis of a Coptic codex of oracles, "retrieving them through a divinatory procedure ascribed by lot."

remained, that is until some doubted! As such, it is entirely likely that Jesus did select twelve, as later practices of those who followed Jesus reflect the practices that the person established; so the sacred and mystical reconstitution of the kingdom of God and Israel's twelve tribes, being rescued from Satan his demons, is suggested and retained by Matthew. However, this does not confirm that twelve went to the sacred mountain. There is no evidence of a spiritual journey, by vision or trance to the sacred mountain here. The trip is portrayed as physical. Yet, this is the place where visionary experiences did occur, including the visionary trance of Kepha, and the visionary experience of John in the *Apocalypse of John the Theologian*. Origen, the theologian and scholar (184 to 254 CE), quotes the *Gospel According to the Hebrews*, where Jesus says that the Holy Spirit had driven him (pulled by the hair) to *Har Tavor*.[80] These traditions continued well into the fourth century.[81] Thus, travel to the sacred mountain is emphasized for generations, as it was most likely a well-known destination to the Matthean community that may have resided in Antioch, Syria.[82] Since both pagans and Jews considered *Har Tavor* a sacred mountain, for the exorcists to physically go to this place (some 17 miles from Capernaum, for example), would constitute substantial risk, i.e., they accepted the risk of being seen, which, since they were hunted, would indicate that their perilous risk was heightened. It is possible that their travel was at night to reduce the chance of discovery (as they did when returning to subsistence fishing). Travel to this sacred mountain by several exorcists would have been suspicious and contrary to the Roman restriction of the gathering of any size group,[83] particularly Galileans. Once they arrived, a vision or encounter occurred, and Jesus spoke to them on the sacred mountain.

Clearly, the context of this tradition is complex. We now turn to risk analysis of Matthew 28:16–20.

Matthew 28:16–20 and Qualitative Risk Analysis

With this context set, we can begin our risk analysis of the unit, employing, first, qualitative risk. In this analysis, the encounter can not be a

---

80. Charlesworth, *James, Jesus, and Archaeology*, 173.

81. Charlesworth, *James, Jesus, and Archaeology*, 173–75.

82. Kloppenberg, *Excavating Q*, 172: "The facts that Q was used by Matthew, whose provenance may be Syrian, and it bears some relationship to the *Gospel of Thomas*, which may have come from Syria (Koester, *Introduction*, 127–28), might invite the conclusion that Q was composed in an area adjacent to Syria."

83. Livy, *The Founding of the City*, 39.14.

countermeasure to the elite, but must heighten the perilous risk of the Galilean exorcists and the conflict with opponents.

Evidence of heightened risks for the Galilean exorcist is layered in the tradition. The travel to the sacred mountain and need to avoid detection and capture shortly after Jesus' crucifixion; the encounter with Jesus and his demand not only to continue itinerant travel and illegal activity as exorcists, but to conduct a very public mystical rite where abundant water was available, i.e., where people would gather, including spies and sympathizers of the Herodians in Palestine (but not out of Palestine). Initiates are to be baptized in the name of a crucified Jewish criminal now identified as the "Son of God," repeating this name and designation in association with a pseudonym of God, Father, as well as the Spirit, making Jesus the Son equal to God, a blasphemy. The danger involved in all of these activities was perilous and, therefore, passes the test of qualitative risk analysis.

Matthew 28:16–20 and the Criteria of Dissimilarity and Embarrassment

In this test, encounters must differ from the needs and influence of the early church on the one hand and first-century Judaism in Palestine on the other.

To begin, the tradition has been redacted to fit the needs of the early church. The presumption of the baptism and use of the names in association with such a public event would fit the contextual world of a Syrian, Matthean community some fifty years after the crucifixion of Jesus. Syrian Antioch became a center of Christian activity at this time, and as noted was the area in which both a primitive version of an esoteric sayings tradition was composed, one that stood behind both Q and Thomas. The "doubt" of some of the eleven would fit the context of a tradition, such as the Gospel ascribed to Toma Didymas, where he, one of the eleven exorcists renamed by Jesus, was identified by a community as the source of these traditions and their authority—a competing tradition to that of Matthew; i.e., why he is typified as the "doubter" in later traditions. The redactor/editor of Matthew would only acknowledge doubt among the eleven if this troubling tradition were not used to mitigate a present risk to that community of significance. Perilous risk of this magnitude must be associated with spurious traditions ascribed to one of the Twelve by the Matthean community, and one that was substantive and considered dangerous, meaning it was persuasive and divisive.

Further, the tradition legitimates the expansion of the practices and the Matthean Gospel tradition into the gentile world, such as Syrian

Antioch,[84] based on a command of Jesus, post-crucifixion. In addition, the use of the words of rite and "Son" and association with Father and Spirit are well-developed Christological titles and a formula, all reflecting a second- or third-generation usage in an equally developed liturgical rite of a Christian community. In this case, the liturgy is a reflection of the Matthean rites. Consequently, the tradition has been adapted to meet the needs of early Christianity.

Is the tradition unique to Palestinian Judaism, particularly with regard to Jesus' demand for charismatic baptism in Matthew 28? This answer is made complex by the extant contemporary sources previously cited, whether from Qumran and among the Essenes[85] to John the Baptist at Aenon.[86] At first blush the command of Jesus to baptize and employ powerful names in a mystical union with the divine, which is very likely a reflection of the original practices of Jesus' band of exorcists, would appear to be distinct from the expectations of Judaism based what can be recovered concerning these sources, including that of John the Baptist.[87] Yet, it is clear that the tradition concerning John has been recast by Josephus to make the Baptist more acceptable to authorities and the literate of a Roman Hellenized society[88] (as opposed to Herod and the Jerusalem elite, whom Josephus portrays as corrupted and evil). Furthermore, the use of the Jewish ritual bath, the Mikveh, to regain ritual purity by immersion (e.g., to enter the Temple) and the practices of John are carefully associated with words such as "virtue,"

---

84. Matthew 17:24–27 correctly identifies two *didrachmae* as exactly equal to the *stater*, the official coin of Greece or Lydia used in the empire, which only occurred in Antioch or Damascus, i.e., the province of Syria. See also Streeter, *Four Gospels*, 500–523.

85. Immersion was used in initiation into the cult, annual commitment and renewal, and then in daily purification—See *The Community Rule, Manual of Discipline* (1QS 5:13–14), and the *Purity Texts* (4Q 274–276). See also Fitzmyer, *Dead Sea Scrolls and Christian Origins*, 19–21 The Qumran initiation and purification rites were full rituals with words and pronouncements.

86. See the introduction to this problem citing various scholars in Johnson, *The Rites of Christian Initiation*, 2–17.

87. Josephus, *Ant.* 18.5.2: "Now some of the Jews thought that the destruction of Herod's army came from God, and that very justly, as a punishment of what he did against John, that was called the Baptist: for Herod slew him, who was a good man, and commanded the Jews to exercise virtue, both as to righteousness towards one another, and piety towards God, and so to come to baptism; for that the washing [with water] would be acceptable to him, if they made use of it, not in order to the putting away [or the remission] of some sins [only], but for the purification of the body; supposing still that the soul was thoroughly purified beforehand by righteousness."

88. The use of virtue, justice, and piety towards God are all Roman traits and likely had nothing to do with the historical John and his charismatic practices, including his baptism.

"justice," and "piety towards God." These are words good citizens of Rome would practice. Consequently, we can not rely on these accounts without placing them in a risk context and evaluating their outcome.[89]

As such, it is certain that there were differing interpretations as to the Jewish and Hellenistic practice and meaning of baptism in the first century, and the use of immersion and water, particularly for conversion, or uniting with the divine.[90] So the question is not necessarily if the Matthean practices were unique to Palestinian Judaism of the first century, as we don't know; but if the Matthean version is simply another expression of this diversity, and, moreover, is a later "Christianized" version of the original understanding and practice of baptism among Jesus' earliest followers,[91] then it can not be distinct from first-century Judaism. Thus, while the tradition in Matthew 28 carries forward a similar charismatic and mystical baptism to that experienced by Jesus, and some of Jesus' exorcists were followers of John before joining Jesus' band,[92] there is little correlation between the rites demanded in Matthew and the practices of the baptism of Jesus that can be recovered. Consequently, the baptism in Matthew 28 is a fully Christian charismatic rite, even distinct from the experience of Jesus recorded in the same Gospel. Indeed, there is no correlation between the charismatic and ecstatic experience of Jesus when baptized by John, which has been shown to have a strong claim to authenticity using various criterion discussed earlier.

With regard to Jesus' demand on his exorcists to remain itinerant and practice ecstatic, mystical rites that are founded on a charismatic act of love, not revenge, we encounter a tradition unique to both later Christian tradition and Judaism. Consequently, employing the criterion of dissimilarity, the tradition found in Matthew 28:16–20 references later Christian baptismal liturgical rites, and so, is not original. Only the command ascribed to their encounter with Jesus that rejects revenge and displaces it with love passes the test.

---

89. See Busse, *To Be Near*, "John the Baptist," 39–42.

90. Cohen, *From the Maccabees to the Mishna*, 43–44; Freyne, "Jewish Immersion and Christian Baptism," 221–46.

91. Particularly given that the baptism of Jesus by John (that has itself been made more acceptable through the redaction of the Markan editors/authors) is an undeniable fact given its difficulty and embarrassment (Jesus needing baptism by John—it had to be explained). Jesus was baptized by John in a ritual act, to which Jesus traced his calling by God, his possession by the Spirit, and being driven to the deserted hills of Judea when demons roamed and faced and conversed with Satan. Baptism was a charismatic event that brought about perilous risk and change, even the risk of demonic possession and death, based on Jesus' baptism. Recovery of this event can only point to the radical transformation that occurred for those baptized by John.

92. John 1:35.

With regard to the *criterion of embarrassment*, one is confronted by the use of the "eleven," a confirmation that one of Jesus' original exorcists had abandoned and betrayed Jesus to enemies, leading to his brutal execution. Certainly, this tradition was an embarrassment to the community in its early years. But here the use of the "eleven" is linked to the "doubt" of some of the eleven; i.e., that they had not seen Jesus on the sacred mountain or that the encounter was not convincing. As we have shown, the embarrassment has been transformed into a polemic against some of the eleven who were outside the Matthean community. The implication is clear—any communities whose traditions are associated with one of these "doubting" exorcists must be considered spurious.

Consequently, there is no longer embarrassment implied by the "eleven" or the betrayal by Judas, only a statement of fact that some of the eleven were not reliant witnesses and dangerous to the Matthean community. Our analysis of risk and mitigation has confirmed that this element of the tradition fails the test of the criterion of embarrassment. Indeed, even the aspect of the command of Jesus to not seek revenge has been so obscured by the tradition's development and application to a later generation of Christians that it no longer represents an embarrassment to the community. Thus, the tradition fails the criterion of embarrassment.

Summary of Risk Analysis

An analysis of Matthew 28:16–20 has isolated the reliable elements of the unit by employing the various criteria of risk analysis. Based on this analysis, the event should not be considered contextually reliable, but reflective of a later Christian liturgical rite and a polemic against some of the original exorcists who did not make central the post crucifixion encounter with Jesus where he was seen. However, the command of Jesus for *agape* versus retribution is distinct from its contextual setting, particularly with regard to encounters with the untimely dead. This piece of the tradition is a reflection of Jesus' post-resurrection instructions to his exorcists.

Matthew 28:16–20 and the Contextual Tests

We now turn to contextual analyses. Here an event must be coherent with the sociological risk setting, including the subsistence struggle of the Galileans, the background from which they came to join Jesus' band of exorcists. The contextual risk tests can be found on pages 118 and 119.

To begin, the unit references the original and surviving exorcists—the "eleven." A twelve- to seventeen-mile traverse through Galilee to and up the sacred mountain would most certainly be fraught with risk. The risk of identification, capture, and execution was real and perilous risk, particularly with the eleven known to have been fellow exorcists of the crucified Jesus. The trip having been made within days or weeks after his execution would heighten that risk of capture.

The post-crucifixion encounter on the mountain is doubted by some of the eleven. For those who accept the encounter as being a post-crucifixion revelation of Jesus, they see him approach and command them not to embrace retribution, but to continue in perilous risk as itinerant charismatics, yet now specifically as *baptists*. Their role as ecstatic exorcists has been significantly altered, and is now focused on building community, the *ecclesiae*. Water immersion required abundant water, or the use of a private *Mikveh*, both dangerous due to the possibility of discovery or betrayal. Immersion was to be performed concurrently with esoteric words and in specific names, in this case, those that elevated Jesus to "Son," and with that, equivalency with God, which might suggest a continuation of Jesus' war on Satan. However, the focus on baptismal sacred rites and not exorcism points to a much different period than that immediately after the crucifixion. Indeed, it is possible to see this encounter as limiting, a recasting of exorcism and ecstatic activity, and thereby alters the specific activity of the exorcists. Finally, the unit presumes that the exorcists had already abandoned a return to subsistent existence as agrarian fishermen, something they had not yet done.

Consequently, while the unit includes contextual elements that are consistent with the majority of tests, the *sitz im leben* is centered in the expanding gentile community, such as Syrian Antioch, among later generations of Christians.[93] As such, this unit fails the contextual tests, but allows that certain elements may warrant consideration as reliable fragments imbedded in it.

Conclusions on the Veracity of Matthew 28:16–20

Based on the risk and analytical criteria employed, combined with contextual analysis, the tradition that stands behind Matthew 28:16–20 should not be considered a reliable post-crucifixion encounter with Jesus in its contemporary setting, but is a reflection on earlier encounters, which may include some actual events. In the context of human risk experience, this encounter with Jesus is therefore unreliable in the original post-crucifixion

---

93. See also Hartvigsen, "Matthew 28:16–20 and Mark 16:9–20," 657–709.

context and setting, and can not be recovered. The Matthean community is facing specific risk challenges. They respond to alternative and emerging communities that ignored the importance of a post-resurrection encounter with Jesus that was material and linked with Jesus' command to baptize—for example, the community of Thomas.

While the tradition does not pass the risk and contextual criteria as noted, one specific element does—an encounter that does not command retribution by one of the untimely dead killed by violence. Instead the exorcists are to continue and charismatically baptize into powerful names *to rescue, provide safety, and mitigate perilous risks to all people, including the enemy—i.e., to love.* There is nothing in contemporary literature relating similar encounters that reject retribution and command love from those killed by violence for their enemies. This element must be considered trustworthy and must also be associated with the call of the risen Jesus. Risk analysis has confirmed that *agape* was the central charismatic power associated with the war on Satan, both before and after the crucifixion, and was the message of Jesus to his inner circle of exorcists, post-crucifixion.

11

Luke

Recovering the Original Risk and Historical Context of Galilean Appearances

In this section the evaluative criteria will be applied to a resurrection encounter in Galilee that is peculiar to Luke. When applied, the criteria will attempt to recover the original risk and historical context of the tradition.

THE VILLAGE OF EMMAUS—NEW CENTER OF THE EXORCISTS' ENCOUNTERS

The material in Luke 24:13-35 is peculiar to Luke, other than perhaps a glancing reference in Mark 16:12.[1] In Luke, two followers of Jesus, one named Cleopas,[2] are heading to a village called Emmaus when they meet

---

1. Mark 16:12 has a similar tradition: Jesus *en hetera morphe,* "he appeared in another form," to two. This tradition does not seem to be reliant on the Lukan tradition, but is distinct and primitive, which indicates this tradition was orally circulated with details known to the Markan reader. Mark 16:12 reads as follows: "Afterward Jesus appeared in a different form to two of them while they were walking in the country." What is interesting about this tradition is that "two of them" seems to indicate two of Jesus' Galilean exorcists, but Cleopas is not listed as one of the eleven. If this tradition and Luke 24:13-35 are related the identification of the eleven is more uncertain, and perhaps this is why the name is omitted in Mark.

2. Attempts to identify Cleopas as Clopas (John 19:25, Mary of Clopas, i.e., her

a stranger,[3] a "lonely sojourner from Jerusalem," on the road. They do not know him. He joins and as they are walking along the road reveals the secret, if not sacred, meaning of events that occurred the same day in Jerusalem concerning Jesus of Nazareth[4] (i.e., the theological meaning of crucifixion and the empty tomb—clearly a useful tradition to the early church). They ultimately recognize the stranger as Jesus when at an evening common meal he blesses and then breaks bread,[5] implying that Cleopas was a member of Jesus' band who had witnessed this practice. Upon recognition, Jesus

---

husband) or later traditions of him being a relative of Joseph by Hegesippus (180 CE, who is said to have received the tradition from the grandson of the apostle Jude; Eusebius, *Ecclesiastical History*, 3.11) are unconvincing. Who Cleopas may be is unknown. However, it is unusual that a name is cited, meaning that the tradition was once tied to a living person well known to the early community said to have encountered Jesus post-crucifixion. Consequently, the name had meaning associated with the oral tradition by way of a strong connection, i.e., such as a nickname or a form of a name given by Jesus as in his normal practice with his exorcists, not necessarily related to the proper name of the person.

3. Luke brings the tradition, which carried the original name of the village of Emmaus, and an exorcist, Cleopas, into his theological program (i.e., of the gospel spreading from Jerusalem to Rome) by artificially placing Emmaus near Jerusalem. This has been shown to be an artificial geographical placement; see Fitzmyer, *Gospel of Luke*, 1562n2c. We must instead see a location in Galilee where the first appearances were said to have occurred (coming from the oral tradition).

4. This recount of events has been thoroughly analyzed due to its striking similarity to the controversial account by Josephus of Jesus in the *Testimonium Flavianum*, such as by Goldberg, "Coincidences of the Emmaus Narrative," 59–77. A comparison of Greek language, structure, and content suggests the tradition of Josephus may come from an independent oral tradition that ultimately was related to the Emmaus tradition in Luke. This analysis, however, as to the relationship between Josephus's account and Luke is outside the scope of our risk analysis study.

5. This is an allusion to the passion narrative tradition, where Jesus "breaks" bread at the Last Supper; but why they would recognize this action as from Jesus is puzzling, particularly since neither of these men is named as one of the remaining eleven exorcists having shared that meal. It was too soon after the crucifixion for the oral tradition of the events at that last meal to have reached them. The answer is quite clear: Jesus' practice of sharing an eschatological meal with his fellow exorcists, i.e., where he prayed and broke bread, was a practice that continued after his death. It was so well known and recognized by early followers in Galilee that they continued this practice (Koester, "Memory of the Jesus' Death," 335–350). Consequently, we can not dismiss this recognition as strictly coming from a later tradition. A post-crucifixion encounter with Jesus by his exorcists (and others) at a common meal would not have been an unexpected setting.

vanishes or disappears (*aphantos*)[6] out of their sight.[7] According to Luke, they return to Jerusalem that same night to let others know they had "seen Jesus," but are not believed.

This tradition has been thoroughly analyzed by scholars, and there is evidence that an earlier tradition stands behind the Emmaus encounter,[8] as there is a close parallel in Greco-Roman literature,[9] and the tradition is problematic in its final form on several levels. For example, why would followers of Jesus be leisurely and openly walking on a road outside of Jerusalem when they were being hunted, or then accept a stranger joining when spies were seeking to capture them? This is incongruous with the perilous risk context. In addition, the Lukan tradition suggests they are heading to a village near Jerusalem, but there are significant problems with this identification in the narrative itself, primarily time and distance and the implied return to Jerusalem that same day, as well as archaeological evidence creating uncertainties as any possible location or identification of a village. There is an Emmaus cited by Josephus, but it is twenty miles west of Jerusalem (also referenced in 1 Maccabees 3:40, 4:3, 9:50), and, while there may be other villages studied by scholars and archaeologists, none adequately match the Lukan account.[10] Interestingly, Josephus identifies an Emmaus, "Ammathus," as a village *on the shore of Galilee*,[11] the very area of Jesus' ecstatic activity,(i.e., where he freed villages and their synagogues from demonic

---

6. *Aphantos egeneto*, which is connected with *ap auton*, making *aphantos* and adverb, a unique construction. "Nowhere else in biblical Greek does *aphantos* occur in classical Greek; it is poetical" (Plummer, *Gospel According to St. Luke*, 557). In other words, the construction is unique to the New Testament and indicates a vanishing or becoming invisible before their eyes. According to Fitzmyer, *ap auton* is "a bit peculiar; but it imitates a phrase often used with the passive of the cognate verb *aphanizein* ('to be made invisible, disappear') in the LXX (Judges 21:16; Job 2:9) . . . In classical Greek the adjective is used of disappearing gods. See Euripides, Hel. 606." Fitzmyer, *Gospel According to Luke X–XXIV*, 1568.

7. See pages 102 and 103 for an example of a Hellenistic tale of a body vacating a tomb to visit a loved one.

8. Fitzmyer, *Gospel of Luke*, 1555–56; this is based on vocabulary and style, and the use of the name "Cleopas," found nowhere else in the New Testament.

9. Plutarch describes how Romulus met with a friend on a road after his death, then vanished after revealing he was now the god Quirinus: Plutarch, *Lives*, 28:1–4, Loeb Classical Library, 1914.

10. Emmaus-Nicolas/Imwas, 18.6 miles west; al-Quebiba, five miles to the northwest of Jerusalem; Abu–Gosh, nine miles from Jerusalem; and Motza (Latin Ammas, Greek Ammaous), five miles.

11. Josephus, *Ant.* 18:36.3, near Tiberias with warm baths.

possession[12]), and where his exorcists likely escaped immediately after the crucifixion (only ten miles, from Capernaum):

> But Vespasian removed from Emmaus, where he had last pitched his camp before the city Tiberias (now Emmaus, if it be interpreted, may be rendered "a warm bath," for therein was a spring of warm water, useful for healing), and came to Gamala.[13]

Galilee is the persuasive location for the village of Emmaus, taken from its original oral tradition and absorbed into Luke near Jerusalem for its theological purposes. We can not forget that the Lukan theological program in Luke-Acts was to demonstrate what Conzelmann (and also similarly in Bovon, Fitzmyer, and others) correctly termed or refers to as "salvation history," i.e., that the gospel of salvation long promised for all nations began in Jerusalem and by divine guidance spread to Rome, the capital of the empire.[14] It is for this redactional purpose that the author-editor of Luke must have the first appearances, as well as the first apostolic preaching and arrival of the Holy Spirit, all occur in Jerusalem.[15] But the resurrection traditions in Mark and Matthew suggest virtually *all* post-crucifixion appearances were in Galilee.[16] Indeed, risk analysis has confirmed that Jesus' male exorcists fled to Galilee after the crucifixion, returning to subsistence existence in hiding, and that it was there the first encounters occurred after the report of Magdalene, who encountered Jesus near the tomb. The author/editor of Luke is developing sacred history, yet Mark and Matthew both support the more risk-centered contemporary events that can be reliably recovered—in Galilee. Consequently, Emmaus must be placed near Jerusalem in Luke-Acts, but the actual encounter is more appropriately placed in Galilee where the post-crucifixion events predominated. That Josephus mentions the village of Emmaus in Galilee, particular one near Tiberias is, therefore, significant. While the location on the western shore of Galilee and proximity to other followers of Jesus would explain why their *phantasm* encounter was shared so quickly (the same day) with the remaining exorcists who were in Galilee,[17] the more important implication, and one that is contextually co-

---

12. Busse, *To Be Near*, 79–80.

13. Josephus, *War* 4:1.3.

14. Conzelmann, *Theology of St. Luke*, 13–14, 18–27, 96, 135, 149–234. Rather than three, Bovon establishes two periods of salvation history; *Luke*, 11. Kummel, *Introduction to the New Testament*, 316.

15. Acts 2:1–13.

16. That is, all encounters and revelations, other than to Magdalene at the tomb.

17. Apparently to those who knew Kepha and had heard his reports of an encounter, which has been shown through risk analysis to have occurred in Galilee, i.e., the first

herent with the risks facing Jesus' followers post-crucifixion, is that the village of Emmaus was considered a safe haven from satanic attack, demonic imperialism, and discovery.

In fact, if a Galilean Emmaus was the destination of these men, it is certain that the perilous risks that permeated an original Galilean-Emmaus-tradition was muted in Luke, as its displacement by the editor/redactor as near Jerusalem acted to eliminate virtually all the contextual perilous risks, i.e., changing a terrorizing escape from capture into a parabolic story of a believer's journey to reward.[18] As risk analysis has demonstrated, recasting traditions to eliminate embarrassment or to mute perilous risks faced by the original exorcists in Galilee often point to later redaction and embellishment, because elements of an oral tradition were still useful to the early community and malleable. Consequently, that an "Emmaus tradition" was retained after decades of oral circulation is evidence that it had Galilean and apostolic origins. Is there additional evidence?

Ecstatic Meals and Prayers of the Exorcists

The action leading to the recognition of Jesus by the exorcist Cleopas is the blessing (*eulogesen*) and breaking (*klasas*) of bread by the traveler (*paroikeis*)[19] at the evening meal. Scholars have long identified this as the communal meal as having been established by Jesus with his exorcists. The meal anticipated the "messianic banquet" to be held in the coming kingdom of God and was practiced during the itinerant activity of Jesus and the exorcists.[20] As such, it was an *eschatological meal* celebrating the presence but still future arrival of the kingdom. It was, therefore, an ecstatic experience of the kingdom emerging around them, yet in "their midst,"[21] and in which they participated:

> Now, is it possible to infer that the Christian community meal has indeed its origin in meals that Jesus celebrated with his disciples?

---

encounter while subsistence fishing at night, and then his visit to the sacred mountain to communicate with Jesus.

18. That is, a countermeasure to perilous risk of believers in a hostile world. The tradition was likely retained by the community, explaining why after decades of oral transmission only residual elements of the original events were awkwardly retained, e.g., the name "Cleopas" and perhaps even the village of Emmaus.

19. The "different form" taken by Jesus according to Mark 16:12, i.e., the traveler who joins the escaping exorcists.

20. Koester, "Memory of Jesus' Death," 335–350.

21. Luke 17:21; *Gos. Thom.*11.3, it is "spread out over the earth and men do not see it."

And my answer to this question is yes. There is indeed good evidence that Jesus celebrated common meals with his disciples and friends. What is told in the reports about Jesus' last meal, as well as in other information, indicates that these common meals must have been understood as *anticipation* of the banquet of God, the banquet in the kingdom of God.[22]

But does this go far enough? When placed in the context of Jesus' war on Satan, where Jesus' exorcisms and daily ecstatic activity were overcoming Satan village by village as he approached Jerusalem to reclaim the Temple,[23] the evening communal meal was much more than just an innocuous "anticipation" of God's arrival. It was instead an ecstatic and powerful countermeasure to evil in the context of perilous risk and the daily threat of counterattack. Jesus certainly instituted it for this reason.[24] Consuming special food, herbs, bread, and wine, combined with apotropaic prayers (much like the Lord's Prayer)[25] and rhythmic songs and incantations, provided protection from demonic attack, not dissimilar, as noted, to multiple examples in the Dead Sea Scrolls and its community.[26] The ecstatic meal united Jesus and his authority with his exorcists. It was *Abbá* and his Spirit who rescued and possessed him, and now protected his fellow exorcists, as it did Paul and his community.[27] Their prayer preserves them from "falling into the hands" of Satan;[28] from being possessed and tormented, just as those that they had rescued. Jesus warned that they could be overwhelmed by the demons that returned seeking retribution.[29] Consequently, the ecstatic meal provided protection from perilous risk of the demonic dangers of the night, while also celebrating the day's victories and union with those who were rescued, the new children of the kingdom of God. Satan and his kingdom

---

22. Koester, "Story and Ritual," my italics.
23. Luke 11:20.
24. Koester, *Introduction*, 96.
25. Jeremias, *Lord's Prayer*, 15.
26. See Lichtenberger, "Demonology in the Dead Sea Scrolls and the New Testament."
27. *Abbá* was the unique and characteristic address of Jesus in his speech about and prayers to God, multiply attested as having originated with Jesus. See Jeremias, *The Prayers of Jesus*, 54–55 (attested in all strata of the tradition—Q, Mark, Matthew and Luke, John and Paul; Paul uses the term *Abbá* in Galatians 4:6 and Romans 8:15, i.e., an Aramaic word in the Greek-speaking world of his itinerant activity is decisive proof that this was the way in which the historical Jesus addresses God). Jesus authorized his exorcists to do the same in their ecstatic prayer, similar to the Lord's Prayer—a unique address in ancient Judaism to God most certainly.
28. Jeremias, *Prayers of Jesus*, 104–06.
29. Similar to Matt 12:45.

were collapsing, "falling as lightning."[30] It was a critical and daily ritual of Jesus and the exorcists, when food was available, who were steeped in battle with Satan to ward off evil. And the apotropaic prayer said at the meal was similar to contemporary Jewish prayers,[31] but was more urgent, reflecting a context of perilous risk.[32] Indeed, the reason the disciples had requested the prayer was because it afforded protection, just as it had for John the Baptist's followers.[33] As noted, it was uttered, perhaps even sung, while holding the bread and breaking it, so as to imbue it with protective power.[34] When it was ingested, the bread and food acted as the communal nourishment against Satan's forces that night, as well as for the next day's battle. The prayer said by Jesus was mnemonic; it had rhythm and rhyme, and was simple.[35] The name of God as *father*, *Abbá*, was invoked by the exorcist at its beginning, identifying their father, the provider of *daktulo theou*, as the one who is "hallowed," i.e., powerful and overwhelming, but intimately available to Jesus and his exorcists. The prayer included an appeal for victory and survival the next day, as it requested another divine meal, i.e., to "deliver the day" to them and bring about the next meal. Finally, there was a petition for continued protection from satanic possession and deception—words, once again, strikingly similar to what is now understood to be the Lord's Prayer that is multiply attested.[36] The final petition was abrupt, pressing, and an affirmation of their source of protection from the "evil one," Satan.[37]

Given the foregoing, the apotropaic prayer taught by Jesus is similar to the following:

30. Luke 10:18.

31. Such as the *Qaddish* and *Shema*; Jeremias, *Prayers of Jesus*, 77–78; but transformed into a charismatic, urgent plea and invocation for protection and power in the face of perilous risk and danger.

32. Jeremias, *Lord's Prayer*, 22.

33. Luke 11:1.

34. See also Chase, "Lord's Prayer in the Early Church," 147–51, in the section, "Deliver us from the Evil One," on "Note on the 'Songs' in St. Luke's Gospel in Relation to Ancient Jewish Prayers."

35. Jeremias, *Lord's Prayer*, 15–16.

36. Koester suggests that the prayers associated with the Eucharist in the *Didache* (last part of the first century CE) may be authentic sayings of Jesus. But these also may be better construed as directly linked to his ecstatic activity and successful war against Satan, defeat of his demons, and the erosion of demonic imperialism (e.g., Jesus' conversion of imperially-licensed tax collectors to his band of exorcists and supporters). These prayers reflect a later theology and eschatology overall in my view. Koester, "Story and Ritual."

37. Jeremias, *Prayers of Jesus*, 106; See also Chase, "The Lord's Prayer in the Early Church," 85–101.

> *Abba*,[38]
> I call on you and invoke your powerful name!
> Your kingdom comes by your power and will!
> Continue to give into our hands victory over your enemies
> and sustain us, your children, with the bread of life tomorrow.
> Protect us from Satan[39] and his demons![40]
> As you have saved us, let us rescue others to be your children!
> Yours alone is the kingdom, authority, and glory.
> Let it be so tomorrow, Amen.

In fact, this form of the prayer is strikingly similar to the earliest version of the Lord's Prayer that has been recovered in Aramaic by scholars.[41] Moreover, there are parallels in the Dead Sea Scrolls to a sacred meal and blessing within the community—the bread, the cup, and the ointment. These were communal elements, but were employed for ritual protection, reflecting similar practices within Jewish mysticism and among the *Therapeutae* (e.g., the origin of Mary the Magdalene).[42] The "pure food" eaten was sacred, perhaps angelic food, affording mystical protection in the end of days as the Essenes prepared for battle against evil, the war against the sons of darkness and evil priest, expected any day, even the next day. These contemporaneous practices have strong parallels to the ecstatic meal instituted by Jesus in his active war on Satan.

The Emmaus event is remarkable, and, in its original form, a critical connection to the original ecstatic, powerful meal practiced by Jesus and his exorcists. In Emmaus, when the bread is broken and the ritual begins, the traveler is "recognized" as Jesus and then disappears. The ecstatic meal no longer anticipates the kingdom of God; it has now come into being, evidenced by the presence of the risen Jesus, who had once said: "For I tell you I will not drink again from the fruit of the vine until the kingdom of God

---

38. Jeremias, *Prayers of Jesus*, 76. The unique call on the name of God using the most unique characteristic of Jesus' prayers, i.e., the address of God as "father," *Abba*, the intimate name of one's father here applied by Jesus to God; a term he allowed his exorcists to employ as well.

39. The original prayer referenced delivery from the "evil one," *apo tou panerou*, i.e., Satan, or *ho paneros*; see also the discussion on the "evil one" being Satan in Sim, *Apocalyptic Eschatology*, 77–78.

40. The context is perilous risk where one lived in the midst of the risk of satanic control; see Jeremias, *Lord's Prayer*, 30.

41. Jeremias, *Lord's Prayer*, 86–89; While Jeremias recreates the earliest version in Luke as the most original, it is missing the petition to protect the exorcists from Satan.

42. See for example, Chestnutt, "The Dead Sea Scrolls and the Meal Formula," 397–401, 404, 405–08.

comes."[43] As such, the Emmaus event confirmed that Jesus was not only active, but was present and available at the ecstatic meals when the bread was broken. He appears at the meal, or is present at the meal, but like the traveler he may be incognito, so beware. To abuse the meal (e.g., to be drunk) is to bring on peril, illness, and death, that is, demons that curse and attack the participants.[44] They are made guilty for the murder of Jesus and receive retribution, much like the attack of the untimely dead on their executioners.

The Emmaus encounter was retained in the oral tradition because it redefined the original ecstatic meal and confirmed that at its practice Jesus was certainly present and could materialize. The meal's focus retained its protective function, but also took an eschatological tenor, looking forward to his return as Messiah. In the earliest stages of post-crucifixion practices in Galilee, Jesus was available,[45] his name carried power,[46] and he continued to direct the war on Satan—the kingdom was still inbreaking, led by Jesus.[47] Ultimately, the story of the passion was linked to the meal, becoming the community sacramental union with the risen Lord, the Eucharist, just as found in Paul's letter to the Corinthians. But all this began with the Emmaus event and this risk context.[48]

Reconstructing the Emmaus Event in its Risk-Based Context

In a recovered tradition that employs risk analysis, the follow reconstruction is suggested: Two men (Cleopas, an exorcist renamed by Jesus, and another unnamed male) flee to the village of Emmaus in Galilee in the evening, having abandoned Capernaum.[49] They have learned that Jesus has been executed as an "evildoer." There is perilous risk—informants, spies, and assassins working for the Herodians and the elite are watching for Jesus' followers (e.g., paid informants, such as Judas or Saul). They expect to find safety in Emmaus of Galilee, a place freed of demons by Jesus in his

43. Luke 22:18.
44. 1 Cor 11:27–30.
45. Matt 18:20.
46. 1 Cor 5:4.
47. Gal 4:6.
48. After Emmaus, the meal was transformed into complex Christological and soteriological rituals to meet the needs of the early church. Indeed, Paul's reference is to a well-developed tradition that he had received points to its thorough development by 54 CE. Its history of development, fully formed in the Gospels, 68–90 CE (i.e., where Jesus predicts his death, his broken body, and shedding of blood for the new covenant with God in the bread and wine), was recast into his last meal in Jerusalem.
49. Or escaping Jerusalem for Galilee after the crucifixion.

itinerant village-by-village war on Satan. There he undoubtedly expelled numerous demons, driving them into the sacred waters of Emmaus (the "healing waters" cited by Josephus), as he had done at the waters of *Beth seda* and *Siloam, and into Galilee*. In Emmaus they find fellow exorcists in hiding who share in the communal meal of protection instituted by Jesus. A stranger joins the two men (a lonely stranger from Jerusalem)[50] on the road to Emmaus. Once in Emmaus, they have an ecstatic experience during a communal meal. Their "eyes" are opened and perceive the traveler as Jesus when he "breaks bread." Jesus, no longer the traveler, then vanishes when recognized. The event is shared with the others. The event is recognized as a resurrection vision and encounter. This event is a both a material manifestation of the risen Jesus, as well as ethereal presence, which, as noted earlier in the study, is contextually coherent with the world of first-century Palestine, particularly by those in ecstatic states, such as during the sacred meal in Emmaus that was originally established by Jesus with his exorcists.

Given this risk context and setting, the Emmaus event originally differed from the needs of the early church and is distinct from Palestinian Judaism. In addition, the event fits all of the contextual risk tests. Consequently, the Emmaus event, when set in the context of Galilee as described, should be considered authentic and reliable and reflects the critical importance of the communal meal as an ecstatic event for the original community of Jesus' followers—Jesus appeared with them during this meal. Its preeminence as the communal post-crucifixion gathering and its association with the experience of risen Lord in Galilee is based on his real presence both now and at the *Parousia*. The tradition was retained and reset near Jerusalem for theological reasons and served later generations of the community by establishing the communal meal as an ecstatic event that celebrates Jesus as Messiah. In its original form, the tradition in Luke reflects a remarkable encounter between Jesus and his exorcists in Galilee during an intense risk period, where the appearance mitigated the threat to his exorcists that he had been annihilated.

---

50. See Plummer, Gospel *According to St. Luke*, 553.

12

John

Recovering the Original Risk and Historical Context of Galilean Appearances

In this section, the evaluative criteria will be applied to two traditions in John associated with resurrection encounters in Galilee. Because these traditions are in Galilee and meet most of the risk criteria, the analysis will be focused on recovering the earliest form and veracity of the encounter. These are clearly reminisces of one who claimed to be a witness, and whom the community believed was present with the risen Jesus. That witness has just died, and the community is memorializing his oral traditions, as well as drawing together various sources, including a "signs" source and the framework of a passion narrative, which is markedly different from that in the Synoptic Gospels. When applied, the criteria will attempt to recover the original risk and historical context of the encounter and the instructions of the risen Jesus to his exorcists and followers.

THE LAKE ENCOUNTER

The original tradition in John 6:16–24 (also Mark 6:45–56 and Matthew 14:22–36) has Jesus walking across the Sea of Galilee at night. It is one of the few accounts found in the Synoptic Gospels to also appear in the Johannine tradition. Jesus' exorcists enter a boat and row against heavy winds toward

Capernaum, leaving Jesus off in the mountains. When they are about three or four miles offshore, they see a figure. Jesus approaches the boat, but the exorcists assume it is a malevolent *phantasm* coming to assault them, i.e., exactly the fear of Galilean fishermen.[1] When Jesus is recognized, he is helped into the boat. Suddenly they find themselves on the shore of Capernaum,[2] suggesting this was a visionary experience or ecstatic trance.[3]

Risk analysis has shown this event to be a post-crucifixion encounter with Kepha that was transposed back into Jesus' Galilean activity.[4] As a post-crucifixion encounter, the lake tradition was problematic. Jesus was at first identified as a malevolent *phantasm*, e.g., a *biaeothanati*, able to curse, punish, and harm, or seek his murderers (perhaps even those that had abandoned him).[5] By placing the event back into the itinerant mission of Jesus, concern that the resurrected Jesus was simply a *phantasm*, a common ghost, was eliminated, as was the potential embarrassment to the community. The editor/author of Luke drops this tradition altogether due its controversial nature, i.e., to ensure that Jesus' appearances post-crucifixion was not confused with simple apparitions, demons, or spirits of the dead common in the Greco-Roman world.[6] Demons and *phantasms* were presumed to haunt

---

1. Risk analysis demonstrated earlier in this study that the fishers-turned-exorcists, including Kepha and others that fled Jerusalem, knew the danger of demonic attack during night fishing, but post-crucifixion they had no choice but to take this risk in order to survive. While terrifying, they could encounter a *phantasm* that would try to drown or possess them. In fact, this tradition presumes such events were feared and well-known, lending credence to its historicity.

2. This event is also found in Mark 6:45–56 and Matthew 14:22–36. In Mark, Jesus is trying to pass by the disciples without notice about 3–6 AM as they fight the strong winds, but the exorcists see Jesus and think he is a *phantasm*. He joins them in the boat and the wind ceases. In Matthew, Jesus sees them in trouble and comes directly to assist. Again, they believe they also see a ghost. Kepha tries to join Jesus on the water but begins to sink, only to be taken by Jesus' hand and rescued. The winds cease.

3. Another aspect of this tradition is the sudden appearance of the boat at the shore when Jesus enters the boat, where this immediate transportation suggests a trance-like experience, and not a physical encounter of any kind. This aspect of the tradition underscores its problematic nature as a resurrection appearance to the early church, but the retention of this aspect of the tradition can only be understood as strengthening the claim that this event was as a post-crucifixion encounter with Jesus.

4. See the discussion by Patterson, *Beyond the Passion*, 113–14; Madden, "Jesus Walking on the Sea."

5. Ogden, *Magic*, 152–53.

6. Patterson believes this was a resurrection event, but was pushed back into the ministry of Jesus because of the controversial nature of Jesus appearing as a *phantasm*

the waters of Galilee, having been cast or expelled there by exorcists (including Jesus),[7] where they found refuge.[8]

That Kepha is prominently mentioned in each version of the tradition, and Jesus appears as a floating or water-walking *phantasm* that consistently interacts with Kepha, suggests this is a post-crucifixion encounter with Kepha. The intense risk setting underscores both the desperate plight of the exorcists, including Kepha, and the terrifying fear he had for retribution, having abandoned and denied Jesus and fled to Galilee. It reports the first encounter between Jesus and Kepha, but in a dream/vision or in a trance, set on the lake in Galilee, where Kepha is reinstated by Jesus, being set safely on the shore of Capernaum. It is this tradition that Kepha reports to other exorcists in hiding, followed by the report that spread among other exorcists: "It is true! The Lord has risen and has appeared to Kepha" (Luke 24:34). They, like he, are not subject to retribution and attack, but acceptance and *agape*. It is a reversal tradition, and as such, is remarkable in its contemporary setting.

While Kepha has been reinstated and is appointed the first witness of the Galilean male exorcists that denied and rejected Jesus, they obviously reengaged in the war on Satan, thereby embracing perilous risk. As such, in the context of human risk experience, this encounter with Jesus is authentic in a post-crucifixion context and setting, and occurred within days of Magdalene's encounter, but before she located Kepha and the other exorcists.

JOHN 21:1–23: THE BREAKFAST ENCOUNTER

The longest and most detailed of the post-crucifixion encounters in the four canonical Gospels,[9] John 21:1–23, has Jesus appearing at dawn along the shores of Galilee and cooking a meal. Consistent with his activity along Galilee pre-crucifixion, he employs animistic powers to direct a larger number of fish into their seine nets, then cooks a charcoal breakfast, inviting Kepha, Toma, Nathanael, Yecob, and Yohannes, and two others[10] to eat—seven male fisher exorcists in all.[11]

---

7. Mark 5:1–17.

8. More discussion will be provided in sections on the waters of Galilee being the home of demons below.

9. Perhaps an appendix to the Gospel; however, all extant manuscripts, including the fragment P66, of John include this section, or what is now John chapter 21.

10. The *Gospel of Peter* has a different list, and only five exorcists. The common disciple between this Gospel and John's is Kepha. See Brown, *Gospel of John*, 1068.

11. Likely these are the only exorcists who regrouped after the crucifixion in Galilee to return, under the protection of kin, to subsistence fishing at night, but without much

These seven have been fishing overnight to avoid detection from informants seeking the followers of the crucified Jesus. However, by doing so they know they risk attack from aggressive lake demons that seek victims at night.[12] At dawn, there is a male figure suddenly standing on the shore.[13] He shouts a question about their catch, and they signal they have caught nothing. The man orders them to move their nets to another spot; this was no small task, but was a familiar order given to them by another charismatic in the past—Jesus (Still, to follow the command of a stranger is surprising). The quantity of the catch is overwhelming, and very specific—exactly 153 fish.[14] "The disciple whom Jesus loved" (the witness of the Johannine community) identifies the figure as Jesus, despite his being over one hundred yards away and in poor early morning light. Kepha dives into the water after putting on his clothes. They meet the man on the shore. Curiously, Jesus is not recognized, just the actions that have taken place identify him, but "they dare not ask him, 'who are you.'"[15] The section ends with this event being the "third" time Jesus was revealed. Obviously, the appearance to Magdalene reported in John was not counted.[16]

This special section of John is likely an appendix to the original Gospel, and its function has shifted attention back to Galilee in an awkward way. As Bultmann notes:

> A still weightier consideration is that in chapter 21 the tradition of the appearances of the Risen Lord in Galilee emerges, and while this is attested by Mark and Matthew it is completely ignored in chapter 20; in chapter 21 it comes without any preparation, without for example any mention being made of the journey of the disciples first from Jerusalem to Galilee. But more! The story in 20:19–29 is related in such a manner that

---

success to support themselves and meet rigorous quotas.

12. See also Brown on the return of the disciples of subsistence fishing; Brown, *Gospel of John*, 1068–69.

13. The figure appears on the shore, similar to the appearance among the exorcists. Why they do not recognize Jesus, even at a distance, is disconcerting. Moreover, when they come to shore and are invited to eat, there is no indication of wounds, and the negative implication that they knew it to be the Lord (but did not ask) suggests that Jesus was appearing in a different form.

14. Commentators have suggested that in the context of first-century Palestine, this was the number of presumed nations of the world, thereby representing the scope of the apostles' mission once commissioned by Jesus to preach the word to the world: Ross, "One Hundred Fifty-Three Fishes," 357, or Grant, "One Hundred Fifty-Three Fishes (John 21:11)," 273–75.

15. John 21:12.

16. For example see Josephus, *Ant.* 4:219.

not only are there no further appearances of the Risen Lord anticipated, but no more could be awaited. After the commissioning of the disciples in 20:22, it is more than surprising that the disciples, instead of bearing testimony, are found fishing in the Sea of Galilee, there to experience a new appearance which now has no real meaning at all.[17]

This awkward construction[18] and placement of the section after John 20 makes suspect any ability to recover an earlier form that is reliable. Instead it must be considered an addition of the Johannine community, one used to address perilous risk issues. For example, there are many difficulties with continuity in John 21:1–14; Kepha's placement in and out of the boat, the broiling fish, and the need to bring catch when breakfast is ready.

This loose combination of elements, all of which are consistent with a Galilean breakfast along the shore with broiled fish, and juxtaposition of scenes suggests an encounter with a stranger, like that in Luke's Cleopas event, that is identified as Jesus on the shore of Galilee. While the event is in Galilee, and clearly identified seven of the male exorcists and their escape to Galilee to night fish, it ends with the assumption by some that it was Jesus. Consequently, the tradition does not create additional perilous risk. Moreover, it is a reminiscence of the "disciple that Jesus loved," and so meets the needs of the Johannine community. There is nothing distinct from ancient Judaism. Consequently, the tradition fails to pass the criteria of dissimilarity and embarrassment. As a result, the event can not be confirmed using these criteria. Nonetheless, because the tradition is reminiscence without any theological program, simply the "third" instance where Jesus showed himself "alive," and is undisputedly from a Galilean witness and is consistent with the "stranger" encounter of Luke, it is likely an authentic resurrection encounter. This tradition demonstrates an example of the variety of encounters experienced by early followers of Jesus in Galilee, and how these experiences reaffirmed for them the need to accept the perilous risk of abandoning a return to subsistence existence and return to the war on Satan. But more, it reflects the power of oral transmission of post-crucifixion encounters to form vibrant communities around these witnesses, who themselves would risk all for the risen Lord.

---

17. Bultmann, *Gospel of John*, 701.

18. Bultmann establishes that the section is not a unity, but is made up of two separate sections that can not have belonged together; Bultmann, *Gospel of John*, 702.

13

Non-Canonical Gospels

Recovering the Original Risk and Historical Context of Galilean Appearances

In this section, the evaluative criteria are applied to two traditions associated with resurrection encounters in Galilee. Both traditions focus on Magdalene, and there is evidence that they may predate the canonical Gospels in their original form. Each provide new instructions from the risen Jesus that differ from those in the Synoptic Gospels. We now turn to these non-canonical Gospels and their encounter traditions, applying risk and contextual texts to access their original form and determine their veracity. The analysis begins with a brief note on the *Gospel of Mary*, which was evaluated earlier in conjunction with Matthew 28:1–10, then turns to the *Gospel of Peter*.

THE GOSPEL OF MARY (*GM*, 30 TO 50 CE)

In the foregoing analysis of Matthew 28:1–10, the *Gospel of Mary* (*GM*) was found to include perilous risk and contextual elements supporting the historicity of Magdalene's post-crucifixion encounter with Jesus. Indeed, GM includes several startling events: Magdalene's confrontation with Kepha and other exorcists as to the legitimacy of her interaction with Jesus post-crucifixion; Kepha's jealously and temper; and Levi's defense of Magdalene as not only equal to the male exorcists, but her becoming male: "But rather, let us praise his greatness, for he has prepared us and made us into men" (*GM* 5:3). Her presence with Kepha and the others at meal indicates that Magdalene was considered equal in authority to Kepha. Furthermore, Magdalene reported to the disheartened exorcists, presumably in Galilee, that (1) Jesus was active; (2) that she had a vision at the tomb; and (3) she then encountered Jesus, not as a ghost, but in a substantive form that was present.[1] It is Magdalene that convinces the Galileans to again abandon subsistence fishing and return to itinerant ministry. She is cited as the authoritative source of Jesus' words and the only exorcist who is fully accepted by Jesus post-crucifixion. Magdalene is portrayed as the leader of Jesus' exorcists. As such, risk and contextual analysis must count Magdalene as one of the Galilean exorcists whose perilous risk was heightened following her encounter with Jesus.[2] While there is no confirmation that Magdalene continued exorcising or absorbing demons in the Synoptic or Johannine traditions, extracanonical traditions confirm that Mary was an active and influential member among the remaining exorcists in Galilee. Despite *GM* being a fragment (the extant copy is from the second to fifth century[3]), risk and scholarly analysis suggests that the traditions likely predate the canonical Gospels, perhaps as early as 30–50 CE.[4]

In sum, a review of the *GM* tradition confirms that Magdalene was believed to have influenced the return to subsistence existence as exorcists and *apostoloi* of Jesus, post-crucifixion. This tradition was an embarrassment to the early church and suppressed and differs from any contemporary accounts of first-century Jewish women. As such, the tradition about Magdalene and her encounter with Jesus in the *GM* (as noted earlier in the study) passes all key tests. Its veracity must be counted as confirmed among the encounters with the risen Jesus.

GOSPEL OF PETER 37–41 (150 TO 190 CE, FROM AN ORAL TRADITION AROUND 30 CE)

The "elders," a Roman centurion named Petronius, and Petronius's soldiers guarding the tomb witness two figures coming from heaven. The two enter

---

[1]. As noted, encounters with the active spirits of the dead included material activity and contact.

[2]. *Gos. Mary* 5:2–7.

[3]. Found in the Coptic Papyrus Berolinesis 8502; Koester notes that the title, "*Gospel of Mary*," appears in the colophon of the scribe or translator, not in the document itself; Koester, *Ancient Christian Gospels*, 21.

[4]. King argues for composition between 30–130 CE; King, *Gospel of Mary*, 148.

a tomb and then and walk out, supporting a third figure with a cross following behind. There is no speaking or identification of the figure, but it is presumed to be Jesus. It is important that these three witnesses are independent (two to three independent witnesses were required to confirm validity in Jewish courts).[5] The disciples are not aware of what has happened. They fled to Galilee to "return to their homes," and Kepha returned to "his nets." Magdalene enters the tomb, encounters a young man, and is told Jesus is risen. She and the other women with her flee.

Risk Analysis of the *Gospel of Peter* (*EvP*)

The *Gospel of Peter* (also identified as *EvP, Euangelion kata Petron*) has divided scholarship as to the date of its composition. Some scholars consider it a late construction (but before 200 CE[6]), and reliant on the Synoptics and Gospel of John.[7] Others, including Koester and Crossan, have argued for a mid-first-century date of composition in Syria and its independence.[8] An earlier date would suggest familiarity with Palestine, although there is little evidence, including ignorance of Jewish religious customs and political tensions during the second temple period (i.e., before 70 CE).[9] Moreover, analysis of the Greek in *EvP* shows that it has some unique vocabulary, distinct from both the Synoptic and Johannine traditions, although it also has Hellenistic and Attic Greek, and sometimes reflects a reliance on Lukan language constructions.[10] There are several other elements that are problematic in establishing a date of composition.

> There are numerous features in these accounts which are obviously secondary: Jesus is condemned and crucified by Herod, while Pilate is completely exonerated; the anti-Jewish polemic seems intensified; the story of Jesus' resurrection from the tomb is told elaborately ... the cross that follows Jesus out of the tomb speaks. Parallels with the passion and resurrection accounts of all four canonical Gospels are numerous. Therefore, the first assessment of the newly discovered document almost unanimously

---

5. Deut 19:15–16.
6. Koester, *Ancient Christian Gospels*, 216, based on fragments from Oxyrhynchus and a citation from Eusebius, quoting Serapion's book.
7. Wright, *Historical Jesus*, 314–15.
8. Koester, *Introduction*, 162–63, 182–83; Crossan, *Cross That Spoke*, 6–9; see also Koester, *Ancient Christian Gospels*, 226–28.
9. See Wright, *Jesus and the Victory of God*, 44–62.
10. Wright, *Historical Jesus*, 321–26.

favored dependence of the *EvP* upon all four Gospels of the New Testament canon and argued for relatively late date in order to explain the uncontrolled growth of legendary features.[11]

However, scholars also notice the lack of *EvP*'s citation of the Old Testament (i.e., to describe the suffering of Jesus as fulfillment of prophecy), which suggests that *EvP* was composed before the canonical Gospels. Matthew, for example, relies heavily on references to support critical events as fulfillment of prophecy and the Torah.[12] In addition, Koester's detailed analysis, comparing *EvP* with canonical Gospels, specifically the mocking of Jesus and the "scapegoat" tradition (i.e., tradition relating Jesus' death as sacrifice, similar to Isaiah's scapegoat references; Isaiah 50:6, Zachariah 12:10[13]), reveals that *EvP* can not be explained as a late and "random compilation of canonical passages."[14] While it may be an independent and early gospel composition, and dating is undetermined, there are elements that suggest an earlier oral tradition may stand behind it.

EvP ends with Mary Magdalene's entry into the tomb, an encounter with a mysterious angelic figure, and a report that Jesus has risen. Mary, terrified that she will be spotted and captured as they approached the tomb, flees, telling no one of the events. Finally, the narrator (Kepha) reports that after the crucifixion the fellow exorcists left Jerusalem among the crowds and returned to their homes in despair. Kepha, Andrew, and Alpheus return to subsistence fishing on Galilee. Here the fragment abruptly ends. While *EvP* has no resurrection encounter and can not be evaluated using standard risk tests of this study, there are several perilous risk elements that merit careful analysis. Some are quite striking and corroborate earlier risk findings of this study. These include:

1. There were no post-crucifixion encounters with Jesus in Jerusalem.

2. Mary approaches the tomb in terror of being discovered and captured.

3. The exorcists go into hiding, then disband, fleeing Jerusalem for the safety of Galilee.

4. They unquestionably believe that Jesus has been annihilated, body and soul, expecting nothing, and know of no death and resurrection predictions.

---

11. Koester, *Ancient Christian Gospels*, 218.
12. Koester, *Ancient Christian Gospels*, 218.
13. Koester, *Ancient Christian Gospels*, 224–25.
14. Koester, *Ancient Christian Gospels*, 227.

5. They do not know or care about the disposition of Jesus' body—they are in fear for their lives—and likely assume it had been thrown into the refuse dump of the city for the animals to consume—the common practice for executed criminals.

6. Jesus' body is guarded by special elders (not only a centurion and his soldiers), indicating that his body was entombed to protect themselves from retribution ("to do us evil" v. 8) or would be used by his followers, who were thought to be "evildoers" and dark magicians.

7. There is no command to remain in Jerusalem, or to wait for the Holy Spirit, or an instance of the conveyance of the Holy Spirit.

8. The elders are understood to be complicit with Pilate, tacitly Roman sympathizers, and a group that Pilate disdained.

9. The exorcists, led by Kepha, return to subsistence fishing.

While *EvP* has no recommitment of the exorcists to the itinerant war on Satan resulting from an encounter with Jesus, and thus no evidence of heightened perilous risks, several of its elements, particularly 2, 3, 4, 5, 6, and 9, betray a level human fear and risk avoidance that would be expected given the devastating circumstances found in our study. Moreover, these *EvP* risk elements are clearly undeveloped, particularly when compared with the Synoptic and Johannine passion and post-crucifixion traditions. As such, they represent both an early and independent tradition that "rings true" from a perilous risk perspective; indeed, they reflect exactly what a devastated group of exorcists whose leader has been murdered by the very evil forces he opposed would do—flee! Consequently, these perilous risk elements within *EvP* evidence the human impact and disaster resulting from Jesus' brutal death. The resulting perilous risks events therefore pass the test of qualitative risk analysis.

Several of these perilous risk events are also distinct from the needs of the early church, and they represent embarrassing traditions. Many of these would never have been created if not well known outside the community. Consequently, the risk elements, particularly 2, 3, 4, 6, and 9, adequately pass the tests of the criteria of dissimilarity and embarrassment. If we adjust our risk analysis to these perilous risk events, the veracity of each is rendered probable.

Contextual Analysis of *EvP*

Turning to the contextual tests, the risk elements are evaluated (2, 3, 4, 6, and 9) in lieu of a post-crucifixion encounter. These must therefore be coherent with the sociological risk setting, including the subsistence struggle of the Galileans, the background from which they came to join Jesus' band of exorcists.

Evaluation of the contextual risk tests, adjusted to the identified perilous risk elements, is as follows:

1. Perilous risk elements related to original members of Jesus' band of Galilean exorcists, those who faced capture, death, and social isolation and starvation, are given priority.

The risk elements in *EvP* pass this test.

2. Perilous risk elements should be consistent with the ecstatic practices of Jesus that engendered the original perilous risk with his opponents.[15] Specifically, encounters that encouraged the remaining exorcists to continue the ecstatic activity of Jesus and his war on Satan are preferred.[16]

The risk elements of *EvP* do not meet this test, but because *EvP* is a fragment, it is certain that the lost section of the Gospel would have reported some form of an encounter and return to either ecstatic or charismatic practices. But what is striking about *EvP* is the clarity as to the devastating impact on the exorcists, and the admission of returning to fishing in Galilee with the absence of a post-crucifixion encounter in Jerusalem. As such, this suggests that the response of the exorcists to a post-crucifixion event would be even more striking, i.e., a stronger emphasis on the perilous risks accepted by the exorcists than what is evidenced in either the synoptic or Johannine traditions. This would suggest that this test is met, but without the complete Gospel we must render it inconclusive.

3. Events near or on the lake of Galilee, particularly related to subsistence fishing, and similar to the animistic control exhibited by Jesus, are preferential (i.e., the remaining exorcists escaped there).[17]

---

15. Koester, *From Jesus to the Gospels*, 231.

16. Koester, *Introduction*, 84: "There is at least no doubt that whatever was experienced was not without relationship to a previous direct or indirect knowledge of or about Jesus."

17. Because of the nature of Jesus' activity there, combined with tradition that the men returned to Galilee to take up their subsistence existence, any activity on or around Galilee relative to how they became followers of Jesus, i.e., as exorcists having witnessed Jesus' ability to employ animistic control (see the previous discussion on how Jesus'

This test is partially met, given the return of the exorcists to subsistence fishing on Galilee.

4. Finally, events that may have led the Galileans to again abandon subsistence existence (i.e., to which they returned for survival post-crucifixion[18]) are also preferred.[19]

This test is not met.

In sum, two of the four contextual tests are met. This renders the contextual tests of *EvP* inconclusive. However, as the document is a fragment, evidence suggests that all four tests may have been met when the document was complete. As such, the likely historicity of the perilous risk events reported in *EvP* noted is strong and supported in an application of the contextual tests.

Conclusions on the Veracity of *EvP*

Based on the risk and analytical criteria employed, combined with contextual analyses, only the selected perilous risk events of *EvP* are considered reliable within their original risk setting and in the context of human risk experience. These events corroborate historical elements of the post-crucifixion response of the exorcists. The *EvP* must be considered an important source in investigation the origins of Christianity.

---

charismatic activity assisted with survival in a subsistence existence), such activities should be given preference.

18. There is ample evidence that the exorcists returned to subsistence fishing after the crucifixion of Jesus and their having fled to Galilee. Both John and the *Gospel of Peter* reference Kepha's decision to return to Galilee and fishing. As Brown notes: "The verb 'to fish' has the form of an infinitive of purpose which is rare in John (iv. 7, xiv 2) and more frequent in Matthew and Luke; McDowell, 430 ff., argues that the present tend of the verb 'to go' expresses more than momentary intention: Peter is going back to his earlier way of life and will stay with it. The point of the story, then, is that Jesus caused Peter to change his mind, especially in vs. 15: 'Do you love me more than these [nets, boats, etc.]?'" Brown, *Gospel of John*, 1068–69. Brown believes that this may be dubious, but it is compelling in a perilous risk context, so we must accept the premise.

19. Slovic, "Trust, Emotion, Sex, Politics, and Science," 280–85. A discussion with Professor Slovic confirms that the human response to perilous risk has not changed in millennia, only the context of that risk. For the Galileans to perceive risk and peril, but accept it as necessary, is a clear test of historicity, when the historical context can be adequately recovered.

14

Summary

Jesus in Galilee

By employing risk analysis and other critical tests and criteria, this study has recovered the most original form of Jesus' activity, practices, and encounters in Galilee, both pre- and post-crucifixion. It is a remarkable and striking set of events that transformed fishers and other Galilean peasants and ecstatics into exorcists, both men and women, all of whom were prepared to suffer annihilation by demonic forces to defeat the kingdom of Satan and inaugurate the kingdom of God. The risks and countermeasures both they and their enemies employed to neutralize the other are now set in their historical context, revealing new and startling insights that demand serious reflection on the risks they took in the first century. Consequently, these results drive to a deeper and fuller understanding of the multi-layered and complex perilous risks taken on by Jesus and these first-century men and women for the sake of the kingdom of God to defeat the rule of Satan, or all was lost.

For the early followers of Jesus who expected nothing after the crucifixion and fled to Galilee in terror fearing demonic retaliation, unexpected multiple forms of encounters recovered in their original risk setting demonstrated he had not been annihilated. Rather, he was active and available to them, allowing the use of his name to continue the war on Satan. Jesus had overcome satanic forces during his activity in Galilee, village by village, and though dark forces believed active in the ancient world attempted to destroy him, including under a deadly curse, they failed, validating by these encounters that he was of God—the risen Lord. He demanded they return to perilous risk activity. For the communities of the resurrection from the tomb (the the Synoptic, Johannine and Pauline traditions), Jesus was Christ, the Messiah to come with the *Parousia*. For other communities (such as the community of Thomas and in other non-canonical documents), he is and was the Living One, whose words are salvific. For the diversity of expressions of belief, practice and faith, Jesus was Lord over all the forces of darkness, and became the Lord of salvation and protective power and authority to safely remain on the side of God. And for this reason, what began in tiny rough-stone villages of Galilee and led a small band of Galilean peasants to follow their risen Lord out into a dangerous world and risk all, brings us to this day, where he is still risen Lord and Savior, both the one available and the one to come, denying the victory of dark forces over his children and *agape*.

Bibliography

Adna, Jostein. "The Encounter of Jesus with the Gerasene Demoniac." In *Authenticating the Actions of Jesus*, edited by Bruce Chilton et al., 279–301. Leiden: Brill, 1999.
Allegro, John. *The Dead Sea Scrolls*. New York: Penguin, 1956.
Anderson, Charles C. *The Historical Jesus: A Continuing Quest*. Grand Rapids: Eerdmans, 1972.
Aune, David. *Prophecy in Ancient Christianity and in the Mediterranean World*. Grand Rapids: Eerdmans, 1991.
Avioz, M. *Josephus's Interpretation of the Books of Samuel*. London: T. & T. Clark, 2015.
Avshalom-Govi, Dina, and Arafan Najar. "Migdal." *Hadashot Arkheologiyot: Excavations and Surveys in Israel* 125 (2013) 121–23.
Bar-Illan, Meir. "Exorcism by Rabbis: Talmudic Sages and Magic." *Da'at* 34 (1995) 17–31.
———. "Infant Mortality in the Land of Israel (in Late Antiquity)." *Faculty.biu.ac*. https://faculty.biu.ac.il/~barilm/articles/to_check/infant.html.
Barr, James. "Abba Isn't Daddy." *Journal of Theological Studies* 39 (1988) 28–47.
Bauer, Walter. *The Greek English Lexicon of the New Testament and Early Christian Literature*. Chicago: University of Chicago Press, 1979.
Bauerenfeind, Otto. *Die Worte Der Demonen Markusevagelium*. Tubingen: Kohlhammer, 2009.
Bazzana, Giovanni. *Having the Spirit of Christ: Spirit Possession and Exorcism in the Early Christ Groups*. New Haven: Yale University Press, 2020.
Beall, Todd. *Josephus's Description of the Essenes Illustrated by the Dead Sea Scrolls*. Cambridge: Cambridge University Press, 1988.
Bellemore, Jane. "Josephus, Pompey, and the Jews." *Historia: Zeitschrift fur Alte Geschichte* 48.1 (1999) 94–118.
Bennema, Cornelius. "The Giving of the Spirit in John 19, 20." In *The Spirit and Christ in New Testament and Christian Theology*, edited by I. Howard Marshall et al., 93–99. Grand Rapids: Eerdmans, 2012.
Ben-Zvi, Yad Yitzhak. *Studies on the Texts of the Desert of Judah 10*. Jerusalem: Magness, 1992.
Bernstein, Peter L. *Against the Gods: The Remarkable Story of Risk*. New York: Wiley, 1996.

Betz, Hans Dieter. *Galatians: A Commentary on Paul's Letter to the Churches in Galatia*. Philadelphia: Fortress, Philadelphia, 1979.

———. *The Greek Magical Papyri in Translation Including the Demonic Spells*. Chicago: University of Chicago Press, 1992.

———. "The Letter to the Galatians." In *The Interpreter's Dictionary to the Bible, Supplementary Volume*, edited by Keith Crim et al, 352–53. Nashville: Abingdon, 1976.

Bohak, Gideon. "Jewish Amulets, Magic Bowls, and Manuals in Aramaic and Hebrew." In *Guide to the Study of Ancient Magic*, edited by David Frankfurter, 388–415. Leiden: Brill, 2019.

Bolt, Peter. "Life, Death, and Afterlife in the Greco-Roman World." In *Life in the Face of Death: The Resurrection Message of the New Testament*, edited by Richard N. Longenecker, 49–77. Grand Rapids: Eerdmans, 1998.

Boobyer, G. H. *St. Mark and the Transfiguration Story*. Edinburgh: T. & T. Clark, 1942.

Borg, Marcus. *The Lost Gospel of Q: The Original Sayings of Jesus*. Berkeley: Ulysses, 1996.

Bornkamm, Gunther. *Jesus of Nazareth*. Translated by James M. Robinson. London: Hodder and Stoughton, 1960.

Bousset, Wilhelm. *Kyrios Christos: A History of Belief in Christ from the Beginnings of Christianity to Irenaeus*. Nashville: Abingdon Press, 1970.

Bovon, Francois. *Luke: A Commentary on the Gospel of Luke 1:1–9:50*. Edited by Helmut Koester, translated by Christine Thomas,. Philadelphia: Fortress, 2002.

Bowker, John. *Jesus and the Pharisees*. Cambridge: Cambridge University Press, 1973.

Boxer, B. M. "Wonder-Working and the Rabbinic Tradition: The Case of Hanina ben Dosa." *Journal for the Study of Judaism* 16 (1985) 42–92.

Brock, Ann. *Mary Magdalene, the First Apostle: The Struggle for Authority*. Cambridge: Harvard University Press, 2003.

Brondos, David. "The Cross and the Curse: Galatians 3:13 and Paul's Doctrine of Redemption." *The Journal for the Study of the New Testament*.

Brooten, Bernadette. *Women Leaders in the Ancient Synagogue*. Brown Judaic Studies 36. Atlanta: Scholars Press, 1982.

Brown, Raymond. *The Community of the Beloved Disciple*. Mahwah, NJ: Paulist Press, 1979.

Brown, Raymond. *The Gospel of John*. New York: Doubleday, 1970.

Brownlee, William. "The Wicked Priest, the Man of Lies, and the Righteous Teacher: The Problem of Identity." *JQR* 72.1 (July 1982) 1–37.

Buckley, Jorunn. "An Interpretation of Logion 114 in the Gospel of Thomas." *Novum Testamentum* 27.3 (1985) 245–46.

———. "Roles of Women in the Fourth Gospel." *Theological Studies* 36 (1975) 688–99.

Bultmann, Rudolf. *Form Criticism*. Translated by Frederick Grant. New York: Harper, 1962.

———. *The Gospel of John: A Commentary*. Translated by G. R. Beasley-Murray, R. W. N. Hoare, and J. K. Riches. Philadelphia: Westminster, 1971.

———. *History of the Synoptic Tradition*. Translated by John Marsh. Oxford: Basil Blackwell, 1972.

———. *Jesus and the Word*. Translated by Louise Pettibone Smith and Erminie Huntress Laterno. New York: Charles Scribner's Sons, 1958.

---. *New Testament and Mythology*. Translated by Shubert Ogden. Philadelphia: Fortress, 1989.

---. *Primitive Christianity in Its Contemporary Setting*. Translated by R. H. Fuller. New York: Meridian, 1956.

---. *Theology of the New Testament*. Edited by Kendrik Grobel. New York: Charles Scribner's Sons, 1955.

Burton, Ernest De Witt. "The Ancient Synagoge Service." *The Biblical World* 8.2 (August 1896) 143–48. https://www.jstor.org/stable/i357554.

Burton, Ian. *The Perception of Risk*. New York: Taylor and Francis, 2000.

Burton, Dan, and David Grandy. *Magic, Mystery, and Science: The Occult in Western Civilization*. Bloomington, IN: Indiana University Press, 2004.

Busse, Roger S. *Enemies of Paul*. Eugene, OR: Wipf and Stock, 2018.

---. *Jesus Resurrected*. Eugene, OR: Wipf and Stock, 2017.

---. "The Son of Man in the Synoptic Tradition." Thesis, Reed College, 1978.

---. *To Be Near the Fire*. Eugene, OR: Wipf and Stock, 2014.

Cameron, Ron. *The Other Gospels: Non-Canonical Gospel Text*. Philadelphia: Westminster, 1982.

Canaan, T. *Aberglaube und Volksmedizin*. Hamburg: L. Friedrichsen & Co., 1914.

---. "Haunted Springs and Water Demons in Palestine." *The Journal of the Palestine Oriental Society* 1 (1920–21) 153–70.

Carter, Matthew. *Matthew and the Margins: A Socio-Political and Religious Reading*. Sheffield, UK: Sheffield Academic Press, 2000.

Castelli, Elizabeth. "Virginity and Its Meaning for Women's Sexuality in Early Christianity." *Journal of Feminist Studies in Religion* 2.1 (1986) 61–88.

Chajes, R. "Rabbis." *Jewish Studies at the Crossroads of Anthropology and History*. Philadelphia: University of Pennsylvania Press, 2011.

Charlesworth, James. *James, Jesus, and Archaeology*. Grand Rapids: Eerdmans, 2006.

---. *Jews and Christians: Exploring the Past, Present, and Future*. New York: Crossroad, 1990.

---, ed. *The Old Testament Pseudepigrapha; Apocalyptic Literature, and Testaments*. Garden City, NY: Doubleday, 1983.

Chase, Frederic. "The Lord's Prayer in the Early Church." In *Texts and Studies: Contributions to Biblical and Patristic Studies, Volume 1, Number 3*, edited by J. Robinson. Cambridge, 1891. Reprint. Eugene, OR: Wipf and Stock, 2004.

Chazon, Esther G. "Hymns and Prayers in the Dead Sea Scrolls." In *The Dead Sea Scrolls after Fifty Years*, edited by James C. VanderKam and Peter W. Flint, 244–70. Leiden: Brill Academic, 1999.

Chestnutt, Randall D. "The Dead Sea Scrolls and the Meal Formula." In *The Dead Sea Scrolls and the Bible: Scripture and the Scrolls, Volume 1*, edited by James Charlesworth, 397–401. Waco, Texas: Baylor University Press, 2006.

Chijoke Iwe, John. *Jesus in the Synagogue of Capernaum: The Pericope and Its Programmatic*. Rome: Gregorian University Press, 1999.

Cicero. *On Divination: Book 1*. Translated by David Wardle. Oxford: Oxford University Press, 2007.

---. *On the Republic, On the Laws*. Translated by Clinton W. Keyes. Cambridge: Harvard University Press, 1988.

Cohan, John. *The Primitive Mind and the Modern Man*. New York: Bentham, 2010.

Cohen, Shaye. *From the Maccabees to the Mishna*. Louisville: Knox, 2006.

Collins, Nina. *Jesus, the Sabbath, and the Jewish Debate.* London: Bloomsbury, 2014.
Combs, Jason. "A Ghost on the Water." *Journal of Biblical Literature* 127.2 (2008) 345–58.
Conzelmann, Hans. *1 Corinthians.* Translated by James W. Leitch, edited by George MacRae. Philadelphia: Fortress, 1975.
———. *An Outline of the Theology of the New Testament.* Translated by John Bowden. New York: Harper, 1968.
———. *The Theology of St. Luke.* Translated by Geoffrey Buswell. New York: Harper, 1961.
Corcoran. "The Roman Fishing Industry of the Late Republic and Early Empire." PhD dissertation, Northwestern University, 1957.
Corley, Kathleen E. *Women and the Historical Jesus: Feminist Myths of Christian Origins.* Salem, OR: Polebridge, 2002.
Costa, Tony. "Exorcisms and Healings of Jesus within Classical Culture." In *Christian Origins and Greco-Roman Culture,* edited by Andrew Pitts and Stanley Porter, 125–45. Leiden: Brill, 2013.
Craffert, Peiter. *The Life of a Galilean Shaman: Jesus of Nazareth in Anthropological-Historical Perspective.* Eugene, OR: Cascade Books, 2008.
Crawford, Jane. "Spies and Spying in Caesar's 'Bellum Gallicum.'" *The Classical Outlook* 89.3 (Spring 2012) 71–74.
Crossan, John Dominick. *The Cross That Spoke: The Origins of the Passion Narrative.* San Francisco: Harper, 1988.
———. *The Historical Jesus.* San Francisco: Harper Collins, 1992.
———. *In Fragments: The Aphorisms of Jesus.* New York: Harper, 1983.
———. *In Parables: The Challenge of the Historical Jesus.* New York: Harper and Row, 1973.
———. *Jesus: A Revolutionary Biography.* New York: Harper, 1995.
———. *Sayings Parallels: A Workbook for the Jesus Tradition.* Philadelphia: Fortress, 1986.
———. *Who Killed Jesus?* San Francisco: Harper Collins, 1995.
Cullmann, Oscar. *The Christology of the New Testament.* Translated by Shirley C. Guthrie and Charles A. M. Hall. Philadelphia: Westminster, 1963.
Culpepper, R. Alan. "John 21:24–25: The Johannine Sphragis." In *John, Jesus, and History, Volume 2,* edited by Paul N. Anderson, Felix Just, and Tom Thatcher. Williston, VT: Society of Biblical Literature, 2009.
D'Angelo, Mary. "Reconstructing 'Real' Women in Gospel Literature: The Case of Mary Magdalene." In *Women and Christian Origins,* edited by Ross Kraemer and Mary D'Angelo, 105–28. New York: Oxford University Press, 1999.
Dalman, Gustaf. *Work and Customs in Palestine.* Translated by Nadia Abdulhadi-Sukhtian. Ramallah, Palestine: Dar Al Nasher, 1987.
Daube, David. "Jesus and the Samaritan Woman." *Journal of Biblical Literature* 69 (1950) 137–47.
Davies, Stevan. *The Gospel of Thomas and Christian Wisdom.* California: Bardic, 2005.
Davies, W. D. *The Setting of the Sermon on the Mount.* London: Cambridge University Press, 1964.
Denaux, Adelbert. *Studies in the Gospel of Luke: Structure, Language, Theology.* Berlin: Tilburg Theological Studies, 2010.

Dickie, Matthew. *Magic and Magicians in the Greco-Roman World*. London: Routledge, 2001.
Dodd, C. H. *Apostolic Preaching and Its Development*. New York: Harper, 1964.
———. *Parables of the Kingdom*. New York: Charles Scribner's Sons, 1961.
Drabek, Tomas E. *Human Systems and Response to Disaster: An Inventory of Sociological Findings*. New York: Springer-Verlag, 1986.
Draper, Jonathan. "The Jesus Tradition in the Didache." In *Gospel Perspectives: The Miracles of Jesus*, edited by David Wenham and Craig Blombert, 269–87. Sheffield, UK: Sheffield Academic Press, 1987.
———. "Weber, Theissen, and 'Wandering Charismatics' in the Didache." *Journal of Early Christian Studies* 6 (1998) 541–76.
du Plessis, Paul. *Borkowski's Textbook on Roman Law*. London: Oxford University Press, 2005.
Duling, Dennis. "Solomon, Exorcism, and the Son of David." *Harvard Theological Review* 68.3/4 (July–October 1975) 235–52.
Dunn, James. *Jesus Remembered*. Grand Rapids: Eerdmans, 2003.
Ehrman, Bart D. *How Jesus Become God: The Exaltation of a Jewish Preacher from Galilee*. New York: HarperOne, 2014.
———. *The New Testament*. Oxford: Oxford University Press, 2004.
———. *Peter, Paul, and Mary Magdalene*. Oxford: Oxford University Press, 2006.
Eisenman, Robert. *The Dead Sea Scrolls and the First Christians*. Edison, NJ: Cascade Books, 1996.
———. *James the Brother of Jesus*. New York: Viking, 1997.
Eshel, Esther. "Jesus the Exorcist in Light of Epigraphic Sources." In *Jesus and Archaeology*, edited by James Charlesworth, 183–85. Grand Rapids: Eerdmans, 2006.
Eusebius. *Ecclesiastical History*. Translated by Kirsopp Lake. London: Cambridge University Press, 1980.
Evans, Craig A. *Jesus and His Contemporaries*. Boston: Brill, 2002.
———. "Jesus and Psalm 91 in Light of the Exorcism Scrolls." In *Celebrating the Dead Sea Scrolls: A Canadian Collection*, edited by Peter W. Flint, Jean Duhaime, and Kyung S. Baek, 541–55. Atlanta: Society of Biblical Literature, 2011.
———. *Jesus and the Remains of the His Day*. Peabody, MA: Hendrickson, 2015.
Farmer, William. *The Synoptic Problem: A Critical Analysis*. London: Macmillan, 1976.
Felton, D. *Haunted Greece and Rome: Ghost Stories from Classic Antiquities*. Austin: University of Texas Press, 1999.
Ferguson, *Baptism in the Early Church*. Grand Rapids: Eerdmans, 2013.
Finkelstein, Louis. *The Pharisees: The Sociological Background of Their Faith, Volumes 1–2*. Philadelphia: The Jewish Publication Society of America, 1946.
Fishoff, Baruch, et al. *Acceptable Risk*. London: Cambridge University Press, 1984.
Fitzmyer, Joseph A. *The Dead Sea Scrolls and Christian Origins*. Grand Rapids: Eerdmans, 2000.
———. *The Gospel According to Luke X-XXIV*. New Haven: Yale University Press, 1985.
Flint, Peter, et al. *The Dead Sea Scrolls After Fifty Years, Volumes 1–2*. Eugene, OR: Wipf and Stock, 2019.
Foerster, Werner. *From the Exile to Christ: A Historical Introduction to Palestinian Judaism*. Translated by Gordon E. Harris. Philadelphia: Fortress, 1964.
Frayer-Griggs, Daniel. "Spittle, Clay, and Creation in John 9:6 and Some of the Dead Sea Scrolls." *The Journal of Biblical Literature* 132.3 (2013) 659–70.

Freyne, Sean. "The Charismatic." In *Ideal Figures in Ancient Judaism—Profiles and Paradigms*, edited by G. W. E. Nickelsburg and J. J. Collins, 223–58. Chico, CA: Society of Biblical Literature, 1980.

———. *Galilee, Jesus, and the Gospels*. Philadelphia: Fortress, 1988.

———. "The Geography, Politics, and Economics of Galilee and the Quest for the Historical Jesus." In *Studying the Historical Jesus: Evaluations of the State of Current Research*, edited by Bruce Chilton and Craig A. Evans, 75–121. New Testament Tools and Studies 19. Leiden: Brill. 1995.

———. "Herodian Economics in Galilee." In *Modeling Early Christianity*, edited by Phillip Esler, 23–46. New York: Routledge, 1995.

———. *Jesus, a Jewish Galilean: A New Reading of the Jesus Story*. New York: T. & T. Clark, 2004.

———. "Jewish Immersion and Christian Baptism: Continuity on the Margins?" In *Ablution, Initiation, and Baptism: Late Antiquity, Volume 1*, edited by David Hellholm, 221–53. Grand Rapids: Eerdmans, 2009.

———. "Urban-Rural Relations in First-Century Galilee: Some Suggestions from the Literary Sources." In *The Galilee in Late Antiquity*, edited by Lee I. Levine, 75–91. New York: Jewish Theological Seminary of America, 1992.

Funk, Robert W., and the Jesus Seminar. *The Acts of Jesus: The Search for the Authentic Deeds of Jesus*. San Francisco: Harper, 1998.

Furnish, Victor Paul. *2 Corinthians*. Garden City, NY: Doubleday, 1984.

———. *The Love Command in the New Testament*. New York: Abingdon Press, 1972.

Gager, John. "The Social Practice of Magic in the Ancient Greco-Roman World." In *Philadelphia Seminar on Christian Origins, Volume 14*, October 5, 1976. http://ccat.sas.upenn.edu/psco/archives/psco14-min.htm.

Gerhardsson, Birger. "Memory and Manuscript: Oral Tradition and Written Transmission in Rabbinic Judaism and Early Christianity." Dissertation, Uppsala University, 1961.

———. *The Origins of the Gospel Traditions*. Philadelphia: Fortress, 1979.

Georgi, Dieter. "Forms of Religious Propaganda." In *Jesus in His Time*, edited by Hans Schultz, translated by Brian Watchorn, 123–31. Philadelphia: Fortress, 1971.

Goldberg, Gary. "The Coincidences of the Emmaus Narrative of Luke and the Testimonium of Josephus." *The Journal for the Study of the Pseudepigrapha* 13 (1995) 59–77.

Grant, R. M. "One Hundred Fifty-Three Fishes (John 21:11)." *Harvard Theological Review* 49 (1949) 273–75.

Graves-Brown, Carolyn. *Dancing for Hathor: Women in Ancient Egypt*. Aukland, NZ: MPG, 2010.

Greenhut, Zvi, "The Caiaphas Tomb in North Talpiyot, Jerusalem." In *Ancient Jerusalem Revealed*, edited by H. Geva, 63–71. Jerusalem: Israel Exploration Society, 1994.

Guijarro, Santiago "The Politics of Exorcism." In *The Social Setting of Jesus and the Gospels*, edited by Wolfgang Stegemann, Bruce J. Malina, and Gerd Theissen, 159–66. Minneapolis: Augsburg, 2002.

Hachlili, Rachel. *Jewish Funerary Customs, Practices, and Rites in the Second Temple Period*. Boston: Brill, 2005.

Hammer, T. "Wealthly Widows and Female Apostles: The Economic and Social Status of Women in Early Roman Christianity." In *Prayer and Spirituality in the Early*

Church: Poverty and Riches, edited by Geoffrey D. Dunn, David Lukensmeyer, and Lawrence Cross, 65–74. Strathfield, Australia: Paulist Press, 2009.
Häkkinen, Sakari. "Poverty in First-Century Galilee." *HTS Theological Studies* 72.4 (2016) 338–39.
Hanson, K. C. "The Galilean Fishing Economy and the Jesus Tradition." *Biblical Theology Bulletin* 27 (1997) 99–111.
———. *Palestine in the Time of Jesus: Social Structures and Social Conflicts*. Minneapolis: Fortress, 1998.
Hartvigsen, Kirsten Marie. "Matthew 28:16–20 and Mark 16:9–20: Different Ways of Relating Baptism to the Joint Mission of God, John the Baptist, Jesus, and their Adherents." In *Ablution, Initiation, and Baptism: Late Antiquity, Early Judaism*, edited by David Hellholm et al., 657–709. Berlin: Walter de Gruyter, 2011.
Haskins, Susan. *Mary Magdalene: Myth and Metaphor*. New York: Metaphor, 1993.
Hengel, Martin. *Crucifixion*. Philadelphia: Fortress, 1977.
———. *The Four Gospels and the One Gospel of Jesus Christ: An Investigation of the Collection and Origin of the Canonical Gospels*. Harrisburg, PA: Trinity, 2000.
———. *The Son of God: The Origin of Christology and the History of Jewish Hellenistic Religion*. Philadelphia: Fortress, 1976.
Horsley, Richard. *Archaeology, History, and Society in Galilee*. Valley Forge: Trinity, 1996
———. "High Priests and the Politics of Roman Palestine." *Journal for the Study of Judaism in the Persian, Hellenistic, and Roman Period* 17 (1986) 23–55.
———. *Jesus and the Spiral of Violence*. San Francisco: Harper, 1987.
———. *The Message and the Kingdom*. Minneapolis: Fortress, 1997.
———. "The Sicarii: Ancient Jewish Terrorists." *The Journal of Religion* 59.4 (October 1979) 435–58.
Horsley, Richard, and John Hanson. *Bandits, Prophets, and Messiahs*. San Francisco: Harper, 1985.
Hull, John M. *Hellenistic Magic and the Synoptic Tradition*. Studies in Biblical Theology, Second Series. London: SCM, 1974.
Humphries, Michael. *Christian Origins and the Language of the Kingdom of God*. Carbondale, IN: Southern Illinois University Press, 1999.
Isaac, E. "(Ethiopic Apocalypse of) Enoch (Second Century BC–First Century AD)." In *The Old Testament Pseudepigrapha; Apocalyptic Literature and Testaments*, edited by James Charlesworth, 5–89. Garden City, NY: Doubleday, 1983.
Iwe, John. *Jesus in the Synagogue of Capernaum: The Pericope and Its Programmatic Character for the Gospel of Mark: an Exegetico-Theological Study of Mark 1:21–28 (Tesi Gregoriana: Teologia)*. Rome: Gregorian University Press, 1999.
Jackson, H. M. "Ancient Self-Referential Conventions." *Journal of Theological Studies* 50 (1999) 1–34.
Janowitz, Naomi. *Magic in the Roman World*. London: Routledge, 2001.
Jenott, Lance. *The Gospel of Judas*. Studien un Texte zu Antike und Christentum. Tubigen: Seibek, 2011.
Jensen, Morten. "Climate, Droughts, Wars, and Famines in Galilee as a Background for Understanding the Historical Jesus." *Journal of Biblical Literature* 131.2 (2012) 307–24.
———. *Herod Antipas in Galilee*. Tubingen: Mohr Siebek, 2005.
Jeremias, Joachim. *Abba*. Gottingen: Vandenhoeck & Ruprecht, 1966.
———. *The Central Message of the New Testament*. Philadelphia: Fortress, 1965.

———. *The Eucharistic Words of Jesus*. London: SCM, 1966.
———. *Jerusalem in the Time of Jesus*. Philadelphia: Fortress, 1967.
———. *Jesus' Promise to the Nations*. London: SCM, 1956.
———. *The Lord's Prayer*. Philadelphia: Fortress, 1964.
———. *New Testament Theology: The Proclamation of Jesus*. New York: Charles Scribner's Sons, 1971.
———. *The Parables of Jesus*. New York: Charles Scribner's Sons, 1972.
———. *The Prayers of Jesus*. Bloomsbury, London: SCM, 1967.
———. *The Problem of the Historical Jesus*. Philadelphia: Fortress, 1964
———. *Rediscovering the Parables of Jesus*. New York: Charles Scribner's Sons, 1966
Jewish Virtual Library. "Jewish Concepts: Demons & Demonology." http://www.jewishvirtuallibrary.org/jsource/Judaism/demons.html.
Johnson, Maxwell. *The Rites of Christian Initiation: Their Evolution and Interpretation*. Minneapolis: The Order of St. Benedict College Press, 2007.
Josephus, Flavius. *Selections from His Works*. Edited by Abraham Wasserstein. New York: Viking, 1974.
———. *Flavius Josephus: Life of Josephus*. Edited by Steve Mason. Leiden: Brill 2003.
Kahneman, Daniel, and Amos Tversky. *Judgment Under Uncertainty: Heuristics and Biases*. Cambridge: Cambridge University Press, 1982.
Kasemann, E. *Testament of Jesus: Study of the Gospel of John in the Light of Chapter 17*. Translated by G. Krodel. Philadelphia: Fortress, 1978.
Kee, H. C. *The Origins of Christianity: Sources and Documents*. Englewood Cliffs, NJ: Prentice Hall, 1973.
———. "Testament of the Twelve Patriarchs." In *The Old Testament Pseudepigrapha; Apocalyptic Literature, and Testaments*, edited by James H. Charlesworth, 775–828. Garden City, NY: Doubleday, 1983.
———. "The Transfiguration in Mark." In *Understanding the Sacred Text*, edited by John Ruemann, 85–94. Valley Forge, PA: Judson, 1972.
Kelly, H. A. "The Devil in the Desert." *Catholic Biblical Quarterly* 26 (1964) 190–220.
Kelber, Werner H. *The Oral and the Written Gospel: The Hermeneutics of Speaking and Writing in the Synoptic Tradition, Mark, Paul, and Q*. Philadelphia: Fortress, 1983.
King, Karen. *The Gospel of Mary Magdala: The First Woman Apostle*. Santa Rosa, CA: Polebridge, 2003.
———. "Women in Ancient Christianity: The New Discoveries." *PBS.org*, 1998. https://www.pbs.org/wgbh/pages/frontline/shows/religion/first/women.html.
Kloppenborg, John *Excavating Q: The History and Setting of the Sayings Gospel*. Minneapolis: Augsburg Press, 2000.
———. *The Formation of Q*. Philadelphia: Fortress, 1989.
Kloppenborg, John, and Marvin Meyer. *Q-Thomas Reader*. Santa Rosa, CA: Polebridge, 1990.
Klutz, Todd. *The Exorcism Stories in Luke-Acts: A Sociostylistic Reading*. Society for New Testament Studies, Monograph 120. Cambridge: Cambridge University Press, 2004.
Koch, Klaus. *The Growth of the Biblical Tradition: The Form-Critical Method*. Translated by S. M. Cupitt. New York: Charles Scribner's Sons, 1969.
Koester, Helmut. *Ancient Christian Gospels: Their History and Development*. Philadelphia: Trinity, 1992.
———. *From Jesus to the Gospels*. Philadelphia: Fortress, 2007.

———. "The Historical Jesus: Some Comments and Thoughts on Norman Perrin's Rediscovering the Teachings of Jesus." In *Christology and A Modern Pilgrimage: A Discussion with Norman Perrin*, edited by Hans Deiter Betz, 81–90. Atlanta: Scholars Press, 1974.

———. *Introduction to the New Testament: History and Literature of Early Christianity, Volume 2*. Philadelphia: Fortress, 1984.

———. "The Memory of Jesus' Death and the Worship of the Risen Lord." *Harvard Theological Review* 91 (1998) 335–50.

———. "One Jesus and Four Primitive Gospels." In *Trajectories through Early Christianity*, edited by H. Koester and J. M. Robinson, 158–204. Philadelphia: Fortress, 1971.

———. "The Origin and Nature of Diversification in the History of Early Christianity." In *Trajectories through Early Christianity*, edited by H. Koester and J. M. Robinson, 114–57. Philadelphia: Fortress, 1971.

———. "Story and Ritual in Greece, Rome, and Early Christianity." Lecture, Harvard University Divinity School, Cambridge, May 30, 1998.

———. "The Structure and Criteria of Early Christian Beliefs." In *Trajectories through Early Christianity*, edited by H. Koester and J. M. Robinson, 205–31. Philadelphia: Fortress, 1971.

Kohler, Kaufmann and Ludwig Blau. "Exorcism." *Jewish Encyclopedia*. https://www.jewishencyclopedia.com/articles/5942-exorcism.

Kraemer, Ross. *Her Share of the Blessings: Women's Religions Among Pagans, Jews, and Christians in the Greco-Roman World*. Oxford: Oxford University Press, 1992.

———. *Maenads, Martyrs, Matrons, Monastics: A Sourcebook on Women's Religions in the Greco-Roman World*. Philadelphia: Fortress, 1988.

Kummel, Werner Georg. *Introduction to the New Testament*. Translated by H. C. Keen. Nashville: Abingdon, 1975.

Lauterbach, Jacob. *Rabbinic Essays*. New York: Ktav Publishing House, 1973.

Layton, Bentley. *The Gnostic Scriptures: A New Translation with Annotations and Introductions by Bentley Layton*. Garden City, NY: Doubleday, 1987.

Leicht, Reimund. "Mashbia' Ani 'Alekha: Types and Patterns of Ancient Jewish and Christian Exorcism Formulae." *Jewish Studies Quarterly* 13.4 (2006) 319–43.

Lesses, Rebecca. "Exe(o)rcising Power: Women as Sorceresses, Exorcists, and Demonesses in Babylonian Jewish Society of Late Antiquity." *Journal of American Academy of Religion* 69.2 (June 2001) 343–75.

Lewis, I. M. *Ecstatic Religion: An Anthropological Study of Spirit Possession and Shamanism*. Middlesex, UK: Penguin, 1971.

Lichtenberger, Herman. "Demonology in the Dead Sea Scrolls and the New Testament." http://orion.mscc.huji.ac.il/symposiums/9th/papers/LichtenbergerAbstract.html.

Litwa, M. David. *Iesus Deus: The Early Christian Depiction of Jesus as a Mediterranean God*. Philadelphia: Fortress, 2014.

Livy. *The Early History of Rome, Books I-V*. Translated by Aubrey de Selincourt. London: Penguin, 2002.

Loftus, Francis. "The Anti-Roman Revolts of the Jews and Galileans." *Jewish Quarterly Review* 68.2 (October 1977) 78–98.

Longenecker, Richard N. *Biblical Exegesis in the Apostolic Period*. Grand Rapids: Eerdmans, 1975.

Lohse, Eduard. *Colossians and Philemon*. Edited by Helmut Koester, translated by William R. Poehlmann and Robert J. Karris. Philadelphia: Fortress, 1971.

Luedemann, Gerd. *The Resurrection of Jesus*. Philadelphia: Fortress, 1994.
Luijendijk, Annemarie. *Forbidden Oracles? The Gospel of the Lots of Mary*. Studien und Texte zu Antike und Christentum 89. Tubingen: Seibeck, 2014.
Luncz, Jerusalem. *ahrbuch zur Beförderung einer Wissenschaftlich Genauen Kenntnis des Jetzigen und des Alten Palästina*, Volumes 1-6. Vienna: Georg Brög, 1881-1903.
Lunn, Nicholas P. *The Original Ending of Mark: A New Case for the Authenticity of Mark 16:9-20*. Eugene, OR: Pickwick, 2014.
Maccini. Robert. *Her Testimony is True: Women as Witnesses in the Gospel of John*. Sheffield, UK: Sheffield Academic Press, 1996.
Madden, Patrick J. "Jesus Walking on the Sea: An Investigation of the Origin of the Narrative Account." *Beihefte zur Zeitschrift fuer die neutestamentliche Wissenschaft* 81 (1997) 30-156.
Magness, Jodi. "Ossuaries and the Burials of Jesus and James." *Journal of Biblical Literature* 124 (Spring 2005) 121-54.
Malina, Bruce, and Richard Robaugh. *Social Science Commentary on the Gospel of John*. Philadelphia: Fortress, 1998.
Mann, C. *Mark: A New Translation with Introduction*. Garden City, NY: Doubleday, 1986.
Marshall, I. Howard. *New Testament Interpretation*. Grand Rapids: Eerdmans, 1977.
———. *The Origins of New Testament Christology*. Downer Grove, IL: InterVarsity, 1976.
Marxsen, Willi. *The Resurrection of Jesus of Nazareth*. Philadelphia: Fortress, 1971.
McCrae, George. "The Jewish Background of the Gnostic Sophia Myth." *Novum Testamentum* 12 (1970) 81-101.
McDowell, Marcus. *Prayers of Jewish Women: Studies of Patterns of Prayer in the Second Temple*. Tubigen: Seibeck, 2006.
Meeks, Wayne A. *The First Urban Christians: The Social World of the Apostle Paul*. New Haven: Yale University Press, 1983.
Meier, John. *A Marginal Jew: Rethinking the Historical Jesus*, Volumes 1-2. New York: Doubleday, 1991.
Mekkattukunnel, A. "The Priestly Blessing of the Risen Christ: An Exegetico-Theological Analysis of Luke 24:50-53." *European University Studies* 23 (2001) 711-14.
Metzger, Bruce M. "The Fourth Book of Ezra." In *The Old Testament Pseudepigrapha; Apocalyptic Literature and Testaments*, Volume 1, 517-60. Garden City, NY: Doubleday & Company.
———. *Lexical Aids for Students of New Testament Greek*. Ann Arbor, MI: University Lithoprinters, 1946.
———. *The Text of the New Testament: Its Transmission, Corruption, and Restoration*. Oxford: Oxford University Press, 1968.
Meyer, Marvin. "Making Mary Male: The Categories 'Male' and 'Female' in the Gospel of Thomas." *New Testament Studies* 31 (1985) 554-70.
Meyers, Eric. "Ancient Synagogues in Galilee: Their Religious and Cultural Setting." *The Biblical Archaeologist* 43.2 (1980) 97-108.
Meyers, Eric M., Ehud Netzer, and Carol L. Meyers. "Sepphoris: 'Ornament of All Galilee.'" *Biblical Archaeologist* 49.1 (1986) 4-19.
Miller, William. "Subordinate Women or Favored Leader: Portrayals of Mary Magdalene in Christian Canonical Gospels." *Constructing the Past* 10.1 (2009). http://digitalcommons.iwu.edu/constructing/vol10/iss1/9.

Mitchell, Matthew. "Matthew 26:73 and the Case of the Disappearing Galilean Accent." *Journal of Biblical Literature* 139.1 (2020) 7–24.
Morris, Michael. *Warding Off Evil: Aprotropaic Tradition in the Dead Sea Scrolls and Synoptic Tradition*. Tubingen: Mohr Siebeck, 2017.
Morrison, Gregg. *The Turning Point in Mark*. Eugene, OR: Pickwick, 2014.
Naggar, Yossi. "Human Osteological Database at the Israel Antiquities Authority: Overview and Some Examples of Use." *Bioarchaeology of the Near East* 5 (2011) 1–18.
Neuser, Jacob. *The Talmud of Babylonia: An Academic Commentary*. Atlanta: Scholars Press, 1994.
Neyrey, Jerome. "The Loss of Wealth, the Loss of Family, the Loss of Honor: A Cultural Interpretation of the Original Four Makarisms." In *Modelling Early Christianity: Social-Scientific Studies of the New Testament in Its Context*, edited by Phillip Esler, 139–49. New York: Routledge, 1995
Nickelsburg, George. *Jewish Literature between the Bible and the Mishnah: A Historical and Literary Introduction*. Philadelphia: Fortress, 1981.
Nickelsburg, George, and J. J. Collins, eds. *Ideal Figures in Ancient Judaism—Profiles and Paradigms*. Atlanta: Scholars Press, 1980.
Nun, Mendel. "Cast Your Net Upon the Waters: Fish and Fishermen in Jesus' Time." *Biblical Archaeology Review* 19.6 (November–December 1993) 46–56, 70.
———. "Let Down Your Nets." *Jerusalem Perspective* 24 (January–February 1990) 11–13.
———. "Ports of Galilee." *Biblical Archaeology Review* 25.4 (July–August 1999) 19–31.
Oakman, Douglas E. "The Archaeology of First-Century Galilee and the Social Interpretation of the Historical Jesus." In *Society of Biblical Literature 1994 Seminar Papers*, edited by E. H. Lovering Jr., 220–51. Atlanta: Scholars Press, 1994.
———. *Jesus and the Economic Questions of His Day*. Studies in the Bible and Early Christianity 8. Lewiston, NY: Mellen, 1989.
Ogden, Daniel. *Magic, Witchcraft, and Ghosts in the Greek and Roman World*. Oxford: Oxford University Press, 2009.
Origen. *Contra Celsum*. Translated by Henry Chadwick. Cambridge: Cambridge University Press, 1953.
Parásso, G.M. "A Lease of Fishing Rights." *Aegyptus* 67 (1987) 89–93.
Parsons, Mikeal. "Narrative Closure and Openness in the Plot of the Third Gospel: The Sense of Ending in Luke 24:50–53." *Society of Biblical Literature 1986 Papers* 25 (1986) 203–22.
Patterson, Stephen J. *Beyond the Passion: Rethinking the Death and Life of Jesus*. Minneapolis: Fortress, 2004.
———. *The Fifth Gospel: The Gospel of Thomas Comes of Age*, Harrisburg, PA: Trinity, 2011.
———. *The God of Jesus*. Harrisburg, PA: Trinity, 1998.
———. *The Gospel of Thomas and Christian Origins*. Boston: Brill, 2013.
———. *The Gospel of Thomas and Jesus*. Santa Rosa, CA: Polebridge, 1993.
———. *The Lost Way*. New York: Harper, 2014.
———. "Paul and the Jesus Tradition: It's Time for Another Look." *HTR* 84 (1991) 23–41.
Pearson, Birger A. *Gnosticism, Judaism, and Egyptian Christianity*. Philadelphia: Fortress, 1990.

———. *The Pneumatikios-Psychikos Terminology in 1 Corinthians: A Study in the Theology of the Corinthian Opponents of Paul and Its Relation to Gnosticism.* Missoula, MT: Society of Biblical Literature, 1973.

Penny, D. L. "By the Power of Beelzebub: An Aramaic Incantation Formula from Qumran." *Journal of Biblical Literature* 114.4 (1994) 620–50.

Perrin, Norman. "The Composition of Mark IX, 1." *Novum Testamentum* 11 (1969) 67–70.

———. *Introduction to the New Testament.* New York: Harcourt Brace Jovanovich, 1974.

———. *Jesus and the Language of the Kingdom.* Philadelphia: Fortress, 1976.

———. *Rediscovering the Teachings of Jesus.* New York: Harper, 1976.

———. *The Resurrection According to Matthew, Mark, and Luke.* Philadelphia: Fortress, 1977.

———. "Towards an Interpretation of the Gospel of Mark." In *Christology and a Modern Pilgrimage: A Discussion with Norma Perrin*, edited by Hans Deiter Betz, 1–4. Society of Biblical Literature: Missoula, MT, 1974.

Petronius. *Petronius-Satyricon, Seneca-Apocolocyntosis.* Translated by Michael Heseltine and W. H. D. Rouse, revised by E. H. Warmington. Loeb Classical Library 15. Cambridge: Harvard University Press, 1913.

Philo. *On the Decalogue. On the Special Laws.* Translated by F. H. Colson. Cambridge: Harvard University Press, 1937.

Pitre, Brant. "Jesus, the Messianic Banquet, and the Kingdom of God." *Letter and Spirit* 5 (2009) 145–66.

Philostratus. *The Life of Apollonius of Tyana.* Translated by F. C. Conybeare. Cambridge: Harvard University Press, 1969.

Pidgeon, Nick, Roger E. Kasperson, and Paul Slovic. *The Social Amplification of Risk.* Cambridge: Cambridge University Press, 2003.

Pliny. *Natural History: Books 28–37.* Translated by W. H. S. Jones. Loeb Classical Library. Cambridge: Harvard University Press, 1963.

Plummer, Alfred. *The Gospel According to St. Luke.* Edinburgh: T. & T. Clark, 1975.

Plutarch. *Plutarch's Lives: Theseus and Romulus, Vol. 1.* Translated by Bernadotte Perrin. Loeb Classical Library. Cambridge: Harvard University Press, 1914.

Raban, Avner. "The Boat from Migdal Nunia and the Anchorages of the Sea of Galilee from the Time of Jesus." *International Journal of Nautical Archaeology and Underwater Exploration* 17 (1988) 311–29.

Raban, Avner, and Elisha Linder. *Marine Archaeology.* London: Cassell, 1975.

Rabinovich, Abraham, "'Jesus Boat' Causes Ripples." *Jerusalem Post,* 1999. https://web.archive.org/web/20091229182509/http://christianactionforisrael.org/isreport/jboat.html.

Reed, Jonathan. *Archaeology and the Galilean Jesus: A Re-Examination of the Evidence.* Harrisburg, PA: Trinity, 2000.

———. "The Population of Capernaum." *Occasional Papers of the Institute for Antiquity and Christianity* 24 (1992) 1–19.

Renan, Ernst. *Vie de Jesus,* Paris: Calmann-Levy, 1960.

Reynolds, Benjamin. *The Apocalyptic Son of Man in the Gospel of John.* Tubingen: Mohr Siebek, 2008.

Robinson, James M. "Jesus: From Easter to Valentinus (Or to the Apostle's Creed)." *Journal of Biblical Literature* 101 (1982) 3–5.

———. *The Nag Hammadi Library in English*. Leiden: Brill, 1988.
———. *A New Quest for the Historical Jesus*. New York: Macmillan, 1968.
———. "On the Gattung of Mark (and John)." In *Jesus and Man's Hope, Volume 1*, edited by David Buttrick, 116–18. Pittsburg: Pittsburg Theological Seminary, 1970.
———. *The Problem of History in Mark*. London: SCM, 1957.
———. "What the Bible Says about Women's Ordination." *ReligiousTolerance.org*. http://www.religioustolerance.org/ord_bibl.htm.
Ross, M. "One Hundred and Fifty-Three Fishes." *Expository Times* 100 (1988) 374–45.
Rothschild, Clare C. *Baptist Traditions and Q*. Wissenshaftliche Untersuchungen zum Neuen Testament 190. Tubingen: Mohr Sieback, 2005.
Rousseau, John. "Exorcism." In *Jesus and His World: An Archaeological and Cultural Dictionary*, 178–79. Minneapolis: Augsburg, 1995.
Runesson, Anders. "Architecture, Conflict, and Identity Formation: Jews and Christians in Capernaum from the First to the Sixth Century." In *Religion, Ethnicity, and Identity in Ancient Galilee*, edited by Jurgen Zangenberg, Harold W. Attridge, and Dale B. Martin, 231–36. Tubingen: Mohr Seibeck, 2007.
Safrai, Zev. "The Roman Army in Galilee." In *The Galilee in Late Antiquity*, edited by Lee I. Levine, 103–14. New York: Journal of Theological Studies Press, 1992.
Sanders, E. P. *The Historical Figure of Jesus*. London: Penguin, 1993.
———. *Jesus and Judaism*. Philadelphia: Fortress, 1985.
———. *Paul and Palestinian Judaism: A Comparison of Patterns of Religion*. London: SCM, 1977.
Sanders, Jack T. *The New Testament Christological Hymns: Their Historical Religious Background*. Edited by Matthew Black. Cambridge: Cambridge University Press, 1971.
Sandmel, Samuel. *A Jewish Understanding of the New Testament*. New York: University Publishers, 1956.
Sawicki, Marianne. *Crossing Galilee*. London: Continuum, 2000.
Schaberg, Jane. *The Resurrection of Mary Magdalene*. London: Continuum, 2004.
Scharlemann, M. S. "Transfiguration." In *The International Bible Encyclopedia, Volume 4*, edited by Geoffrey Bromiley, 886–88. Grand Rapids: Eerdmans, 1988.
Schiller, Arthur. *Roman Law: Mechanisms of Development*. New York: Mouton, 1978.
Schmithals, Walter. *Gnosticism in Corinth: An Investigation of the Letters to the Corinthians*. Translated by John E. Steely. New York: Abingdon Press, 1971.
Schweitzer, Albert. *The Mysticism of Paul*. Baltimore: John Hopkins University Press, 1998.
———. *The Quest of the Historical Jesus*. Translated by F. C. Burkitt. Baltimore: The Johns Hopkins University Press, 1998.
Sefaria. "The William Davidson Talmud." https://www.sefaria.org/william-davidson-talmud.
Shillington, George. *Jesus and Paul Before Christianity: Their World and Work in Retrospect*. Eugene, OR: Cascade, 2011.
Shurer, E. *The History of the Jewish People in the Age of Jesus Christ, Volumes 1–2*. Revised and edited by G. Vermes et al. Edinburgh: T. & T. Clark, 1979.
Sim, David C. *Apocalyptic Eschatology in the Gospel of Matthew*. Cambridge: Cambridge University Press, 1996.
Slovic, Paul, and Elke Weber. "Perception of Risk Posed by Extreme Events." Paper presented at the Risk Management Strategies in an Uncertain World conference,

Palisades, NY, April 12–13, 2002. https://Ideo.columbia.edu/chrr/documents/meetings/rountable/white_paper/slovic-wp.pdf.

Slovic, Paul, et al. "Risk as Analysis and Risk as Feeling: Some Thoughts about Risk as Affect, Reason, Risk, and Rationality." In *Risk Analysis* 24.2 (2004) 311–22.

———. "Trust, Emotion, Sex, Politics, and Science: Surveying the Risk Assessment Battlefield." *Risk Analysis* 19.4 (1999) 689–700.

Smith, David. *"Hand This Man Over to Satan": Curse Exclusion and Salvation in 1 Corinthians 5*. London: T. & T. Clark, 2008.

Smith, Morton. *Clement of Alexandria and a Secret Gospel of Mark*. Cambridge: Harvard University Press, 1973.

———. *Jesus the Magician*. San Francisco: Harper, 1978.

Snapp, James. *The Authenticity of Mark 16:9–20*. Ebook. 2007. www.textexcavation.com/snapp/PDF/snappmark.pdf.

Sorenson, Eric. *Possession and Exorcism in the New Testament*. Tubingen: Mohr Siebeck, 2002

Stein, Robert H. "Is the Transfiguration (Mark 9:2–8) a Misplaced Resurrection Account?" *The Journal of Biblical Literature* 95.1 (March 1976) 88–89.

Sterling, Gregory. "Jesus as Exorcist: An Analysis of Matthew 17:14–20; Mark 9:14–29; Luke 9:37–43a." *Catholic Bible Quarterly* 55.3 (July 1993) 467–93.

Strange, James F., et. al. "Has the House Where Jesus Stayed in Capernaum Been Found?" *Biblical Archaeology Review* 8.6 (1982) 26–37.

Strauss, David Friedrich. *The Life of Jesus Critically Examined*. Edited by Peter C. Hodgson, translated by George Elliot. Philadelphia: Fortress, 1972.

Streeter, B. H. *The Four Gospels*. London: McMillan Press, 1951.

Strugnell, John. "A Plea for a Conjectural Emendation in the New Testament with a Coda on 1 Corinthians 4:6." *Catholic Bible Quarterly* 36 (1974) 555–558.

Suggs, M. Jack. *Wisdom, Christology, and Law in Matthew's Gospel*. Cambridge: Harvard University Press, 1970.

Tacitus. *The Annals of Tacitus*. Edited by Henry Furneaux. 2nd edition. Oxford: Oxford University Press, 1965.

———. *Tacitus: The Histories*. Translated by Clifford H. Moore. Cambridge, MA: Harvard University Press, 1956.

Talbert, Wendell Lee. *Idol Meat in Corinth: The Pauline Argument in 1 Corinthians 8 and 10*. Society of Biblical Literature Dissertation Series 68. Atlanta, 1985. Reprint, Wipf and Stock: Eugene, OR, 2004.

Taylor, Joan. *The Body in Biblical, Christian, and Jewish Texts*. London: Bloomsbury Academic, 2014.

———. "The Name Iskarioth." *The Journal of Biblical Literature* 129 (2010) 369–85.

Taylor, J. E., and Davies, P.R. "The So-Called Therapeutae of 'De vita contemplativa': Identity and Character." *Harvard Theological Review* 91.1 (1998) 3–24.

Thatcher, Tom. "I Have Conquered the World." In *Empire in the New Testament*, edited by Stanley Porter and Cynthia Long Westfall. Eugene, OR: Pickwick, 2011.

Theissen, Gerd. *The Social Setting of Pauline Christianity: Essays on Corinth*. Edited and translated by John H. Schutz. Philadelphia: Fortress, 1982.

Theissen, Gerd, and Annette Merz. *The Historical Jesus: A Comprehesive Guide*. Translated by John Bowden. London: SCM, 1997.

Throckmorton, Bruce, Jr., ed. *Gospel Parallels: A Synopsis of the First Three Gospels*. New York: Thomas Nelson, 1957.

Todt, H. E. *The Son of Man in the Synoptic Tradition.* Translated by Dorothea M. Barton. London: SCM, 1963.
Tomson, Peter. "The Johannine 'Jews.'" In *Anti-Judaism in the Fourth Gospel,* edited by Reimund Bieringer, 197–99. Louisville: Knox, 1963.
Twelftree, Graham. *In the Name of Jesus.* Grand Rapids: Baker Academic, 2007.
———. *Jesus the Exorcist.* Peabody, MA: Hendrickson, 1993.
van der Toom, Karel, and Pieter Willem van der Horst. *Dictionary of Demons and Deities in the Bible.* Boston: Brill, 1999.
van Wahlde, Urban. *Gnosticism, Docetism, and Judaisms in the First Century.* London: T. & T. Clark, 2015.
Vassiliadis, Petros. "The Eucharist in the New Testament Ecclesiology." In *Einheit der Kirche im Neuen Testament,* edited by Anatoly Alexeev et al., 121–46. Tubingen: Mohr Siebeck, 2005.
Vermes, Geza. *The Changing Faces of Jesus.* New York: Viking, 2001.
———. *The Dead Sea Scrolls in English.* London: Penguin Books, 1990.
———. *Jesus the Jew: A Historian's Reading of the Gospels.* London: William Collins, 1977.
———. *Post-Biblical Jewish Studies.* Leiden: Brill, 1975.
Wachsmann, Shelley. *The Sea of Galilee Boat: A 2000-Year-Old Discovery from the Sea of Legends.* Cambridge: Perseus, 2000.
Wahlen, Clinton. *Jesus and the Impurity of Spirits in the Synoptic Gospels.* Tubingen: Mohr Siebeck, 2004.
Webb, Robert T. *John the Baptizer and Prophet.* Eugene, OR: Wipf and Stock, 2006.
Weeden, T. J. "The Heresy That Necessitated Mark's Gospel." *Zeitschrift fur die neutestamentliche Wissenshaft* 59 (1968) 145–48.
Wells, George. *The Historical Evidence for Jesus.* Amherst, NY: Prometheus Books, 1982.
Wuellner, Wilhelm. *The Meaning of "Fishers of Men."* New Testament Library. Philadelphia: Westminster, 1967.
Winkelman, Michael. "Shaman and Other 'Magico-Religious' Healers: A Cross-Cultural Study of their Origins, Nature, and Social Transformations." *Ethos* 18.3 (1990) 308–52.
Witmer, Jesus, The *Galilean Exorcist.* London: T. & T. Clark, 2013.
Wrede, William. *The Messianic Secret.* Translated by James C. G. Grieg. Cambridge: James, 1971.
Wright, David F. *The Historical Jesus.* Edited by Craig Evans. London: Routledge, 2004.
Wright, N. T. *Jesus and the Victory of God.* Philadelphia: Fortress, 1997.

Subject Index

Abbá
    invoked by an exorcist, 186
    Jesus accepted risks for his, 62
    as the unique and characteristic address of Jesus, 185n27
    used to address one's own father, 44–45n98
    Yacob as the child of, 67n22
Abba Hilqiah, 10
Abraham, 51n136, 55, 58n183
"affect heuristic," xiiin1
agamoi demons, 4
agape, salvific love
    acceptance of, 192
    as the central charismatic power of the war on Satan, 179
    command of Jesus for versus retribution, 177
    democratized, 137
    differentiating Jesus' exorcists, 169
    as more than an attitude for Jesus, 56–57
    as the only mitigation to evil and demonic powers, xix
    post-crucifixion encounter with Jesus demanding, 168–69
    power of immune from demonic control, 57
    power to mitigate evil, xixn11
    practice of, 55
    from those killed by violence for their enemies, 179
aggelos, 141n108
agrarian production regions, in the Middle Eastern Roman provinces, 14
Agrath bat Mahalath, queen of demons, 45
allegories, Therapeutides thought and taught in, 87
amulets, 95n40, 96, 99n57, 153
ancient world, mass visions and trances in, 164–79
Andreas (the "warrior"), left a subsistence life, 67
angel of God, at the tomb, 154
angelic figures, appearing in the metamorphosis, 146
angels, 1, 6n32, 27, 124
animals, Jesus' ability to control, 35n16
animistic control of Jesus, 135, 200, 200n17
animistic powers, of Jesus, 126n37, 192
annihilation, of the threat of Jesus, 91
anointing, a decaying body, 153
Antipas. *See* Herod Antipas
aoroi demons, seeking revenge to haunt the living, 4
Apocalypse of John the Theologian, visionary experience of John in, 173

SUBJECT INDEX

Apollonius of Tyana, 140n102, 141n102
apostles, xiv, 171
apostoloi, 155
apostolos, 79
apotropaic prayer, 74, 186–87
appearances post-crucifixion, of Jesus, 191
appendix, of Mark, 112
Aretas of Petra, 6
arreta remata, "unutterable words," Paul heard, 141
ataphoi demons, 4
Athronges the Shepherd, 44n90
authority, 42, 122, 126
   for esoteric wisdom sayings and practices, 167
   exchanging powerlessness for, 71
   of the "finger of God," xvi, 83, 169
   of Herod Antipas, 93
   of Jesus, 8n45, 11, 39, 43, 45n99, 68, 69
   of Jewish women, 78
   of Junia, 85n141
   of male charismatics, 155
   of Mary Magdalene, 79, 83
   over death, 47
   over demonic forces, xvii
   of Paul, 155, 165
   of Phoebe, 89
   of Solomon, 50
   spittle of an exorcist imbued with, 9
   of "super apostles" (*huper apostolon*), 124
   of those who controlled the water's inhabitants, 23
   Toma ("my twin") equal to Jesus in, 67n22
   of women of rabbinic families, 159
Autocratoris, north of Nazareth, 14n2
awakening, revealing one's true state, 171
Azazel, testing Abraham, 58n183

banishment, Jesus survived his, 60
baptism
   as the essential rite for the "super apostles," 170–71
   fraught with danger, 137
   by John, 6n30, 169n64, 176n91
   linked with the demand to continue itinerancy, 137
   as a mystery rite of unification with the divine, 167
   in the names of the Father, Jesus, and the Holy Spirit, 123
   practice and meaning of, 176
   for the purification of the body, 175n87
   as a substantive transformational rite, 169
   uniting one with the Spirit of God, 138
baptismal rites, 6, 178
the baptized, received the gift of the Holy Spirit, 128n50
Bar-Jesus, blinding of, 133
Beelzebul, 11–12, 11n67, 34n14, 95, 129
Be'er-la-hai-ro'i, "The-Well-Of-The-One-Who-Seeth," 24
beth hesda, Jesus intentionally at the pool, 27
Bethsaida (fish house) village, 16, 70
Bethsaida ("house of the fish god"), 35
bi(ai)othanatoi demons, 4
"blasting," serpents killed by, 126
blindness, Jesus casting out demons causing, 46n109
boats, of the fishers, 66, 191n3
bodily mutilation, of Jesus followed by cursed crucifixion, 103
body of Jesus, 96, 97
both Marys, 151–53, 154
bread, plea for one's daily, 20
bread and food, as communal nourishment, 75, 186
bread and wine, ingesting, 107
breakfast encounter, in John, 192–94
"brood of vipers," as a demonic accusation, 31n41
Bultmann, Rudolf, xix, 144–45, 152n7
burial, as immediate, 96–97

Caiaphas, Joseph, tomb of protected from evil attack, 96

SUBJECT INDEX 223

canonical Gospels, *EvP* composed before, 198
canonical sources, obscuring Mary's role among Jesus' band, 82
Capernaum (Nahum's village), 16
 descriptions of, 35n23
 Jesus confronting the elite from Jerusalem in, 29n31
 Jesus' village and center of activity in battling demonic forces, 48n118, 62n213
 as a poor peasant area, 19
 population of, 35, 35n20
carobeam, tree inhabited by demons, 25–26
"cat of nine tails," 103n78
catch quotas, of Galilean fishers, 20
centurion Petronius and soldiers, guarding the tomb, 116
Cephas, 20n38. *See also Kepha* (Peter)
Cephas's mother-in-law, in Capernaum, 46n109
ceremonial initiations, common for healers, 58n185
charismatic activities
 commanded by Jesus, 129–30
 commission linked with continuation of, 123
 of Jesus and the men he trained, 122
 of Jesus in his battle with demonic imperialism, 131
 Paul linking his to those of the apostles, 133
 in the "signs" statement in Mark, 112
charismatic authority
 of Jesus as different, 69
 Junia imbued with, 85n141
charismatic exorcism, 128
charismatic practices, xiii, 122
charismatic techniques, by Jesus, 132
charismatic women, 85
charismatics
 breathing on snakes with fire, 126
 encounters with Jesus, 169
 evaluating contemporaneous of Jesus' time, 131
 Jesus commanding to raise-up serpents, 125
 in northern Palestine during the first century, 10
 sayings and practices of, 132n56
Charito and Demostratus, parents of Philinnion, 100–101
chief priests, guards of the tomb reporting to, 98
child, Jesus casting out a demon from, 46n109
children, 17, 53
"choker," expelled demons into waters, 67n22
Choni Ha-Me'aggel (Choni the Circle Drawer), 10, 131
chora, agricultural area surrounding a city, 20n34
Chorazin ("the little village" or "farm village"), 36
cistern water, 30n36
cities, ancient as parasitic, 20n34
Cleopas, attempts to identify as Clopas, 180–81n2
clothing, of exorcists, 39, 75, 103
cloud, covering of, 145
coherence, criterion of, 138
cold water, 29, 29n32
collector of taxes, in Alexandria, Egypt, 66n19
commission
 Jesus giving, 113
 tied solely to Kepha in John, 123
common meals, 73–74, 73n61, 184, 185
composition date, for the *Gospel of Peter*, 197–98
comprehension, lack of, meeting the criterion of embarrassment, 94n31
confrontations, with demons as hostile, 50
contemporary setting, establishing, xviii
contextual analysis, 30, 177–78, 200–201
contextual coherency tests, 117–19, 134–36
contextual risk analysis, xiv, xviii

224 SUBJECT INDEX

contextual risk tests, 148, 160, 200
contextual tests, 134–36, 147–49, 159–62, 178
continuity, difficulties with in John 21:1–14, 194
cooperatives, of fishers, 21
core risk issues, uncovering, xvn2
core tradition
    of Mark 9:2–8, 146
    of Matthew 28:1–10, 158
countermeasures, xivn2, 61
criminals, bodies of not cleaned and rewrapped, 97
crucifixion
    annihilated a Jew, both body and soul, xviii
    curse of, 76n91, 92–95
    neutralizing retribution by the dead, 42n76
    as a Roman punishment, 93n22
    as a troubling event, 131
crucifixion nails, in the family tomb of Joseph Caiaphas, 99n57
curse tablet, from Selinus, 125n32
curses
    accepted as the norm, 1
    exorcists casting deadly, 39
    of Germanicus, 127n45, 127n46
    in secret language, or on hidden tablets, 125

danger of refusal, to embrace being an *apostolos*, 142
dark forces, xviii, 202–3
dark magicians, 7, 7n36
dark powers, of Jesus feared by the elite, 105
daughter of Jairus, cast out of death by Jesus, 46n109
David, 7n38, 9
dawn, when evil spirits and demons no longer roamed, 99
the dead. *See also* untimely dead
    buried with personal items, 97
    crucifixion neutralizing retribution by, 42n76
    encounters with in the ancient world, 111
    excluded from Hades wandering desolate places, 4
    gentle righteous given white robes in Revelation, 98n54
    Herod Antipas considered Jesus a conjurer of, 85
    Herod Antipas fear of retribution of, 91
    Jesus known for reanimating, 109
    restless spirits of, making demands on the living, 168
    "sleeping," raising at judgment, 41
    spies reported Jesus raising, 41
    vacating tombs, 100–102
    wicked, demons as active spirits of, 12
dead bodies, stealing and manipulation of, 109
Dead Sea Scrolls, 7n38, 187
deadly charges, brought against the Galilean exorcists, 106
deaf and mute man of Bethsaida, Jesus commanded not to reenter his village, 125n33
death
    authority over almost unheard of in Judaism, 47
    having no meaning any longer, 166
    Jesus called souls back to their bodies, 105
debts, forgiveness of, 20
Decapolis, Jesus refused access to, 39n51
deception, as an evil force, 93
demon(s)
    absorbed and trapped by a pool of water, 27
    accepted as the norm, 1
    agape completely neutralized, xix
    allowed to attack Paul, 142
    appealing to God against Jesus, 50n125
    appearing as deformed and decaying bodies, 4–5
    attempted possession by, 11
    attempting to take control of Jesus, 49, 49n119, 62n213
    binding of, 59n192

calling Jesus by name, 48
categories of malevolent, 4
coming out of Mary Magdalene, 83
commanding to enter special clay, 28
confirming the presence of, 50n127
confrontation with, 51, 63, 71–77
control of, 8n44, 12, 44, 46n109
detached at death, 5
disabled by Jesus, 48n118
drawing out through the nostrils, 8
driving people into desolate places, 2n9, 12n73
evoked by magicians, 5
expelling, 6n32, 46n109, 49, 72–73, 189
feared waters, 27, 27n16
forcing into a desolate place, 9
forcing to identify by name, 7
freeing when followers invoke Jesus' name, 123
haunting the waters of Galilee, 191–92
hazard of from drinking water at night, 25
intense, hostile, and violent conflicts with, xvii
Jesus aggressively casting out, 53
Jesus conversing with, 39
Jesus faced off against countless, 62
Jesus identifying and silencing, 124
Jesus's control of, xiii–xiv
labeled and categorized by the ancients, 3
language of, 124
living in the interior of the earth, 26
multiplicity of Jesus' encounters with, 47
no longer holding control over villagers, 63
possessed and then killed their victims, 2
resisted Jesus at virtually every exorcism, 48
returning back to those exorcised, 53n149
roaming near tombs, 2–3
seeking victims at night, 193
shouting at Jesus, 54, 54n151
speaking through their victims, 54
taking control by knowing its name, 7n42
techniques for exorcising, 131
turning on the exorcist, 53n149
violently resisting and trying to possess and destroy Jesus, 38
demoniacs, attempting to intercept Jesus, 51
demonic activity, perpetual fear of, 18
demonic attack
    common meal provided protection from, 185
    constant risk of, 20
    facing from winds, waves, ghosts, and malevolent spirits, 21
    Jesus resisted, 58
    mitigating the perilous risk of, 34
demonic control, land under, 18
demonic curses, 125. See also curses
demonic encounters, scope and breadth of, 47
demonic exorcisms, multiple in Galilee by Jesus, 91
demonic expulsion, 124
demonic forces, xvi, xvii, 151
demonic imperialism
    brought on by the occupying forces, 17
    continuing Jesus' war on, 123
    displacement of, 40
    High Priest and Antipas as the embodiment of, 37
    Jesus mitigating and driving from the villages, 69
    Jesus rejected, 6
    overwhelmed every aspect of life, 32
    proliferation of, xvi
    threat of, 30
demonic oppression, augmented by the elite and religious hypocrites, 56
demonic pollution of the land, expulsion of, 138
demonic retaliation, expected by followers of Jesus, 202
demonic spirits, as voracious and active at night, 2

SUBJECT INDEX

Di manes, left physical evidence of their presence, 3
Dialogue of the Savior, 82
Didache, 186n36
diet
   of bread, olives, and fish, 33n6
   of exorcists, 39
disabled people, waiting for waters to move, 27
disciple whom Jesus loved, 82n124, 193
disciples, 87, 113, 143, 194
dissimilarity, criterion of, 117, 118n26, 130–31, 147, 157–59
dissimilarity and embarrassment, failing to pass the criteria of, 194
divine authority, of those who controlled the water's inhabitants, 23
divine curse, 94, 141
divine rescue, peasants waiting for, 17
doubt, troubling oral tradition of, 165
"drinking," from Jesus as a union with him, 30

early Christian movement, Magdalene's prominent place in, 158
early church, would have not created a negative tradition, 51n135
Easter events, localized in and around Jerusalem in Luke, 111n8
economic and political power, end of the elite's, 43
ecstatic activities
   encouraged remaining exorcists to continue, 118
   of Jesus as remarkably perilous, 62
ecstatic exorcists, focusing on building community, the *ecclesiae*, 178
ecstatic experiences
   among Jesus' Galilean exorcists, post-crucifixion, 142
   during a communal meal, 189
   of holy men and exorcists, 11
   of Kepha, 148–49
   of Paul, 141
   of Simon (i.e., Kepha), James, and John, 112
   of the two Marys, 154

ecstatic meal, 185–86, 187
ecstatic mountain experiences, 140
ecstatic practices, of Jesus, 40, 135, 148
ecstatic prayer, similar to the Lord's Prayer, 185n27
ecstatic response, 37–38n41
ecstatic transportation, 146
ecstatic visions, of Jesus, 39n57, 57, 112, 140
ecstatics, 18, 48
Egyptian *goetes*, Jesus as, 44, 105
elders, understood to be complicit with Pilate, 199
Eleazar the Exorcist, 8, 10
the "eleven," doubt of, 164, 177
Elijah, 47n115, 144–45, 146
Elisha, 47n115
the elite. *See also* religious elite
   believed in demons and dark forces, 6
   charged Jesus' exorcists with stealing his body, 108
   dire warning to, 56
   extinguishing the new threat of an active Jesus, 106
   Jesus' Galilean exorcists as a perilous risk to, 104
   living in Sepphoris aligned with Rome, 15
Elymas, Jewish sorcerer blinded by Paul, 5
embarrassment, criterion of, 51n135, 71n45, 94n31, 103, 110, 117, 131–34, 147, 159
Emmaus event, 182, 187, 188–89
Emmaus of Galilee, 26, 29, 180–89
Emmaus travelers, returning to Jerusalem, 113
empty tomb, elite threatened by, 106
encounters with Jesus post crucifixion, 149n141, 200
entrapment in a tomb, 101
epitropos, 78, 78n106. *See also prefect* (governor of Judaea)
eschatological meal, 184
eschatological tenor, of a meal, 188
esoteric sayings tradition, composed in Syrian Antioch, 174

SUBJECT INDEX   227

Essenes, 28, 37, 98n54
euangelion, inaugurating the rule of God, 36
Euangelion kata Petron (*EvP*). See *Gospel of Peter* (*EvP*)
the Eucharist, began with the Emmaus event, 188
Eusebius, 143n121
Eutychus, resuscitation of, 133
evaluative risk criteria, applied to two resurrection encounters in Mark, 120
evening communal meal, as a countermeasure to evil, 185
evil, plea for protection from, 20
evil forces, 1, 7–13, 23
"evil one," prayer referencing delivery from, 187n39
"evildoer" (*kakourgos*), Jesus as, 41, 41–42n76, 43, 157
"evildoers," 76, 95
EvP. See *Gospel of Peter* (*EvP*)
excommunication, Choni threatened with, 10
exorcisms
   considered illegal in the Roman world, 133
   of Jesus, xvii, 31n41, 35, 46–49, 46–47n109
   methods and techniques of Jesus' in Galilee, 46–49
   multiplicity of Jesus' public, 38
   outcome of, 57n178
   overcoming Satan village by village, 73
   pattern of Jesus's, 49–52
   at Qumran, 9
   reliability of the tradition of about Jesus, 37n34
   sequences in ancient literature, 50n127
   spell from the eighth Book of Moses, 9n48
   tactile aspect of Jesus,' 52–54
exorcists (*exorkistes*). See also Galilean exorcists
   absorbing demons and keeping them, 83–84n131

   accepted as the norm, 1
   all of Jesus' closest followers became, 67–68
   allowed entry to control demons, 33–34
   altering the specific activity of, 178
   animistic powers over snakes, 126
   believed crucifixion was annihilation, 94, 137
   believing that Jesus has been annihilated, 198
   bound together in a war on Satan, 61
   celebrating with the villagers freed of satanic control, 73
   confrontation with demons, 71–77
   continuing the perilous mission of Jesus, 130
   controlling evil forces, 7
   countering demonic forces, 18
   distinguishing Jesus from other, 55–57
   ecstatic meals and prayers of, 184–88
   ecstatic post-crucifixion encounter, 142–43
   encounters with Jesus post-crucifixion, 154
   entering a village in pairs, never alone, 72
   entering into ecstatic trances and seizures, 39
   entrance of intended to be striking, 55
   EvP's clarity as to the devastating impact on, 200
   fled Jerusalem to the safety of Galilee to hide, 136
   forcing a demon to confess its name and origin, 9
   frequented warm springs, 26–27
   going into a trance, 7
   hid behind locked doors post-crucifixion, 110–11
   how to destroy, 90–103
   invited to eat with Jesus, 192
   invoked Jesus' name to take control of demons, 45

228   SUBJECT INDEX

exorcists (*continued*)
  Jesus commanding to raise-up serpents, 125
  Jesus defining the practices of his legitimate, 121–38
  Jesus instructing to find "who is worthy" in the village or town first, 55
  Jesus' instructions to in Mark, 120–21
  Jesus meeting on a Galilean mountain in Matthew giving the great commission, 113
  Jesus' own employed his name to expel demons, 45
  Jesus sent followers as, 54n156
  mountain in Galilee familiar to, 140
  named by Jesus, 67n22
  negotiating with a demon, 11
  not always successful in expelling demons, 71, 71n45
  number of itinerant, two generations later, 72n52
  performing acts in the name of Jesus, 91
  primary role of, 168
  rabbis as, 5
  reliance of lower castes on, 123n21
  returned to subsistence fishing, 118n29, 199
  risk of being trained as essential to survival, 69
  risks for, 123
  rowing against heavy winds toward Capernaum, 190–91
  seeing Jesus thinking he is a *phantasm*, 191n2
  seeking to communicate with Jesus' spirit, 154
  socially marginalized in the ancient world, 38–39
  some of Jesus' chosen not having or not accepting a post-crucifixion encounter, 165
  techniques used by, 8
  travel to by, 173
  vulnerability of, 71n46, 75
  witnessed Jesus' animistic control, 118n28
  witnessing demons being drawn out with the aid of powerful angels, 27
expulsion techniques, of Jesus, 28n26
extracanonical traditions, on Mary Magdalene, 160–61, 196

families, 19, 59, 65
family
  Jesus not supporting his own, 59
  rejection of Jesus by his own, 60, 60n201
fasting, implying a state of ecstatic experience, 125n31
fear, of Jesus and his claims to authority, 39
female *apostoloi*, primitive belief in a risen Jesus, 156
female Jewish healer and ascetic, Mary Magdalene as, 85
fevers, as demonic possession, 132n58
"finger of God"
  accessing the authority of, 83
  identifying possession of the power and spirit of a god, or God, 11
  Jesus claiming the authority of, xvi
  Jesus made claim to his power by, 105
  Jesus possessed by, 8n45, 45, 58, 62
  replaced with the "Spirit of God" in Matthew 12:28, 11n64
  what Jesus had termed, 138
first century, recovering the risk context of life in, 2–7
fish
  control of, 46n109
  directing into nets, 23n3
  Galilean exported to other sale-points, 16n15
  hope that the exorcist held sway over, 34
  as important to subsistence existence, 70
  in incantations and magic, 70n42
  Jesus directing into nets, 30, 34n14, 47n109

fish oil, extracted to create sought after sauces, 77
fish sauces, Galilean as highly sought, 16
"fish tower," in Magdala, 77
fishers
　abandoned their trade to be trained by Jesus as exorcists, 30
　Galilean as desperately poor, indebted, and at risk, 21
　Galilean turned exorcists, 42
　kept enslaved to debt, 66
　knew that demons and evil inhabited the land, 68
　living with bountiful surplus as completely errant and foreign to Jesus' world, 18–19
　responded without hesitation to the invitation of Jesus, 70
　rituals mitigating risks from demonic attacks, 22
　willingness to embrace deadly risk, 70
fishers-turned-exorcists, knew the danger of demonic attack during night fishing, 191n1
fishes, number of 153 as the number of presumed nations of the world, 193n14
fishing
　controlled by the ruling elite, 16
　as subsistence survival in Galilee, 20–22
fishing boat, 21, 21n43
fishing cooperatives (*koinonoi*), 21, 66
fishing rights, sold to brokers (*telonai*, "tax collectors," or "publicans"), 16
followers, of Jesus, 61–62, 64, 102, 105–6, 113, 123
food, provided protection from demonic attack, 74
forces of darkness, Jesus as Lord over all, 203
foreign gods, 37, 37n38
foreign occupation, burden of, 33
forgiveness, 56

form critical analysis, of the metamorphosis, 139–40
"the fortress," as Mary's exorcist name, 83
"Fourth Philosophy," led armed resistance against Rome during the Jewish rebellion, 67n22
Fridays, bathing children on as harmful, 24
Frumentarii, 43n81

Gadara, refusing Jesus entry, 51
Galatians, written after the council of Jerusalem, 141n104
Galilean appearances, risk and historical context of
　in John, 190–94
　in Luke, 180–89
　in Matthew, 150–79
　in non-canonical gospels, 195–201
Galilean charismatics, opponents seizing every opportunity to kill them, 127
Galilean exorcists. *See also* exorcists (*exorkistes*)
　encounters with members of Jesus' band of, 117, 148
　evidence of heightened risks for, 174
　expectations of, 103
　of Jesus not threatening the elite, 101
　perceived as capable of retribution against the elite, 108
　as the source for oral traditions for private exorcisms, 131
　trained by Jesus, 64–89
Galilean peasants, 16, 17, 33, 64
Galilean rebels, fate of under the Romans, 42n77
Galilean villages, relied on local exorcists, 38
Galilean waters, demonic infection of, 63n215
Galilean women, encounters with Jesus, 117n25
Galileans, 65, 103, 107

230 SUBJECT INDEX

Galilee
  burden on to rebuild Sepphoris, 15
  command of Jesus to meet him in, 140
  fishing as subsistence survival in, 20–22
  inhabited by phantasms, demons, and evil spirits, 32
  Jesus in, 32–63, 202–3
  kin protected the exorcists in, 109
  as the persuasive location for the village of Emmaus, 183
  proliferation of pagan worship in, 37n38
  socio-economic risk conditions in, 14–22
  villagers of as *ptochos*, the truly destitute, 20
  villages of, 35–36
  world of first-century, xviii
Gamaliel II, requested the healing of his ill son, 10
"game wardens," scrutiny of, 21
garments
  of Jesus and his exorcists, 54–55
  touching Jesus's, 52
gender, shed at baptism in early baptismal rites, 86
gentile righteous dead, given white robes in Revelation, 98n54
gentile world, expansion into, 174–75
Gerasene demons, possess swine, 27n21
Germanicus, 127, 127n45, 127n46
Gethsemane, as a place of protection from demonic forces, 136n77
ghost (*phantasms*), 2, 3, 5, 95–96n40. See also phantasm(s)
glossolalia, 124
gnosis of Jesus' wisdom sayings, 166
God
  address of as "father," 187n38
  alone as king, 137
  chose Paul from his mother's womb, 141
  one sitting quietly in the presence of, 39n59
  speaks and identifies Jesus as "my son," 146
gods, accepted as the norm, 1
goetes (sorcerer)
  accepted as the norm, 1
  controlling evil forces, 7
  described, 1n2
  Jesus as, 44, 105
gospel, as a verb, 138
Gospel of Mary (*GM*), 81–82
  chapter 5, 161
  chapter 9, 161–62
  found to include perilous risk and contextual elements, 195
  post-crucifixion encounter with Jesus, 116
  reporting Magdalene's discussion with Kepha, 160
Gospel of Peter (*EvP*)
  conclusions on the veracity of, 201
  contextual analysis of, 200–201
  ending with Mary Magdalene's entry into the tomb, 198
  as an important source in investigation of the origins of Christianity, 201
  post-crucifixion encounter with Jesus, 116
  risk analysis of, 197–99
Gospel of Philip, on Mary as a close companion of Jesus, 81
Gospel of the Egyptians, recorded in Clement of Alexandria's *Stomateis*, 86n145
Gospel of Thomas
  Jesus defending Mary in, 87
  on Jesus helping adherents to become unified, 86
  on the leading role of Mary Magdalene, 81
  on Magdalene's discussion with Kepha, 160
  relationship of Q with, 173n82
  suggesting ecstatic experiences not reliant on an empty tomb, 166
  water as an efficacious metaphor for life, 30

SUBJECT INDEX   231

gospel traditions, suppression of women in, 151n5
Gratus, Valerius, 100
grave robbing, 104, 106, 108–9
Greco-Roman women, similarities with Magdalene's role, 159
greetings, not traditional on the road, 55, 75
Pope Gregory I, 83n126
guarding, the corpse of Jesus and the tomb, 96–100, 152n9

Hagar, escaping danger from Abraham's wife, Sarai, 24
Hainina ben Dosa, 10
Hanan the Hidden, continued Choni's charismatic practices in Galilee, 10
handkerchiefs, 133, 133n63
Hanina, 131
Hanina ben Dosa, 125
Har Tavor, mountain in Galilee, 67n21, 146n130, 172, 172n76, 172n77, 172n78, 173
"healer," Mary Magdalene as, 83–84
"healing waters" of Emmaus, 29
Hellenistic magician, Jesus as, 44, 105
Hellenized Jews and gentiles, looking for protection and safety, 22
herbs and spices, brought to carry out ecstatic prayer near a tomb, 154
Herod Antipas
  accused by Jesus, 38
  assumed the spirit of John the Baptist was taken by Jesus for retribution, 91, 169n63
  aware of the risks of retaliation from Jesus' ghost, 93n24
  built Tiberias on the shores of Galilee, 15
  built two new opulent cities, 14
  considered Jesus a conjurer of the dead and dangerous threat, 85
  fear of infiltration into his inner circle, 78–79
  fear of John, 90–91n6
  fear of retribution of the dead, 91
  feared Jesus' retributive powers, xiv
  having no authority to crucify, unless he colluded with the Romans, 93
  John's murder by, 37
  licensed overseers of, protected by Roman soldiers, 20
  sought to annihilate Jesus, 58
  supported Jesus' crucifixion, 94
  terrified of an attack as retribution, 6
  terrified of Jesus, 44, 93n26
  used spies, 43n81
Herod the Great, 15, 93n22
High Priest, xiv, 37, 98n54
historical conflict, xiiin1, xivn2
Holy Spirit, giving Jesus unlimited authority, 169
"home," of Jesus as Capernaum, 34n11
hot springs, 6n32, 25
hymns, attributed to David, 9

"I come to bring the sword," referencing a special brass sword, 61n208
illness, associated with demonic possession or evil, 128
immersion, performance of, 178
incantation bowls, for capturing demons, 27n16
incantations, of exorcists, 7, 39
infection, of death, 47
inhabitants of waters, 23n3, 26
initiates, baptizing in the name of a crucified Jewish criminal, 174
initiation and purification rites, at Qumran, 175n85
innocent victims, demons seeking out, 4
instructions, of Jesus to his exorcists, 72
Isis, tricking Re, 28n27
itinerant ecstatics, living conditions of, 84
itinerant exorcists, continued Jesus' conflict, 169
itinerant life, of peasant exorcists, 76

232 SUBJECT INDEX

Jacob, return to Shechem from Paddam Aram, 24n4
Jairus, meeting Jesus, 52n141, 55n158
James, reports of the death of, 91n7
Jannaeus, Alexander, crucified eight hundred Jews, 92
Jerome, on Mary Magdalene-called the tower, 79
Jerusalem
   destruction of as a sign of the *Parousia*, 143
   elite of, xvi, 16–17, 18, 104
   Mary Magdalene remaining in, 156
   no command to remain in, 199
   no post-crucifixion encounters with Jesus in, 198
   rejecting the elitism of, 57
Jesus
   approaching in his historical context, 1–2
   associating with or calling him "master" as a perilous risk, 42
   clothing of, 55
   devastated by the murder of John the Baptist, 12n76
   encountering the Samaritan woman, 24n4
   expelled from Nazareth, 35n19
   experienced trances and visions, 149
   forbidden from entering villages, 34n10, 36n33
   in Galilee, 32–63, 202–3
   as a guest in Kepha's home, 34n10, 60n202
   known for reanimating the dead, 109
   left Nazareth for Capernaum, 35n18
   meaning of events in Jerusalem concerning, 181
   as never explicitly tied to speaking in tongues, 124
   recovering the first-century world of, xiii–xix
   risk-based dimensional view of, 62
   suspended baptism after the execution of John, 137
Jesus (baptism of), 176, 176n91
Jesus (battle agains demons and Satan)
   acknowledging his control over demons as from God, his *Abbá*, 44
   acknowledging the power of the angel(s) to capture demons, 27
   assaulted demonic forces village by village in Galilee, xvii
   authority over the demons, 43
   as available and continuing to direct the war on Satan, 188
   battled evil forces to reclaim the land for God, 13
   believed to be possessed by a demon, 40n63
   bound Satan, 59n193
   confrontation with demons in villages, 36
   control of demons, xiii–xiv, 62n213, 91
   control over the waters of Galilee, 69
   conversed multiple times with Satan, 45
   on demonic forces attempting to overtake the kingdom of God, 12
   driven into demon-controlled lands in the desert wilderness of Judea, 57–58
   employing powerful substances, 28
   exorcised all demons but one, 11
   on the "finger of God" leading the expulsion of demons, 102n73
   given a room and board for having exorcised a demon of fever, 35
   identification of by a demon attempting to take control of Jesus, 48n118
   multiple conversations with Satan, 58
   neutralizing serpents, 126
   personal contact and special words to expel death, 47–48
   on successful expelling of demons and spirits, 54

SUBJECT INDEX 233

techniques to affect exorcism and
overcome evil spirits, 48
techniques to expel demons, 28
at war with Satan, 58–59
Jesus (body of)
covered with magical herbs,
amulets, and written spells, 153
exorcists not knowing or caring
about the disposition of, 199
guarded by special elders, 199
special treatment of, 95–96
taken by his enemies to ensure his
annihilation, 153n16
Jesus (commands of)
to be baptized of water and the
spirit, 29
to continue the conflict with Satan
and his demons, 126–27
cursing Bethsaida, Korazim, and
Capernaum, 39n60
to his exorcists, 121–22, 168
to Kepha to feed his sheep, 115n17
to the women to tell the male
exorcists, "Go to Galilee where
they will see me," 155
Jesus (divinity of)
accepted risks for his *Abbá*,
demanding *agape*, 62
as the Christ, the Messiah, 203
claiming he would return after
three days, 91n8
claiming his authority as directly
from God, 8n45
as the divine Son of Man, 147
as enthroned with God in the third
heaven, 146, 149
given by "the finger of God" after
his baptism, 11
as greater than Solomon, 8n45
on his authority of God by his
"finger," 45n99
making equal to God, 174
muzzling the wind and waves, 68
not invoking the name of Solomon,
Moses, or another exorcist, 50
offering salvation to those who
heed his words, 82
renamed the Son of Man, 67n22

revealing his true self-his glory,
139
as still risen Lord and Savior, 203
Jesus (exorcism and)
acknowledging exorcists practicing
in Galilee, 11
appearance as an exorcist when
entering a town or village, 54–55
different from any contemporary
exorcist or ecstatic, 38
entering villages when allowed, 36
as a first-century Jewish peasant
exorcist, xviii
on his exorcisms as proof, 38, 43
instruction to other exorcists,
51n136
performed exorcisms on the
Sabbath, 60
protected his exorcists with specific
practices, 74
selected and trained subsistence
fisher peasants to became
apprentice exorcists, 36, 66
sending exorcists into villages, 71
sent followers as exorcists, 54n156
sharing an eschatological meal,
181n5
witnessed in trances, 39
Jesus (family relationships)
broke with kin and family, 59–60
failing to provide support for his
kin, 35n17
left his kin and family behind in
Nazareth, 59
not behaving like other
contemporary Jewish sons, 59
proclaimed those with him as his
kin, 87
public rejection of his kin, 60n201
rejected by his brothers and sisters,
35n17
Jesus (healing by)
affected several cures with the use
of his hands, 128
feeling "power had gone forth from
me," 52
laid his hands on Kepha's mother-
in-law, 132

234 SUBJECT INDEX

Jesus (healing by) (*continued*)
   readmitting those he freed from possession back into fellowship, 55
   taking the possessed aside in private, 28n24
   using spittle, 9n53
   when unsuccessful, 53n148
Jesus (Mary Magdalene and), 88, 116, 160
Jesus (post-crucifixion appearances)
   appearing at dawn along the shores of Galilee and cooking a meal, 115, 192
   appearing to the exorcists despite the doors being locked, 115
   causing Peter to change his mind, 118n29
   encountering in Galilee post-crucifixion, 110–19
   Galileans having no expectation of encountering, 111
   Kepha encountering the spirit of, 163
   not recognized, 193n13
   recognized at an evening common meal, 181
   taking the followers to Bethany, blessing them, and then parting, 114
Jesus (walking on water), 29–30, 63n216, 68, 114n13, 191
Jesus (war against the elite)
   accusing Antipas and the Jerusalem religious establishment of being possessed, 38
   betrayed by an assassin funded and paid by the Sanhedrin, 99
   considered as a deceiving dark magician, 31n41
   as a danger to his enemies, 91
   exposing himself to retribution and death by his charges of hypocrisy, 56n167
   guarding the corpse of, 96–100
   as the liberator destined to free Galileans from demonic imperialism, 102n73
   as more dangerous in death than in life if not dispatched correctly, 95
   placed in the tomb of a member of the Sanhedrin, 97
   portrayed as a deceiver empowered by Satan, 40
   quickly identified by elitist sympathizers, 40
   rejected demonic imperialism, 6
   seen as a dangerous deceiver, 45
   using the spirit of John to deceive Antipas's subjects and incite rebellion, 93
   warned his opponents that he would not be annihilated, 94n31
Jesus' exorcists
   activities of fraught with physical peril and risk, 131
   fled to Galilee after the crucifixion, 135
   not fearing any poison, 127
   unfamiliar with any concept of a post-crucifixion return, 102n73
   urgency to neutralize post-crucifixion, 104–9
Jewish hospitality, tradition of, 55
Jewish ritual bath, regaining ritual purity by immersion, 175
Jewish ritual priests, *kohen*, as the likely guards Jesus' tomb, 98
Jewish women, 65, 78. *See also* women
Joanna, the wife of Chuza, Herod Antipas's householder, 78
Johanan ben Zakkai, 154n20
John, Gospel of
   appearances of the Risen Lord in Galilee, 193
   portrayal of Mary Magdalene, 80, 80n116
   post-crucifixion encounters, 114–15
   reporting the resurrection of Lazarus, 47n113

John Hyrcanus, 33n3
John the Baptist
  asked his followers to give away
    their second tunic, 75n82
  beheaded during a drunken party,
    90, 175n87
  condemned the Jerusalem elite as
    demonic and possessed, 6
  as a critic of the Jerusalem and
    Temple elite, 57
  Herod Antipas's fear of, 90–91n6,
    93
  immersed Jesus in waters of the
    Jordan, 29, 131
  on the Jerusalem religious elite as
    the progenitors of the crisis,
    18n25
  Jesus as the return of, 105
  and Jesus believed to be dangerous
    ecstatics and exorcists, 58
  murder of, 6
  mutilation of his body, 93
  practice of renaming adherents
    likely originated with, 67n22
  as second cousin to Jesus, 37n36
  tradition of recast by Josephus
    to make the Baptist more
    acceptable to authorities, 175
Jonah-Zebedee cooperative, peasant
  sons of Kepha, Andrew, Jacob,
  and Yohannes, 66n18
Joseph (Mary's husband), 35n17, 92
Joseph of Arimathea, 96, 99, 99n58,
  100, 152n7
Josephus, Flavius
  account of Jesus in the
    Testimonium Flavianum, 181n4
  acquaintances crucified during the
    Jewish rebellion, 92n15
  citing examples of demons being
    drawn into the water, 29n33
  on the defeat of Herod's army by
    Aretas of Petra, 6
  depiction of Sepphoris, 15
  describing the powers of the warm
    waters in Galilee, 25
  on the destruction of the Temple,
    xviin5
  Herod and the Jerusalem elite
    portraying as corrupted and
    evil, 175
  identifying Emmaus as a village on
    the shore of Galilee, 182
  incidents of possession and
    exorcism, 8
  Testimonium Flavianum, 116, 181n4
  on villages and cities in Galilee,
    16n11
Judah Aristobulus, 33n3
Judaism, Tiberias eventually becoming,
  15n9
Judas, the son of bandit Eleazar,
  rebellion of, 15
Judas *Iscariot*
  betrayed Jesus, 107, 131
  as "the choker," 67n22
  chose Gethsemane as the place
    where Jesus' charismatic
    powers were limited, 44n96
  compromised the secret nighttime
    retreat in Gethsemane, 106
  infiltrated Jesus' band of exorcists,
    43
  killed prior to the encounter on the
    mountain, 172
  "kissed" Jesus as an ancient curse
    used to infect and disable an
    opponent, 98
  possession of by Satan, 11
Judas of Gamala, tax revolt of, 92
Judas the son of Hezekiah, rebellion
  of, 44n90
Judean desert, 3, 105
Junia, 85n141, 89, 151n4, 151n5, 156

katakrino, implying both immediate
  judgment and punishment
  from a divine curse, 137
Kepha (Peter). *See also* Shimon Kepha
  abandoned Jesus, 107
  assumed Jesus' body had been
    thrown into the city dump, 103
  communities claiming as the sole
    source of their legitimacy, 81
  decision to return to Galilee and
    fishing, 118n29

236 SUBJECT INDEX

Kepha (continued)
    diving into the water, 115, 193
    encounter with Jesus, 113n12, 138, 145, 163
    fled to Galilee immediately after the crucifixion, 148
    as leader of the male exorcists, 145
    Magdalene's confrontation with, 195
    male-dominated communities linked to, 87
    mentioned in each version of the tradition of Jesus walking on water, 191n2, 192
    never considered as "doubter" in early Christianity, 165
    publicly denied even knowing Jesus, 94
    questioning and breaking the trance, 145
    as a rare name in the Hebrew scriptures, 20n38
    reinstatement of, 115n17, 192
    seeing a figure standing on the shore, 115
    subject to capture and death, or attack by demons, 163
    thrust back into the perilous risk of serving his master, 145
    visionary trance of, 173
    witnessing necromancy, 48
"keys," fpr accessing the authority of the "finger of God," 83
"kicking the dust" off their feet, 70
King, Karen, 81–82
kingdom of God, 11, 31, 40, 57
kingdom of Satan, neutralized and disbanded by Jesus' risk mitigations, xix
Kittim (*ktyym* or *kty'ym*), as a strong, greatly feared military power, 37n40
Koester, Helmut, 89, 129, 129n53, 167

lake encounter, in John, 190–92
lake of Galilee, 15, 118, 148, 200
land, now under demonic control, 18
Lares, of the family, 3

larvae, 3
last will be first, and the first last, 56
laying on of hands (*keiris epithesousin*)
    as common to Jesus' practice of exorcisms, 129
    in conjunction with demonic exorcism, 130–31
    fraught with risk and danger, 129
    of Jesus, 156n28
    Jesus committing his exorcists to do, 127–28
    for Luke becoming the ordination of apostles or leaders, 132n56
    as practiced by Jesus passed into obscurity very early, 134
Lazarus, 44n95
Legion, 12n74, 31, 46n109, 63n215, 68n25
leper, in Capernaum, 46n109
letters of Paul, confirming the role of first-century women, 85n141
Levi, 67n22, 82, 162, 195–96
Lewis, I. M., 83
life expectancy, xviii, 18
liturgy, as a reflection of the Matthean rites, 175
Living One with salvific words, Jesus as, 203
"living waters," 30n36, 57
locations, named in honor of a direct encounter with God and angels, 24
locked rooms, Jesus' sudden appearances in, 101
Lord's Prayer, earliest version of, 187
lots, divination by used to complete the Twelve, 172
love, *agape*. *See agape*, salvific love
love, mercy, and forgiveness, practice of, 56
love or eroticism, poisons engendering, 127
love potion, considered a type of "poison," 127n44
lower classes, crucifixion "inflicted" on, 93n22
lower regions, places having a direct connection with, 26

SUBJECT INDEX   237

Lukan theology, smoothing over the abandonment of Jesus, 172n76
Luke, Gospel of
    leaves out the sending of the disciples to Galilee, 111n8
    making Mary Magdalene possessed, 83
    omitting Mary Magdalene's encounter with Jesus, 80
    placing Emmaus near Jerusalem, 181n3
    post-crucifixion encounters, 113–14
    recasting the final encounter with Jesus in Jerusalem, 135
    working out his conception with the help of geographical information, 111n8
luxuries, absolutely none for Galilean peasants, 19

Machetes, loved one of Philinnion, 100, 101
Madaurensis, Lucius Apuleius, accused of using magic, 3n12
Magdala (the tower) village, 16, 77. *See also* Tarichaeae
"Magdala Stone," oldest Menorah found to date in Israel, 77, 77–78n101
Magdalene, meaning "high one" or "fortress," 158
Magdalene (*Maria he kaloumene Magdalene*, or in Hebrew, *Maryam*). *See* Mary Magdalene
magicians (*magoi*)
    accepted as the norm, 1
    controlling evil forces, 7
    including dark magicians practicing black magic, 1n1
    Judaism forbade, xviiin10
    needed to drive out demons, 3
male
    Mary Magdalene becoming, 116n19, 160n38
    together with the female as neither male nor female, 86n145
male exorcists, 103, 107, 155

male Jewish peasants, no rights in the Roman world and kept in debt, 65
male-dominated hierarchical church, devaluing the role of Mary Magdalene, 88
malevolent demons, termed "restless," 4
malevolent spirits, 1, 70, 93
man with "unclean spirit," living near tombs, 51n133
the marginalized and dispossessed, Jesus and, 56
Mark
    including Mary Magdalene, 80
    wrote accurately, 143n121
Mark (Gospel of)
    appendix of, 112
    authentic reflection of the earliest activity of Jesus' exorcists post-crucifixion, 133n62
    confirming that Jesus' followers met with him in Galilee, 140n98
    manuscripts varying in resurrection appearances included, 120–21
    post-crucifixion encounters, 112, 120–49
Mark 9:2–8, 139, 140, 149
Mark 16:9–20, missing in a number of ancient manuscripts, 121
Mark 16:12, 180n1
Mark 16:17–18, 131, 134–37
Marxsen, Willi, 111
Mary, *the Magdalene* ("the tower," "fortress," or the "high one"), 36n30, 79
Mary Magdalene
    accepted and lived with the other males, 88
    accepted the perilous risk of going to a tomb before dawn, 84, 107, 150–51, 163, 198
    accepting the deadly risk of conjuring or communicating with Jesus, 85, 156
    as an active and influential member among the remaining exorcists in Galilee, 89

Mary Magdalene (*continued*)
   as an apostle, 155n25
   becoming like a male, 86
   considered an exorcist post-crucifixion, 160
   control of at least seven demons, 83
   conversing with Jesus as if an equal, 81
   discussing the words of the Savior, 161
   as an embarrassment to the early church, 196
   encountering Jesus, 79, 113, 114, 156, 160, 163
   given a title designating her authority over demons, 83
   as identifiable, 156–57
   impact on Jesus' teachings, 87
   as an itinerant ecstatic and exorcist, 84, 151
   in Jesus' band, 77–89
   knew where his body had been taken, 103
   as the leader of Jesus' exorcists, 196
   made subservient to the traditions associated with the male exorcists, 79, 159
   "ministered (*diekonoun*)" to Jesus and his exorcists, 78
   never questioning Jesus' use of allegories and parables, 87
   omitted as one of Jesus' leading exorcists, 72n50
   overcoming a multitude of demons, 67n22
   Paul not citing, 151n4
   perilous risk following her encounter with Jesus, 160
   presence with Kepha and the others at meal, 196
   role of dangerous to certain Christian communities, 81
   seeing the Lord in a vision, 161
   subsistence existence of, 158
   suppressed and relegated to Gnostic wisdom literature, 87
   as a Therapeutae, 86
   tradition of exorcism of demons from, 158n32
   travelled with Jesus and the other male exorcists, 80
   as well-respected as Kepha, 88
   witnessed the crucifixion, the place of burial, and had a vision of the risen Lord, 82

Mary of Clopas, 180–81n2
Mary the Magdalene and "the other Mary," having the first ecstatic encounter with Jesus post-crucifixion, 150–56
Mary the Mother of James and Salome, 153n13
"master" of the Sabbath, Jesus as, 57
material substance, as the sign of a departing demon, 7
Mattaym, tax collector licensed under Antipas, 68
Matthew (Gospel of), 113, 114n15, 132
Matthew 28:1–10, 150–63
Matthew 28:16–20, 177, 178–79
Matthew 28:17, 168
the meal, transformed after Emmaus, 188n48
men and women, brutal attacks on by Pilate, the elite, and their spies, 152
mercy, *eleos*, 55, 56, 57
messianic age, inauguration of, 73
"messianic banquet," 73, 184
messianic rebellions, 43–44n90
metamorphosis of Jesus, of Jesus as a post-crucifixion encounter, 139–49
miqvaot, collected rainwater for ritual purification, 30n36
"miracles," of Paul, 133
mob, in Gethsemane, 106
money, carried by exorcists, 72n49, 72n54
Moses, 58n183, 139n91, 144–45
Mt. Tabor (*Har Tavor*)
   held to be sacred by Jews and Pagans, 172, 172n76, 172n77, 172n78, 173
   sacred to Jesus, 146n130

where Jesus escaped, 67n21
mud and saliva, application of, 128
mud or clay, mixing spittle with, 9–10
mutilation, of bodies, 90n5, 93, 103
mystical encounter, with Jesus' words as the "living" one as salvific, 166
mystical rites, 174, 176

"name," of Jesus as "above" all spirits, 106
Nazareth, 35n18, 127n47
necromancer, Jesus as, xviii
necromancy
    furthest thing from the minds of the Galileans, 106
    of Jesus derived from Beelzebul, xiv
    Jesus openly performed, 91
    Jesus' practice of, 40–41
    as the most illegal and controversial, 47
    public practice of, 45–46
    raising Lazarus as an illegal act of, 44n95
    Roman and Jewish laws expressly prohibited, 41
    witnessing, 48
negotiated settlement, as usually temporary, xvn2
neutralizing practices, used against Jesus, xviii
"new tongues," interpreted as foreign languages, 124
night work, arranged for Kepha, 148
non-canonical gospel accounts, of encounters with Jesus, 116
non-canonical Gospels and writings, never emphasizing retribution, 101
non-canonical literature, honoring the role of Mary Magdalene, 81
northern Israelites, distinct from Judeans, 65

Old Testament, lack of *EvP*'s citation of, 198
opponents of Jesus, xvi, 125

oral tradition, 24, 181n4, 198
Origen, 173
ossuaries, measurements of, 97n48
overseers, lining their own pockets, 21

pagan sources, as void of post-crucifixion encounters with Jesus, 116
Palestinian Jews, deaths of, 90
palsied hand, man with, 46n109
parable(s)
    of Jesus, 30, 43n84, 56n169, 77n95
    Therapeutides thought and taught in, 87
paradise, 141
paralyzed man, lowered down to Jesus, 46n109, 52
Parousia, 143, 167, 170
passion narrative tradition, 111, 181n5
"patron to Judaism," supporting the synagogue, 78
patrons, wealthy widows became, 65
pattern
    of entry required for exorcists, 72
    of Jesus' exorcisms, 49–52
Patterson, Stephen, 191n6
Paul. *See also* Saul of Tarsus
    accused of being a false apostle or a charlatan, 170
    appealing to Kepha as witness to the resurrection of Jesus, 156n27
    charismatic powers of, xiv
    considering himself as equal to Kepha, 142
    curse on an adulterer, 142
    defending the legitimacy of his apostleship, 155–56n27
    describing exorcisms, 133
    ecstatic experiences of possession, "Christ in me," 137
    on ecstatic visionary and trance experiences, 149
    finding it unnecessary to speak in tongues, 124
    "gospel" of the death, burial, and resurrection of Jesus, 171
    on his being a true apostle, 133n62

240   SUBJECT INDEX

Paul (*continued*)
  on his ecstatic experience, 141
  identifying Jesus as Jesus *Christos*, 67n22
  on Kepha and Yohannes as "the pillars," 145
  knew of Jesus' exorcisms, 133
  muting opponents' claims to legitimacy, 165–66
  on neither "male nor female" adherents, 86
  practiced the use of Jesus' name in rites, 169n66
  rejected by the "super apostles," and earlier by men (false brothers, *psuedadelphous*), 168
  statement that "And if Christ be not risen, then is our preaching vain, and your faith is also vain," 111n9
  stating he saw Jesus with his own eyes, 166
  on the tension between claims of authority of various post-resurrection encounters, 165
  traced charismatic and divine authority to Kepha's encounter, 155
  on women as exorcists in the Jesus movement, 151n4
  on women remaining silent as a later emendation, 89
Pauline community, devalued baptism, 172
Pauline *ecclesiae*, with baptism as optional, 171
"peace" coins, *eirenopolis*, demonstrated allegiance to Caesar, 15
peasant exorcists, 60–61, 71
peasant Galilean Jews, understood malevolent and retributive ghosts, 102n73
peasants
  burial of, 90n3
  chosen by Jesus to join with him and assist, 60–61
  inability to control the safety of the waters, 30
  not voluntarily supplying labor for the elite, 21
  struggling for survival under severe oppression, xiii, xvi
peasant's body, placement into an expensive elitist's tomb and then the sealing it up, 96
perilous risk
  associated with any affiliation with Jesus, 103
  behavior authenticating the Markan tradition, 130
  elements, 198, 200
  of a Galilean-Emmaus-tradition muted in Luke, 184
  human response to, 118n30
  in a refusal to accept encounters as divine, 142
  risk analysis identifying a perception of, xivn2
  surrounded the Galilean exorcists, 107
Perrin, Norman, 138
personal items, dead buried with, 97
persuasive letters, of the super apostles, 167n54
Peter. *See Kepha* (Peter)
Petronius, Roman centurion witnessing two figures coming from heaven, 196–97
phantasm(s). *See also* ghost (*phantasms*)
  accepted as the norm, 1
  controversial nature of Jesus appearing as, 191n6
  encounter in Emmaus shared quickly, 183–84
  exorcists seeing Jesus as, 114n13
  floated over the waters seeking victims, 33
  haunting the waters of Galilee, 68, 191–92
  pulled from the dead pool of wandering souls for retribution, 93

Philinnion, leaving her tomb (after six months), 100
Philo (*Da Vita Contemplativa*), on the Therapeutae, 86
Phlegon, 100, 154
Phoebe, 89, 151n5, 156
physical appearance, of an exorcist, 55
Piso, 127n45
Pistis Sophia, on Jesus instructing his disciples, 81n118
plants, growing near waters to be avoided, 25–26
Pliny, writings of, 116
poison, drinking unharmed, 127
"poisons," as evil potions and concoctions, 127
Pompey the Great, conquered Jerusalem, 33n3
Pontius Pilate
  acceding to demands that Jesus be crucified, 76n91
  approaching as unimaginable in the recovered risk context, 99
  fifth Roman governor, 32n1
  fully supported Jesus' crucifixion, 94
  imperialism under, 151n3
  interrogating Jesus as a dark magician, 76n91
  knew Jesus' reputation as an exorcist and necromancer, 42n76
  turning the guards over to the chief priests, 98
  used the ruse of releasing Jesus so his spies and assassins could identify and kill Jesus' followers, 43n81, 100n63
  wife fearing contact with Jesus, 76n91
population
  of Capernaum (Nahum's village), 35, 35n20
  of Tiberias and Sepphoris, 15–16
possession
  accepted as the norm, 1
  demonic, 11, 61, 128, 132n58
  ecstatic experiences of, 137
  fear of, 2
  first-century Jewish peasant accused of, xviii
  identifying with the "finger of God," 11
  incidents of reported by Flavius Josephus, 8
  Jesus' insistence on readmitting those he freed from, 55
  of Judas *Iscariot* by Satan, 11
  petition for continued protection from, 186
  spirit, 38n47, 58n185
possession trance, 157, 157n30
post-crucifixion encounters with Jesus
  demanded continuation of perilous practices, 135
  engendering a radical decision, 130
  in the four canonical Gospels, 111, 112–15
  of Kepha, 146–47
  of Paul, 130, 166
  reports of treated as *leros*, nonsense, 155
  traditions in Matthew associated with, 150
  transposed back into Jesus' Galilean activity, 191
  traumatizing as evidence of a risk event, 110–12
post-crucifixion events, 144, 200
post-crucifixion set of demands, Mark 16:17–18 as a contextually reliable, 136–37
poverty, 21, 69
powerlessness, exchanging for authority, 71
prayer
  apotropaic, 74, 186–87
  appeal for victory and survival the next day, 186
  earliest version of the Lord's Prayer, 187
  ecstatic, 154, 185n27
  and fasting expelling a demon, 125
  Jesus taught to the Galilean exorcists, 20
  preserving them from "falling into the hands" of Satan, 185

prayer (*continued*)
    protection afforded by, 74
    referencing delivery from the "evil one," 187n39
    "secret" in heavenly language, 125n31
    verbal, 39n59
predictions, of Jesus, 94–95, 102n73
prefect (governor of Judaea), 32n1
priestly ruling families, chosen by Rome, 33n3
primitive community, indispensable role of women in, 89
procurator. See *prefect* (governor of Judaea)
production quotas, 14, 16
protection, afforded by prayer, 74
public exorcisms, employing Jesus' name in, 123
publicani, 34, 34n15
"pure food," affording mystical protection, 187
Pythagoras, 125

Q, 18, 36, 173n82
qualitative risk analysis. See also risk analysis
    application of, xvn2, 122
    of Mark 9:2–8, 143–45
    of Mark 16:17–18, 129
    of Matthew 28:1–10, 156–57
    of Matthew 28:16–20, 173–74
    for post-crucifixion encounters, 117
Quirinus, crucified Jews in Galilee, 92
Qumran literature, confirming belief in exorcisms and knowledge of demons, 9

Rabbinic tradition, confirming the pervasive activity of demons, 5
rains, 24, 26
raising up of snakes, 132n56
reality, embracing an altered perspective of, 1
religious ascetic, exorcist or prophet, marking the entrant as, 55
religious elite. See also the elite
    doomed to judgment, 56n167
    equated by Jesus with vipers and serpents, 125n36
    Jesus' woes on, 43n84
    on Mary Magdalene, 84
    sent spies with questions to trap Jesus, 43n81
religious leaders' homes, Jesus heading to in each village, 55n158
restlessness, of demons, 4
resurrected Jesus, as nothing more than a ghostly experience, 114
resurrection
    appearances as a reflection of theological intent, 111
    characterization of Jesus' seeking to comfort those he loved, 101
    encounter with Kepha lost and recast in Mark, 147
    no expectation of a general, 167
    as the salvific event associated with Kepha, 87
    traditions in Mark and Matthew, 183
retribution
    crucifixion neutralizing, 42n76
    Galilean exorcists perceived as capable of bringing, 108
    Herod Antipas assumed the spirit of John the Baptist as taken by Jesus for, 91, 169n63
    Herod Antipas terrified of, 6
    Jesus exposing himself to, 56n167
    Kepha facing, 163
    not ascribed to Jesus' exorcists post-resurrection, 101
    phantasm(s) pulled from the dead pool of wandering souls for, 93
    rejecting, 179
    villages fear of denomic-Roman, 42
return of Jesus, to continue the war on Satan and demonic imperialism, 102
risen Jesus
    defining his legitimate apostles as charismatics and exorcists, 121
    encountered as a *phantasm*, 114n15

SUBJECT INDEX 243

instructions from differing from those in the Synoptic Gospels, 195
ordering a mystical baptism of unification with powerful, divine names, 169
risk, of following Jesus, 61
risk analysis. *See also* qualitative risk analysis
adjusting to perilous risk events, 199
application of following a distinct pattern, xiv
identifying a perception of "perilous risk," xivn2
of the post-crucifixion encounters, 117–19
reading and understanding texts from Jesus's world, xiv
roots of, xiiin1
studying the origins of Christianity through, xix
risk conflict, accepting the salvific wisdom sayings of Jesus, 170
risk context, of Jesus' countermeasure to free Palestine and Galilee from evil, 53
risk criteria, for post-crucifixion encounters, 117
risk elements, 199, 200
risk environment, recapture of, xiiin1
risk events, distinct from the needs of the early church, 199
risk motivation, of Mary Magdalene's visit to the tomb, 151
risk perception, of the elite, 104
risks and risk mitigations, neutralizing the threat of the other, xiii
ritual acts, "in the name of" as intentional, 169
ritual clothing, power of, 98n54
ritual guard, at the tomb, 98
ritual Jewish baths (*miqva'ot*), in Magdala, 78
ritual pattern, followed by Jesus, 49
"the rock," as *Petros* in Greek, 20n38
rock-hewn tomb, of Jesus was intended to be a trap, 96
rolling stone, removable with great strength, 97–98
Roman army, occupation of, 32n2, 33n3
Roman guard at the tomb, as unlikely, 98
Roman officials, licensed overseers protected by Roman soldiers, 20
Roman religion, embedded in Palestine, 33n3
Roman soldier's paralyzed servant, healed by Jesus' command alone, 46n109
Roman world
as completely alien to our own, 1
illegal magicians of, 63, 63n218
Roman wrath, as perilous, 62
Romanization, of Jerusalem's elite, 17
Roman-licensed brokers, controlling fishing, 66
Romans
brought foreign gods and demons into the land, xvi–xvii
crucified Jews in Galilee, 92
disapproving of magicians and sorcerers, 7n36
royal official's son, Jesus' healing while at some distance away, 10n60

Sabbath, demons vulnerable on, 49
sacred fish, employed in rites, 70
sacred gifts, waters as, 23
sacred space, Jesus entering and exorcising demons, 78n101
sacred waters, 24, 29
sacrifice of Jesus, breaking the curse of death, 170
safety, to avoid being expelled, 20
saliva. *See also* spittle
application of with mud, 128
creating an ointment, 9–10
of Jesus absorbing or drawing out demons, 28
mentioned in cures, 9n55
salvific esoteric sayings, 167
Samaritan woman, tradition of Jesus and, 157n31

sandals, unclear that Jesus is prohibiting, 75n83
Satan
  attempting to possess exorcists, 74
  employing all means to succeed, 12
  entering Judas's heart, 11n66
  "falling like lightning," xix, 63, 138, 185–86
  Jesus as an agent of, for the elite, 105
  Jesus at war with, 38
  Jesus conversed with, xvii, 58, 91, 105
  Jesus driving from the land, 37n34
  known to employ demons, 11
  prayer referenced delivery from, 187n39
  seeking his victims, 74n71
  shown as powerless, 126
satanic forces, 42, 151n3
Saul of Tarsus, 67n22, 108, 152. *See also* Paul
sayings
  created difficulties for the early church, 131
  of Jesus, 171
  spoken by demons to Jesus, 50n125
sayings-wisdom salvation tradition, as "doubters," 172
"scapegoat" tradition, relating Jesus' death as sacrifice, 198
Sea of Galilee, Jesus walking on at night, 114, 190
sealed container, placing bodies in, 95
sealed tomb, guards of, 153
secret knowledge, of Mary Magdalene, 82, 87
"secret" prayer, in heavenly language, 125n31
Sepphoris, built by Antipas, 14–15
serpents and scorpions, crushing or blasting, 126
servants, those in power becoming, 56
seven, in Jewish tradition, 83n128, 84
"seventy" exorcists, sending of, 72n54
sewage, carried out and dumped, 19
shamans, able to produce group visions, 139

sheep gate, may have been near the Temple, 27n17
Shimon ben Yonah, renamed "the Rock" by Jesus, 20n38
Shimon Kepha, 67, 67n22. *See also* Kepha (Peter)
"signs" (*semeia*)
  evoking, 123
  of Jesus, 121
  Mark and Luke identifying as exorcisms, 132n59
  in a post-crucifixion encounter in Mark, 122
  statement attributed to the risen Jesus and addressed to his exorcists, 112
Siloam, waters of, 29
Simon, 5, 67n22
Simon of Perea, 44n90
sin and judgment, Jesus demanded a change in the view of, 56
"sins," presumption of, 128
sitz im leben of the first century, uncovering, xix
six days, in the Gospel of Mark, 139, 139n91
slavery, selling children into to satisfy debts, 17
"sleeping" dead, raising at judgment, 41
snakes, as the personification of Satan, 125
socio-economic risk conditions, in Galilee, 14–22
sociological risk setting, coherence with, 117, 147–48, 159–60
soldiers
  guarding the tomb, 116
  not executed for falling asleep, 98
  protecting licensed overseers, 20
  witnessing two figures coming from heaven, 196–97
Solomon, 8–9, 8n44
Solomonic practices and teachings, exorcists invoking, 50
Solomon's sword, 98n56
soma (body), with a material presence, 3
Son of God, 144
Son of Man, 144, 144n124

SUBJECT INDEX 245

Songs of the Sage (Songs of Maskil), 9
sorcerers (*goetes*). *See goetes* (sorcerer)
"sorceresses," crucified in Askelon, 92
sorcery, enticing Israel to apostasy, 40n68
"speaking in new tongues (*glossais*), 124
spell scrolls, widely used in the ancient world, 96
spells, accepted as the norm, 1
spells, amulets, and other means, sealing a ghost into a tomb or grave, 95n40
spells and curse tablets, poisons combined with, 127
spices, carrying at night as difficult, 153
spies
    assigned to track Jesus, 40
    Mary Magdalene watched by, 84–85
    recruiting paid from the local populace, 43n81
    reported Jesus raising the dead, 41
    sympathetic to Rome and the Jerusalem elite, 43
    witnessed Jesus controlling all classes of malevolent demons and spirits, 105
spirit, of Jesus ritually entrapped, 96
spirit and body, uniting as strictly forbidden, 41
Spirit of Christ, Paul possessed by, xiv
Spirit of God, denied the annihilation of Jesus, 138
spirit possession, 38n47, 58n185
spirit transportation, 166
spirits, 12, 83n129
spittle. *See also* saliva
    combined with other techniques of manipulation, 53
    of an exorcist thought to be imbued with authority, 9
    Jesus using, 9n53, 53, 128
springs, dangerous on Wednesday evenings and nights because of demons, 19
springs and waters, in Galilee as possessed by spirits and demons, 25
staff, as a common feature in Palestine for travelers, 75n84
stone, rolling back could require two or more men, 98
stone tomb, placement in a sealed, xviii
storm over Galilee, Jesus stilling and rescuing Kepha from drowning, 29
style of life, of Jerusalem's elite, 17
subsistence existence
    encounters led the Galileans to again abandon, 118, 136, 148, 201
    of fishers, 192n11
    of peasants, xvi
subsistence laborers, welcoming peasant exorcists, 76
"super apostles" (*huper apostolon*), 124, 155, 167, 167n54, 168, 170–71
supporters, of Jesus as small in number, 42
supporting Jesus, risk of, as too great, 40
swords, present when Jesus was taken, 98
synagogue(s)
    Jesus' practice of entering, 50–51
    located in Galilee, 17n22
    in Magdala, 78
    remaining near a cleansed, 51n137
Synoptics, reporting young individuals, 47n113
Syrian Antioch, 174
Syrophoenician women, Jesus' exorcism of, 47n110

Tacitus, writings of, 116
tactile aspect, of Jesus' exorcisms, 52–54
Talmud, references to Jesus in, 116, 116–17n24
tamarisk, of the Jordan Valley as *makruh*, "loathsome," 26
Taricheaeae, famous for its salted and pickled fish, 35
Taricheae, Magdala also known as, 77
tashlikh prayers of the Jews, recited next to a body of water, 25

taxation, of fishers allowed no surplus, 21
taxonomy, of ghosts, 3
techniques, Jesus employed in encounters to expel demons, 53
Telchines, inducing clouds and rain, hailstones and snow, 63n218
tenant/landlord relationships, harsh in Galilee, 20
Tertullian of Carthage, 5
Tertullianus, Quintus Septimius Florens, father of Latin theology, 5n23
Testimonium Flavianum, alluding to Jesus being seen alive again, 116
testimony, of a woman not carrying weight, 151n4
Tetrarch, or "ruler of a quarter" of Palestine, 37n37
theological program, of Luke as Christianity's expansion, 137
Therapeutae (the origin of Mary the Magdalene), 187
Therapeutides, 86–87, 158
thirty pieces of *arguria*, 44
Thomas
    abandoned Jesus, 107
    charismatic nature of, 159n36
    later known in ancient Christianity as "the doubter," 171–72
    refusing to accept that Jesus is active and risen, 115
three-day return, of Jesus only remembered by his enemies, 110
Tiberias (city), 15
Tiberius (emperor), 15, 127n45
Tibullus, 63n218
time, finding a safe to ritually "destroy" Jesus, 41
Toma ("my twin"), 67n22, 68, 167, 167n52
tomb
    examples of the dead vacating, 100–102
    going to having nothing to do with anointing a decaying and mutilated body, 153–54
    guarding, 96–100
    of Jesus found empty three days after he was crucified, 106
    not provided to peasants or the poor, 100n64
    with a single entrance selected for Jesus, 97
touching with hands, as a powerful charismatic act to drive off evil, 128
traditions
    of post-crucifixion encounters, 111
    relating to Magdalene's encounter meet the criterion of embarrassment, 159
    as reminiscence without any theological program, 194
trance-like experiences, 166
trances
    in the ancient world, 164–79
    Jesus entered into, 39, 39n57
    Mary Magdalene entering into, 163
transfiguration. *See also* metamorphosis of Jesus
    as most likely a post-crucifixion encounter, 112
troubling events, examples of, 131
true self, reuniting of with the divine, 166–67
tunic, Jesus said to have worn a single, 75n82
Twelve
    eventually gathered and selected by Kepha, 149n140
    names of varying in canonical lists, 172
twin. *See* Toma ("my twin")
two Marys, 151–53, 154

unclean spirits, as demons in Mark, 12, 12n71
untimely dead. *See also* the dead
    able to curse, punish, and harm, 95
    Antipas's fear of, 93
    fear of the return of, 92

retributive attack on enemies, 153n15
"upper room," Galileans hiding in, 106

vacancy, among the Twelve filled by casting lots, 149n140
Varus, 42n77, 43n86
verbal confrontation, with demons in the synagogues of Galilee, 51
verbal prayer, as only the first stage of prayer, 39n59
Vespasian, 8, 9n55
village leaders, accused Jesus of being of Satan, 59
villagers
  going to extraordinary measures to reach Jesus, 52
  no better than chattel slaves, 16
  some not allowing Jesus or his exorcists to set foot in their village or region, 42
villages
  along the lake of Galilee, 16, 64, 86
  burden on nearby in Galilee, 15
  Galilean peasants huddled in, 33
  of Galilee, 35–36, 38
  Jesus' condemnation of, 137, 137n83
  Jesus entering when allowed, 36
  Jesus forbidden from entering, 34n10, 36n33
  Jesus sending exorcists into, 71
  Josephus, Flavius on, 16n11
  rejected Jesus out of fear of demonic-Roman retribution, 42
  settled around waters, 25

War Scroll, 11n63
warning, of Jesus meeting the criterion of dissimilarity, 102
water
  discussion about drinking living, 29–30
  drawing on certain days and times, 5–6
  drawn only on certain days and never at night, 19
  immersion in requiring abundant, 178
  of Jesus considered powerful, transformative, and able to commute his authority to others, 28n25
  as a place to contain demons, 27n16
water and food, consumption of at certain times, 19
waters
  in the ancient world as inhabited, 23
  fishers taking significant risks on, 66
  importance and danger of in the ancient world, 26
  including the lake of Galilee as places for trapping demons, 3
  mastery of was regarded with awe, 68
  sacred and haunted, 23–31
waters of Galilee
  filled with demons and spirits, 57n181, 62–63n214
  Jesus and, 29–30
  Jesus held mastery over, 63
  as the refuge of demons, 68
weather and wind, immediate changes of, 68
Wednesday evenings and nights, springs especially dangerous on, 24
wells, exorcism of in later rabbinic tradition, 23n2
white robes, as protective garb, 98n54
"who is worthy," finding in the town first, 75
wicked dead, demons as active spirits of, 12
widows, rights of, 65
wife
  of Germanicus, 127n46
  of Pontius Pilate, 76n91
witnesses, authentic demonstrating charismatic practices, 163
woman
  making herself male, 87

woman (*continued*)
   touching Jesus' garment to be healed, 46n109
women
   authority of, 159
   bringing children and infants to Jesus to touch him, 52–53
   brutal attacks on by Pilate, the elite, and their spies, 152
   charismatic, 85
   coming to the tomb hoping for contact with Jesus, 154n20
   directly linked to healings, 151n4, 159n35
   encountering Jesus on the road, 155
   Galilean, encounters with Jesus, 117n25
   having virtually no rights, 65
   holding monetary power and even religious authority, 78
   in Jesus' band, 77–89
   with male exorcists originating with Jesus, 85n141
   in Paul's list, 89
   of rabbinic families said to have had charismatic authority, 159
   suppression of in gospel traditions, 151n5
   Therapeutrides included as equals, 86
   tradition of first conversing with the risen Jesus, 155
wonder worker, Hainina's fame as, 10

Yacob
   as the child of *Abbá*, 67n22
   witnessing necromancy, 48
Yecob and Yohannes (renamed by Jesus, *Boanerges*, "sons of power/the thunderers"), 67–68, 67n22, 70–71, 165
Yeshua, "son of Mary," 35n17
Yohannan, witnessing necromancy, 48

Zakkai, Johannan ben, 10
Zealot extremists, *sikarioi*, the "knife men" or "assassins," 37

Scripture Index

OLD TESTAMENT

Genesis
3:14	125n36
15	58n183
16:7–14	24n5
33:18–20	24n4

Deuteronomy
18:10–11	xviiin10
19:15–16	197n5
20:23	92n19
21:16	41n71
21:22–23	41n72, 76n91

Judges
13:6	7n42, 12n75
21:16 LXX	182n6

1 Kings
17:17–24	47n115

2 Kings
4:32–37	47n115

Job
2:9	182n6
30:6	20n38

Psalms
89:12	172n76
95:5	11n67

Song of Songs
7:9	41n71

Isaiah
26:19	41n71
35:10	24n6
50:6	198
61:2	40n64

Jeremiah
4:29	20n38

Daniel
12:2	41n71

Hosea
5:1	172n76

Zachariah

12:10	198

DEUTEROCANONICAL BOOKS

1 Enoch

	144
10:4	59n192

1 Maccabees

3:40	182
4:3	182
9:50	182

Book of Jubilees

10:3–8	59n192
10:8–11	58n183
22:1–17	11n67

IV Ezra

	144

Tobit

8:3	9n51, 59n192

PSEUDEPIGRAPHA (OLD TESTAMENT)

eighth Book of Moses

	9n48

Testament of Solomon

	98n56
2:1	7n42, 12n75
3:5–6	11n67
3:6	7n42, 12n75
4:3–4	7n42, 12n75
5.11	6n33, 27n16
6:1–4	12n68
11:6	27n16
22	2n9, 12n73

Pesik

140a	98n56
R15	98n56

DEAD SEA SCROLLS

1QH

5:9, 13–14	74n71

4Q286 (4QBer a)

7.2.1–4	11n67

4Q510–112n5

4QpHos

1	74n71

4QpNah

1:5–7	74n71
11Q	112n5

The Community Rule, Manual of Discipline

1QS

5:13–14	175n85

Genesis Apocryphon

11Q5	7n38

Hymn Against Demons

4Q560	2n5, 7n38

Pesher Nahum

4Q	169
3–4 II	92

SCRIPTURE INDEX 251

Purity Texts
4Q
274–276   175n85

Qumran Hymn
11Q ps
27.9–10   9n49
11Q5   9n49

Songs of the Sage **or** *Songs of Maskil*
4Q510–511   2n7, 9

Temple Scroll
11QT
LXIV, 7–13   92

War Scroll
    11n63

"wicked priest" Pesher Habakkuk
1QpHab
1:13   18n25
8:8–12   18n25
9:9   18n25
12:3–5, 8–9   18n25

ANCIENT JEWISH WRITERS

Josephus

Antiquities of the Jews
2, 5, 8, 45–48   8n43, 29n33
4:219   115n16, 193n16
8:2.5   50n128, 154n20
8:45–48   7n40, 10n58
8:46–49   8n46
8:60–62   90, 152n10
9:2, b1   12n68
10   43n86
13:14   92n16
14:2.121   10n59
14:22–24   10n57
14:61–70   33n3
14:143   78n106
14:158–60   37n39
15.8.1   17
17:6.7   69n37
17:8.3   96n43, 153n17
17:10   92n13
17:10.10   42n77
17:271   15n4
18:1–10, 23   44n90
18:1.1–10, 23   92n14
18:2.2   69n37
18:3.2   78n107
18:3.3   152n10
18:5.2   58n190, 91n6, 175n87
18:26–8   92n13
18:27   15n5
18:36–38   15n8
18:36.3   182n11
18:60–62   69n37
18:63–64   116n23
18:85–87   42n77
18:85–89   152n10
18:109–18   37n37
18:109–19   6n34
18:118   12n76
20:8, 4–5   xviin5
20:9   91n7
20:102   37n39

Apion
2:205   97

Jewish War
1:8, 9   77n97
1:128, 141, 143, 145–147, 149–51
    33n3
1:204.5   37n39
2:4.2.3   69n37
2:5.2   42n77, 69n37
2:175–177   43n81, 69n37
2:254–57   37n39
2:433   44n90
2:443–48   37n39

SCRIPTURE INDEX

Jewish Wa(continued)r

2:510	65n10
4:1.3	25n8, 183n13
4:400–405	37n39
6:3	12n72
7:6, 3	2n3

Life

76	92n15
235	16n11

Testimonium Flavianum

	116, 181n4

Philo

Da Vita Contemplativa

	86

Embassy

302	152n10

Special Laws

3.159	66n19

RABBINIC WORKS

Bikkurim

3:3	97
65c	97

Leviticus Rabbah

24:3	23n2

Miam. Yad.
Evel

12:8	97

Midrash

Teharot

11.6	19n31
.6	25n10

Mishnah

Ketubbot

4.12a	65n13

Shabbat

6:6, 9–10	99n57

Ta'anit

3:8	10n59

Terumot

1:1	51n133

Pesachim

	112
p. 1	6n32, 25n9

Sem.

8.1	91n8

Sh. Ar. YD

361:4	97

Talmud

Ketubbot

105a	65n6

Menahot

85a	36n26

Mishnah Erubin

53b	xviiin9

Pesahim

112b	19n30

Sanhedrin

6:6	96
43a	45n106, 58n189, 67n22, 105n11
90b	41n71
91b	41n71

SCRIPTURE INDEX

Tosefta Hullin

2:22f	45n105
2:22f, 62–64	105n11
2:22f, 114–115	105n11

"Treatise Berachoth

fol. 3a	9n51

Testament of the Twelve Patriarchs

Testament of Asher

1:9	12n71

Testament of Levi

5:6	12n71
18:12	12n71

Testament of Simeon

3:5	12n71
4:9	12n71

Tosefta

Terumot

1:3	51n133

NEW TESTAMENT

Matthew

	44n98, 71, 75, 81, 114n13, 118n29, 120, 132, 132n57, 132n59, 140, 144n121, 159, 160n37, 164n41, 169, 183, 191n2, 201n18
3:4	39n50
3:7	57n180
3:13–17	37n35
4:1–11	3n15, 11n62
4:8	140
4:10	2n4
4:12–13	35n18
4:13	34n11
4:18–22	35n16, 126n37
4:19	40n65
4:20	70n40
5:41	65n5
5:44	55n164
6:5	69n37
8:1	140n100
8:14–5	34n12
8:14–15	34n10
8:16–17	49n120, 52n138
8:29	51n134
8:34	34n10
9:13	56n173
9:18, 19, 23–25	103n76
9:19	103n76
9:23–25	103n76
9:27–31	46n109
9:35	72n54, 78n103
10:1	67n21
10:1, 9–11, 14	72n54
10:2	164, 164n42
10:5–15	54n156, 71
10:7–9, 10a, 11–13	54n155, 72n53
10:9	72n49, 72n52
10:10	75n84, 157n29
10:10a	54n155, 72n53
10:11	75n85
10:11–13	51n136, 54n155, 72n53
10:41	29n32
11:7–19	12n76
11:20	137n84
11:20–24	36n31, 39n55
11:20–25	39n60
12:1	36n32, 61n209
12:1–21, 22–37	40n66
12:8	57n177
12:22–25, 46–47	62n210
12:22–37	40n66
12:27	11n61, 38n46, 45n99, 62n212, 75n81
12:27–28	59n198
12:28	11n64, 43n84
12:38–42	94n33
12:39	43n84
12:43	45n102, 105n8
12:43–45	9n51

Matthew (continued)

12:45	53n149, 57n179, 74n66, 74n70, 142n114, 185n29
12:46–47	62n210
12:46–50	60n201
12:50	87n150
13:19	74n72
14:1–12	91n10
14:2	58n191
14:13–14	12n76
14:22–23	29n35
14:22–36	21n46, 114, 114n13, 190, 191n2
14:23	140n100
14:36	52n142, 55n160
16:4	43n84
16:19	83n125
16:24–28	94n30
17:1–8	137n82
17:14–21	71n45
17:17	43n84
17:19	122n12
17:24–27	21n41, 34n14, 175n84
17:27	35n16, 126n37
18:1–5	56n171
18:20	188n45
20:16	56n170
22:37–39	55n164
23:1–36	56n167
23:14–36	43n84
23:33	125n36
26:53	28n22
26:73	103n79, 152n11
27:35	97n47
27:55	152n6
27:61	152n9
27:62—28:15	96n46
27:63	102n75
28	171, 175, 176
28:1–8	88n152
28:1–10	84n132, 113, 150–63, 195
28:7	140n96
28:9	101n68
28:11–20	108
28:12–14	98n53
28:16–20	113, 123n15, 135n73, 164–79
28:17	110n3, 149n140, 168
28:18	169
28:63	110n4

Mark

	44n98, 71, 81, 114n13, 120, 131, 132, 132n56, 132n57, 132n59, 133n62, 138, 139, 140, 144n121, 150, 160n37, 180n1, 183, 191n2
1:9–11	37n35, 169n64
1:12–13	3n15, 11n62
1:16–20	35n16, 60n204, 126n37
1:17	40n65
1:18	70n40
1:21–26	49n119
1:21–28	29n31, 48n118, 62n213
1:22	56n168
1:23–25	50n131
1:24	xviin8, 50n125
1:29–31	34n10, 34n12, 46n109, 132
1:32–34	46n109, 49n120, 52n138
1:35	140n100
1:39	32, 47n109
1:40–45	46n109
2:1	34n11, 60n202
2:1–12	46n109
2:4	52
2:23	36n32, 76n87
3:31–35	61n205
3:1–5	46n109
3:10	52n142, 55n160
3:11	xviin8, 50n125
3:13–19	67n21, 140n99, 146n130, 148n139, 164
3:13–19, 31–35	61n205

SCRIPTURE INDEX

3:14	122n11, 122n13	6:45–56	21n46, 63n215, 68n25, 114, 114n13, 190, 191n2
3:15	36n30		
3:17	68n24		
3:20–25	52n140	6:46	67n21, 140n101, 146n130
3:21	53n149, 60n201, 62n210		
		6:51–52	94n31
3:27	31n42, 71n47	6:53–56	46n109
3:31–35	60n203, 73n64	6:56	52n142
3:35	35n17, 60n201, 87n150	7:24–31	47n110
		7:31–35	46n109
4:35–41	46n109	7:31–37	10n56, 28n24
4:40	94n31	7:32	127n47
5:1–9	33n9	7:32–35	28n26, 128, 129
5:1–17	31n42, 54n150, 192n7	7:33	28n23, 156n28
		7:34	39n59, 39n60, 124n29
5:1–20	3n11, 46n109, 69n33		
5:5	3n10	8:4, 14–21	94n31
5:7	xviin8, 50n125	8:11–12	94n33
5:17	36n33, 39n51	8:22–26	9n53, 10n56, 28n24, 46n109, 53n148, 128, 132
5:19	55n162		
5:21–24, 35–43	46n109		
5:21–43	52n141	8:23	28n23, 156n28
5:22–24	103n76	8:24—10:47	147
5:25–34	46n109	8:27—10:52	144
5:35–43	46n109, 55n158	8:28–30	102n73
5:36–43	2n4	8:28–34	31n43
5:38	97	8:31	94n31, 94n33, 102n74
5:39–42	48n116		
5:41	124n29	8:31–32	144n122
6:3	35n17	8:33	94n31
6:3–5	59n197	8:34	76n92
6:4	58n191	8:34—9:1	94n30
6:5	127n47, 128n49	8:34–35	63n219
6:6b–13	72n49, 72n54	8:38	144
6:7–13	54n156, 67n21, 71, 122n13	9:1	170n67
		9:1, 38	36n30
6:8	72n49	9:1–8	147
6:8–9	75n84	9:2–8	112, 137n82, 139–49, 140n95, 164, 164n43
6:9	72n52, 103n80		
6:10	72n56, 76n86	9:2–10	94n31
6:11	70n43, 75n80	9:8	141
6:14	43n89, 105n4, 122, 122n14	9:14–29	46n109, 71, 71n45
		9:18–20	76n88
6:14, 15	93n25	9:19	62n210
6:14–29	90, 91n10	9:28	122n13
6:15	93n25	9:30–32	144n122
6:16	41n71, 169n63	9:31	94n31, 94n33
6:17	85n141	9:38	36n30, 122n12

Mark (continued)

9:38–39	62n210, 123n17
9:38–40	11n61, 45n104
9:41	29n32, 56n165
9:42	53n146
10:13–16	53n144, 55n163
10:14b	53n145
10:32–34	94n31, 144n122
10:34	102n74
10:38	82n124
11:12–25	39n60
11:25	69n37
11:28	40n66
12:31	56n172
14:50	107n22
14:58	123n20
14:66–72	107n18
14:68–72	94n31
14:70	152n11
15	79
15:40	79
15:41	80n114
15:43	100n65
15:43–46	99n60
15:47	79
16:1	79
16:1–2	152, 153n13
16:1–8	84n132, 112, 120–21
16:7	112n11, 140n96, 140n97
16:9	80, 83n131
16:9–10	88n152
16:9–20	112, 121–30, 132, 135, 136
16:12	180, 180n1, 184n19
16:15	137
16:15–16	137–38
16:16	137
16:17	132
16:17–18	121, 121n8, 123, 125, 129, 137, 138, 142, 145
16:19–20	132n56

Luke

	44n98, 71, 81, 118n29, 120, 132, 132n57, 132n59, 144n121, 180, 181n4, 183, 191, 194, 201n18
1:36	37n36
2:14	44n94, 105n7
3:11	75n82
3:21–22	37n35, 74n68
4:1–3	3n15
4:1–13	11n62
4:14–30	35n19, 59n197
4:16–20	65n7
4:19	40n64, 52n142, 55n160
4:20–30	59n198
4:21–36	49n119
4:24–28	59n199
4:29	39n62, 59n196
4:33	12
4:38	60n202
4:38–39	34n12
4:38–40	2n4
4:38–41	34n10
4:39	60n202
4:40	127n47, 128
4:40–41	49n120
5:1–11	34n14, 46n109
5:2–11	35n16, 126n37
5:4	35n16
5:4–6	18n24, 34n13, 69n36
5:11	70n40
5:16	140n100, 148n138
6:1	36n32
6:12	140n100, 148n138
6:12–19	164
6:17–19, 53–56	52n142
6:19	55n160
6:24–26	51n132
6:27–36	55n164
6:53–56	52n142
7:1–10	46n109
7:11–15	103n76
7:11–17	41n74
7:36–50	83n126
8:1–3	79n111, 84, 160
8:2	67n22, 79n109, 88n152
8:2–3	83, 83n126

8:21	60n201	11:14–22	53–54n149
8:25–33	52n142	11:14–28	12n68
8:26–37	54n150	11:15	43n88, 105n3
8:26–39	3n16, 33n9, 63n215, 68n25	11:15–17	34n14
		11:19	11n61, 38n46
8:30	12n74	11:19–20	59n198
8:39	55n162	11:20	38n43, 40n66, 40n69, 41n76, 43n84, 44n97, 45n99, 57n175, 57n182, 59n198, 73n65, 185n23
8:46	52n143		
8:55	156n28		
9:1	67n21		
9:1–6	54n156, 71, 72n54, 122n12		
9:2	78n103	11:24	9n51, 12, 49n123, 58n184
9:3	72n52, 75n84, 157n29	11:24–26	9n51
9:7	43n89, 105n4	11:27–28	73n64
9:7–9	91n10	11:29	43n84
9:23–27	94n30	11:29–32	94n33
9:28–36	137n82	11:31	8n45, 50n129
9:29	146n131	12:39	74n72
9:32	146n129	13:15	56n165
9:32–34	46n109	14	57n176
9:51—10:15	42n78	14:1–14	57n176
9:51–56	36n33	14:7–14	77n95
9:54	70n44	14:15–24	77n95
9:60	61n206	15:1–7	56n169
9:62	142	15:11–32	56n169
10:1–16	54n155, 72n52, 72n53, 72n54	16:7	111n8
		17:1–2	56n166
10:8–10	55n157, 72n55	17:20–21	38n43, 57n174
10:9	129n52	17:21	73n63, 184n21
10:13	137n84	18:15–17	53n145
10:13–15	36n31, 39n55	18:33	95n37
10:14	129	20:9	43n84
10:17	77n96, 123n17	20:20	43n82
10:17–20	73n62	20:20–26	43n81
10:18	38n43, 39n57, 57n174, 59n194, 74n73, 135n72, 186n30	22:3	11n66, 74n72
		22:18	188n43
		22:35	70n39
		22:54–62	94n32
10:18–19	42n79	22:58	152n11
10:19	54n154, 126	23:1–11	84n132
10:20b	54n153	23:8	93n26
10:25–37	56n169	23:11–12	94n28
10:27	55n164	24	80n115
10:29	83n126	24:1	152
11:1	74n76, 186n33	24:10	88n152
11:2–4	69n37	24:11	103n77

Luke (continued)

24:13–35	113, 180, 180n1
24:16	111n8
24:34	113, 113n12, 138n87, 145n128, 155n26, 192
24:34 ESV	145n126
24:34 NIV	145n126
24–35	12n76
24:36–39	113
24:36–49	101n67
24:37	110n2
24:44	110n5
24:49	136n78, 155
24:50–53	114

John

	44n98, 81, 131, 164n41, 193, 197, 201n18
1:35	176n92
3:5	29n34
4:1–42	157n31
4:5–6	24n4
4:7	118n29, 201n18
4:10	30n37
4:46–50	10n60
5	27
5:1–4	27n20
5:4	26n15
6:7	11n66
6:16–24	21n46, 114, 190
7:1–9	60n201
7:37–39	30n37
9:1–10	28
9:3	128n48
9:6	10n56, 128, 156n28
11	47n113, 97
11:1–44	34n12, 103n76
11:16	42n80
11:33	39n58, 124n29
11:39	153n14
11:46–47	44n95
11:46–47, 53–54	41n72
11:48	125n35
11:53–54	41n72
12:6	70n39
13:27	11n66
14:2	118n29, 201n18
18:2–3	98n55
18:4–6	106n12
18:17	152n11
18:20	76n91
18:28, 30	41n76
18:29–30	40n66
18:30	41n76, 43n87, 105n2
19:23–24	55n159, 75n82
19:25	180n2
19:25–27	82n124
19:26–27	107n23
19:34	28n25
19:38	99n62
19:38–42	96, 153
20	193
20:7	101n70
20:11–19	114
20:17	101n69, 160n37
20:18	88n152
20:19	101n67, 107n17, 110n2
20:19–23	115
20:19–29	193
20:21	80n116
20:22	194
20:24–29	164n41
20:25	155
20:25–27	107n19
20:26–29	115
21	192n9, 193
21:1–3	136, 136n76
21:1–4	33n9
21:1–14	34n14, 194
21:1–23	115, 192–94
21:3	135n70
21:4–11	47n109
21:6	35n16, 126n37
21:6–8	34n13, 69n36
21:11	193n14
21:12	193n15
21:15–24	115n17
21:18	123n16, 142n111
:15	118n29

SCRIPTURE INDEX 259

Acts	132n56, 133, 166n47
1:12–26	172
2:1–13	124n26, 183n15
2:4	122n9
2:22	138n85
4:32—5:11	39n55
5:12–16	148n136
5:15	122n9
7:54–60	108n27, 142n112
8:3	142n112
8:4–15	39n55
8:14–17	148n136
8:17–18	128n50
9:1–19	166n47
9:17	128n50
9:32	151n4
9:33, 34, 36–41	148n136
9:34	148n136
9:36–41	148n136
10:9–16	39n57
10:10	146n132, 154n22
13:4–12	39n55
13:6–11	133n67
13:6–12	5n24
14:3	134n68
14:9–20	134n69
18:17–18	132n56
19:12	133n64
20:9	133n66
28:3	122n9, 125

Romans	
8:15	44n98, 185n27
16	156
16:3	85n141
16:6	85n141, 151n4, 158n38
16:7	85n141, 151n4, 151n5
16:12	85n141
16:15	85n141
16:25	166n49

1 Corinthians	
	155, 157n30, 165, 168n57, 170
1:10, 11	85n141
1:11	85n141
1:13	169n65
1:14, 17	170n69
1:17	170n69
2:8	171
2:9	167n55
4:8	170
4:15	170n68
5:4	169n66, 188n46
5:5	142
5:17	170n71
7:1–12	166n49
7:12	137n80
9:1	166n48
9:5	54n156, 151n4
9:16	130n54, 142n113
11	75n78
11:5	89
11:23	137n80, 166n49
11:27–30	188n44
12:2	166n48
12:8	166n49
12:10	133
13	xixn11, 56n172
13:1	124n28
13:2	166n49
13:8	124n25
14:2	166n49
14:8	124n27
14:32	137n80
14:34	89
15	151n4
15:1–3	170
15:1–5	113, 149n141, 172
15:1–8	155
15:1–9	124n27, 165
15:1–9, 50–54	166n48
15:5	138n87, 164n42, 166n49
15:14	111n9
15:44	170
15:50–54	166n48
15:51	47n114
16:22	39n55

2 Corinthians

	133, 165, 168n57, 170
3:1	167
11:3	125n36
11:5	170
11:5–6	124n23
11:24–26	142n112
12	141n104, 142, 145, 146, 151n5
12:1–4	137n81
12:1–7	166n49
12:2	151n4
12:2–4	141
12:7	141n108, 142n115
12:11–12	133n62
12:12	133n61, 133n62, 138n85

Galatians

	141n104, 168n57
1:8	39n55, 141n109, 171n74
1:13, 23	142n112
1:15	141n106
1:15–16	166n47
1:16	141n107
1:23	142n112
2:4	39n55
2:4, 11–13	168n58
2:9	145n127, 148n135, 165n44
2:11–13	168n58
2:20	137n79, 142n111
3:1–4	133
3:13	92n19
3:27–28	86n145
3:28	85n141
4:6	44n98, 185n27, 188n46

Ephesians

	106n13
1:21	106n13

1 Thessalonians

4:13–18	47n114
4:16	170n67
4:17	166n49

Hebrews

	173
6:2	128n50

1 Peter

4:15	42n76
5:8	74n71

2 Peter

1:15–18	146
1:17–18	172n78

1 John

| 5:6 | 28n25 |

Revelation

	98n54
7:9–17	98n54
12:9	125n36

APOCRYPHA (NEW TESTAMENT)

The Apocalypse of Abraham

| 14:1–14 | 58n183 |

Apocalypse of John the Theologian

| | 173 |

Apocryphon of James

| 14:25–26 | 139–40n92 |

Codex Berolinensis

| 8502 | 88n153 |

SCRIPTURE INDEX

Dialogue of the Savior

5	82

Gospel of Mary

	81, 88n153, 116, 160, 161, 195–96
1–6	84n133
5	82, 161
5:1	161
5:2	161
5:2–7	196n2
5:3	161, 196
5:4	161
5:5	161
5:6	161
5:7	161
5:8	161
5:9	161
5:10	161
5:11	161
9	161–62
9:1	162
9:2	162
9:3	162
9:4	162
9:5	162
9:6	162
9:7	162
9:8	162
9:9	162
9:10	162
20:17	160n38

Gospel of Peter

	98n52, 118n29, 192n10, 195, 197–201, 201n18
12:50—13:57	84n132
37–41	116, 196–97

Gospel of Philip

	88n153
59:6–11	81
63:30—64:9	81
70.13–17	86n145

Gospel of Thomas

	30, 71, 87, 160, 164n41, 166, 167, 167n51, 167n53, 171, 174
8	30n38
10.8	30n39
11.3	184n21
14.2	54n156, 71
17	171
21	81n118, 81n119
22	86
35	71n47
82	61n207
113	73n63
114	81, 81n118, 86, 87, 88n154, 155n25, 159n36

Pistis Sophia

	81n118, 88n153
2–3	139n92

Testaments of the Twelve Patriarchs

Testament of Naphthali

8:4–6	58n183

Q AND SIMILAR SOURCES

Q

	n98, 71
10:4–9	54n156, 71
11:13–14, 17–20	31n40
11:19–20	59n198
11:24–26	9n51

EARLY CHRISTIAN WRITINGS

Apocalypse of James

	155n25

Clement of Alexandria

Stomateis

3.13.93	86n145

Dialogue of the Savior

	155n25

Eusebius

Ecclesiastical History

3:39:9	127n42
3.11	181n2
3.39:14–17	143n121

Origen

Against Celsus

4	9n47
6:40	105n11
8.25	11n67

Tertullian of Carthage

De Anima

56–7	5

Scorpiace

12.3	42n76

GRECO-ROMAN LITERATURE

Apuleius

De deo Socratis

15	3

Celsus

	108n28

Cicero

On Divination

1.57	2n8

Codex

Justinianus

IX.8.7	42n76

Theodosianus

IX.16.4	42n76

Hipplytus

Haer.

6.34.1	11n67

Horace

Satirea

1.8	127n43

Livy

The Founding of the City

39.14	173n83

Lucian

Pharsalia

6.413–587	126n40

Philopseudes

11–13	126n40
16	4n17, 9n52

Ovid

Amores

2.1.23–28	126n40

Papyri Graecae Magicae (PGM)

IV

1017–19	7n42, 12n75
44–5	59n192

VIII

6   48n118, 62n213

Paulus

Sententiae

5.19.2	93n22
21.4	93n22
23.2, 16	93n22
25.1	93n22
30b.1	93n22

Pausanias

2.65–11   68n28

Petronius

Satyricon

131   8n29

Philostratus

Life

4.8   2n9, 12n73

Phlegon of Tralles

Mirabilia I   101n71, 154n23

Pliny

Epistles

10:96   116n21

Natural History

28:7   28n29

Plutarch

Lives

28:1–4   182n9

Strabo

Geographica

16.2.45   35n24

Suetonius   108n28

Tacitus

Annals

15:44	108n26, 116n20
II.69	42n76

Histories

4.81   9n55

The Twelve Tables, Crimes

Table VII.3 and 15	41n72, 123n19
Table VIII.9	41n72, 123n19

Virgil

Aeneid

6   4n21

Xenophon of Ephesus

Ephesiaca

5.9.7–9   3n14

www.ingramcontent.com/pod-product-compliance
Lightning Source LLC
Chambersburg PA
CBHW050842230426
43667CB00012B/2105